CRIMINAL JUSTICE
A PEACEMAKING PERSPECTIVE

John R. Fuller
State University of West Georgia

Allyn and Bacon
Boston • London • Toronto • Sydney • Tokyo • Singapore

This book is dedicated to
Amy Hembree
whose husband I blissfully am.

Editor-in-Chief Social Science: Karen Hanson
Editorial Assistant: Elissa Schaen
Marketing Manager: Karon Bowers
Composition and Prepress Buyer: Linda Cox
Manufacturing Buyer: Suzanne Lareau
Cover Administrator: Linda Knowles
Cover Designer: Suzanne Harbison
Production Administrator: Robert Tonner
Editorial-Production Service: Shepherd, Inc.

Copyright © 1998 by Allyn and Bacon
A Viacom Company
Needham Heights, Massachusetts 02194

Internet: www.abacon.com
America Online: keyword: College Online

Library of Congress Cataloging-in-Publication Data

Fuller, John R.
    Criminal justice : a peacemaking perspective / John R. Fuller.
        p.   cm.
    Includes bibliographical references and index.
    ISBN 0-205-20043-5 (alk. paper)
    1. Criminal justice, Administration of.   2. Law enforcement.
    3. Reconciliation.   I. Title.
    HV7419.F87   1998
    364—dc21   97–26200
                                                     CIP

Printed in the United States of America
10 9 8 7 6 5 4 3 2   01 00 99 98

CONTENTS

PREFACE

This book was written as an alternative to the standard introduction to criminal justice text. Even though there are several very good texts on the market, I have long been dissatisfied with the scope and emphasis of books that seem to restrict the examination of the study of criminal justice to the criminal justice system. In my opinion, the introduction to criminal justice courses should encompass a broader range of issues than is found in studying simply the workings of the police, courts, and correctional systems. Criminal justice is an exciting field of study, and this book includes coverage of some of its contested issues such as drug use, capital punishment, gun control, and violence.

A second, and more important, distinguishing feature of this book is the way it puts criminal justice issues in context by contrasting two policy perspectives. The war on crime and peacemaking perspectives are utilized to highlight the disparity in how criminal justice issues are conceived, attacked, and resolved. This book uses the war on crime and peacemaking perspectives as ideal types of policy models to illustrate the range of opinion on crime issues. That this dichotomy may have limitations, I am well aware. Nevertheless, the war on crime and peacemaking perspectives are advanced as vehicles to explore how the criminal justice system can act as a double-edged sword in its attempt to protect and serve.

While some textbooks may take a neutral stance (as Joe Friday says in *Dragnet,* "Just the facts, ma'am), my biases in this book are clearly stated and their limitations freely acknowledged. In discussing controversial criminal justice issues, policies, and programs, I do not pretend to know all the answers. Positions (sometimes extreme) are taken to stimulate thinking and discussion and as a general rule the peacemaking perspective is advanced over the war on crime perspective. This book will serve its primary purpose not by the reader arriving at the same conclusions as the author, but by being inspired to think critically about the issues.

The book is divided into fourteen chapters. Chapter 1 discusses the nature of crime. Chapter 2 presents the war on crime perspective, and Chapter 3 presents the peacemaking perspective.

Chapter 4 discusses the rule of law and the place of the victim in the criminal justice system. Chapter 5 covers issues of law enforcement. Chapter 6 deals with the criminal court system, and Chapter 7 deals with the problems of corrections.

Chapter 8 deals with drug use and its suppression and treatment. Chapter 9 is concerned with the problems of violence in society. Chapter 10 describes the issue of gun control in the United States. Chapter 11 covers the debate on capital punishment. Chapter 12 deals with the problems of youth crime and gangs.

Chapter 13 highlights how crime in other cultures differs from crime in the United States. Chapter 14 presents a reaffirmation of the peacemaking perspective.

An Appendix is presented that discusses some problems and issues of a career in the criminal justice system. Finally, there's an appendix listing sites on the World Wide Web that will be of interest to students of criminal justice.

Throughout the book, the theme of comparing and contrasting the war on crime and peacemaking perspectives is preserved to enable the reader to develop some perspective on the complexities of social control in a democratic society.

ACKNOWLEDGMENTS

I wish to thank several people who helped in the inspiration and production of this book. First, the outside reviewers commissioned by Allyn and Bacon who read all or parts of the manuscript and provided numerous helpful comments:

Cynthia Line, Holy Family College
David O. Friedrichs, University of Scranton
Jo Ann Marie Scott, Ohio Northern University
Pelgy Vas, Fort Hays State University
Angela D. West, Indiana State University
Rom Haghighi, The University of Texas–Pan American

I also wish to thank my colleagues who either read parts of the manuscript, loaned me materials from their personal libraries, or discussed particular issues and made helpful suggestions. They include Jane McCandless, Marc LaFountain, Sheila LaFountain, Bruce DiCristina, Eric Hickey, and my department chair Ted Simons. I also wish to thank Karen Hanson, the Social Sciences Editor-in-Chief of Allyn and Bacon, and her team of editors and production people.

Finally and foremost, I wish to thank two individuals who worked tirelessly in helping me write this book. The first is my research assistant, Dana L. DeSandre, who slaved for two years looking up resources and proofreading manuscript. The second is my wife, Amy, to whom this book is dedicated. Words cannot express the many contributions in the myriad of ways she made to this endeavor.

1

THE NATURE OF CRIME
IN THE UNITED STATES

© Tony Freeman/PhotoEdit.

Learning Objectives

After reading this chapter, the student should be able to:

- Explain how definitions of crime are in dispute.
- Describe three conditions necessary for a behavior to be considered a crime.
- Differentiate between types of crime.
- Explain what is meant by the dark figure of crime.
- Explain why so much crime goes unreported to authorities.
- Describe the range of criminal acts measured by the Uniform Crime Reports (UCR).
- Understand the relative prevalence of the (UCR) eight index crimes as measured by the crime clock.
- Understand the strengths and weaknesses of victimization studies.
- Understand the strengths and weaknesses of studies of self-reported crime.
- Describe how the media reports and sometimes distorts the question of crime in the United States.
- Appreciate how crime and freedom are intricately related.

Key Terms

Folkways	Political Crime
Social Mores	Juvenile Delinquency
Norms	*Parentis Parens*
Laws	Dark Figure of Crime
Socialization Process	Victimization Studies
Violent Crime	Self-Reported Crime Studies
Property Crime	Crime Clock
Victimless Crime	Index Crimes
White-Collar Crime	

DEFINING CRIME

The first step in developing an understanding about the extent and impact of crime in this country is to construct a definition of crime. One would think the problems of definition were settled long ago and that there is a clear consensus on what is, or what should be, considered crime. Unfortunately, this is not the case. There is considerable debate on what actions should be proscribed and what society should do with offenders. The problems of definition spill over into problems of politics and organizational behavior. Crime is a socially constructed problem, which means that definitions change as new or reconsidered issues arise. The classification of behaviors into crime is constantly in dispute and is a large part of the public's perception of the criminal justice system's ability to seem disconnected, unfair, and unable to effectively combat crime.

In order to understand how crime is defined we must first recognize that the law is just one of the mechanisms of social control that bonds the social fabric of society. Most of us do not break the law because our behavior is controlled by less restrictive features of social control such as **folkways, social mores, norms,** and **laws.**

Imagine how chaotic society would be if only laws influenced our behavior. An individual would be constantly ensnared in the formal net of social control, called the criminal justice system. The fact of the matter is, almost all the factors that govern our relationships with other people are regulated by processes and institutions other than the law. The criminal justice system may be the most visible and the arena of last resort, but it handles only a very small fraction of disputes among individuals and between individuals and their government.

At the most basic level, crime occurs when a law is violated. For this to happen several things need to have occurred:

1. There needs to be an agreement among citizens that certain behaviors warrant suppression by society.
2. Duly authorized representatives (lawmakers) need to discuss the behaviors, delimit what constitutes the behavior, codify (enact a law), and proscribe the penalty(ies).
3. Other duly authorized representatives (law enforcement officers) must become aware of the behavior, and, using their considerable discretion, determine that the behavior violates an enacted law.

There are many other ways in which disputes are settled that fall short of invoking the criminal sanction. Each family, school, workplace, and other social institution has its own mechanism for regulating behavior and handling conflicts. We are all socialized to some extent into society through these social institutions where we learn to submit to authority and work together in forming meaningful communities. The very way we act in public is a result of the **socialization process** designed to ensure we engage in behavior that is appropriate. From the table manners taught to us when we are very young to the etiquette, manners, and forms of deference to our elders we pick up in early childhood, the process of training in correct behavior is lifelong. We internalize these rules, conventions, norms, and polite ways of doing things as we grow up, and the criminal law is the final secular proscription that controls our behavior.

What constitutes correct behavior can vary enormously from culture to culture. One need only travel abroad to see how people of other countries view a matter as simple as standing in a line and waiting one's turn. While people in England will wait in line for a very long time and enforce the rule about "cutting in," people in north Africa do not respect the western conception of a line at all, and forming a pushing mob instead of an orderly line is the norm (Henslin 1996, 70).

Whether we realize it or not, the vast majority of our behavior is rulebound. The internal disciplines adopted by each of us dictate how we interact, and in a society that has been successful in transmitting its socially approved codes of behavior, we believe that we choose our behavior where in reality the behavior has been drilled into us.

Whose Definitions?

Let's step back a minute and consider how some behaviors are defined as crime and others are not. The differences between crafty business practices and crime are not always clear and sometimes take a court of law to determine. As each of us attempts to maximize the money we keep when we do our taxes, we run the risk of fines or imprisonment if the Internal Revenue Service disagrees with our interpretation of the tax code. Depending on where we stand on the socioeconomic ladder we may think the tax laws unduly penalize us and require too little from others. We may be right. Tax laws, like all laws, are developed in an historical and social context where people attempt to protect their own interests. The criminal laws display the same bias toward those who are able to have their voices heard when laws are made.

To a large extent, our legal system defines criminal behaviors as those that threaten the interests of the people who are best able to influence the legislature. The disparities in penalties between different offenses and the actual harm done to society is sometimes striking. Reiman (1995) demonstrates how those with financial resources are able to influence not only the criminal justice system but also the legislature. The result is a complex set of laws and criminal justice practices that seem weighted against the poor, people of color, and children (Rothman 1995).

One recent example of this disparity is the curious case of crack cocaine. There are some rather obvious patterns in cocaine use where individuals in the African-American community use crack cocaine and those in the upper-middle-class white community use powder cocaine. Legislatures in some states have passed laws making crack cocaine subject to penalties that are much more severe than the penalties for powder cocaine. The result of the contrast in how different types of cocaine are handled by the criminal justice system is that a disproportionate number of African-Americans are arrested and imprisoned for cocaine use.

Why Clear Thinking about Crime Is Important

The United States is experiencing a crisis in the confidence that citizens have in its institutions. The traditional family is besieged by broken homes and divorce, schools fail to teach even the most basic skills, doctors get rich performing unnecessary surgery, lawyer jokes are appreciated by everyone (even lawyers), and the shift from a manufacturing economy to an information economy is transforming the relationship workers have with employers. The downsizing in the workforce being done in many corporations has signaled a change in the ethos of loyalty and job security that workers have had to their jobs. Now individuals can no longer expect to work for the same company for their entire career. Our institutions do not enjoy the respect they once did (Currie and Skolnick 1997).

The criminal justice system is subject to intense criticism because as other institutions fail to deliver on their promises and expectations, the criminal justice system becomes the institution that must eventually be employed. It is interesting to note that for some people the system seems to be too lenient on criminals. They look at what they perceive as a revolving door of the criminal justice system where offenders serve only a fraction of their sentences and are back on the street, often victimizing new people. Other people see the criminal justice system as being overly oppressive and discriminatory against people without economic means. The disparities in sentencing depending on how much money and how many resources the offender can muster are viewed as evidence that the criminal justice system is simply a tool of the rich to preserve their privileged position in society.

It is important then for the students of the criminal justice system to understand not only how the system operates, but also to appreciate why the system defines crime as it does. Additionally, it is important to recognize that in our democratic institutions laws and practices can be held up to higher standards, such as the Constitution and human rights, and that laws and the criminal justice system can, and should, be reformed when injustices are discovered.

In studying what we define as crime, three themes are readily apparent. First is the emphasis on crimes of personal violence such as homicide, rape, armed robbery, and assault. These crimes affect everyone, and we all agree they are undesirable behaviors. Poor people fall victim to these crimes much more often than do rich people, and we would expect the criminal justice system to enforce these laws uniformly regardless of who is the victim.

Second, we have a set of laws that deal with property. Burglary, larceny, and motor vehicle theft are crimes that carry heavy penalties but do not result in the same type of social harm as personal violent offenses. The amount of property stolen is not as important in determining the penalty as the manner in which it was taken and the extralegal factors associated with who the offender and victim are.

Third, there are a range of laws that do not directly relate to either personal violence or property but have to do with behaviors some people consider undesirable. Laws concerning alcohol and drug use, prostitution, and gambling all involve the moral order of society. These will be discussed in more detail in subsequent chapters, but it is useful to note how these laws may not have the support of large portions of the population and that the enforcement of these laws is at times selective and discriminatory.

TYPES OF CRIME

When we talk about the high rate of crime in the United States, it is important to keep in mind that we are talking about a wide range of behavior that cannot be reduced to short, comprehensive statements. Therefore, it is useful to consider some of the differences between various types of crime.

1. *Violent crime.* This category of crime receives the most attention from the media and politicians. Homicide, rape, and assault are of concern to all citizens because of the potential for bodily harm that drastically impacts quality of life. Compared to other crimes, the rate of violent crime is actually quite low, but the public demands violent criminals be dealt with in the most severe manner the law allows.

2. *Property crime.* While some violent crimes such as armed robbery clearly involve the theft of property, the category of property crime refers to theft without the use of force. Burglary, larceny-theft, motor vehicle theft, and arson do not put the victim's life in direct danger so these crimes are not considered as serious as violent crime and, for the most part, do not carry as heavy a penalty. In 1994 the value of property stolen was estimated by the Federal Bureau of Investigation to be $15.1 billion with the average loss per offense estimated at $1,248.

3. *Victimless crime.* Drug use, prostitution, and gambling are good examples of victimless crime. The rationale behind such terminology is that in a free society people should be able to engage in behaviors that do not hurt other people. According to an old saying, "my right to wave my fist in the air ends where your nose begins." I should be free, therefore, to wave my fist all I want as long as I don't touch your nose. If I want to engage in an economic transaction where I pay for sex then, according to some people, I should be able to. As long as the prostitute is an adult and I pay her or him the agreed-upon price, then our transaction should be a private matter and not the concern of the government. Some people will argue that there are victims to prostitution, drug use, and gambling because of the impact these behaviors have on the moral order of society. It is interesting to note how many state governments are getting into the gambling business through the use of lotteries. Apparently, who the victim is is not as important as where the money goes.

Crime is sometimes a form of collective behavior. (© AP/Wide World Photos.)

4. *White-collar crime.* When business takes unfair advantage of consumers and competitors it can do immense damage to individuals and society without public knowledge that a crime has even been committed. When corporations conspire to fix prices on products, the public will pay the inflated price thinking that is what the marketplace has determined is fair. Likewise, unsafe or defective products may be sold to the public as a result of companies cutting corners in the manufacturing process. White-collar criminals, however, are not treated as severely by the criminal justice system as other types of criminals. First, they are not as visible as other criminals. White-collar criminals are seemingly legitimate business operators who are providing needed goods and services. "Let the buyer beware" has enormous currency as a warning for dealing with the economy, and a certain amount of false advertising, large profits, and planned obsolescence are tolerated in the corporate world.

5. *Political crime.* Like white-collar crime, political crime is of relatively low visibility. The influencing of legislation to favor one's own concerns is part of the political process and it becomes a crime under only the most serious and flagrant violations of the law. Some politicians have put their own finances and power before the public welfare and have, in essence, sold their vote to the highest bidder. A number of laws speak to just how far politicians can go in accepting money or favors from those who have an interest in legislation. Given the millions of dollars it takes to run for a major political office, it is not surprising that politicians are often found stepping outside the law to generate money. Campaign finance-reform efforts have limited how much money an individual can contribute ($1,000). Now, political action committees (PACs) are the major fund-raising tools used by interest groups. So far all the efforts to diminish the influence of money on who gets elected have failed. In the United States big money talks, and the buying and selling of political influence, although changed, is still a major problem.

    6. *Juvenile delinquency.* Young people are subject to an additional set of laws because of their status as minors. This extra surveillance is a double-edged sword for juveniles because although they are treated differently by the criminal justice system, they are often treated more harshly. The juvenile justice system was conceived as an alternative to the criminal justice system so that youth would not be punished with adults. The idea was to save the child, and it was with the best intentions that the juvenile justice system was designed to help children. There are two issues that critics contend make the juvenile justice system problematic. The first is the issue of status offenses. Because of their age, juveniles have laws that apply to them and not to adults. Under-age drinking, mandatory school attendance, obeying parents, and sometimes even curfews are all behaviors for which adults are not held responsible. It is true that most of the time these types of infractions are handled within the family, but the juvenile justice system is there to help the parent or guardian ensure compliance. The second issue that critics of the juvenile justice system find problematic is the reduced due process available to the juvenile offender. Because the ultimate goal of the juvenile justice system is to help or treat the youth rather than to punish, many of the procedural safeguards provided by the Constitution do not apply to juveniles (Fuller and Norton 1993). The juvenile justice system acts as ***parentis parens,*** or parent of the country, in deciding what is in the best interest of the child. In recent years, the juvenile court has taken steps to ensure the youth is afforded more due process rights, especially if a serious crime is involved and the youth is likely to be incarcerated for a long time. Still, the issue of due process rights are of concern because of the vulnerability of youth and the serious crimes they sometimes commit. One way of dealing with this issue for very serious crimes is to transfer the case to the adult court where not only are due process rights rigidly enforced but more severe penalties are possible. This practice is used sparingly and for only the most sensational and serious cases.

CRIME TRENDS

Problems in the Measurement of Crime

As can be seen from the variety of behaviors that are considered crimes and the different impacts they have on society, it is impossible to talk about the

FIGURE 1.1   Dark Figure of Crime (Crime Index + Dark Figure of Crime = True Crime Rate).

crime rate in the United States in any meaningful way without looking more closely at how we measure crime and some of the problems in comparing crime rates. One thing we do know is that our measures of crime can only approximate the amount of crime that actually exists. A great deal of crime goes unreported for one reason or another. Criminologists refer to this as the **dark figure of crime** (see Figure 1.1).

Why is there so much unreported crime? There are several reasons that are tied to how the criminal justice system is perceived to operate by the public. First, the victim may be afraid to report the crime. This is especially true in cases of domestic assault or child abuse. Women and children put themselves in added danger if the criminal justice system simply inflames the anger of the man without solving the problem. Second, the victim may be embarrassed to report the crime. Rape victims or male victims of domestic assault often feel that scrutiny by police and court personnel is an added insult to the injury of the crime. Third, the victim may think the criminal justice system can do little to solve the crime. This is especially true of larceny and burglary cases. Unless an insurance claim is involved, the victim may feel it is not worth the time and effort to report a crime where there is little likelihood of an arrest. Fourth, the victim may be blameworthy in some way. The victim may have been involved in selling drugs and was robbed. This victim is unlikely to report the crime to the police. Fifth, the victim may have little faith that the criminal justice system will respond in a satisfactory way and may decide to dispense justice in his or her own way. The crime is not reported because the victim plans to "fight fire with fire" and get revenge by committing a crime on the person(s) thought responsible.

There may be other reasons for the underreporting of the actual amount of crime but this list serves to suggest why we cannot be certain exactly how much crime occurs. Does this mean that it is useless to try to measure crime? The answer is no. It is very important to attempt to measure crime even though we understand we can never be totally accurate. There are many reasons for trying to measure crime and we can be reasonably confident that we are approximating a reasonable guess when we use more than one measure of crime.

Uniform Crime Reports, Victimization Studies, and Self-Reported Crime

In this section, three measures of crime are considered in order to give a triangulation effect. That is, by looking at the amount of crime from different angles we can compensate to some extent for the incomplete picture any one measure may give us. The three measures include one official measure, the Uniform Crime Reports (UCR) published by the U.S. Government Printing Office, and two unofficial measures: **victimization studies** and **self-reported crime studies** that are administered by either research agencies or university professors. Each of these measures has its own strengths and weaknesses, and it is only by considering them together than we can be confident that we are close to measuring the true extent of crime. Also, because of the repeated use of these measures of crime, we can observe some stability in crime rates, which suggests a certain degree of reliability in the way indices account for crime. If there were wide fluctuations in our measures of crime, we might think our way of assessing crime was subject to significant measurement error. By refining the measures we ensure that differences are actually variations in crime and not problems in how we measure it.

Uniform Crime Reports

The Uniform Crime Reports are the most comprehensive and complete measures of crime available. The need for national crime statistics led the International Association of Chiefs of Police (IACP) to develop the Uniform Crime Reports in coordination with the Federal Bureau of Investigation in the 1920s. The most difficult aspect in generating these statistics is getting the over 16,000 city, county, and state law enforcement agencies to define, measure, and provide the statistics in an equivalent manner so that what is being called "crime" reflects behaviors that all agencies agree upon, rather than simply differences in reporting.

At the broadest level, the Uniform Crime Report divides crime into two main categories, Part I offenses and Part II offenses. Part I offenses are considered to be the more serious and can be assumed to be reported to the police more often than the Part II offenses. Eight crimes are included in Part I offenses:

- Murder and nonnegligent manslaughter
- Forcible rape
- Robbery

- Aggravated assault
- Burglary
- Larceny-theft
- Motor vehicle theft
- Arson

The Uniform Crime Reports for 1995 show there were 13,867,143 Part I offenses reported, which is a 0.9 percent decrease from the 13,989,543 offenses reported in 1994. By way of illustration, the Uniform Crime Reports provide a **crime clock** to show how often each of these crimes are committed in the United States if they were uniformly spread out over the year (see Figure 1.2).

This "crime clock" should give one pause to think about just how much serious crime there is in the United States. Even the most cursory review of this clock, however, shows that for the eight Part I offenses, murder and forcible rape occur at a significantly lesser rate than the other crimes. In terms of personal safety, it should be apparent that the crude rates of Part I offenses actually mask the nature of crime and produce an inflated picture of just how dangerous it is in the United States.

When the rate of crime as measured by Part I offenses is viewed over a 20-year period it does not show a consistent pattern (see Figure 1.3). Crime rates fluctuate rather than continue to rise as one might expect from the political rhetoric.

Even the rate of violent crime seems to be improving from its peak in 1991 of 758.1 crimes per 100,000 people to its 1994 mark of 684 violent crimes per 100,000 people (see Figure 1.4).

Of the Part I offense the most improvement over the past 20 years has been in burglary where, from a peak in 1980 of 1,684.1 crimes per 100,000 people, it has dropped to 987.6 crimes per 100,000 people in 1995.

Why the crime rate fluctuates as it does is subject to considerable debate. The most pressing question that can be asked is "do the policies and practices of the criminal justice system have any measurable effect on the rates of crime?" That question will be dealt with in some detail in later chapters so it is enough to say here that the rates of crime do go up and down, and any explanation needs to consider random fluctuations and crime displacement, as well as policies aimed at particular crimes.

Part II offenses consider a much broader range of crimes. The 21 crimes included in the Part II offenses include white-collar crimes such as embezzlement, forgery and counterfeiting, and fraud; vice crimes such as prostitution, gambling, sex offenses, driving under the influence, and drug abuse violations; and offenses aimed at juveniles such as vandalism, disorderly conduct, curfew and loitering laws, and runaways. Part II offenses are considered less serious than Part I offenses and together give a picture of the level of public safety and compliance with the norms of society.

The Uniform Crime Reports provide a measure of the rate of crime for each jurisdiction. The rate of crime is calculated as the number of offenses

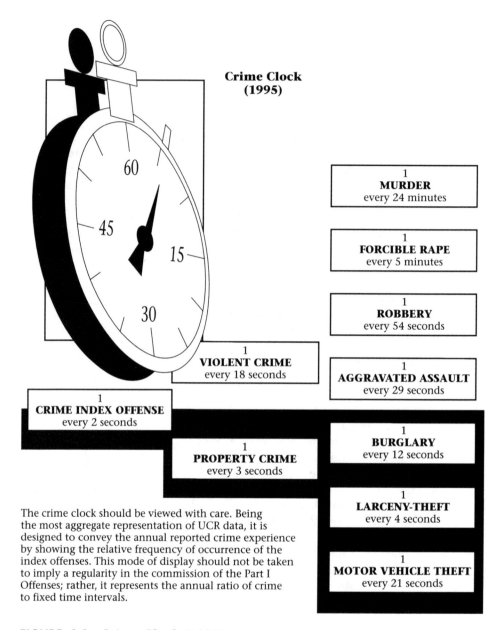

Crime Clock (1995)

1 **MURDER** every 24 minutes	
1 **FORCIBLE RAPE** every 5 minutes	
1 **ROBBERY** every 54 seconds	
1 **VIOLENT CRIME** every 18 seconds	
1 **AGGRAVATED ASSAULT** every 29 seconds	
1 **CRIME INDEX OFFENSE** every 2 seconds	
1 **PROPERTY CRIME** every 3 seconds	
1 **BURGLARY** every 12 seconds	
1 **LARCENY-THEFT** every 4 seconds	
1 **MOTOR VEHICLE THEFT** every 21 seconds	

The crime clock should be viewed with care. Being the most aggregate representation of UCR data, it is designed to convey the annual reported crime experience by showing the relative frequency of occurrence of the index offenses. This mode of display should not be taken to imply a regularity in the commission of the Part I Offenses; rather, it represents the annual ratio of crime to fixed time intervals.

FIGURE 1.2 Crime Clock (1995).

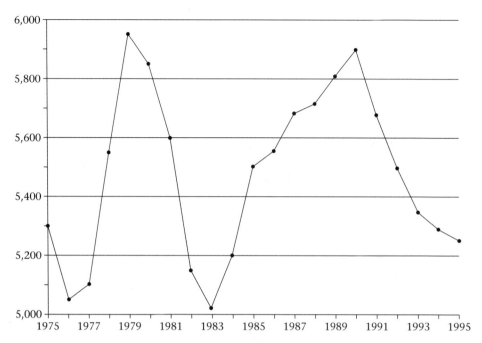

FIGURE 1.3 Index of Crime in the United States, Total, 1975–1995
(Rate per 100,000 People).

Source: Federal Bureau of Investigation. 1994. *Crime in the United States*. Washington, DC: Government Printing Office, p. 58.

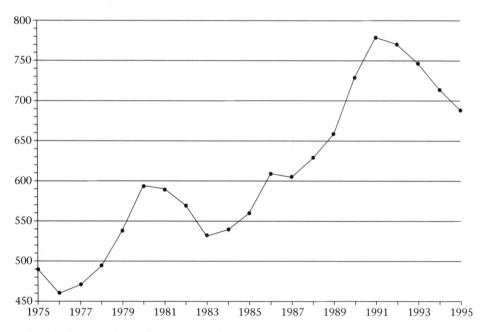

FIGURE 1.4 Index of Crime in the United States, Violent Crime, 1975–1995 (Rate per 100,000 People).

Source: Federal Bureau of Investigation. 1994. *Crime in the United States*. Washington, DC: Government Printing Office, p. 58.

that occur for each 100,000 people and allows criminologists to compare one jurisdiction to another. If only the number of crimes was measured, then the larger cities would appear much more crime-ridden than smaller cities because of their larger population. The crime rate gives a more accurate picture of the true level of crime but, as noted previously, it is only an approximation of the dark figure of actual crime.

Despite the enormous effort and good intentions that go into producing the Uniform Crime Reports, there are critics who contend that the UCR gives an incomplete and inaccurate picture of crime in the United States. Jeffrey Reiman (1995) argues the official statistics reflect primarily the crimes of the poor and neglects the behaviors of corporations and wealthy individuals. Price-fixing, environmental crimes, tax fraud, and other offenses that poor people seldom have an opportunity to commit are not included in the Uniform Crime Reports even though they can do significant harm to the community. Similarly, when wealthy people are detected committing these acts, they are not arrested, prosecuted, or imprisoned with the same vigor as offenders of the eight **index crimes.** Reiman believes the Uniform Crime Reports give a distorted mirror of the crime in society.

> . . . *the general public loses more money by far . . . from price-fixing and monopolistic practices and from consumer deception and embezzlement than from all the property crimes in the FBI's Index combined. Yet these far more costly acts are either not criminal, or if technically criminal, not prosecuted, or if prosecuted, not punished, or if punished, only mildly. In any event, although the individuals responsible for these acts take more money out of the ordinary citizen's pocket than our Typical Criminal, they rarely show up in arrest statistics and almost never in prison populations (1995, 55).*

In terms of violent crimes, Reiman argues that the loss of life from unsafe working conditions in factories and mines is attributed to accidents; however, the employers are morally culpable. Many of these accidents are preventable, but the employers are not held responsible by the criminal justice system the way a mugger or a rapist is. Consequently, according to Reiman, the way we measure and prosecute crimes is biased in favor of the rich at the expense of the poor.

Another criticism of the Uniform Crime Reports is they are not so much a measure of crime as they are a measure of police activity. Again, the dark figure of crime is unknown (and for all practical purposes unknowable). The police decide what behaviors are defined as crime and because the decisions they make are subject to a great deal of discretion, we can be confident only in their reporting and arrest activities and not in the actual level of crime.

Despite these problems with the Uniform Crime Reports, it is important to recognize that there are some compelling reasons to take them seriously and base public policy on them. First, in the almost 60 years of measuring crime in this manner a baseline measure has been developed. Any radical change in a jurisdiction's crime rate cannot be automatically assumed to be a reflection of criminal activity. Changes in definitions and recording practices must first be considered because the crime rate customarily changes only within a certain range. Drastic changes should be explainable by measuring changes of such obvious crime waves that there is little question as to why there is such an observable increase or decrease. In short, the UCR has developed a baseline measure that allows for the recognition of the relative stability of crime rates.

Victimization Studies

We turn now to an entirely different way of measuring crime. The Uniform Crime Reports can consider only crimes that are reported to the police. Victimization studies attempt to tap into the dark figure of crime by asking people if they have been a victim of crime, and if so, whether it was reported to the police. Clearly not everyone in the nation is asked about their victim status so the rate of crime in the United States can only be approximated through victimization studies. Using survey research, the National Crime Victimization Survey (NCVS) asks individuals about a wide range of circumstances surrounding their victimization. This is especially rich and useful information because it comes directly from the crime victims and includes not only information about them, but also information about the offender(s), the nature of the crime, and the response of the police if the crime was reported.

Like the Uniform Crime Reports, victimization studies have limitations. First, victimization studies do not measure all crimes. Prostitution, drug use, public drunkenness, and gambling, often considered victimless crimes, are not included in victimization studies. Also, many people are not aware that they have been victims of some white-collar crimes such as embezzlement or forgery. Obviously, homicide is a crime where there is not going to be victim reporting. Nevertheless, victimization studies provide an alternative measure of crime that can provide a different dimension of the actual incidence of criminal behavior.

Other limitations of victimization studies include the problem of memory. Asking people about crimes that have happened up to one year ago is problematic. People forget many of the minor infractions that may have happened and remember or even exaggerate the major ones. This can give a distorted picture of the actual level of victimization. Another problem is telescoping. This involves people thinking a crime happened more recently than it actually did because it is so distinct in their memory. A crime may have happened two years ago but the individual may report it as happening in the last year because it made such an impact on their life it seems to them to be more recent. Additionally, individuals may not report crimes where they have been partially at fault or the actual facts are embarrassing to them. These are called errors of deception and can result in an underreporting of victimization.

Self-Report Studies

So far we have discussed measuring crime by looking at what activities are reported to law enforcement (UCR) and asking victims what has happened to them (NCVS). Criminologists use a third method of measuring crime to develop a different perspective on this multifarious problem. Self-report studies ask individuals what unlawful behaviors they have committed. Of course, the very first limitation of this method is the problem of lying. People are very hesitant to admit unlawful behavior even if they are confident they will not be held responsible for it. Most individuals are too embarrassed and ashamed to confess to committing serious violations of the law. Nevertheless, under the right kind of research methods, criminologists have been able to develop studies where individuals, particularly youths, have provided useful data concerning their criminal activities. Examples of nationwide self-report studies are the National Youth Survey and the efforts by the National Institute of Drug Abuse, which has been monitoring the tobacco, alcohol, and drug use of teenagers since the mid-1970s.

One of the most enlightening discoveries of these self-report studies is that almost all youths engage in some type of delinquent behavior. William Chambliss, in his classic article on the Saints and the Roughnecks (1995), demonstrates how the infractions of lower-class youth are much more likely to get recorded in official statistics gathered by law enforcement agencies than are the transgressions of middle- and upper-class youth. Self-report studies are one of the most effective ways in which to discover how widely delinquency actually occurs across the population. The less serious the offense, the more likely someone will admit to the behavior, and for very serious offenses we can reasonably expect that there will be a significant underreporting error. By using self-reported crime studies in conjunction with official law enforcement statistic and victimization studies, a more complete picture of the dark figure of crime has been developed.

CRIME AND THE MEDIA

The impression most people have of crime is not informed by the Uniform Crime Reports, victimization studies, or self-reported crime studies. The picture most people have of crime comes from two other sources: their own experience and the media. Those who have been a victim of crime, especially a violent crime, will have a relationship or association with crime that colors their judgment and makes them extremely fearful even when circumstances do not warrant such a level of concern. This is understandable and healthy to the extent that the victim changes his or her behavior and takes precautions. It is regrettable to the extent that the victim overreacts and withdraws trust in others and passes up opportunities to go places and do things that they formally enjoyed. For some people, the trust and sense of security will come back slowly, and for others the emotional results of victimization will be lifelong.

The impression of the risk of crime presented by the media is more problematic than that garnered from personal experience. The media distorts the level and severity of crime as a matter of policy to attract readers and viewers (Hickey 1997). Crime is good business for the media, especially if it is unusual, gory, grotesque, sensational, lurid, or scandalous. The impression of crime one gets from the media can be so out of touch with the actual danger and risk of crime that it has the effect of driving people from the streets. The media has a tendency to concentrate on the most sensational crimes and to report the story numerous time until a new shocking story comes along.

While it is unfair to lump all news organizations together under the rubric of media, the average reader or viewer does not differentiate between media outlets and forms an opinion about crime based on an overall impression of the news, which includes local, state, national, and international reporting. The fear of crime generated in many people is not comparable to the actual risk of crime they are exposed to in their neighborhoods. The effect of the media coverage is to make every crime seem, to some extent, a local crime. Compared to other stories available to the media, it is the violent crime that gets reported.

> There is no dispute that the mass media is enamored with crime and violence. Violent crime is a major theme in both news and fictional media presentations, with 20 percent or more of television broadcast time often devoted to crime-related topics . . .
>
> Perhaps the most disturbing aspect of this proliferation of crime-related programming is that the presentations rarely resemble reality. Only the most sensational and horrific offenses make their way into the media. Violent crime, particularly murder, is overrepresented in comparison to its actual occurrence in the real world . . . (Doerner and Lab, 192–193).

This overexposure of violent crime in the media has two negative effects. The first effect is to make people unreasonably fearful for their safety. The impression of crime makes individuals alter their behavior by staying off the streets and out of public places. The overexposure is good for the private security industry and companies that sell deadbolt locks, car alarms, and mace. The second effect of the media crime coverage is to present violent crime as typical, so that young people start to model that behavior. Homicides, assaults, and rapes presented by the media have lost their impact and are no longer shocking. Media-depicted violence may desensitize the public toward violence and may prompt an increase in it. Doerner and Lab (1995, 193) conclude, ". . . there is little doubt that the mass media plays some role in the high levels of violence in society."

CRIME AND FREEDOM

In order to understand the extent and nature of crime in society we must develop a sense of perspective. Crime is a serious social issue, but it is also an issue about which a great deal of overstatement, myth, and inaccurate perceptions exist. If we listen to the most vocal among us, we will get a distorted view of the level and seriousness of crime. There is such a thing as a healthy fear of crime, where we take reasonable precautions aimed at prevention and we use the criminal justice system in a sensible way to apprehend and punish or treat the offenders. We should be careful, however, not to "throw the baby out with the bathwater." In the case of crime in the United States, this cliché can be taken to mean we should be careful in our concern for crime in that we do not react in such a way that we fundamentally alter the positive aspects of our society. We enjoy tremendous freedoms in this country and a certain level of crime is one of the unintended consequences of those freedoms.

While the objective is to reduce the level of crime without abridging those freedoms, we need to understand the danger in pursuing one objective at the expense of another. In times of war we willingly (but temporarily) give up some freedoms for a higher cause. The question we must continually ask ourselves is "does the level of crime we are experiencing warrant giving up some of the freedoms we enjoy as citizens?" How we answer this question tells us much about how we view society. It is not good enough to say, "I am willing to give up all of your freedoms to protect me, but none of my freedoms to protect you." In our democratic society, we must agree on how the law and the criminal justice system can best protect us all from crime while at the same time preserving the freedoms that symbolize the quality of life in the United States. The following two chapters on the war on crime and the peacemaking perspectives illustrate the tension in trying to accomplish these two goals simultaneously.

CRITICAL THINKING QUESTIONS

1. Discuss why so much of the crime in society goes unreported. What crimes are the most likely to be reported? What can be done to encourage citizens to report more of the crimes they know about?

2. Compare and contrast the strengths and weaknesses of the Uniform Crime Reports, victimization studies, and self-reported crime studies.

3. Discuss the different types of crime. Which do you consider to be the most reprehensible?

4. What behaviors that are not crimes today would you like to see be made crimes? What penalties should be attached to your new crimes?

SUGGESTED READINGS

Blumstein, Alfred. 1993. "Making Rationality Relevant—The American Society of Criminology 1992 Presidential Address." *Criminology 31*(1): 1–16.

Currie, Elliot, and Jerome H. Skolnick. 1997. *America's Problems: Social Issues and Public Policy*, 3rd ed. New York: Longman.

DiCristina, Bruce. 1995. *Method in Criminology: A Philosophical Primer.* New York: Harrow and Heston.

Hickey, Eric W. 1997. *Serial Murderers and Their Victims*, 2nd ed. Belmont, CA: Wadsworth.

Miller, Alden D., and Lloyd E. Ohlin. 1985. *Delinquency and Community: Creating Opportunities and Controls.* Beverly Hills: Sage.

Reiman, Jeffrey. 1995. *The Rich Get Richer and the Poor Get Prison: Ideology, Class and Criminal Justice*, 4th ed. Boston: Allyn and Bacon.

Rothman, David J. 1995. "More of the Same: American Criminal Justice Policies in the 1990s," in Thomas G. Blomberg and Stanley Cohen, eds. *Punishment and Social Control.* New York: Aldine De Gruyter, pp. 22–44.

Vaughn, Michael S. 1993. "Listening to the Experts: A National Study of Correctional Administrators' Responses to Prison Overcrowding." *Criminal Justice Review 18*(1): 12–25.

2

WAR ON CRIME PERSPECTIVE

© Bob Daemmrich/Stock Boston.

Learning Objectives

After reading this chapter, the student should be able to:

- Define what is meant by "war on crime."
- Explain why the war on crime is a metaphor.
- Appreciate the conceptual limitations of metaphors.
- Understand how law enforcement agencies are quasi-military bureaucracies.
- Explain how the war on crime has altered the sentencing patterns in the courts.
- Describe the differences between an indeterminate sentence and a determinate or fixed sentence.
- Explain how the war on crime has made prison more punitive.
- Appreciate how measurements of crime are often simply measurements of criminal justice agencies' outputs.
- Describe how our efforts to combat skyjacking have impinged on our freedoms.
- Explain how the forfeiture laws allow law enforcement agencies to confiscate money from suspects without the protection of due process.
- List 15 issues or areas where the war on crime has infringed on individuals' rights and freedoms.
- Understand why citizens are losing confidence in their institutions because of the war on crime.

Key Terms

Metaphor	Determinate Sentence
Quasi-Military Bureaucracies	Skyjacking
SWAT	Sky Marshals
Career Criminals	Forfeiture Laws
Sentencing Patterns	War on Crime Perspective
Indeterminate Sentence	Militarization of Civil Society

In Chapter 1 we saw how complex crime is as a social phenomena. It includes many types of behaviors, some of which most of us agree should be discouraged and suppressed and some of which many of us violate from time to time without feeling especially guilty or deviant. Hopefully, we gained an appreciation for how complicated and involved any solution to these behaviors is going to be. If we listen to the politicians and the media the solution to crime is not all that hard to determine. All we need to do is "get tough" on crime and "declare war" on the criminals and the drug dealers. By untying the hands of the police, appointing judges who do not "coddle" criminals, and giving long prison sentences without parole and/or executing more people, we can make our society safe for the good citizens.

WAR AS A METAPHOR

Fortunately, war is just a **metaphor.** It is political rhetoric used to mobilize the population to attack a social problem. Lyndon Johnson declared a war on poverty in the 1960s with his Great Society programs. Poverty is still with us. War has also been declared on illiteracy, illegitimacy, and drugs. These are all social problems whose solutions require creative ideas, financial resources, and fundamental changes in our institutions (Kozell 1991). Moreover, these problems are extricably ingrained in the populace. Realistically we cannot wage war on ourselves. War is an inappropriate metaphor to employ in addressing these social problems.

Why is the war metaphor so popular in political rhetoric? What do we really mean when we declare war on a social problem? Finally, what are the implications for our society when war is declared? In addressing the warlike administration on the problem of drugs, Czajkoski contends:

> *It seldom happens that the concept of a warlike approach to a national problem is explicitly expressed. Among the characteristics implied in the notion of coping with a problem by declaring war on it are extra effort, expediency, ruthlessness, sacrifice, and subordination of the individual. It is the last mentioned characteristic that is especially troubling to students of justice and to the mind of a liberal, at least the old-fashioned liberal who regards the rights of the individual as paramount (1990, 125).*

At one time in this century, war was the solution to a problem that everyone could agree upon. World War II had the almost universal support of Americans, and almost all willingly made great sacrifices to promote the war effort (Dyer 1985). For the generations of Americans who experienced World War II, it seemed that a concerted effort could solve any problem. The enemy of the Allied powers formed a sufficiently serious and villainous problem, about which there was little disagreement that extreme measures should be taken to ensure victory. And, in fact, extreme measures were taken that some Americans have come to regret. As Czajkoski points out, the internment of Japanese-Americans was an excessive policy that has parallels in the policies of today's war on drugs.

> *The intensification of the war on drugs and the planning for a cabinet-level drug czar occurred at the same time as the nation was putting the finishing*

touches on reparations to the Americans of Japanese descent who were bru-
tally interned at the beginning of World War II. The quickly established war
mentality after Pearl Harbor clouded any concern with due process or elemen-
tary fairness—after all, there was a dangerous war to be won (1990, 126).

War is a popular metaphor precisely because it envisions the crime problem to be so serious as to require drastic policies and extreme measures. After
all, who is going to be willing to sacrifice and expend resources for a problem
that is not perceived to be all that bad? The war metaphor is also popular
because it implies that the sacrifices are going to be temporary. Once the war
has been won then things can presumably return to normal. When dealing
with a war on crime, however, the sacrifices we make may be more permanent
than we are willing to tolerate. Once our rights in a democratic society are
willingly given up they may be difficult to reestablish. Therefore, a critical
look at what the war on crime in U.S. society actually entails is in order.

What Would a Real War on Crime Look Like?

The war on crime in the United States is being waged on many fronts with a
variety of policies, programs, tactics, and strategies. Many criminal justice
agencies are involved and several other institutions such as schools, churches,
and corporations are pledged to contribute whatever efforts they have available to combat illegal behavior. But are the efforts to curb crime really worthy
to be called a war? No, not by a long shot. What passes as a war on crime is
nothing more than selective enforcement of some high visibility crimes,
which serves to help politicians get elected and to undermine our democratic
institutions (Bertram et al. 1996; Manning and Redlinger 1986).
    A true war on crime would turn the United States into a police state. The
liberties afforded by the Bill of Rights would need to be suspended and the
individual citizen would be exposed to the whim and caprice of the police,
prosecutors, and judges. It is politically and practically impossible to wage an
actual war on crime because to do so would mean we would have to wage war
on ourselves. War as a metaphor is appropriate when there is an external
enemy but is misleading when it is applied to social problems such as crime
and drug use. Let's look at some of the policies that fall under the rubric of
the war on crime and discuss what is not being done that a true war on crime
would entail.

Law Enforcement

This is the area where the war on crime is most visible and for good reason.
Law enforcement agencies are structured as **quasi-military bureaucracies**
(see Chapter 5). There are uniforms, inspections, ranks (captain, sergeant etc.),
and weapons. But even given the quasi-military nature of law enforcement,
the war on crime initiative has increased the military overtones of this institution. Now **SWAT** (Special Weapons and Tactics) teams dress in camouflage

The police sometimes face situations that require a military-type response.
(© David Woo/Stock Boston.)

fatigues or all-black uniforms. They wear flack jackets and carry automatic weapons. Some law enforcement agencies have armored vehicles and helicopters. The line between the military and local police forces gets blurred when such resources are employed. In terms of tactics, law enforcement agencies often mimic the military. Roadblocks, drug sweeps, and undercover intelligence efforts all are reminiscent of military strategies during wartime.

Courts

The war on crime as waged by the court system entails several features that differentiate it from the normal processing of cases. One good example of this is the manner in which **career criminals** are handled. Career criminals are offenders who have been convicted of serious crimes in the past and now meet strict definitional requirements that allow the courts to treat them in special ways and apply more severe sanctions to their cases. We will deal with career criminals in a later chapter on courts, but suffice it to say here that they are dealt with in a more severe and adversarial manner. Another aspect of the war on crime that can be seen in the courts is the emerging sentencing patterns. In the past two decades we have seen a retreat from the **indeterminate sentence,** which vested broad discretion in the judges and parole boards to dispense sentences that take into consideration both the legal circumstances of the crime and offender (seriousness of offense and prior record) and the extralegal characteristics of the defendant (probability of further offending and likelihood of rehabilitation). Today, in an effort to limit discretion and treat offenders in a more equivalent manner, the indeterminate sentence has been replaced by **determinate** or **fixed sentences** (Albanese 1984). This has led to longer sentences for a broad range of offenders and the need to build more prisons. In discussing the "three strikes" legislation in California, Skolnick (1995, 23) explains how this type of sentencing impacts prisons and the state budget.

> *To pay for a fivefold increase in the corrections budget since 1980, Californians have had to sacrifice other services. In 1984, California devoted 14 percent of its state budget to higher education and 4 percent to prisons. In 1994, it gave 9 percent to both.*

Corrections

Overcrowding has had a detrimental impact on not only prisons but also on probation, parole, and diversion programs. There simply are not the resources to do what these agencies are designed to accomplish. But the war on crime has influenced corrections in other ways. The correctional component of the criminal justice system has gotten more punitive as a result of the war on crime perspective. From the new maxi-max prisons, which do little more than warehouse prisoners, to the intensive supervision probation and parole programs that increase the requirements and sanctions of offenders, the war on crime has made corrections less helpful and more threatening to offenders (Blomberg and Lucken 1994). In fact, the very idea of treatment in prisons has been co-oped to allow for greater punishment.

> *If we look to the penological methods in use at the present time we can see that therapy in prisons is often indistinguishable from punishment. The actual consequences accruing to those individuals being treated in reality differ very little from the consequences accruing to people being punished. The reality of punitive measures which subject individuals to involuntary deprivations of their freedom is not altered by the fact that the motives inherent in the decision are of reform or contribution to the individual's well being (Selva 1980, 271–272).*

There should be little debate that the criminal justice system in the United States has purposefully and dramatically made the move toward a more punitive posture in dealing with the criminal offender (Reuter 1992; Rosenbaum 1991). In some ways this has been at the request or even the demand of citizens who are affected by crime, but in many ways the move toward declaring a war on crime has been motivated by politicians and the media who see the issue of crime as serving their own agendas (Kaminer 1994).

The war on crime has impacted on everyone in society in ways that may not be readily apparent but that undermine the safety and welfare of victims of crime and innocent bystanders. Because of the aggressive stance of law enforcement and the courts, the level of tension on the street has increased to the extent that criminals are more likely to fight rather than be arrested and face the types of mandatory penalties now on the books. Drunk driving provides an interesting example of how the war on crime can increase the danger to citizens. Because of the accelerated penalties for driving under the influence of alcohol or drugs, drivers sometimes will attempt to flee rather than stop when law enforcement officers try to stop them. The traffic hazards resulting from high-speed pursuits expose unsuspecting motorists and pedestrians at risk of getting struck by both the vehicles of the drunk driver and the law enforcement officer.

The increased risks associated with drug trafficking mean that the level of danger for law enforcement officers is greatly increased. Rather than look at long mandatory sentences in prison with little or no chance of parole, drug dealers are tempted to use extreme measures to ensure they do not get apprehended. All of a sudden human life becomes cheap and the killing of witnesses or law enforcement officers can look like a reasonable policy to the drug dealer who risks losing not only his or her freedom but also a lucrative income from the drug trade. The higher price of drugs associated with the increased risks resulting from the war on crime perspective makes drug trafficking an activity that jeopardizes the safety of the community even more than the prospect of the problems associated with simple drug use (Tobolowsky 1992). It is the war on drugs, not the drugs themselves, that make the streets of the city so dangerous for citizens and law enforcement officers (Sweet 1996).

Has the War on Crime Worked?

Evaluating a social policy such as the war on crime is a difficult task. What indicators do we look at to determine if the policies are effective in attaining our desired goal? The central problem of evaluating criminal justice policies is determining if a policy actually impacted on the problem or if other factors are responsible for any changes. Measuring crime-control strategies is in essence measuring something that does not happen. Given normal fluctuations in the crime rate, changes in the economy, shifts in demographics, and other social programs aimed at factors associated with crime, it is extremely difficult to credit a criminal justice policy with a reduction in crime.

One way to attempt to measure a criminal justice system strategy is to look at the output of criminal justice agencies. For instance, if one wishes to assess the effectiveness of a drug enforcement project the number of arrests or the amount of drugs seized would be tallied. The problem with using this kind of measure is that we are not really determining the impact of the project on the drug problem at all: we are simply measuring the output of the criminal justice agency. Despite impressive numbers of arrests or tons of seized drugs, the project may not be making a dent in the amount of drugs available on the street. A good analogy to illustrate this point is the practice during the Vietnam War of the military to claim progress based on how many of the enemy were killed. Body count became the indicator of choice for the military, which led to a false sense of progress and also to a perversion of the entire mission for Americans serving there. Because dead Vietnamese got included in the body count whether they were allies or enemies it made little difference to the U.S. officers who were evaluated on the body count their troops amassed.

Rather than trying to measure the real goal of the U.S. involvement in Vietnam, the "winning the hearts and minds" of the people, the military substituted an indicator they could measure: body count (Luttwak 1985). Of course, as we all realize now, the American people were misled about the progress of the war and, even more problematic, great injustices in the form of war crimes were imposed on the Vietnamese people (Lewy 1978).

Reducing the level of crime in the United States entails some of the same problems of measurement as winning the hearts and minds of the Vietnamese people. The fundamental issue becomes telling the "good guys from the bad guys." Criminals do not conveniently label themselves by wearing uniforms so that they can be readily distinguished from the law-abiding citizens. In an effort to detect, apprehend, and punish the criminal, we all too often trample the rights and privacy of individuals who have not violated any laws.

There is an additional problem in attempting to determine if we are winning the war on crime by looking at the output of criminal justice agencies, and that is crime displacement. Increased arrest rates or quantities of drugs captured may signify victory over crime in one sense but may actually result in the criminal enterprise moving to an adjacent location. The production of marijuana is a good example of how law enforcement activity has not been effective in stemming the drug trade. The increased border surveillance that was effective in preventing marijuana from being smuggled from Mexico and the Caribbean has had the unintended consequence of spawning a robust domestic marijuana-growing industry (Weisheit 1992). While customs, the border patrol, and the DEA can claim a victory of sorts in stemming the flow of marijuana into the country, they have not solved the problem but simply forced a mutation of it into what some people would claim to be a more serious form of marijuana production. Where a few U.S. citizens were involved in the importation of the drug, now many are making their livelihoods growing and selling it domestically. We have not only failed to win the war on marijuana, we have caused a displacement effect which has made it one of the most profitable cash crops in the country and has strained the resources of local criminal justice agencies to deal with other crimes (Potter et al. 1990).

Skyjacking

It is sometimes tempting to conclude that little can be done to address criminal behavior by public policy and that we should throw up our hands in despair and simply give up. This would be a mistake because there are steps that can be taken to curb specific criminal behaviors that can not only be effective but can also be accepted by the majority of citizens (Etzioni 1993). **Skyjacking** serves as a useful example of what society can do to stem or curb actions that we find so unacceptable that we are willing to go to great extremes. Criminals and political terrorists found the airline industry suscep- tible to extortion by a single individual who would hijack, or in this case, sky- jack an entire planeload of people with a handgun or the threat of a bomb. For a period of time in the 1960s it seemed like a monthly occurrence on the evening news that someone had skyjacked a plane and demanded to be flown to Cuba. In one particularly well-publicized case a man (popularly known as D. B. Cooper) skyjacked a plane in the northwest and, after receiving a large sum of money, bailed out, never to be seen or heard from again. He was either a very talented criminal who had a well conceived plan or a fool who risked his life jumping out of a jet at 30,000 feet and fell to his death. In any event, the D. B. Cooper case demonstrates how a crime can capture the attention of the nation and how skyjacking became so visible that it was decided some- thing drastic needed to be done about it.

A number of options to stop skyjacking were suggested, including placing **sky marshals** on every plane to "ride shotgun" as used to be done on the stagecoaches of the old west. It was pointed out, however, that this policy of placing armed guards on each plane could cause more problems than it solved. The last thing the airlines wanted were gun battles at 30,000 feet. A bullet piercing the fuselage of a jet at that altitude would cause decompres- sion that could cause the plane to crash. Other options included physically frisking each passenger before they were allowed to board each plane, but this was considered not only demeaning but also too costly in terms of time and personnel required.

The solution to skyjacking, as everyone who travels by air now knows, was to x-ray all carry-on luggage and to electronically search everyone who gets on a plane. Technology was developed that allows the airline industry to process thousands of passengers boarding hundreds of flights each day. Still, when this procedure was first proposed, there were many who objected to what they felt was an invasion of their privacy by the electronic search and the x-ray examination of their luggage. It was decided that skyjacking was such a serious problem that the traveling public would be willing to sacrifice a little privacy for the security of flying and not having the plane they were on skyjacked.

Skyjacking, then, is an example of what society can do to protect itself if it is willing to make hard decisions and choose between competing values, in this case between privacy and safe flying. However, in other ways it is a mis- leading example of how effective public policies can be in stopping crime. The resources required to stop skyjacking were expensive and extensive but because of the nature of the problem they were able to be concentrated in a very small locale. All skyjackers must board the plane at the airports so the airline industry was able to funnel all passengers through natural bottlenecks leading from the terminal to the departure ramps. Resources therefore could be concentrated and everyone boarding a plane could be inspected.

How does the experience of stopping skyjackers translate to stopping other types of crime? Unfortunately, not very well. People are willing to sacrifice a certain amount of privacy to be able to engage in the relatively rare behavior of flying in an airplane, but they are not willing to expose themselves to this type of intrusive surveillance and inconvenience to go about their daily routines. With the exception of getting on airplanes, entering certain high-risk buildings such as Congress and some federal courthouses, there is little that can be done under our current system of laws that can effectively protect us from violence and is not also greatly intrusive on our civil rights.

COSTS OF THE WAR ON CRIME

When the founders of the United States wrote the Constitution they almost immediately amended it by adding the Bill of Rights, or the first 10 amendments. The Bill of Rights spells out what rights the individual has in relation to the government. It is designed to preserve the freedom of the individual from intrusive government interference. Only in extreme circumstances, such as a state of war, can the guarantees of the Bill of Rights be suspended. When we use the metaphor of declaring a war on crime we need to guard against infringing the freedoms afforded by the Bill of Rights, because as we have already discussed the war on crime is not truly a war but rather an approach to a social problem.

Human and Civil Rights

There are several strategies employed by the criminal justice system to get tough on crime. Many of these strategies are legitimate ways the system can become more effective. The use of computers to keep offenders from falling through the cracks in the system, the deployment of more law enforcement officers, and the concentration on the truly violent offender are all strategies the criminal justice system can and should use that do not infringe on the rights of citizens. There are other strategies of the war on crime that cause concern. In an effort to get tough on crime, politicians have enacted laws that change the nature of the balance between the rights of the citizens and the procedural laws that guide law enforcement. These new laws, or new interpretations of old laws, while aimed at the criminal, also impact on law-abiding citizens in a way that some criminologists find problematic (Kalstein et al. 1992).

A few examples are useful to illustrate how the criminal justice system, in an effort to wage war on criminals, often involved innocent citizens. Drug dealing, for reasons of security, is a cash business. Drug dealers cannot use checks and credit cards because the paper trail would make their arrest and conviction too certain. Money used in drug deals can be confiscated by law enforcement officers without their having to prove it was the cash that was actually used to buy drugs.

In 1991, a landscaper from Nashville, Tennessee bought an airline ticket with cash to go to Houston, Texas. The ticket agent tipped off the DEA that a customer had a large sum of cash on him and this landscaper, who is an African-American, was searched. While no drugs were found, the $9,600 cash discovered inside his wallet was confiscated because the DEA suspected its purpose was to purchase drugs even though he had no criminal record. The landscaper contended he was on the way to buy shrubbery and that it is a common practice to pay cash, even large amounts of cash, in the landscaping business. Nevertheless, his money was confiscated, and he had to hire an attorney to get it back from the government. The airline ticket agent was paid a reward for tipping off the DEA that the man had a large amount of cash on him. The landscaper is quoted as saying, "I didn't know it was against the law for a 42-year-old man to have money in his pocket" (Levy 1996, 3).

In another case, a woman and her friend were driving south on Interstate 95 and were stopped in central Florida. The law enforcement officer found $19,000 in her purse, which she contends was to be used for repairs to her home which was damaged by Hurricane Hugo. The officer concluded the money was to be used for drugs and confiscated it without arresting her or even taking her name. She followed the officer back to the police station, filed a complaint, hired an attorney, and learned it was the officer's right to act as he did. Based on her attorney's advice, that it was extremely expensive to contest a forfeiture case, she settled out of court by allowing the sheriff's department to keep $4,000 of her money.

One would expect that if Interstate 95 is used to transport drugs from Florida, where they enter the country, to the northeast cities of New York, Philadelphia, and Boston, where they are presumably sold on the streets, that the law enforcement officers would stop cars headed north to try to intercept the drugs. Because the **forfeiture laws** allow the law enforcement agencies to keep the cash that is confiscated they target traffic headed south and assume that any large amounts of cash found is destined for the drug trade. Many people innocent of any crime and without intention of engaging in behaviors harmful to society are stopped and their large amounts of cash taken by law enforcement authorities based simply on some stereotypic profiles of what drug dealers look like. These profiles impact on the young and minorities, and the burden of proof then falls on them to prove the cash is not to be used for drugs. This is extremely expensive and difficult to accomplish, and the result is that law enforcement agencies end up with a great deal of cash.

On one hand it is easy to see why legislators would pass such laws that make it easy for law enforcement officers to target the cash used in drug trade. Drug dealers go to great lengths to avoid getting caught, and the public demands that something be done. A war-on-drugs mentality suggests that any tactic that is useful is legitimate because, after all, the goal is to keep drugs off the streets and out of the playgrounds of our cities. On the other hand, however, the expanded freedoms of law enforcement have some unintended consequences. Overzealous police can substitute the goal of reducing cash available for drug buys with the goal of generating cash to supplement their own coffers.

In addition to the laws concerning forfeiture, there are other practices used by law enforcement agencies engaged in the war on crime that overstep what reasonable individuals consider to be appropriate limits of the reach of the law. Christina Jacqueline Johns, in her book *Power, Ideology, and the War on Drugs: Nothing Succeeds Like Failure* (1992, 90–127), details many of the ways in which the war metaphor translates into policies that infringe on the rights of individuals.

1. *The right to privacy and searches.* Johns refers to cases where the Supreme Court has expanded the ability of government agents to intrude on the privacy of citizens through search and seizure and increased surveillance. These include cases that validate aerial surveillance; searches in airports without probable cause of people who fit a drug-courier profile; warrantless searches of automobiles and inside compartments; surveillance of suspects with electronic devices placed inside cars, briefcases, or trunks; the acquisition of warrants to search private homes based on anonymous tips; police inspection of bank records without customer consent; and the reading and inspecting of contents of a person's trash without warrant or probable cause. As an example of how intrusive some of these searches have become, Johns refers to a policy in 1989 where the DEA conducted raids in 46 states of stores specializing in the sale of indoor garden supplies. These legitimate businesses had their records seized by the DEA who were looking for customers who might be cultivating marijuana indoors.

2. *The right to free speech.* Many of the indoor garden supply stores targeted by the DEA had advertised in pro-marijuana magazines such as *High Times* or *Sinsemilla Tips*. Even though the equipment they sold was available to marijuana growers in many stores in every community, these stores were targeted because they advertised in a perfectly legal pro-marijuana magazine.

3. *The right to financial privacy.* Because criminals must somehow turn their ill-gotten cash into legitimate assets, banks are under constant pressure to cooperate with law enforcement officers attempting to detect money laundering. The government can freeze bank accounts of persons whom they suspect of illegal activities.

4. *Illegally gathered evidence: The exclusionary rule.* The exclusionary rule prohibits the use of evidence in criminal cases if that evidence was not obtained legally. In the Anti-Drug Abuse Bill of 1988, flawed evidence is permitted to be used if that evidence was gathered by law enforcement officials in good faith. While many citizens support this closing of a legal loophole, it is important to realize that law enforcement officers do not always act in good faith and should be held to a high standard of procedural law.

5. *Drug testing.* The war on drugs has captured the imagination of the public to such an extent that procedures that would have been dismissed as outrageous a generation ago are accepted as necessary today to ensure public safety. Drug testing of prisoners, employees, athletes, and students has become widespread in American society. It is probably true that if drug testing were less expensive it would be even more pervasive. From a legal point of view, drug testing is problematic because of the Fourth Amendment right against unreasonable search and seizure. When an individual is required to submit bodily fluids that could be incriminating, it becomes an issue of legal questionability and, to many, an abuse of the power of the state to intrude into the affairs of citizens. Clearly, there are different contexts of drug testing and some, such as the testing of airline pilots for intoxication, are agreeably legitimate. Those who promote the **war on crime perspective,** however, have proposed or actually implemented drug-testing policies that go far beyond what is required to protect society. For instance, there was a bill being considered by the Georgia legislature that would require the random drug testing of everyone associated with education in the state. Teachers, professors, administrators, custodians, every student, and even food service workers would be subject to unannounced, mandatory drug testing. It was only the prohibited cost of such a widespread program that prevented it from being passed into law.

One of the problems with drug testing for the purpose of public safety is that the tests do not measure intoxication as much as they measure lifestyle. Because traces of drugs like marijuana stay in the body for weeks, a drug test cannot detect if the person's judgment and motor functioning are impaired or if the person simply used the drug sometime in the past. In the case of breathalyzer tests to detect the blood alcohol level to determine if someone is dangerous behind the wheel of an automobile, a significant case can be made since the public safety is being protected. Drug testing for other illicit substances cannot make this claim for the protection of public safety and are therefore contentious issues to those concerned about constitutional protections.

Drug testing has become more widespread in the private sector than in public life. Private corporations are not governed by the same rigid guarantees of rights as are public institutions. Private corporations can test employees as part of preemployment screening or randomly while they work for the company. Employment in a private business is not a right and more restrictive requirements can be imposed on employees. It is good public relations for private employers to promote a drug-free environment and they are able to pass the cost of the drug testing on to the consumer. One of the real successes of the war on crime perspective is the way in which it has changed the mindset of the population concerning drugs. It has convinced people to accept restrictions on their liberties from many different quarters.

6. *Due process and the rights of defendants.* There is a major assault taking place on the rights of those suspected of illegal behaviors in this country. The mood of the public is to close what they perceive are loopholes in the crimi-

nal law which allow criminals too many protections from the efforts of law enforcement officials. The public believes that victims have less rights in the criminal justice system than the offenders and some politicians play up this attitude in their campaigns. As previously mentioned, the exclusionary rule that makes evidence illegally gathered has been modified if the court determines the law enforcement officers acted in good faith. Other due process provisions that are under attack include Miranda warnings, where suspects are advised of their right to an attorney before they talk to police and possibly incriminate themselves, the limiting of legal appeals of offenders on death row, and the provisions that allow some drug offenders to be handled in civil procedures rather than criminal courts. The criminal justice system can be very confusing to people and the rules of procedure often seem to and sometimes actually do allow the guilty to escape punishment. In an effort to prevent some seeming miscarriages of justice, the due process rights of everyone are being reconsidered in state legislatures in many states across the country as well as in Congress.

7. *Public housing.* The war on crime, especially the war on drugs, has hit those living in public housing more severely than those renting or owning their own residences. Because those living in public housing are often the victims of crime and lack the resources to move if the environment is unsafe, it seems reasonable to expect the government to do what it can to ensure the safety of the residents. However, when law enforcement authorities start treating residents of public housing projects with fewer due process rights it becomes a matter of concern to those attentive to issues of social justice. The Anti-Drug Abuse Bill of 1988 contained provisions that would allow residents to be evicted from their homes if illegal activities, such as drug dealing, occurred on the premises. It did not matter if the residents themselves were innocent of any criminal violation—as long as their children or guests committed a crime in public housing projects, the residents could be expelled. Additionally, drug sweeps through the projects were performed with military precision which, rather than being targeted at specific offenders, were aimed at all the residents simply because they were residents of the public housing projects. This can be seen not so much as a war against crime or drugs but as a war against the poor. Imagine the protests if the police conducted such drug sweeps through the more affluent neighborhoods in the city.

8. *The family.* The war on crime has had a detrimental impact on some families. Children indoctrinated by schools with the message that all drug use is bad have reported their parents to the police. Such behavior, once thought to be the fantasy of novels like George Orwell's *1984,* has become so commonplace that it no longer surprises us and seldom is covered by the media except on a very local basis. Some will argue that children reporting their parents is a good thing. Homes where illegal drugs are used are considered unfit homes, so the thinking goes, and parents need to stop using their drugs or face losing their children. Others will argue that recreational drug use is a private matter and that the state should keep its intrusive surveillance out of the

home especially when it takes the form of recruiting children through indoctrination. A similar problem is when parents monitor the behavior of their children as part of the war on crime. Home-administered drug testing kits are available for parents to determine whether their children are using illegal drugs. While few would argue that it is desirable for parents to prohibit drug use, testing one's children seems to violate the bond of trust that families work so hard to establish. The family is a fundamental but fragile institution that is critical to the healthy functioning of society. The efforts of the state to intervene in the dynamics of family life, even for such important matters as combating crime, should be done with great care. Once the delicate trust of family members is broken, all kinds of problems can result, many of which the government are incapable of resolving.

9. *Women, the unborn, and drugs.* One of the most popular images used in the war on drugs is the "crack baby." There is some debate as to whether the crack baby syndrome is a real problem or the result of media hype perpetuated by the war on drugs. What is being called an epidemic of babies addicted to crack cocaine resulting from the mother's drug-using behaviors during pregnancy may possibly be an equally worrisome example of fetal alcohol syndrome. Because many women who use crack also drink alcohol, it is difficult to separate the effects of each (Currie 1993). Regardless, the problem is a medical tragedy and should not be handled by the criminal justice system. The prenatal care available to poor women in the United States is inadequate to begin with, and imposing sanctions from the criminal justice system is going to prevent women from trying to seek what little medical help is available. Education and treatment are the answers to the crack baby and fetal alcohol syndrome problems, not imprisonment. The issue is further complicated by the abortion debate. The view that life begins at conception adds a new variable of fetal rights into the drug abuse issue. Where do the rights of an unborn child and the mother converge? The answer to that dilemma lies not in prosecution but in prevention.

10. *Expansion of the death penalty.* One of the most fashionable weapons advocated by supporters of the war on crime is the expansion of the use of the death penalty. In addition to limiting the number of appeals available to offenders sentenced to death, the circumstances for which someone can receive the death penalty have been changed. The Anti-Drug Abuse Bill of 1988 included provisions where the death penalty could be given to any person "engaging in a drug-related felony offense, who intentionally kills, or counsels, commands, or causes the intentional killing of an individual and such killing results" (Johns 1992, 110, quoting *Congressional Quarterly,* 1988). Some individuals have advocated the expansion of the death penalty to drug kingpins whether any death occurs or not. The rationale of the supporters of the war on crime perspective is that drugs do great social harm, that sometimes people die from drug overdoses, and the drug dealers and suppliers should bear the responsibility even though they may be several times removed from the final transaction. Those who make the big money from the importation or manufacturing of illegal drugs should be held accountable and punished accordingly for their profitable behaviors. Only in this way can drug dealers be deterred from engaging in such lucrative enterprises.

11. *Harsher punishments.* There is a public perception that the United States is soft on crime and this leads to more and more people engaging in criminal activities because they believe that when caught they will be treated leniently. This is not the case, however, because the United States uses incarceration as an instrument of social control in a way not equaled by other developed nations in the western world.

12. *Dangerousness and preventive detention.* One of the most unjust myths concerning crime in this country is that we can accurately predict which individual will be a danger to society and that by placing these people in detention we can prevent a significant amount of crime. Prediction scales and tables have been developed that are supposed to accomplish this task and have the added feature of imposing more uniformity into the decision-making processes of the criminal justice system. While limiting the disparity between offenders sharing similar characteristics (seriousness of offense, prior record) is a worthy goal, the problem arises when extralegal factors (sex, race and ethnicity, social class) are taken into consideration. According to Decker and Salert (1987), preventive detention does little in terms of protecting society and, by taking such variables as unemployment into account, has a discriminatory effect. While criminologists can make some realistic predictions based on group characteristics, they cannot, with any degree of accuracy, predict individual behavior. Thus, preventive detention predictions are based on who people are rather than on what they do.

13. *Student loans and the right to education.* The war on crime has enlisted the aid of schools to combat illegal drug use. Students face the loss of loans from the federal government if they are convicted of drug offenses and they are subject to expulsion if they sell or possess drugs on campus. While most people will agree that schools should be free from drugs, the zero-tolerance programs imposed by some schools and universities require resources to be directed away from academic and student service activities toward enforcement efforts whether there is a demonstrated drug problem or not. Additionally, athletes are subject to drug testing based simply on their status of being on a school team. These policies reject the value of presumption of innocence and require students to prove their conformity to school drug policies. This war-on-crime mentality flies in the face of the goals of education to teach students to learn to make important decisions for themselves.

14. *Workplace surveillance.* Drug testing in the workplace is only one of the techniques used by employers to enforce drug policies promoted by the war on crime perspective. Undercover private security agents pose as workers attempting to buy drugs and detect drug use in the workplace. Again, there is a legitimate need for corporations to ensure a safe and healthy work environment for all employees, but the lengths to which some companies have gone to detect unlawful behavior, even when they have no reason to suspect it, violates the sense of fairness and privacy that is part of living in a democratic society.

15. *The militarization of civil society.* One of the premier hallmarks of the war on crime perspective is the **militarization of civil society:** the military rhetoric, the actual use of the military, and the quasi-military nature of civilian programs used to deal with domestic crime. While we previously stated that the phrase "war on crime" is a metaphor, there are distinct military overtones and tactics used to apply the metaphor. These include the actual use of the military to attempt to seal the borders to stem the influx of drugs and illegal immigrants, the use of state National Guard and Army Reserve units to detect and destroy the domestic marijuana crop, and the use of the military model of discipline in boot-camp prisons. There is a widespread belief that the war perspective can be transposed from the international arena to the domestic one. The massive funds spent on the defense industry are now up for grabs with the demise of the former Soviet Union. While a strong defense will always be required, the mission of the military is subject to debate and the type of training exercises are undergoing constant change. Combating domestic crime is an attractive real-life training arena and an efficient way to capitalize on money that has already been allocated. There is a real danger to employing the military model to the domestic crime situation, however. We need only look to other countries to see some of the problems when the simplistic goal of using superior force (very useful on the battlefield) is used to control a civilian population. Military dictatorships have features that are inconsistent with democratic values. The founders of the United States were careful to specify the relationship between civil and military life precisely for the reasons of avoiding the problems inherent in military police states.

As we can see from this list of issues, the war on crime perspective is not without its own set of concerns. While many of these issues represent policies and programs that when used with moderation and proper oversight can help reduce the incidence, costs, and suffering caused by crime, many of these policies fail to make our streets, homes, and institutions safer and have the unintended consequences of increasing crime while at the same time dismantling the procedural and legal safeguards that make this a nation built on freedom, liberty, and justice.

Are People Losing Respect for U.S. Institutions?

U.S. institutions have been relatively stable and effective throughout our history. While there is often a time lag while our institutions catch up to social change in society, they can be characterized as flexible in accommodating to the will of the people. Institutions do, however, seem to take on a life of their own. The policies and laws in the United States are aimed at the traditional nuclear family when contemporary conditions dictate that even when there are two parents in the home they both be employed. The institution of the traditional family is more of an ideal than a reality in this country and issues such as government-supported daycare remain unfunded because politicians, and much of the public, do not want to recognize that the family is not what it used to be or rather what we would like to believe it used to be.

From the church to the military to medical care to education, all of our society's institutions are feeling the stresses of modernity (Etzioni 1993). The pace of social change is so rapid that it is almost impossible for our institutions to keep up with the needs of citizens. Alvin Toffler coined the term "future shock" to account for how the ways we thought and did things in the past, and increasingly in the present, are not sufficient to account for the massive changes coming in the near future. A simplistic war on crime will not make the streets safer and represents a substantial threat to the glue that holds our institutions together, the rights of people to be protected from their government.

Distrust of the criminal justice system can be seen in many segments of society. The rise of domestic groups like the Freemen in Montana, militia groups in many states, and angry citizens who turn to internal terrorism point to a rejection of the legitimacy of the government. In the inner cities, many view the police as an invading army that dispenses street justice based on race, age, and class differences. Courts appear to favor the wealthy and prisons are reserved for those without means. Many criminal justice professors assign their classes to read Jeffery Rieman's scathing *The Rich Get Richer and the Poor Get Prison (1995).*

It is the central thesis of this book that the war on crime is doomed to failure not just because it is ineffective, but also because it is morally bankrupt. To use a medical analogy, domestic crime cannot be removed by radical surgery because too many of the good cells are intertwined with the bad. What is needed to deal with the cancer of crime is both a cure that reforms the bad cells and, more importantly, a vaccine that prevents cells from getting sick in the first place. For our society and the criminal justice system this can be translated to envision both an environment of social justice where everyone is given the opportunity to succeed through legitimate means, and an emphasis on reform and rehabilitation where those who have committed crimes are permitted to reconcile with those they have injured and with society as a whole.

It will be argued in this book that the war on crime, while fought by good people with noble motivations, is an inherently flawed strategy. What is needed to address both crime and many other social problems related to crime is a new and more effective way to address deviance in our society. Chapter 3 presents such a strategy to address crime. A peacemaking perspective that concentrates on social justice and nonviolent conflict resolution is put forth as an alternative to the war on crime. While this may appear to be a radical departure from the way crime is currently confronted, many of the tenets of the peacemaking perspective are presently employed to some degree in many agencies, programs, and jurisdictions. What this book attempts to do is present the peacemaking perspective as a coherent and related whole so the student can see the connections between the many efforts of courageous individuals who are working to make our society safer by making it more socially just.

CRITICAL THINKING QUESTIONS

1. Discuss why the phrase "war on crime" is a misleading metaphor to describe the workings of the criminal justice system. What would a real "war on crime" entail?

2. Debate just how important is the issue of waging a war on crime. What are the likely casualties of such a war in terms of human and civil rights?

3. Air travelers routinely submit to electronic body searches in order to be allowed to get on an airplane. What other invasions of privacy would you be willing to incur to fight a war on crime and drugs?

4. Discuss whether the war on crime and drugs increases or decreases the public's confidence in its institutions. What is the relationship between the war on crime perspective and the democratic values ingrained in the U.S. system of government?

SUGGESTED READINGS

Bertram, Eva, Morris Blackman, Kenneth Sharpe, and Peter Andreas. 1996. *Drug War Politics: The Price of Denial*. Berkeley: University of California Press.

Czajkoski, Eugene H. 1990. "Drugs and the Warlike Administration of Justice." *The Journal of Drug Issues 20*(1): 125–129.

Etzioni, Amitai. 1993. *The Spirit of Community: The Reinvention of American Society*. New York: Touchstone.

Johns, Christina Jacqueline. 1992. *Power, Ideology, and the War on Drugs: Nothing Succeeds Like Failure*. New York: Praeger.

Kozol, Jonathan. 1967. *Death at an Early Age*. New York: Bantam.

Kozol, Jonathan. 1991. *Savage Inequalities*. New York: Crown.

Manning, Peter K., and Lawrence J. Redlinger. 1986. "Invitational Edges of Corruption: Some Consequences of Narcotic Law Enforcement," in Thomas Barker and David L. Carter, eds. *Police Deviance*. Cincinnati: Pilgrimage, pp. 40–69.

Reuter, Peter. 1992. "Hawks Ascendant: The Punitive Trend of American Drug Policy." *Daedalus 121*(3): 15–52.

Skolnick, Jerome H. 1995. "Gangs and Crime Old as Time; But Drugs Change Gang Culture," in Malcolm Klein, Cheryl L. Maxson, and Jody Miller, eds. *The Modern Gang Reader*. Los Angeles: Roxbury, pp. 222–227.

Tobolowsky, Peggy M. 1992. "Drugs and Death: Congress Authorizes the Death Penalty for Certain Drug-Related Murders." *Journal of Contemporary Law 18*(1): 47–73.

Weisheit, Ralph. 1992. *Domestic Marijuana: A Neglected Industry*. Westport, CT: Greenwood.

3

THE PEACE PERSPECTIVE

© Fritz Henle/Photo Researchers, Inc.

Learning Objectives

After reading this chapter, the student should be able to:

- Define the peacemaking perspective.
- Trace the religious and humanist, feminist, and critical traditions from which the peacemaking perspective is drawn.
- Describe how the peacemaking perspective is relevant to other levels of analysis as well as other institutions.
- Describe how the peacemaking perspective is not soft on crime.
- Explain how the peacemaking perspective requires reforms outside the criminal justice system.
- Describe the peacemaking heritage of Tolstoy, Gandhi, and Dr. Martin Luther King, Jr.
- Explain how the peacemaking perspective is a personal philosophy as well as a government policy.
- Describe how government policy needs to be a model for personal behavior.
- Explain how in comparison to the war on crime perspective, the peacemaking perspective has a more optimistic conception of human nature.
- Understand the peacemaking pyramid paradigm (P^3).

Key Terms

Peacemaking Perspective	Peacemaking Pyramid Paradigm (P^3)
False Consciousness	Racism
Religious Traditions	Sexism
Humanist Traditions	Ageism
Feminist Traditions	Correct Means
Patriarchy	Ascertainable Criteria
Critical Traditions	Categorical Imperative
Hegemony	Vigilantism
Satyagraha	Bill of Rights
Civil Rights Movement	Collective Violence
Nonviolent Social Protest	

When someone hits us, our normal reaction is to hit back. The same can be said for society's strong right arm, the criminal justice system. When a criminal assaults the law, our patterned response is to strike back, swift and hard, to show both the individual and others who may be watching that there are unpleasant consequences to crime. This response is so ingrained in our society that seldom do we question if there is any other way to reply to criminal behavior. Many people who have had experience with crime, particularly violent crime, believe in harsh responses. Criminals are viewed as the enemy and the war metaphor is considered the appropriate model to guide society's response to criminal activity. As demonstrated in the previous chapter, there is a long history of retribution and revenge which suggests to many people that criminal behavior is best prevented or deterred by certain, swift, and harsh punishment. We have also discussed the limitations of this approach and now turn to a radically different method.

In this chapter, we advance an alternative perspective for addressing the problems of crime. A peacemaking model of criminal justice is beginning to emerge in both the criminal justice system and academic criminology that challenges the war perspective as an effective and humane policy approach. The peace perspective emphasizes social justice, conflict resolution, rehabilitation, and a belief that people need to cooperate in democratic institutions in order to develop meaningful communities. The peace perspective is an inclusive policy model which aims at empowering all individuals and giving them an opportunity to control their destinies (Trebach 1990; Quinney 1993; McDermott 1994).

The peace perspective operates at many different levels and all have an influence on the criminal justice system. Figure 3.1 illustrates the relationship between peacemaking in criminal justice and the broader concept of the perspective. Each level of analysis or each institution could be broken out in more detail but is provided here simply as a guide to show how comprehensive the **peacemaking perspective** is.

1. There is an international/global level which envisions an interconnectedness between all living things. Taking care of the environment and opposing war are concerns of peacemakers at this broad level.

2. At the institutional/societal level, peacemaking looks at systems of government (democracies vs. dictatorships), economic systems (capitalism vs. communism), and religious systems (Christianity, Islam, . . .). The peace perspective looks at how our schools, churches, families, criminal justice systems, and other institutions develop and implement rules, policies, and norms which structure the interactions among citizens.

3. At the interpersonal level, the peace perspective looks at how individuals treat each other in resolving conflicts and dispensing power and privilege. The Golden Rule, "Do onto others as you would have them do onto you," is a simplified but accurate way to think about the peacemaking perspective at this level.

4. Finally, there is an intrapersonal level that considers how we treat ourselves. Thoreau said, "Most men lead lives of quiet desperation." The peacemaking perspective encourages us to be gentle with ourselves, to forgive our own transgressions and learn to make peace with our souls.

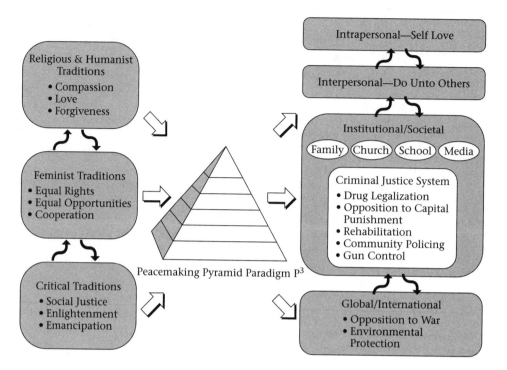

FIGURE 3.1   Peacemaking and the Criminal Justice System in Context.

The aspect of the peace perspective that sets it apart from other models of the criminal justice system is that the peace perspective requires consideration of the entire range of contributing influences, from the global to the intrapersonal. The peace perspective forms a pattern of living which permeates all human interaction and forces individuals to consider not only immediate problems but also the etiology of those problems and the consequences of proposed solutions (Currie 1989).

One of the problems in considering the peace perspective is that people envision it as being soft on crime. This perception is understandable in that the peace perspective does not use the rhetoric of the war perspective. The peace perspective, with its more inclusive view of the crime problem, looks to transform both the individual criminal and the institutions that produced this type of individual. It is a mistake to think of the peace perspective as being soft on crime, because in many ways it is very firm in how it deals with antisocial behavior.

The important message that people fail to understand about the peace perspective is that it demands justice not only on the part of the individual but also on the part of the institution. To the extent that our institutions are patriarchal, racist, and have a social class bias, the peace perspective can cast an uncomfortable light on our social problems. By requiring social justice, the peace perspective does not excuse crime, but rather looks both at the individual's culpability and at the contribution of the institutions of society. Only by transforming both can we hope to develop effective, fair, and humane responses to the problems of crime.

Peacemaking has also been criticized from the other direction by those who contend that the perspective does not go far enough in examining how the power structures of society make for unjust and inhumane relations. In reviewing what one peacemaking book had to say about race relations and class conflict, O'Malley (1993, 255) took peacemaking theorists to task from a Marxian perspective.

> *Such well-meaning peace-makers might not go down so well in communities in which black people are ghettoized and brutalized, partly because they might be seen as trying to cool the rage that fuels a just struggle. This is not meant to ridicule the peace-makers—since the rest of us have failed, we have no grounds for derision. Rather, it is to point to the old problem that pacifism is regarded as liberal, as easiest for those with a full stomach, to whom love for a rather abstract humanity is untroubled by the LAPD and the rent-man's bootboys. It is such an obvious problem, and such a vulnerable Achilles heel for a book—and a movement—of this kind, that it is genuinely surprising not to see such issues addressed.*

O'Malley raises a pivotal component in the peacemaking perspective by highlighting the fact that how one is impacted by injustice goes a long way in determining how one reacts. To the extent that Marxism envisions a struggle between the haves and the have-nots, O'Malley sees peacemaking as a naive and foolish policy, almost what Marx would term **false consciousness.** But people who employ the peacemaking perspective are not so blindly innocent. They do not simply wish and pray that crime will go away, and they are painfully cognizant of the suffering of both the victims and their offenders. The peacemaking perspective is a courageous philosophy which looks beyond the violence we do to each other and attempts to understand and address the causes for that violence. Then, and only then, can we develop lasting solutions to crime. The peacemaking perspective does not grow from a vacuum. In later chapters, the peacemaking perspective is employed to address several of the most serious issues in the criminal justice system. There are several strands of long-established ways of knowing, from different cultures, which coalesce to form the peacemaking perspective.

PEACEMAKING TRADITIONS

The peacemaking perspective in the criminal justice system is not well organized and developed at this point in time. Many individuals work in relative ignorance of others who share similar concerns, ideas, and problems

(Pepinsky 1994). The reasons for this lack of cohesion rest partly in the vastly different traditions from which peacemakers have come. For the purposes of trying to tie together peacemaking tradition we look to the structure developed by Harold Pepinsky and Richard Quinney in their collection of readings, *Criminology as Peacemaking*. They group together different viewpoints on peace into religious and humanist, feminist, and critical traditions. While not exhaustive, or even mutually exclusive, this division of viewpoints offers a useful guide in understanding the widespread and complex history of efforts to reduce tension and promote peace between individuals and groups.

Religious and Humanist Traditions

Many of the world's great religions are concerned with peace. While critics of religion point out religious wars and religious intolerance as being instruments of power that do not promote peace, most observers would agree the tenets of belief systems of religions promote a world view that conceives of people living in meaningful communities characterized by harmony, mutual cooperation, and peace. An important feature of religions is a longing for the value of life. According to many religions, our existence is not accidental and meaningless, but rather part of some greater plan which reaffirms life as not only sacred but also as having a purpose and meaning which transcends our mortal existence. Each religion puts its own spin on the cosmic questions: Who are we? Why we are here? What is the plan for humankind? However, the important point to observe is how the similarities of religions outweigh their differences. As for morality, religions provide a divine guide.

> *The intellectual and emotional sides of religion affect behavior. Religion has always been linked to morality, though moral systems differ greatly from place to place. Whether morals can exist without religion or some supernatural belief has been debated, but at least all religions have important moral commandments. The famous laws of Hammurapi of Babylon, which date from about the eighteenth century B.C., gave royal, feudal, legal and social prescriptions, but were said to have been received from the god of justice (Parrinder 1971, 10).*

The legal and social prescriptions dictating social justice and respect for life are the peacemaking traditions that religions provide to vast numbers of people. While not all religions concern themselves with these ideas to the same degree, we can see that religions provide a perspective on life that includes peace as a central feature (Ross and Hills 1956; Smith 1958).

In Christianity, the 10 commandments provide a moral code which embraces a peaceful perspective. Taken literally, as some people do, the commandment, "You shall not kill," embraces a peacemaking philosophy which argues against not only war, but against crimes of murder and even against capital punishment on the part of the state. Clearly, the peacemaking perspective, with its **religious traditions,** challenges not only the behavior of individuals but also the behavior of institutions of social control.

Religious traditions also alert us to the universal qualities that all human beings possess. In the criminal justice system offenders are viewed as being different from other citizens. Our academic studies divide criminals from a control group of "good" subjects and look for small but statistically significant differences in physical, emotional, social, economic, and a vast array of other characteristics to demonstrate loosely constructed ideas about the causes of crime. Criminals are no different from the rest of us and religion helps us keep this important notion in mind.

There are **humanist traditions** which also embrace a peace perspective. Humanists believe it is possible to live a moral life without religious theory as a basis. Humanists envision a relationship between people as being fair and peaceful because it is in peoples' best interest to treat one another as they wish to be treated. Based on an assumption about human nature that optimistically envisions people as basically good, the humanist tradition imagines a world where people cooperate for the benefit of all. Without the historical cleavages of religion, the humanists construct a relationship among people that is inclusive and tolerant of opposing viewpoints. While religion is one of the institutions that cements society together, it is also one of the organizations that divides groups of people and provides the rationale for discrimination, hate, and war. Religious zealots throughout history have caused immense amounts of pain and suffering.

Feminist Traditions

In the past 30 years, women have had a tremendous impact on the functioning of the criminal justice system. While the women's movement has influenced all the institutions of American society, it is the criminal justice system that a feminist perspective has most directly challenged the patriarchal authority of men (Knopp 1991).

Domestic violence is the best example of how the women's movement has changed our attitudes about the relationship between women and men. While there is still work to be done in improving the status of women in society, the consequences of domestic violence is an area that has signaled a new attitude toward gender relations in society.

According to the feminist perspective, justice should be blind to sex. Women and men should have the same opportunities made available to them by the law. There is a long history of subjugation of women that remains to be overcome in both behavior and attitude, which the feminists are addressing. **Patriarchy** is perpetuated by the gender-role socialization in our society, which emphasizes mutually exclusive patterns of behavior for women and men. The problems with this gender role socialization are that women are subjugated both in the work place and at home (Caufield 1993; Hochschild 1993; Mainardi 1993; Reskin 1993). Women devalued in society are victims of male attitudes and behaviors, a result of a long history of patriarchy so ingrained that many people do not even question it.

Feminists look at the structure of society to be a function of male privilege and propose to transform the process of allocating resources to one of meritocracy. That is, individuals will be rewarded based on what they do rather than who they are. According to the feminist perspective, women are able to compete with men when the social systems of society give them a fair footing. The inequities between the sexes we witness now are a result of the unequal opportunities allocated to women. Historically, women have been excluded from prestigious and high-paying occupations, have been paid a fraction of what men earn in comparable work, and are bound to the home by custom and children. These conditions have resulted in women finding themselves victims of a culture created by men for the advantage of men. Being female will no longer be an adequate justification for being denied full rights of participation in the concerns of society.

More important for the peace perspective, feminists reject the masculine processes that result in patriarchy. The masculine model of power and domination which are taught in the sport and business cultures produce a dysfunctional individual who is incapable of interacting in a peaceful and cooperative way. The feminist model, in contrast, is more conducive to the development of human potential without regard to sex and rejects the idea that power is the path to fulfillment. The feminists want their share of power, but they do not want to exercise it in the manner that men do. Lacking masculine socialization, women are able to repudiate the culture of domination that is so much a part of boys' and men's worlds.

Critical Traditions

Like the feminist tradition of peacemaking, the critical tradition focuses on power and domination as the instruments of social control that require attention by reformers. Where feminists see patriarchy and male domination as problematic, the critical theorists see several other influences causing social inequities.

Foremost among the concerns of critical theorists is the concept of social class. Karl Marx laid the groundwork for a number of critical theorists with his critique of capitalist society. The inherent contradictions in capitalism are responsible for a social system that relegates certain groups of people to perpetual poverty (Anderson 1991). The upward mobility which is a prime idyllic feature of capitalism is, according to Marx, simply a matter of false consciousness. That is, individuals buy into the myth of upward mobility in capitalist societies, but in actual fact only a relatively small number of people really improve their social class. The myth of upward mobility is perpetuated by the ruling powers because it is necessary for the functioning of society for everyone to work toward this goal.

Critical theorists look at a number of societal issues besides class, such as race, sex, and age, but the central focus of all these investigations is on how power is defined and distributed in society. Students are challenged to examine how information and knowledge is controlled by those in power and it is used to enhance the dominant worldview. Marcuse (1976, 302) illustrates this theme in his essay on tolerance.

> *The toleration of the systematic moronization of children and adults alike by publicity and propaganda, the release of destructive and aggressive driving, the recruitment for and training of special forces, the impotent and benevolent tolerance toward outright deception in mechanizing, waste, and planned obsolescence are not distortions and aberrations, they are the essence of a system which fosters tolerance as a means of perpetuating the struggle for existence and suppressing the alternatives. The authorities in education, morals, and psychology are vociferous against increase in juvenile delinquency; they are less vociferous against the proud presentation, in word and deed and pictures, of ever more powerful missiles, rockets, and bombs—the mature delinquency of a whole civilization.*

The critical tradition has special significance for the peace perspective because the war perspective is so entrenched in our society. To challenge the war perspective requires us to reexamine what many believe to be obvious truths. The critical tradition holds that many obvious truths are simply the successful implementation of dominant power structures into our ways of thinking and perceiving (Taylor et al. 1973). This **hegemony** extends to how criminological knowledge is produced by the privileging of one method of research over others. DiCristina (1995) calls for an anarchic criminology which greatly expands the problems, methods, and goals for the study of crime.

Age is one of the characteristics of individuals that those in power have used to allocate resources and roles in a purposeful way. Both the young and the old are victimized by laws and social conventions that restrict their opportunities to succeed. There are plausible reasons for restricting some rights of people based on age. For instance, in driving an automobile very young people do not have the maturity and judgment while elderly people may lack the physical skills. However, when one looks at maturity and judgment or deteriorating physical skills, age is an artificial criteria. Some young people may be very mature and some middle-aged people may be very immature. Age is not a perfect measure of maturity, and some other indicator could be used to decide when a person should be granted this privilege. Likewise, age is an imperfect indicator of physical skills, and those who advocate restricting driver's licenses to those over a certain age unless they pass more rigid tests than the rest of drivers are guilty of the same type of assumptions as those who use age to restrict younger drivers.

The critical theorist would contend that the debate over driving age has another dimension. Competition in the labor force is a latent function of restricting rights because of age. By passing laws that make it more difficult for the young and the old to compete in the workforce, power is preserved for those in other age categories. The critical theorist sees the construction of driving laws as having economic as well as safety implications and, by looking at the economic implications of the law, we can better understand why laws are constructed as they are.

There are several overlapping features with critical theory and feminist perspectives when looking at the issue of social justice. Critical theory is inclusive of many of the features of the way feminists critique the social order and is sympathetic to the concerns of feminists for the way sex is used in society to allocate status and privilege. The critical theorist differs from the feminist in her or his scope of inquiry. In addition to sex, class, race, and age, a number of other factors may be included in the critical theorist's investigation.

Taken together, the religious and humanist, feminist, and critical traditions provide a substantial foundation for the peacekeeping perspective. But more work needs to be done if this model of public policy is going to seriously challenge the dominant war on crime model currently in vogue. The peacekeeping model must tie together these three perspectives and apply them directly to the problems of the criminal justice system. In addition, the peacekeeping perspective needs to be articulated at all levels of the criminal justice system and be presented as a unified and comprehensive approach, rather than as a gimmick program inserted into an otherwise punitive system.

PEACEMAKERS WHO CHALLENGED INJUSTICE

Before we address these goals, however, it is useful to paint a picture of just how successful and desirable the peacemaking perspective can be. This is not a new idea. Many efforts at peacemaking within society have been attempted, and there is much to learn from these efforts. For our purposes here, we will briefly review the work of three enormously courageous individuals who dedicated their lives to fighting social injustice in a peaceful way. Leo Tolstoy, Mahatma Gandhi, and Martin Luther King, Jr., all fought for social change in their time through peacemaking methods. Each has left a legacy of inspiration that is maybe more significant than the actual impact each had on the society of their time.

Tolstoy

Count Leo Tolstoy (1828–1910) is an inspirational figure in the peacemaking tradition because he rejected the success of the material world and attempted to live the latter part of his life as he felt a Christian should (Wilson 1988). He was a literary giant of his time and is best known for his still popular novels *War and Peace* and *Anna Karenina*. He wrote not only novels but also short stories and a vast amount of nonfiction dealing with the social problems of his time (Tolstoy 1967). A very complicated spiritual person, he interpreted Christ's teachings for himself and eventually, and probably inevitably, was excommunicated by the Russian Orthodox Church. Tolstoy was antiwar and in a number of essays preached nonviolence as the only ethical way to conduct one's life. He would ask what Jesus would do on any specific occasion and then make his decision or give his answer based on that criteria.

Tolstoy's fame brought letters and visitors from around the world, including the noted Italian criminologist Cesare Lombroso. There were differences in how these two men viewed the nature of crime and punishment.

> *When Lombroso tried to explain to Tolstoy his theory of the "delinquent man" whose responsibility was attenuated by heredity, illness and environment, the author of* Resurrection *scowled at him and burst out, "It's insane! All punishment is criminal! (Troyat 1967, 579).*

By today's standards, Tolstoy appears in some ways to be an almost comic figure. In a manner reminiscent of Don Quixote, he fought against entrenched and powerful interests and cultural traditions to do what he thought was right. Like the fictional Man of La Mancha, Tolstoy fought against injustice and promoted a sense of moral behavior which was deemed impractical and naive by his contemporaries. However, Tolstoy has had a lasting impact on the literature of the peace perspective. His extremely powerful and insightful letters and essays about peace transcend the circumstances in which they were written and contain universal messages which render them as important today as when they were written. Also, Tolstoy is important because he tried to live his ideals. As feminists are apt to say, "the personal is the political," and no one struggled with trying to match his actions with his words as much as Tolstoy. He gave up his writing career at the height of his popularity, renounced his worldly possessions (his wife had everything put in her name and took over running the affairs of his estate), worked in the fields, wore peasant clothes, and made his own sandals.

He gave sums of money to people and causes for working for peace and consistently spoke out against tyranny and oppression. Unfortunately he could not always practice on a personal level what he sought in his philosophy. His life is filled with contradictions and broken promises. Because he and his wife each kept diaries, their marriage is one of the best documented love/hate relationships ever recorded. By today's standards he could be regarded as the type of man who inspired the women's movement with his oppression, ridicule, and psychological abuse of his wife. Nevertheless, he articulated a philosophy of social change through peaceful tactics which embodied his conception of how a truly Christian person should act.

Gandhi

Mohandas K. Gandhi (1869–1948) was an Indian lawyer and a political and religious figure who made a huge impact on his country. He has inspired people worldwide with his ideas about nonviolent protest and the simple way in which he lived his life. When he was a young man dealing with racism in South Africa he read Tolstoy and in a letter asked his advice on how to deal with the oppressive government that eventually would evolve into apartheid. Gandhi and the elder Tolstoy continued to correspond until the latter's death. Later, Gandhi started a commune in South Africa called Tolstoy Farm (Payne 1969).

Gandhi shared with Tolstoy a dream of social justice brought about by peaceful protest against unjustified government policies. Gandhi also shared with Tolstoy an effort to live simply and consistently with his moral ideals. In this, Gandhi was more successful than Tolstoy. Gandhi is looked upon today as achieving an almost saintly quality in his actions in an otherwise very secular and hedonistic avaricious world of international politics. While some would contend that Gandhi was a bad husband and a worse father, they fault him mainly as being too concerned with his larger visions of social justice at the expense of interpersonal family affairs.

What did Gandhi mean by nonviolent social protest? Why is this a tactic that should concern the student of the criminal justice system? Nonviolent social protest and passive resistance are part of Gandhi's overall concept of **Satyagraha,** which is a strategy where the victims of unjust power relationships confront their oppressors with the immorality of the association between them. Clearly, the way this is done most of the time is through forceful revolution where the oppressor is violently overthrown and a new government is put in place. The American and Soviet revolutions are examples of how this tactic can result in different circumstances for the people. There are countless other examples of countries where revolutions have been successful in overthrowing the established order. Some countries seem to make revolution the standard practice in changing the head of state.

Gandhi's nonviolent revolution is aimed not so much in the immediate overthrow of the government but more at the reform of the government by illustrating to the world, and to the government itself, the iniquitous and unethical way it treats its people. The key is nonviolence. By embarrassing the government through sit-ins, peaceful marches, prayer meetings, and sometimes by hunger strikes, the oppressed can state their case to the world in a way that demonstrates their moral superiority. When the state uses force to disrupt the nonviolent protest, it plays into the hands of the challengers. Using force on peaceful demonstrators makes for interesting and newsworthy coverage by the press and causes the dominant social classes to question the ethical position their police are defending.

Gandhi's method is to make the oppressors examine their actions in the harsh glare of public discourse. When decent people see how the instruments of the state (police and army) are used to violently suppress peaceful demonstrations, it causes them to reexamine their position. This method seldom works immediately. The police are simply carrying out the policies of those in power and often have their full support. The trick is to get the police to overreact to the peaceful protest and to use excessive force. This not only embarrasses the power elite but it also brings new protestors to the battle. Over a period of time, and after several such demonstrations, the issues start to get seriously considered by the governing class. If a person is willing to stand up and confront authority in a peaceful way and risk getting physically attacked, it adds legitimacy to his or her case. One must feel very strongly to provoke attack from the government and not fight back.

By provoking social change in this way, Gandhi attempted to demonstrate that the means used predetermine the end that can be attained. In other words, violence begets violence, and only by using nonviolent confrontation can the cycle be broken (Naess 1965).Outside observers viewing such behavior tend to believe that looking at the issues may be warranted in order to understand this seemingly foolish but courageous behavior.

Gandhi used this tactic in South Africa to confront the racist policies aimed at Indians and in his homeland of India to confront the policies of the English empire. In both cases, Gandhi believed the oppressors were engaged in immoral behavior, and by challenging their policies he could peacefully force them to change their method of government or their political policies (Fischer 1950; Payne 1969).

Martin Luther King, Jr.

Dr. Martin Luther King, Jr. (1929–1968) was an American civil rights leader who became a pivotal figure in the 1950s and early 1960s when he led the United States through one of the most significant periods in its history. The **Civil Rights Movement** challenged the segregation laws in the South and ushered in a period of tremendous social upheaval and change. The Civil Rights Movement and the protests against the U.S. involvement in Vietnam rocked the social fabric of the country and altered the process in which many individuals engaged the government. Until he was assassinated in 1968, Dr. King led the vanguard of organizations and groups of individuals attempting to influence social and political policy in the United States.

Like Gandhi, Dr. King also used the strategy of **nonviolent social protest.** Drawing on the ideas of Tolstoy and Gandhi, he led people of color and their supporters against an outdated and unjust social structure which allocated positions and rights based on race. It is beyond the scope of our purposes here to fully document the racial policies of the south in the first part of the century, but suffice it to say that by today's standards it was a system that was inconsistent with the ideals of the American people and the Constitution.

When Dr. King and his supporters found a community engaging in racially biased behavior they would target that community for peaceful protest. In a society accustomed to having people of color "know their place," the white citizens and local authorities in the South would resort to violence to break up the demonstration. Police batons, fire hoses, and police dogs were used on the protestors by the states in an attempt to preserve the established order. Captured on national television, these tactics backfired, and the injustices of the system were held up for an international community to condemn.

Nonviolence is an important part of the peacemaking perspective.
(© Patricia Hollander Gross/Stock Boston.)

Often the tactics employed by Dr. King and his followers forced them to break laws which they believed to be unjust. In his famous "Letter from Birmingham Jail" (King 1963), he explains his philosophy of breaking the law in order to make conditions more just.

> *You may well ask, "Why direct action? Why sit-ins, marches, etc.? Isn't negotiation a better path?" You are exactly right in your call for negotiation. Indeed, this is the purpose of direct action. Nonviolent direct action seeks to create such a crisis and establish such creative tension that a community that has constantly refused to negotiate is forced to confront the issue. It seeks so to dramatize the issue that it can no longer be ignored. I just referred to the creation of tension as a part of the work of the nonviolent resister. This may sound rather shocking. But I must confess that I am not afraid of the word tension. I have earnestly worked and preached against violent tension, but there is a type of constructive nonviolent tension that is necessary for growth. Just as Socrates felt that it was necessary to create a tension in the mind so that individuals could rise from the bondage of myths and half-truths to the unfettered realm of creative analysis and objective appraisal, we must see the need of having nonviolent gadflies to create the kind of tension in society that will help men to rise from the dark depths of prejudice and racism to the majestic heights of understanding and brotherhood.*

It is clear in this excerpt from Dr. King's writings that this form of civil disobedience was a deliberate and carefully thought-out tactic. It is based on an understanding of social change and on the moral vulnerability of the racist laws that existed in the United States. The demand for social justice requires the institutions of the state to embrace laws and policies that are consistent with the ideals that they profess. Dr. King and his followers simply asked that the ideals of the U.S. government be extended to all its citizens and not allocated according to race. For the peacemaking perspective, Dr. King's tactics are as important as his goals.

1. Active nonviolent resistance to evil
2. Not seeking to defeat or humiliate opponents, but to win their friendship and understanding
3. Attacking the forces of evil rather than the people who happen to be doing evil
4. Willingness to accept suffering without retaliating
5. Refusing to hate the opponent
6. Acting with the conviction that the universe is on the side of justice (King 1958, 101–107)

Martin Luther King presented a model for social change that was not adopted by all oppressed people. Some turned to violence as a method of challenging the system, and in the long hot summers of the 1960s many cities were scared by race riots which threatened to escalate into long and protracted civil unrest. Groups like the Black Panther Party, the Student Nonviolent Coordinating Committee (SNCC), and the largely white middle-class Weathermen used violent tactics to influence government policies and promote their own agendas. Young militant individuals who sought the same goals as Dr. King became impatient with the pace of social change and embraced violent means to startle and stun the country with the degree of frustration experienced by many victims of the discriminatory laws. Dr. King's legacy is that of the high road of morally superior nonviolence challenging an unjust system, rather than succumbing to the temptation to "fight fire with fire" and strike back with violence as so many of his contemporaries counseled.

A second basic fact that characterizes nonviolence is that it does not seek to defeat or humiliate the opponent, but to win his friendship and understanding. The nonviolent resister must often express his protest through noncooperation or boycotts, but he realizes that these are not ends in themselves; they are merely means to awaken a sense of moral shame in the opponent. The end is redemption and reconciliation. The aftermath of nonviolence is the creation of the beloved community, while the aftermath of violence is tragic bitterness (King 1958).

The United States would have been perilously endangered if Dr. King had not led his people in such a nonviolent manner. The injustices done to people of color in the United States were (and in many ways still are) in need of redress, and it is fortunate that the religious underpinnings of Dr. King's philosophy embraced the principles of nonviolence and peacemaking.

The works of Tolstoy, Gandhi, and King have important implications for the criminal justice system of today. Even though they were concerned with challenging unjust government policies, the ideals of the peacemaking philosophy can be applied by society's institutions to reduce the level of conflict on the street. One of the important elements of the peacemaking perspective which we will stress is the fact that the components of the criminal justice system have criminogenic influences themselves. That is, in fighting crime, the police, courts, and correctional systems can cause people to break the law. They sometimes escalate the level of tension or violence, causing unintended consequences, whereby crime is shifted from one type or location to another.

There is an old joke about the cause of divorce: marriage. To the extent that crime is socially constructed, we can say laws cause crime. The criminal law sometimes overreaches into areas where many people think it should not be applied. The so-called "victimless crimes" of gambling, prostitution, and drug use enjoy support from many individuals who engage in these activities or simply believe these behaviors are not the concern of the government.

By waging a war on crime, the criminal justice system labels individuals as the enemy and polarizes their behavior into that of the outlaw. That is, people are disconnected from the mainstream of lawful society by the criminal justice system, and obstacles are placed in their path as they try to engage in lawful employment, commerce, or social discourse.

THE PEACEMAKING PYRAMID PARADIGM (P³)

The peacemaking perspective has a long history in international affairs but is relatively new when applied to the criminal justice system. Many of its principles have been implemented to various degrees in some jurisdictions but the philosophy of peacemaking has not enjoyed the recognition and support that the war on crime perspective has enjoyed. The problem with the peacemaking perspective's lack of acceptance by criminal justice practitioners and the general public is the boundaries of peacemaking have not been staked out, and its many facets have not been clearly articulated and fastened by criminologists.

This is an immense project, one that can be only started here, but one that is an important area for scholars and practitioners to address. It is important because of the failure of the war on crime perspective and because of the need to transform the criminal justice system into one that deals with crime and its causes in a socially healthy manner. To this end, the **peacemaking pyramid paradigm (P³)** is offered (see Figure 3.2). P³ is a beginning, not an

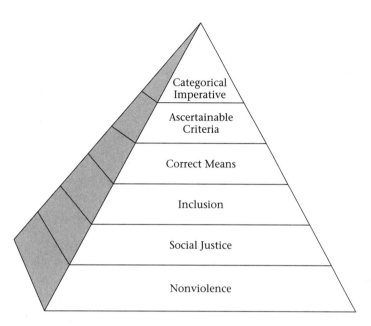

FIGURE 3.2 Peacemaking Solutions to Criminal Justice Problems: Peacemaking Pyramid Paradigm P³.

end. It is put forth to stimulate conversation about the potentials of the peacemaking process and not as a rigid doctrine.

   As a model for considering solutions to criminal justice problems, P³ is formulated as an ideal type in the Weberian tradition. By this, we mean it is a model for comparison regardless if any criminal justice policy can achieve all its conditions. To the extent any situational criminal justice policy works its way up the pyramid, we can say that it is more or less a peacemaking solution.

   1. *Nonviolence.* The base of the pyramid represents the most basic peacemaking principle: nonviolence. The criminal justice system ought not to use coercion, excessive force, or capital punishment in the name of justice. In the tradition of Gandhi, Tolstoy, and Dr. Martin Luther King, Jr., the tenets of nonviolence are fundamental to the peacemaking perspective. No matter what other laudable features a public policy entails, if violence is condoned, it is not a peacemaking policy.

   2. *Social justice.* Solutions to criminal justice problems must be consistent with the concept of social justice if they are to be considered peacemaking solutions. Socially unacceptable relationships such as **racism, sexism,** and **ageism** need to be addressed by any peacemaking perspective solution. A nonviolent resolution to a problem is not enough of that solution lets stand a social injustice that allows the powerful to dominate a victim. For example, in a domestic assault case, the sexism of a husband who insists on controlling his wife's life to the extent that he keeps her financially and emotionally dependent represents an instance of social injustice that would need to be addressed by the peacemaking perspective. Simply having the police respond to the call for service and taking the abusive husband into custody is not a sufficient solution to the problem. A peacemaking solution would entail social services to the family to not only prevent the violence from recurring but also to help the husband and wife achieve a relationship of mutual respect and support whereby the wife is freed from the confining bonds of traditional gender relationships.

3. *Inclusion.* Any solution to a criminal justice problem has several entities that are affected. A peacemaking solution includes the participation and input from all concerned parties. This inclusion begins, first and foremost, with the offender and the victim. Peacemaking solutions are not simply handed down from authorities but are fashioned from those involved through processes of negotiation, arbitration, and mediation. The Chinese examples of *Bang-Jiao* and *Tiao-Jie* are models of how inclusion of the victim, offender, government, and the state can work together to construct solutions that promote the ideals of prevention and rehabilitation. One way the war on crime has worked against the inclusion ideal is the creation of determinate sentencing. In the interests of uniformity, the mandatory sentencing crusade has stripped judges of their discretion to fashion a sentence to fit the circumstances of the crime and the offender. Determinate sentencing also excludes the interests of the victim, the judgment of the prosecutor, and ignores the potential of community resources to help resolve the problem. A peacemaking solution cannot be constructed by legislators intent on deterrence and punishment as they pass legislation.

4. *Correct means.* Gandhi emphasized that solutions to problems must be arrived at through **correct means.** This entails not only nonviolence, social justice, and inclusion but also what could be considered in the Western context as due process. Justice in the United States is bound to guiding principles found in the Constitution that ensure individuals' legal safeguards against questions of self-incrimination and the right to face accusers and to present evidence and witnesses that support his or her case. The principle of correct means embraces these legal safeguards and encourages the arrival at peacemaking ends through means that protect standards of legal and social justice.

5. *Ascertainable criteria.* A rational decision-making process needs to be based on **ascertainable criteria** that all involved can not only understand, but can agree are valid and trustworthy. When one side of the disagreement holds the power to define and manipulate the factors on which the dispute hinges, then an unfair situation exists and a peacemaking solution is impossible. Much of the rhetoric of the U.S legal system is conducted in such a technical parlance that only attorneys can understand the proceedings. A peacemaking solution ensures that not only are offenders represented by counsel but also that counsel explains the procedures and variables on which decisions are based. This takes extra time and resources in terms of educating

offenders and victims and, in some jurisdictions, it takes translators to ensure the workings of the criminal justice system are understood by the multicultural population. If knowledge is power, we must ensure that the powerful do not use their education and technical expertise to control the criminal justice process.

Categorical Imperative

The philosopher Immanuel Kant developed a test of ethical behavior that he entitled the **Categorical Imperative.** Kant said that in deciding actions individuals should apply this axiom: "Act only according to that maxim whereby you can at the same time will that it should become a universal law" (Kant 1995, 45). From a peacemaking perspective, this means that solutions to particular criminal justice problems should entail underlying moral reasoning so that the solution would be applicable to other times and places. Kant's categorical imperative attempts to establish principles that transcend the peculiar circumstances of individual cases and can serve as guides to moral behavior. Kant argues that the foundation of the categorical imperative is that human beings should be regarded as ends in themselves and not simply as means to someone else's ends. For the peacemaking perspective this means that solutions to problems must be structured in such a way that any resolution could theoretically be transposed to other situations and be applied without treating people as means.

The peacemaking pyramid paradigm (P^3) requires that we start at the base with nonviolence and construct solutions to the criminal justice problem by working up the steps toward a solution that could stand as a categorical imperative. Again, this model is an ideal type, and, in many instances, the solution may not be able to progress very far up P^3 but the quest is to attempt to progress as far up as possible so as to arrive at solutions that can be embraced by all concerned.

RATIONALE FOR THE PEACEMAKING ALTERNATIVE

The war on crime model of criminal justice policy is intent on identifying, separating, and punishing criminals. Just about all of us break one law or another, and the crucial issue with the war on crime perspective is the question: Who gets caught and brought into the criminal justice system? It is clear there are some patterns as to who is selected for attention by the criminal justice system that are independent of the actual harm the offender presents to society. Street crime is punished more severely than white-collar crime. Individuals with resources can afford private attorneys and can minimize their punishments where poor people cannot. Age, sex, race, appearance, and commitment to conventional lifestyles all are extralegal factors used in criminal justice system decision-making. To a great extent, those with power use the criminal justice system to maintain the status quo. A form of war is declared on anyone who challenges the power structure.

According to the war on crime perspective, anyone can be successful in the U.S. system and therefore there is no need to commit crimes. By working hard, deferring gratification, and sacrificing, anyone can "pull themselves up by their bootstraps" and become prosperous according to the American dream. The institutional structures in society are in place to ensure even competition whereby those with ambition and talent will rise to the top. Those who sink to the bottom are therefore unlucky at best, but more often considered lazy, shiftless, and stupid. Crime is viewed as a shortcut to the American dream used by those who are unable or unwilling to compete in the conventional manner.

The peacemaking perspective does not share the same assumptions about opportunity in society as the war on crime perspective. The playing field is not level, according to those who dispute the war on crime perspective. For the most part, we can predict which groups or individuals will find themselves in trouble with the criminal justice system based not on what individuals do but, more interestingly, on who they are. Because punishment is distributed based on these extralegal factors rather than on seriousness of offense, those who employ the peacemaking perspective look to reform of society's institutions as much as to the reform of the individual offender.

The revolving door of our criminal justice system should alert us to some problems in how we administer justice in the United States. While it is not fair to blame all of society's failures on the criminal justice system, it is noteworthy that it does fail to prevent offenders from coming back within its clutches. Being caught and punished by the criminal justice system does not deter offenders from violating the law again. As a matter of fact, some observers contend that the more contact a person has with the criminal justice system the more antisocial, dangerous, and crime prone he or she becomes (Schur 1973).

The peacemaking perspective can be envisioned as operating at different levels of the criminal justice problem. At the interpersonal level, the peacekeeping perspective would conceive of dealing with the criminal offender in a "kinder and gentler way" than imagined by the war on crime model of criminal justice policy. The peacemaking perspective looks at the offender as a human being who has committed unacceptable behaviors but still has worth. Rehabilitation (and in many cases habilitation) would be the goal of the peacemaking perspective rather than punishment.

Because most offenders will be returned to the street, the peacemaking perspective seeks to help the situation by making the offender better able to compete. Job training, literacy classes, drug and alcohol treatment, and interpersonal relations instruction all can assist the offender to adjust to a life of freedom better than the punishment and deterrence methods of the war on crime perspective (Cullen and Gilbert 1982).

As stated previously, the peacemaking perspective also focuses on the institutional level where social justice is the major concern. Sexism, racism, and ageism are all barriers to equality and, to the extent these problems can be addressed, there is a greater opportunity to prevent unlawful behavior resulting from alienation. If the institutions of society are fair and just it will be easier to convince individuals that progress can be made through democratic processes. Social learning theory is our model here. How can we expect potential criminals to obey the law when the law is used as an instrument of coercion by those who have the power to define and enact the law? The solution to most problems of democracy is more democracy (Irwin 1980). Giving individuals the feeling they have some influence in making the law is the best way to get them committed to obeying the law. Therefore, the political process needs to be reformed, or at least made to represent all people rather than just the powerful.

Critics of the peacemaking perspective can point to the immediate problems of dealing with criminals who are already dangerous, violent, and antisocial. They will charge the peacemaking perspective with being unable to address the pressing problems of crime on the street and state that society simply cannot wait for the criminals to be transformed by education and understanding. The critics can further indict the peacemaking perspective as not having the answer to the career criminal who is not so much a victim of inequality but someone who has made a cold and calculated choice to break the law and take unfair advantage of people. Add to these concerns the problems of dealing with the mentally ill offenders who are a danger to themselves and others, and we can understand why the critics of the peacemaking perspective would have little faith in the potential of this type of policy.

The peacemaking perspective is viewed as naive and soft on crime by those who adopt the war on crime model. This is mainly a misunderstanding of what the peacemaking model proposes. It recognizes that crime is a real and immediate problem and that some offenders are not yet ready to be released into society. But the peacemaking model has an optimistic view of human nature and differs with the war on crime model mainly in where the locus of responsibility for crime is to be found. The peacemaking perspective does not advocate doing away with the criminal justice system, it simply conceives of reforms in the laws, the way the system operates, and in the overall goal of the government's instruments of social control.

The purpose of the criminal justice system is to resolve conflict. When individuals or parties have disputes, the criminal justice system settles the issue within a process of justice. Without the independent third-party involvement of the criminal justice system, individuals would "take matters into their own hands" and resolve conflicts by force. Revenge, violence, **vigilantism,** and domination of the weak by the strong would be the result of not having a legal mechanism to resolve disputes. The peacemaking perspective emphasizes the conflict reduction aspect of the criminal justice system rather than enhancing conflict, as does the war on crime model.

Three process for applying the peacemaking perspective are already well established in the criminal justice system.

1. In many law enforcement agencies community policing is a fast-growing model of law enforcement practice. Community policing aims at reestablishing the connection between the patrol officer and the citizen.

2. Many courts have alternative dispute resolution programs designed to avoid costly litigation, involve the offender and the victim in reaching a mutual agreement, and avoid the stigma of formal court processing.

3. In the correctional system there are many new and innovative programs aimed at providing services to offenders to make them better able to compete in society.

The police, courts, and corrections each have a chapter devoted to how they operate, so we will simply say here that the peacemaking perspective is something which the criminal justice system has been doing for a long time but has not been recognized as being a fundamental objective. The apprehension, conviction, and punishment of offenders has been the chief preoccupation of the criminal justice system, and this has caused the country to squander its resources and talents on a war on crime perspective which does not accomplish either its goal of making society safe or its duty to perform its mission to protect the civil and human rights of the citizens.

The peacemaking perspective does something else that the war on crime model does not. It takes a broader look at human interaction and proposes that human worth and dignity be emphasized in all associations between people. The dynamics between parents and children, wives and husbands, bosses and workers, professors and students, and institutions and citizens can all be guided by the peacemaking perspective. While it is outside the scope of responsibility of the criminal justice system to address all these types of relationships the principles do pertain to each type of interaction. The conflict orientation engendered by the war on crime model can be witnessed in each of the relationships as one of domination and exploitation. In fact, many, if not most, of the problems we see in interpersonal relationships can be attributed to the behaviors resulting from a war on crime model of social interaction.

GOVERNMENT POLICY AS A MODEL OF BEHAVIOR

When the founders wrote the Constitution of the United States they neglected a very important point. While they set up a mechanism to govern they forgot to specify how far the limits of power of the state over the citizens should extend. This oversight was corrected by the first 10 amendments of the Constitution, the **Bill of Rights** (Peltason 1976). The Constitution protects the citizen from abuse by the state, something the founders were very concerned with given the problems with King George III and their observations of many abuses of human and civil rights across Europe.

Democracy was conceived as an experiment, and it was not altogether certain that the relationship between the citizen and the state could be worked out in such a way that citizens could enjoy the fruits of liberty and the state could govern effectively. The experiment is still unfolding, and the Bill of Rights is still the guidebook in resolving disputes between the needs of the state and the desires of the people.

Two issues should concern us here as we envision the peacemaking perspective. First, how do we keep the government under control? Second, how do we influence the government's style of interaction with its citizens? The first concern is accomplished through procedural law. The second concern is problematic. The bureaucratic clerk of the large government agency is renowned as one of the great afflictions of contemporary life; even worse, the incompetent or corrupt government functionary who violates the public trust. The ethos of service is a quality that appears to be diminishing in many occupations, but no more so than in public service.

It is important for social institutions to have the support of the citizens. This is especially true for the criminal justice system where lack of commitment results in harm to individuals and society. When law-abiding citizens began to view the police and courts as the enemy of the people, as happens from time to time (recently in a dramatic manner when the Rodney King verdict was announced and several cities across the nation experienced **collective violence**), it becomes difficult for the police to do their job and protect life and property (Fuller 1993). One commission on the violence of the 1960s charges that some of the urban riots were caused by the police (Skolnick and Fyfe 1993, 78). Clearly, society would have benefitted a great deal more if the police had the support of the people and did not alienate large segments of the population.

The question we ask at this point is how does the peace perspective help us deal with the antisocial criminal who refuses to abide by the laws of society? Given our need to protect our personal safety and property, how do we police the streets, adjudicate criminal cases, and treat or punish offenders in a manner consistent with the principles of the peacekeeping perspective? Is this philosophy for dealing with crime no more than a utopian pipedream, or does it have relevance for the day-to-day workings of the criminal justice system?

The peacemaking perspective does have an answer to these troublesome questions. It may have the only answer to crime in our age which gives hope to victims and offenders and preserves our democratic values. The morally bankrupt and hopelessly inefficient war on crime perspective, which we discussed in Chapter 2, is not the path that will lead to a better life for anyone.

In the following chapters we will look at how the major components of the criminal justice system (police, courts, and corrections) have used the war on crime perspective in ways that have not only failed to reduce the level of crime but also have made the criminal justice system the adversary of a large segment of the population. We will also look at how these components of the criminal justice system employ aspects of the peacemaking perspective. Alternatives to typical criminal justice system practices such as community policing, arbitration and conflict resolution outside the courts, and the recognition that treatment and rehabilitation are still major goals and objectives in the correctional field all fall under the rubric of peacemaking practices.

CRITICAL THINKING QUESTIONS

1. Discuss the three intellectual traditions from which the peace perspective draws its inspiration. Besides the religious and humanist, feminist, and critical traditions can you think of other intellectual sources for the peacemaking perspective?

2. We often hear the phrase "the personal is the political." Should we hold our governmental policies to the same standards of morality as we expect of individual personal behavior?

3. In addition to Tolstoy, Gandhi, and Dr. King, what other individuals should be considered in our discussion of peacemakers?

4. What is the peacemaking pyramid paradigm (P^3)? How is this model useful in understanding the peacemaking perspective? How do the principles of P^3 differ from the war on crime perspective?

SUGGESTED READINGS

Anderson, Kevin. 1991. "Radical Criminology and the Overcoming of Alienation: Perspectives from Marxian and Gandhian Humanism," in Harold E. Pepinsky and Richard Quinney, eds. *Criminology as Peacemaking.* Bloomington, IN: Indiana University Press, pp. 14–29.

Caulfield, Mina Davis. 1993. "Imperialism, the Family, and Cultures of Resistance," in Alison M. Jagger and Paula S. Rothenberg, eds. *Feminist Frameworks: Alternative Theoretical Accounts of the Relations between Women and Men,* 3rd ed. New York: McGraw-Hill.

Cullen, Francis T., and Karen E. Gilbert. 1982. *Reaffirming Rehabilitation.* Cincinnati: Anderson.

McDermott, M. Joan. 1994. "Criminology as Peacemaking, Feminist Ethics and the Victimization of Women." *Women and Criminal Justice* 5(2): 24–44.

Parrinder, Geoffery. 1971. *World Religions: From Ancient History to the Present.* New York: Facts on File Publications.

Payne, Robert. 1969. *The Life and Death of Mahatma Gandhi.* New York: Smithmark.

Quinney, Richard. 1993. "A Life of Crime: Criminology and Public Policy as Peacemaking." *Journal of Crime and Justice* 16(2): 3–9.

Taylor, Ian, Paul Walton, and Jock Young. 1973. *The New Criminology: For a Social Theory of Deviance.* New York: Harper and Row.

Trebach, Arnold S. 1990. "A Bundle of Peaceful Compromises." *The Journal of Drug Issues* 20(4): 515–531.

Troyat, Henri. 1967. *Tolstoy.* Garden City: Doubleday.

4

CRIMINAL JUSTICE AS A SYSTEM

© Erin Newrath/Stock Boston.

Learning Objectives

After reading this chapter, the student should be able to:

- Explain why the criminal justice system is not really a system.
- Understand that responsibility for various criminal behaviors are divided by political jurisdictions.
- Appreciate how the terms "due process" and "justice" are related.
- Describe how the criminal law is a form of social control.
- Explain the difference between substantive and procedural law.
- List the various sources of law.
- Describe how the U.S. Supreme Court acts as the country's court of last resort.
- Appreciate how the victim of crime can be further injured by the criminal justice process.
- Describe how victim and witness assistance programs can assist victims in dealing with the criminal justice system.
- Describe the advantages and disadvantages of locating victim and witness assistance programs in the prosecutor's office.
- List the various services that may be provided by victim and witness assistance programs.

Key Terms

Criminal Justice System	Procedural Law
Jurisdiction	Supreme Court
Representational Democracy	Invisible Wounds
Mala In Se	Victim and Witness Assistance
Mala Prohibita	Program
Due Process	Crisis Intervention
Substantive Law	Personal Advocacy

The **criminal justice system** is one of the most important institutions in society. In preliterate societies the work of criminal justice system was performed by the family, clan, or tribe. As societies developed more complex divisions of labor the criminal justice system evolved to settle disputes and formally affirm the values of each society. The most significant function of the criminal justice system is the maintenance of social control (Vago 1988, 11). As the institution of last resort, the criminal justice system provides a forum to do the "dirty work" of society, reining in deviant members and attempting to change undesirable behavior either through punishment or treatment. Additionally, and perhaps most importantly, the criminal justice system provides a setting where individuals can present their grievances and have a court decide guilt or innocence. Without a criminal justice system, society would be in chaos with various individuals and groups meting out their own justice without the benefit of the rule of law. Finally, law also provides a social engineering function that provides for social change in society.

The term criminal justice system is a bit of a misnomer. Perhaps calling it a criminal justice *nonsystem* would better illustrate its structure and function. The word "system" implies a set of interrelated parts that mesh smoothly together in a process that works in harmony to produce a desired result. Anyone familiar with the U.S. criminal justice system recognizes this is not the case. The criminal justice system is a collection of loosely related agencies that share clients. Each agency has its own mission, goals, and organizational imperatives that prevent it from working with other agencies in a manner that could be termed systematic.

An example of the differing agendas of agencies in the criminal justice system can be seen in the tension that exists between law enforcement agencies and the courts. One mandate of the police is to apprehend law violators and turn them over to the courts for processing. The courts must determine guilt or innocence according to the rule or law which specifies exactly how the offender is to be handled. Sometimes the behavior of the police is called into question, and the defendant is released based on procedural mistakes. The police are looked on as bungling fools by the courts and the judges are seen as liberal do-gooders by the police. This tension between components of the criminal justice system acts as a form of checks-and-balances mechanism helping to ensure that defendants are not railroaded through the system.

The problem of applying the term "system" to the criminal justice system is further compounded by the issue of **jurisdiction.** The responsibility for dealing with criminals is divided across different levels of government. Local, state, and federal police, courts, jails and prisons each have authority for enforcing certain provisions of the criminal law, and each has its own minisystem of bureaucracies that deal with enforcing the law. The lines of distinction between the various levels of government involved in the criminal justice system are clear, but oftentimes coordination and cooperation between agencies is needed. There is also an oversight function where appeals to a higher level are permitted.

OVERVIEW OF THE CRIMINAL JUSTICE SYSTEM

Making of Laws

The system of government in the United States is not a pure democracy. It is a **representational democracy** where citizens elect individuals to represent their interests in conducting the business of government. The making of laws is a very contentious activity because a consensus must be achieved among those vested with the responsibility of representing the interests of the populace. Providing the legal code that governs the conduct of public and private affairs is an ongoing process as myriad and diverse groups seek to have their perspectives considered in the law. We can witness the ebb and flow of changing standards of acceptable conduct by seeing how laws change to reflect the views of not only the majority, but also the groups who have the power to exert their desires on the community. One need only look at the laws concerning issues such as drug (decriminalization and recriminalization) and alcohol use (prohibition and its repeal) or abortion to see how the making of laws reflects changing shifts in the power of various groups in society. There are some behaviors where there is a strong consensus that they are criminal acts in themselves. Crimes such as murder, rape, and assault are ***mala in se,*** or inherently wrong. Other acts are considered ***mala prohibita,*** or wrong because they are prohibited by the law. These would include the more contested behaviors such as gambling, drug use, and prostitution, which may be legal in some jurisdictions and illegal in others.

Arriving at a consensus in making the law is never easy. Various groups strive to have their interests reflected in the language of the law (Vago 1988). When dealing with the criminal law, the exact behaviors prohibited and the schedule of penalties for offenses can be in dispute, even for laws regarding behaviors where one would think there would be no problem developing a consensus. For example, organizations such as the North American Man/Boy Love Association and the Paedophile Information Exchange attempt to influence laws concerning the sexual relationships between adults and children (Baker 1995, 363).

Apprehending Offenders

Law enforcement officers are vested with the responsibility for enforcing a broad range of laws passed by Congress and state legislatures. While the duties of the police are varied, the popular image of police work is catching lawbreakers. In fact, this constitutes only about 10 percent of law enforcement activity but it is vitally important and subject to procedural rules that specify how they can legally do their job (Greene and Klockers 1991). A distinction can be made between reactive and proactive police work. In reactive policing, law enforcement officers respond to citizen complaints or to illegal behavior they witness themselves. Proactive policing refers to efforts of the police to structure events so they can catch violators in the act of committing a crime. Sting operations where law enforcement officers buy drugs or stolen property or pose as prostitutes are designed not to make individuals break laws, but to structure situations where those who would and do commit crimes do so in the presence of law enforcement (Klockers 1991).

The apprehending of offenders is not as easy as the popular media suggests. In order not to become a police state, Americans have instituted a number of rules that dictate how law enforcement officers can do their job (Sutton

1991). These rules, regulations, procedures, and policies are designed to ensure that the police are not so overzealous in the pursuit of offenders that they violate constitutional rights to due process. Perhaps the most pivotal function of law enforcement is the decision the police officer makes in deciding when to invoke the criminal justice sanction. Not all complaints or behaviors witnessed by the police are deemed significant enough to insert the case into the criminal justice system. Law enforcement officers use their individual judgment or discretion in deciding what actions to take in each circumstance. The discretion is guided both by the policies of the department derived from criminal law and by a host of extralegal and personal factors that mean individual police officers may handle cases differently (Brooks 1993). Controlling discretion and ensuring a uniform pattern to the application of the criminal justice sanction is vital to the development of public confidence in law enforcement.

Justice and Due Process

To some, the criminal justice process seems like a game rather than a pursuit of the truth. The complex divisions of labor and responsibilities between agencies and individuals involved in the criminal justice process appear to work against the smooth functioning of the system and the resolution of conflicts in a manner that can satisfy most people. Recent sensational criminal trials such as the O. J. Simpson case have elevated the visibility of the way courts operate and have added to the frustration of those who believe the courts give defendants too many rights that seem to impede the application of justice. The truth is an evasive value, and the Simpson case illustrates the lack of agreement in this country as to how well the criminal justice system accomplishes determining guilt or innocence. Race seems to be the best indicator of how someone feels about the criminal justice system's handling of the Simpson case. Whites report they believe he "got away with murder," while African-Americans believe the criminal justice system, in a rush to judgment, charged O. J. Simpson in the murder of his former wife and her friend Ronald Goldman because the victims were white and Mr. Simpson is African-American.

Regardless of how one feels about the outcome of the O. J. Simpson case, it provides a very valuable service to the criminal justice system by exposing just how complex the functioning of the system can become. While it is true that the case was not only atypical but so beyond the normal functioning of the criminal justice system as to be misleading, it is also true that some people who had little interest in the criminal justice system before the case became fascinated with how the process works and have tried to become more informed about criminal law.

It is sometimes tempting to think of the terms "justice" and "due process" as being incompatible. In its narrow conception, justice is thought of as "getting what one deserves." Due process is the application of justice according to specific procedures that ensure that the result is derived at in a fair and impartial manner. As important as arriving at the right or just decision is, it is equally important that the public has confidence that the criminal justice system itself operates within the law. In a police state, individuals are not protected from the arbitrary behaviors of criminal justice professionals who are unfettered in their pursuit of offenders. The determination of guilt or innocence may be easier in a society where police can search anywhere they choose whether they have reason to suspect illegal activity or not, but in this society the police will quickly lose the cooperation of the public when it is felt that human and civil rights are being abused.

Crimes and Jurisdiction

As mentioned previously, the United States has a system of criminal justice that spans several layers of jurisdiction. Different agencies located at different levels of government divide the responsibility for enforcing the vast complex of laws applicable to the citizenry.

At the broadest level is the federal government whose agencies include the Federal Bureau of Investigation (FBI), the Bureau of Alcohol, Tobacco and Firearms (BATF), the Drug Enforcement Agency (DEA), and the enforcement branches of a host of other agencies vested with the responsibility of overseeing the laws for specific areas such as the postal service or the stock market. Federal laws apply to everyone, and the system of federal courts and prisons ensures uniformity in how individuals are treated. Additionally, the federal courts provide oversight and appeal functions for state courts.

It is at the state level that most of the action of criminal courts takes place. Each state legislature enacts criminal laws that cover the behaviors we most often think of as criminal. For instance, except for some exceptions, murder is a crime covered by state jurisdiction, and conviction will result in the offender being sentenced to a state prison. The exceptions include the murder of a federal officer, murder on federal land such as a military base or Native-American reservation, or murder while committing some other federal crime. These exceptions mean the case will be tried in a federal court and the offender(s) could be placed in a federal correctional system. Then, depending on the circumstances, the jurisdiction for similar behaviors can end up at different levels of the criminal justice system.

Law enforcement agencies are found at all levels of government but it is at the local level that the bulk of police activity takes place. City police and county sheriffs constitute the vast majority of law enforcement officers employed in the United States. They are responsible for enforcing the laws in their jurisdictions and make most of the arrests in the criminal justice system. Depending on the crimes involved their cases are processed by the local or state courts.

If this discussion of jurisdictions sounds a bit confusing, it is because the structure of the criminal justice system is complex and asymmetrical. This means that there is no consistent pattern to how state and local government divide responsibilities for criminal justice activities; therefore, no encompassing statements can be made about who does what. Historical circumstance has as much to do with the structure and functioning of the criminal justice system as any rational plan of organization. As we said previously, the term "system" as applied to the criminal justice system can be misleading. Agencies have an overall goal of working together to protect the public and deal with offenders, but they do not fall under any overall coordinating organization. Police, courts, and correctional agencies can be found at all levels of government, and because they work together in such an amorphous relationship, there is considerable conflict and tension between them. Offenders often fall through the cracks in this nonsystem of criminal justice as it lumbers along answering to the agendas of various agencies, politicians, and the public.

RULE OF LAW

Law is a form of social control. It is the last type of social control utilized when others have failed to settle disputes. But it is also much more than the ultimate form of social control. It is also a guide that helps define and interpret other forms of social control such as rules, customs, and norms. In modern societies, the law is part of a process in which the government as a representative of the collective of individuals legislates, litigates, and adjudicates the agreed-upon pattern of behavior, public order, and formal relationships and interactions between individuals. The complete scope of the law is well beyond the purpose of this book, but is important to understanding the place that criminal law holds in the complex of social control mechanisms. It is sufficient to recognize at this point that the criminal law is only one realm where the formal rule of the state dictates, confines, or guides the interactions of individuals (Vago 1997).

As a function of social control the criminal law plays a pivotal role in the maintenance of meaningful communities. Where tradition and custom fail the criminal law is there to provide a method for determining socially correct behavior and settling conflicts. Were it not for the criminal law we would each be compelled to seek justice in our own way. Such vigilantism would perpetuate conflicts rather than resolve them. In order to adequately understand the criminal law, it is necessary to recognize that the state is not considered a neutral party. The state as a representative of the people is a contestant in the criminal justice process, and the criminal law treats the state as a participant whose role must be carefully circumscribed in order to protect the ideals of fairness and justice. To this end, the criminal law proscribes not only what behaviors are forbidden but also the process in which the state can detect, apprehend, and adjudicate those who violate the criminal law (Vago 1997).

Substantive Law

The **substantive law** can be envisioned as the "thou shall nots" of the criminal law. There are a number of behaviors that society has deemed so undesirable that it is willing to forbid and use the criminal justice system to discourage. These behaviors are specified in the federal and state criminal codes and include the acts that most of us agree constitute crimes against each other or the state. The most obvious and the ones where the greatest consensus can be found are murder, rape, assault, larceny, and other behaviors that are measured by the Uniform Crime Reports. Congress and the various state legislatures are fairly uniform in deciding what the substantive law is, but there are some variations that illustrate how differing community standards find their way into the substantive law.

Gambling is a good example of how different jurisdictions can conceive of a behavior in varying ways. Virtually all jurisdictions have some laws concerning gambling. The most liberal are states like Nevada that legalize a broad range of gambling behaviors, but only under the strict rules of a gaming commission that regulates how the gambling industry operates. Corporations are allowed to operate casinos where a variety of gambling games are played according to rules that both protect the consumer and ensure the state gets its cut of the profits. To say gambling is legal in Nevada does not mean that anyone can gamble any way they choose. In order to open a gambling establishment one must acquire the proper licenses and permits and operate according to a set of requirements that ensure a certain level of fairness. To do otherwise is a crime and, in a state like Nevada where gambling is a major industry, violating the law can be considered a serious crime.

In other states, gambling is permitted in much more limited circumstances. Corporations are not allowed to develop gambling enterprises because the state reserves that lucrative industry for itself. In the past decade or so capital-starved states have developed lotteries to tap into this source of easy money. These state legislatures seem to feel gambling is justified only when it is administered by the government and the profits are used to offset expenses normally paid for by taxes. For instance, the state of Georgia has gone so far as to use lottery profits to fund its Hope Scholarship program, which offsets tuition at its state colleges and universities for all students who maintain a B average.

Still other states continue to prohibit gambling altogether. This example makes clear the variations in the substantive law across the nation. Similar but not quite so dramatic variations can be seen for behaviors such as drug use, sex offenses, and increasingly, abortion. It would be a mistake, however, to conclude that the variations between states in terms of the substantive law are immense. For the most part there is a consistency among the states in what behaviors are legal or illegal.

Procedural Law

The most contested portion of the criminal law is not what behaviors are finally deemed legal or illegal but how the law is enforced by the criminal justice system. One of the primary strengths of the U.S. democratic system is the protection citizens are given from overzealous agents of the government. On one hand we want law enforcement officers, prosecutors, and prison administrators to do their jobs of protecting the public and dispensing justice competently but, on the other hand, we do not want them to violate the legal, civil, and human rights of those whom they are protecting.

Procedural law specifies how the agents of the state can perform their duties in such a way that they do not violate the rights of citizens. The source of the rights stems mainly from the Bill of Rights, which are the first ten amendments to the Constitution of the United States. Of particular interest to our discussion of the criminal law are the first, second, fourth, fifth, sixth, eighth, and ninth amendments. They are:

Amendment I: "Congress shall make no law respecting an establishment of religion, or prohibiting the free speech thereof; or abridging the freedom of speech, or of the press; or the right of the people peacefully to assemble, and to petition the Government for a redress of grievances."

Amendment II: "A well regulated Militia, being necessary to the security of a free state, the right of the people to keep and bear Arms, shall not be infringed."

Amendment IV: "The right of the people to be secure in their persons, houses, papers, and effects, against unreasonable searches and seizures, shall not be violated, and no Warrants shall issue, but upon probable cause, supported by Oath or Affirmation, and particularly describing the place to be searched, and the persons or things to be seized."

Amendment V: "No person shall be held to answer for a capital, or otherwise infamous crime, unless on a presentment or indictment of a Grand Jury, except in cases arising in the land or naval forces, or in the Militia, where in actual service in time of War or public danger, nor shall any person be subject for the same offense to be twice put in jeopardy of life or limb, nor shall be compelled in any criminal case to be a witness against himself, nor be deprived of life, liberty, or property, without due process of law; nor shall private property be taken for public use, without just compensation."

Amendment VI: "In all criminal prosecutions, the accused shall enjoy the right to a speedy and public trial, by an impartial jury of the State and district wherein the crime shall have been committed, which district shall have been previously ascertained by law, and to be informed of the nature and cause of the accusation; to be confronted with the witnesses against him; to have the compulsory process for obtaining witnesses in his favor, and to have the Assistance of Counsel for his defense."

Amendment VIII: "Excessive bail shall not be required, nor excessive fines imposed, nor cruel and unusual punishments inflicted."

Amendment XIV: "All persons born or naturalized in the United States and subject to the jurisdiction thereof, are citizens of the United States and of the State wherein they reside. No State shall make or enforce any law which shall abridge the privileges or immunities of citizens of the

United States; nor shall any State deprive any person to life, liberty, or property, without due process of law; nor deny to any person within its jurisdiction the equal protection of the law."

As one can see from these amendments, the manner in which the criminal justice system implements the criminal law is restricted. Additionally, there are other ways in which the criminal justice system is prevented from being too aggressive in enforcing the criminal code. These other limitations on the criminal justice system include:

State constitutions: Each of the 50 states has its own constitution that can further specify how criminal cases may be processed. While no state can strip suspected offenders from the rights provided for in the federal constitution, the state constitution can add protection to the process and make it even more difficult for the criminal justice system to process or prepare criminal cases.

Federal and state statutes: Often a federal or state law will provide additional procedural requirements that are beyond those provided for in the federal or state constitutions. For example, in juvenile cases there is no constitutional right to a jury trial for juveniles, but some states can extend this right by passing a statute that would apply only to jurisdictions in that state.

Case law: Sometimes confused with common law, case law is another example of how the rules of criminal procedure come from many different sources. Case laws are the gradually-developed legal principles that evolved through judicial decisions. It is different from laws passed by legislative bodies and represents what some call "unwritten" law or "judge-made" law. When one hears of legal precedent guiding a judge's decision, it is case law that is being referred to.

Court rules: State supreme courts may dictate rules on how certain procedures and pleading are to be handled in lower courts. These rules have the force of law in that the lower court must follow them in order to be in compliance. Violation of the superior court rules can be grounds for an appeal so they can further restrict how the criminal justice system processes cases.

The rules of criminal procedure are complex and may seem to some as overly restricting the criminal justice system's ability to process cases and dispense justice. Given our previous discussion of the criminal justice system as a nonsystem and the myriad rules and laws circumscribing how criminal justice officials are allowed to operate, it is easy to understand how many individuals might become frustrated by the legal system. It is important to remember, however, that the procedural law is not there to provide loopholes for criminals to slip through and to hinder the application of justice. The procedural law protects citizens from what the founders of the United States feared the most: a state that did not respect the civil and human rights of its people and used the criminal justice system as a weapon of tyranny rather than one of freedom.

The Supreme Court

The United States has a dual court system. There is a federal court system and a state court system, although it may be more accurate to say there are fifty state court systems that each perform special functions for their jurisdictions. The **Supreme Court** is the highest court in the federal court system and is also the court of last resort for the state system (although, in reality, only a very small fraction of cases make it all the way through the appellate system to the Supreme Court). The Supreme Court is composed of nine justices, all of whom are appointed by the president (subject to the "advise and consent" function of the Senate) for life terms. At present, there are judges sitting on the Supreme Court who have been appointed by Presidents Nixon, Ford, Reagan, Bush, and Clinton. Historically, Supreme Court justices have been white males, but now there are two females, Sandra Day O'Conner and Ruth Bader Ginsberg, and one African-American, Clarence Thomas.

Each year thousands of cases are presented to the Supreme Court from various lower federal and state courts, but only about 100 of them are considered. At least four justices must agree to hear a case and for those that are not considered the decision of the immediate lower court in which the case originated is left undisturbed.

THE VICTIM AND THE CRIMINAL JUSTICE SYSTEM

It is perhaps trite to say we would not have a criminal justice system if it were not for the victim of crime. It is obvious that the victim is a centerpiece in the foundation for the rationale for a criminal justice system but, judging by the functioning of the system, it sometimes appears that the victim has been left out. Once a case is inserted into the criminal justice system the victim is reduced to the role of witness, useful only in helping officials process the case. The role of the victim as the complainant who has a stake in the case and who wants some kind of input or control has been ignored by a criminal justice system more concerned with processing cases than with providing victims with a sense of justice.

Being a victim of crime can be a traumatic experience. It can affect individuals in a number of ways, and the impact can last a surprisingly long time. For some people, the hurt, shame, or loss of security never goes away, and they live the rest of their lives with the shadow of crime affecting the way they behave on the street, causing them to barricade themselves behind locks and barred windows at home, and even affecting how they associate and socialize with new acquaintances. The violation can create **invisible**

wounds and private anguish for the victims. According to Bard and Sangrey (1986), "victims of personal crime often express their sense of having been attacked in a sacred, inner place." It takes a long time for people to develop the healthy sense of who they are that allows them to become an outgoing and trusting person. One unfortunate victimization experience can devastate positive feelings about themselves and other people.

> The part that has been hurt is the private inner space that defines our being. The self is as real as a person's hand or heart, but it isn't physical. It has no anatomical site. It can be conceptualized as invisible, but within—some call it the soul; other, the spirit; the ego. The self encompasses everything that a person means when he or she says "I" (Bard and Sangrey 1986, 11).

Loss of self also occurs from the loss of personal possessions. We normally think of material objects as replaceable, especially if there is insurance, but many times the possessions have a special or symbolic meaning. It is a mistake to think of losses from theft only in dollar amounts. Gifts from loved ones have meanings far beyond their monetary value. The loss of a wedding ring worn for 40 years can have a devastating effect on a widow who may believe she has desecrated the memory of her husband by losing the ring.

Perhaps the most traumatic impact on a victim of crime is how relationships with others are affected. Once someone is a victim of an armed robbery on the street it is very difficult to resume a pattern of living where going out is taken for granted. Now each excursion into the street is looked on as a strategic dash from one safe haven to another. This can cause strain with companions who may understand the victim's concerns at one level but cannot fully comprehend the depth of fear and mistrust such victimization can cause. In more serious crimes this disruption can go on for years. The invisible wound may not even be fully understood even by the victim. There may be a general uneasiness or uncertainty about venturing into new experiences that lingers with the victim long after the victimization has presumably passed.

As if the crime committed were not traumatic enough, the victim's experiences in dealing with the criminal justice system can add insult to the injury. Only recently has the criminal justice system made a concerted effort to develop programs aimed at assisting victims and witnesses in dealing with the criminal justice system. Without some forethought in how cases are processed, the consequences for victims can be as unnerving as the crime itself.

> Interviewers learned that common problems for system participants included time loss, a corresponding reduction in income, time wasted waiting needlessly inside the courthouse, and transportation problems. In addition, court appearances for subpoenaed witnesses translated into lost wages—a significant concern for many people. Waiting conditions were

another critical problem. . . . In one particular case, a sexual assault victim took a seat before the trial began. A number of other people shuffled in and out waiting for their cases to begin. A few minutes later, much to her chagrin, the victim realized her suspected assailant was sitting next to her (Doerner and Lab 1995, 48).

Why has the criminal justice system seemed so unconcerned with the plight of the victim? Why have so many victims reported they were dissatisfied with the way their cases were handled? What dangers does the criminal justice system face in the future if victims and witnesses of crime do not cooperate because they feel the government is more interested in the rights of the accused than in the rights of the victim?

Part of the problem with how the victims and witnesses are treated by the criminal justice system can be traced to the structure of the criminal justice institution. As we previously discussed in this chapter, the criminal justice system is not really a system in the true sense of the word but is actually several different agencies all working on a different part of the criminal justice process. Each agency has its own mandates, internal demands, reward systems, and ways of keeping score. Each agency has its own agenda in terms of trying to preserve its own discretion. The victims of crime have to interact with all of these agencies and often find themselves and their interests shuffled between agencies or, all too often, slipping between the cracks. Before the advent of victim/witness assistance programs, every agency had some responsibility for promoting the interests of the victim and this meant that no agency had final responsibility.

The first criminal justice agency the victim normally comes in contact with is law enforcement. The speed at which the police respond, how carefully they listen, and how much they seem concerned with the victim's plight all influence how the victim views their efforts. If the police are uncaring, seem bored, or imply they have other more important work to do, the victim will feel even more distress from the crime. Normally the police are not so insensitive to the victim's plight, but sometimes their complex job gives them the appearance of not caring. Part of the problem is perspective. To the victim, their crime is the most important event to happen in that city for the whole day and nothing less than the full mobilization of all police resources is expected.

To the police officer, the crime the victim has just suffered may be routine and the prospects for an immediate arrest slight. The most useful activity for the police officer is to make a detailed and factual report that requires the victim to relate in a calm and considered manner what has happened. This apparent lack of urgency on the part of the police officer is sometimes interpreted by the victim as a lack of caring. Police officers who have been on the street for any length of time have been exposed to a good deal of suffering and trauma. The blood and carnage from automobile accidents alone desensitize police to the shock of violence. Police, ambulance attendants, and

Victims of crime have a variety of needs including help in negotiating the criminal justice system. (© Mark Richards/PhotoEdit.)

nurses develop a type of emotional armor around their feelings that can appear as indifference to those who are experiencing crime.

> At its worst, this protective armor becomes inflexible and impenetrable. The officer is truly indifferent to the victim's plight. He or she depersonalizes victims, treats them as objects to be processed as quickly as possible. A self-protective officer can become entirely detached from any human feeling for the victim. Since the victim is a person who has recently been treated like an object by the criminal, this behavior in the part of a police officer is sure to make the victim feel even more violated (Bard and Sangrey 1986, 120).

After the case is processed by the police it moves to the court system. There always exists a bit of tension between the police and the courts, who are responsible for obtaining a conviction within a very strict definition of the rule of law. The police often feel they have risked their lives to arrest suspects only to have the courts let them off on some technicality or a plea bargain. The courts criticize the police for not processing the case correctly and violating the accused's rights to the point that any conviction would be over-turned on appeal. Into this tension between the police and the courts steps the vulnerable and unsuspecting victims who still expect the criminal justice system to behave as a system.

The prosecuting attorney has the most contact with the victim in the criminal justice system. The prosecutor represents the people (that is, the entire society) and not just the victim. A criminal act is a violation against society, and the accused is answerable to all of us as represented by the prosecutor. The case is effectively taken away from the victim who may have revenge as a motive more than justice, and given to the state in the form of the prosecutor who presses the case forward in a fair and impartial way based on the law rather than on emotions. At least, this is the way it is supposed to happen. The prosecutor has a host of demands placed on her or him which dictate that cases be processed in an orderly fashion. For victims, the work of the prosecutor can appear to be arbitrary and uncaring.

There are two decisions made in the courts that upset many victims and cause them to lose faith in the criminal justice system. The first is when after being charged with the crime, the accused is given a chance to make bail or is released on his or her own recognizance. Because of the presumption of innocence that is a cornerstone in our criminal law, unless the state can present convincing evidence that the accused is dangerous or likely to flee the jurisdiction, temporary release is granted in most cases. This is partly because the state does not have sufficient jail space and does not want to feed the many individuals who are accused of crimes but are not considered dangerous or escape risks. Victims may feel threatened by having their attacker back on the streets while the case is pending, but from the perspective of the prosecutor, the law and available resources prevent keeping most offenders in jail until their cases are over.

In addition to letting suspects out on bail, the decision that really upsets victims of crime is the practice of plea-bargaining. To the victim, a plea-bargain is a perversion of justice and a slap in the face. The plea-bargain is seen by the victim as the prosecutor being soft on crime and as rejecting the victim's interests in the case. There are many reasons why a prosecutor will plea-bargain a case. According to Bard and Sangrey (1986, 123–24), the reasons include:

1. The prosecutor may be aware of mitigating circumstances that call for leniency in a particular case.
2. The prosecutor may believe that the evidence is insufficient to sustain one charge but sufficient to sustain a lesser charge; in such cases he or she may plea-bargain to ensure a conviction.
3. Most often the plea-bargain is for the convenience of the government. There are simply too many cases going through the court system and the prosecutor must make deals in order to dispose of a great number of them.

Victims also can get disillusioned by the court proceedings. The workings of the court calendar are subject to a variety of delays and changes that, while routine to court workers and attorneys, can be very frustrating to victims and witnesses of crime. The various pretrial hearings, arraignments, discovery motions, and jury selection proceedings can leave victims and witnesses confused and perplexed. While the defendant will have an attorney to guide him or her through the maze of court proceedings, the victim must rely on a prosecutor who is too busy to explain the intricacies of the case. Often the case is disposed of through a plea-bargain between the prosecutor and the defense attorney with little or no input from the victim. It is not surprising, then, that victims feel the criminal justice system does not adequately express their sense of outrage over the crime that has been committed against them. Bard and Sangrey (1986, 134) conclude:

> Our law requires evidence of guilt. It requires the presumption of innocence for the accused. It surrounds defendants with safeguards so they cannot be deprived of their freedom capriciously. These are necessary and proper rules. But all the intellectualizing in the world cannot prevent crime victims from feeling terribly wronged when the criminal justice system fails to satisfy their need for justice. There just isn't any way to soften the blow.

There are, however, some ways the criminal justice system can react to the victims' concerns so that they do not feel completely abandoned. The criminal justice system can take steps with the victims' interests expressly in mind to make the process more understandable, less inconvenient, and less alienating. What some jurisdictions have done is to establish programs aimed at aiding victims and witnesses of crime.

Victim and Witness Assistance Programs

There is a real threat to the system of justice in a country when the victims and witnesses to crime do not report it to law enforcement and do not participate in the court process because they have lost faith in the system. When victims and witnesses perceive the criminal justice system as being more concerned with the suspects than themselves, they tend to become cynical about the whole process. Suspects are provided public defenders when they cannot afford a private attorney, but victims are represented only by the prosecutor who has a broader agenda than catering to their needs for a satisfactory closure to the case. Prosecutors, as we have already mentioned, sometimes incur the wrath of victims and witnesses because of plea-bargaining and the need to make decisions on which cases to prosecute the most vigorously. Additionally, the prosecutor's knowledge of the norms of justice in the jurisdiction may be at odds with what the victim thinks should happen to the case. For instance, if someone assaulted your mother, you would not care about their being a first-time offender or any other mitigating circumstances the prosecutor might consider. You would want a severe sentence, or you would feel the system is not working as it should. Maintaining the cooperation of citizens has become a problem, and **victim and witness assistance programs** are designed to help them negotiate the criminal justice system and provide input into how their case is decided.

Most of the victim-witness assistance programs are located in the prosecutor's office to ensure the cooperation of victims in the court proceedings. There is some justification in placing these programs within the prosecutor's office, but there are also some drawbacks to this organizational structure. The advantages to having the victim-witness program in the prosecutor's office include:

1. Prosecutors are in the best position to keep the victim informed about changes in the court calendar. As part of the court workgroup (this includes defense attorneys, the public defender, judges, and clerks) the prosecutor participates in plea-bargaining, postponements or continuances, and can best predict when victims and witnesses may be needed to testify.

2. Prosecutors are in the best position to press the interests of the victim in the court proceedings. The prosecutor is familiar with the crime and how it has impacted on the victim. While the prosecutor represents the state, she or he is also representing the victim and can respond to arguments put forth by the defense attorney.

3. The prosecutor must answer to the victim in cases of plea-bargaining. By having the victim-witness program in that office the prosecutor will feel an obligation to make deals to which the victim can consent. Placing the victim witness program in a different organization distances the prosecutor from the victim.

There are also some organizational reasons to place the victim-witness program somewhere other than the prosecutor's office.

1. The prosecutor represents the interests of the state first and the victim second. When these interests conflict, the victim will feel cheated by the system and lose faith in the criminal justice system.

2. The prosecutor must give at least the appearance of neutrality and cannot press the victim's interests as well as an advocate from another agency.

3. The prosecutor is interested in getting convictions in big or important cases and may expend victim-witness program resources on those cases that fit her or his immediate priorities rather than on what is best for the victim of a less politically useful case.

4. Placing the victim-witness program in the prosecutor's office may limit the types of victims served. Only those cases that have suspects that are going to court are of real interest to the prosecutor. Victims in cases where no one has been arrested are not as useful to the prosecutor and may receive little or no service.

5. What about witnesses for the defense? If the goal of the system is to promote justice then victim-witness programs placed under the control of the prosecutor's office and funded by tax money may give an unfair advantage to the state. Perhaps the victim-witness program, in the interests of fairness, should notify all witnesses when court proceedings are changed.

Regardless of where the victim-witness program is organizationally housed, there are services provided that not only help the criminal justice system maintain the trust and cooperation of victims and witnesses but, more importantly, help those individuals. Reducing the suffering caused by the crime and reducing the confusion and frustration of dealing with the criminal justice system are the objectives of victim-witness programs. Each victim may have different needs and the programs must be able to provide a wide range of services. According to Doerner and Lab (1995, 53–54), these services include:

- *Crisis intervention.* Crime is a traumatic event for most victims. Especially in cases of violent crime, the victims and their families may need assistance in dealing with transportation to the hospital, notification of relatives, money to buy meals after a robbery, and advice on when the criminal justice system will deal with the case.
- *Follow-up counseling.* The traumatic nature of crimes such as sexual assault may require ongoing counseling until the case is brought to court and in some cases long afterward. Counseling services may be provided by victim-witness program staff or by referral to a psychologist. Some programs have established support groups to help victims deal with the crimes committed against them.
- *Personal advocacy.* Often the victim is too traumatized to effectively plead his or her side of the case to the police, prosecutor, judge, or others. The victim-witness program staff member will assert the interests of the victim in the repeated telling of the crime's impact on the victim. Victims can grow tired of pleading their woes and feel that others perceive them as whining, where a professional staff member can advocate the victim's best interests.
- *Employer and landlord intervention.* Victimization can have far-reaching and long-lasting effects. If the crime was committed in the workplace or apartment, the employer or landlord may see getting rid of the victim as a solution to future violence. The victim-witness staff member can intervene to convince the employer or landlord that the victim is just that, *the victim,* and that it would be morally unethical to fire or evict the victim.
- *Property return.* In cases of theft or armed robbery the victim's stolen property is used by the criminal justice system as evidence. Many times the property is kept from the victim for long periods of time as the case winds itself through the court process. The victim-witness program staff member can sometimes expedite the return of property to the victim when the state has concluded the case.

- *Intimidation protection.* Victims and witnesses can be subject to intimidation from offenders or their family and friends. Sitting outside the courtroom waiting to testify can be frightening for the victim when the offender who is out on bail or a family member is pestering them to drop the charges. Additionally, the defense attorney may give unsolicited advice to victims and witnesses in depositions that can border on intimidation. The victim-witness staff member can act as a buffer between the victim or witness and protect them from intimidation.
- *Referral.* The victim-witness staff member is knowledgeable about the community resources available to the victim. Often the trauma of the crime will create problems such as excessive drinking that can be helped with counseling, and the victim-witness staff member can assist in the referral.
- *Restitution, compensation, and witness fee assistance.* Depending on the case and jurisdiction, there may be ways the victim-witness program staff member can help the victim or witness recover money from the offender or the state. The judge may order the offender to pay restitution to the victim, and the staff member can help the court in deciding on the appropriate amount. Some states have programs that use tax dollars to compensate victims of crime and pay fees for witnesses. The requirements for such compensation always require paperwork, and the victim-witness staff member can assist in this task.
- *Court orientation.* For many victims and witnesses, their case represents the first time they have had to go to the courthouse. Seemingly little issues like parking, finding the correct courtroom, and even what to wear are likely to be the subject of questions for the uninitiated. The victim-witness program can answer these questions as well as help the victims and witnesses anticipate what types of questions to expect from the prosecutor and the defense attorney.
- *Court transportation and escort.* Some victims and witnesses may need transportation to the courthouse and help and support during the proceedings. Victim-witness program staff members will guide the victims and offer emotional support and counsel.
- *Public education and legislative advocacy.* The victim-witness staff members are responsible for advertising their services to the public. They will speak at service organizations such as the Kiwanis, Rotary Club, Chamber of Commerce, and other organizations that support the community. Another important function for the victim-witness program staff members is to educate the politicians who make laws concerning the victims of crime. By speaking to legislative members and committees, the victim-witness staff member can sensitize the legislators to the concerns of the victims and generate supportive laws and financial resources for the program.

As can be seen from this list of functions provided by victim-witness programs, the criminal justice system can do much to relieve the suffering of the crime victim and ensure that she or he is not further victimized by insensitive or uncaring court officials. Not all jurisdictions have such comprehensive programs and not all program staff members have the professional training to be effective. Nevertheless, it seems that victim-witness programs have become an important feature in the criminal justice system and will continue to advocate on behalf of citizens who find themselves caught up in the problems of being a victim of crime.

One note of caution about the role of the victim in the criminal justice system is warranted. While the victim's interests and impact are important to the goal of achieving justice, they should not be the determining factor. From a peacemaking perspective, the inclusion of the victim should allow for a reconciliation between the victim and the offender rather than the simple revenge of the victim.

CRITICAL THINKING QUESTIONS

1. Discuss how the criminal justice system cannot really be considered a system. What changes in organizational structure would it take to make it a system? What are the advantages and disadvantages of making such changes?

2. Describe the differences between substantive and procedural law. How is each important to the workings of the criminal justice system?

3. Discuss how the victims of crime may be further injured by the workings of the criminal justice system. Which victims are most likely to have unpleasant interactions with criminal justice personnel.

4. What are the differences between the interests of the state and the interests of the victim in a criminal case? What are the dangers of allowing the victim to have too much to say in determining how the offender is dealt with by the criminal justice system?

SUGGESTED READINGS

Doerner, William, and Steven Lab. 1995. *Victimology.* Cincinnati: Anderson Publishing.

Greene, Jack R., and Carl B. Klockers. 1991. "What Police Do," in Carl B. Klockers and Stephen D. Mastrofski, eds. *Thinking about Police: Contemporary Readings,* 2nd ed. New York: McGraw-Hill, pp. 273–284.

Klockers, Carl B. 1991. "The Modern Sting," in Carl B. Klockers and Stephen D. Mastrofski, eds. *Thinking about Police: Contemporary Readings,* 2nd ed. New York: McGraw-Hill, pp. 258–267.

Vago, Steven. 1997. *Law and Society.* Upper Saddle River, NJ: Prentice Hall.

5

POLICE AND PEACEMAKING

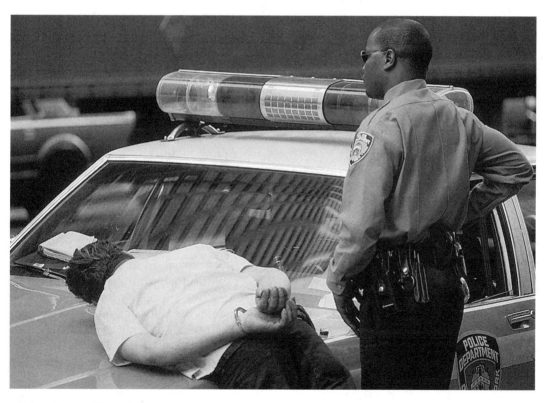

© Robert Brenner/PhotoEdit.

Learning Objectives

After reading this chapter, the student should be able to:

- Describe the paramilitary nature of police organizations.
- Explain the differences between discretion exercised by a police officer and a military soldier.
- Describe James Q. Wilson's styles of policing.
- Explain how the use of force is at the core of police work.
- Describe how a peacemaking perspective can be applied to how police exercise their use of force.
- Define the mission of SWAT teams.
- Describe some of the unintended consequences of SWAT teams.
- Define community policing.
- Describe some of the strategies used in the community policing concept.
- Describe some of the obstacles to community policing.
- Explain why there may be resistance on the part of the police officer to community policing.

Key Terms

Police Discretion	Zero Tolerance
Watchman Style	Police Use of Force
Legalistic Style	Police Riots
Service Style	Community Policing
Styles of Policing	

The war on crime and peacemaking perspectives can most visibly be observed in the area of law enforcement. The resolution of conflict, the decision to arrest or not arrest, and the deterrent effect of the police presence all can be examined by the war on crime and peacemaking perspectives. While politicians may call for untying the hands of the police so they can fight the criminal, simplistic rhetoric that clearly espouses the war on crime perspective, many police officials and countless law enforcement officers practice the peacemaking perspective in the course of their daily routine.

The war on crime perspective is more apparent because it results in high profile police initiatives such as SWAT teams, drug crackdowns, and measurable arrest rates, but peacemaking activities may be more effective in making the streets safe. Police working with concerned citizens, churches, schools, and other government agencies have the capacity to transform communities.

Peacemaking efforts can not only make the streets safe, but also meet the needs of citizens in such a way that suffering is reduced, conflicts are resolved, and people feel that justice is being done.

THE PARAMILITARY NATURE OF POLICE INSTITUTIONS

The institution to which law enforcement is most often compared is the military (Bittner 1980). This should not be surprising given the weapons, uniforms, hierarchical command structures, and social isolation associated with each of these occupations. Even the nomenclature of law enforcement is reminiscent of the military, with titles like "captain" and "sergeant," missions termed "patrol," and a central command structure called "headquarters."

Just as war is a problematic analogy for the nature of law enforcement, so too is the military model a misleading indicator. There are some distinct differences between the military and law enforcement that makes the comparison deceptive (Skolnick and Fyfe 1993).

Command and Discretion

A fundamental aspect of law enforcement involves the nature of discretion. **Police discretion** is the latitude or flexibility the officer has in deciding how an incident should be handled. While there is certainly a good bit of training in the police academy on the policies and procedures used by the force which greatly limits the individual officer's decision, the fact remains that the core of police work revolves around how the officers interpret situational variables in deciding if and how to invoke the criminal justice sanction. The discretion used in police work is exercised at the lowest level of command, the individual line police officer, as opposed to the military where the greatest discretion is vested at the higher levels of the organization (Bittner 1980). A private in the army is so closely supervised that she or he need not make important decisions. The private in the army need only follow orders in fulfilling the clearly defined mission. James Q. Wilson (1972) contends that law enforcement agencies are more similar to some social service departments than they are to the military.

> *The police have a complex, not a simple task; they work alone or in pairs, and not under continuous supervision; and they cannot let the client be the sole judge of their non-service function. These attributes are not unique. Schoolteachers, welfare workers, doctors in a hospital, and parish priests in the Catholic church share them and as a result, school superintendents, welfare supervisors, hospital administrators, and bishops share the police chiefs' special concern for the problem of discovering, evaluating, and modifying the ways their organization's operative deal with clients.*

The mission of the police officer is ambiguous; many contingencies cannot be foreseen. Police officers are required to use their own discretion in a way that the military model of organization does not encourage. For example, in the traditional military battlefield situation the soldier fires on the enemy when ordered to do so. Obedience rather than decision-making is required. The police officer, by contrast, has no clear enemy. The police officer must interpret the behaviors of suspects and victims and then apply the law and departmental policies. The police administrator makes policies at a very broad level but cannot predict every situation the line officers find themselves in so they cannot make rules to cover all the discretion-making possibilities. Wilson (1972) explains how discretion is unavoidable in law enforcement.

> *In fact, as all police officers and many citizens recognize, discretion is inevitable—partly because it is impossible to observe every public infraction, partly because many laws require interpretation before they can be applied to all, partly because the police can sometimes get information about serious crimes by overlooking minor crimes, and partly because the police believe that public opinion would not tolerate a policy of full enforcement of all laws at the time.*

Central to this problem of discretion-making is the concept of the *enemy* embedded in the military model. On the battlefield the enemy is relatively easy to identify. He or she wears a different uniform and is physically located some distance away. In the Vietnam War the concept of the enemy became confusing to the U.S. troops. It was hard to tell the Vietnamese who were on our side from the enemy, and this resulted in mistakes and atrocities that point to the failure of the traditional military model to guide discretion (Karnow 1983). The nature of police work is much more like the Vietnam War than the traditional military situation. Unfortunately, the criminal does not wear a uniform that would allow the police officer to readily distinguish him or her from the law-abiding citizen. Furthermore, there is no identifiable battlefield where law enforcement takes place. The criminal and the respectable citizen are practically indistinguishable from each other, and the law enforcement officer must use experience, training, and judgment to decide how and when to enforce the law.

The military model is useful for directing large groups of soldiers toward a central target in a coordinated manner. It is less useful for supervising a large number of loosely-related individuals engaged in an infinite number of tasks. Criminal behavior cannot be addressed in the same ways as military behavior.

Varieties of Police Styles

Not all police officers have the same style of enforcing the law and not all law enforcement agencies are alike. Historically there have been some discernable patterns in the way that law enforcement agencies relate to the public. James Q.

Wilson identified three styles of police behavior: **watchman style, legalistic style,** and the **service style.** These styles are important because they set the tone of civility between the police and the public. The ability of the police to become involved with citizens is a pivotal issue in how effective they can be in addressing crime. Thus, it is useful to consider how Wilson's typology of police styles treats police discretion in interacting with the public.

The Watchman Style

Wilson makes a distinction between two types of police activities: law enforcement and order maintenance. Law enforcement involves a violation of the law in which only guilt needs to be determined. Order maintenance involves deciding if there is a legal infraction (and many times there is), deciding who is culpable, and deciding whether to invoke the criminal justice sanction. The watchman style is more concerned with maintaining order by allowing the police officer to ignore many minor offenses, tolerate a certain amount of vice and gambling, and be concerned with using the law not to regulate behavior but to preserve the social order in such a way that most citizens (especially the most powerful) are satisfied. The watchman style is a remnant from the past when police forces were a private concern that protected the property of individuals rather than served the public. A certain standard of public order is expected, and the police use discretion in maintaining the standard depending on some extralegal factors such as social class, race, and demeanor.

The Legalistic Style

This style of policing is concerned with applying the law to more situations than the watchman style. Rather than just keeping a lid on things, the police officer using the legalistic style will use less discretion by writing more tickets, making more arrests, and urging more citizens to sign complaints rather then work things out informally. The legalistic-oriented police officer applies a single standard to all citizens and does not consider race and class to be factors in deciding whether to arrest or to handle the situation informally. The legalistic style signifies a change from the watchman style to the degree in which the police officer interacts with the citizens. While it is an oversimplification, it may be useful to think of the legalistic type of police officer as riding in a squad car and the watchman style as walking a beat. The opportunity for the legalistic police officer to consider individual differences in citizens and situations is reduced when one works from a car rather than intermingling with the merchants and people on the street.

The Service Style

The service style of policing shares some of the characteristics of the other two styles but includes an emphasis of service to the community. According to Wilson, the service style police officer will take seriously all requests for either law enforcement or order maintenance (unlike police with a watchman

style) but are less likely to respond by making an arrest or otherwise imposing formal sanctions (unlike police with a legalistic style).

Wilson found these three **styles of policing** distributed across eight
communities. The region of the country in which the community was
located, the history of the police department, and the characteristics of the
community all influenced what style of policing the community displayed.
What is important to understand from Wilson's research is that there is a
range of policing styles and the particular style a community adopts is, in
part, a policy decision made by the politicians and the police administrators.
The style of policing then filters down to the street-level officer through regulations, training, rewards, and example.

As with any typology, Wilson's style of policing are not mutually exclusive and exhaustive. That is, there may be other styles in other cities and there
is some degree of overlap between the styles. A police officer may have a
watchman style and work in a department that is legalistic or service-
oriented. A department may adopt one type of style for certain situations and
another for a different situation. For example, police may be given very little
discretion in dealing with domestic assault cases and may be given broad discretion in handling complaints about street people.

In the 30 years since Wilson wrote about policing styles much has changed
in the country and in the nature of police work. Still, the core dilemma of when
and how to use police discretion remains and the idea that the police department can help structure the use of discretion continues to be relevant. As with
many aspects of society, technology has changed the ability of police managers
to supervise the street-level officer. Improved communications have made it
possible for shift supervisors to stay in constant contact with their police officers and to assure that the policies of the department are implemented. The
increased visibility of the officer's actions serves to limit greatly the discretion
that can be employed in any given situation (McKenzie 1990).

The implications of the competing war on crime and peacemaking perspectives for police styles are important to understanding current law enforcement issues. To a great extent, the war on crime (and particularly the war on
drugs) has transformed policing styles. Policies such as **zero tolerance** have
required police to become more proactive in enforcing the law. When the
police use such tactics as drug dogs, roadblocks, and sting operations to find
crime this ensures that when police find transgressions of the law they will
proceed with formal legal processing. Conversely, a department can ensure
that the system can manage its resources better by monitoring department-
approved discretion much more closely. Hence, the organizational imperatives of the police agencies can be brought to bear on specific police concerns.

Police Use of Force

At the core of the police role is the mandate to use physical force and violence
in the interests of society. It is the job of the police to decide when and how

force should be used, and it is understood that the police will employ force when other methods of resolving conflicts fail. While it is certainly true that there have been abuses of the use of force by the police it is also true that for the most part the police have been guided by the law, police procedures, and public opinion in curbing their use of excessive force. The police are not a gang that victimizes society for its own purposes, but rather a group of authorized officers who use force on behalf of the citizens so they do not need to use force for themselves. Bittner (1980, 39) characterizes the police role in the use of force as, "It makes more sense to say that the police are nothing else than a mechanism for the distribution of situationally justified force in society." So central to the police mandate is the authority, capacity, and willingness to use overpowering resistance that Bittner conceives of our understanding of the use of force by the police as the primary and final solution to ongoing conflicts.

> *There can be no doubt that this feature of police work is uppermost in the minds of people who solicit police aid or direct the attention of the police to problems, that the persons against whom the police proceed have this feature in mind and conduct themselves accordingly, and that every conceivable police intervention projects the message that force may be, and may have to be, used to achieve a desired objective. It does not matter whether the persons who seek police help are private citizens or government officials, nor does it matter whether the problem at hand involves some aspect of law enforcement or is totally unconnected with it (Bittner 1980, 40).*

So how does a police officer decide when to use force and how much force is acceptable? There is great variability in the answer because each police force sets policies to guide their officers and each officer brings to the job his or her own personality and temperament. To make a blanket statement on how and how much force should be used ignores the fact that these decisions are made in relative isolation and in a very short time span. With the exception of television programs such as "Cops," there is no instant replay that allows the researcher to examine the incidents of **police use of force** to find the situational exigencies that prompt the use of force.

Of interest to our discussion of the war on crime and peacemaking perspectives as they relate to the issue of the use of force by the police is Bittner's claim that the institutionalized use of force by the police rest on one's conception of the police role.

> *It appears that in our society two answers to this question are acceptable. One defines the targets of legitimate force as enemies and the coercive advance against them as warfare. Those who wage this war are expected to be possessed by the military virtues of valor, obedience and* esprit de corps. *The enterprise as a whole is justified as a sacrificial and glorious mission in which the warriors' duty is "not to reason why." The other answer involves*

an altogether different imagery. The targets of force are conceived as practical objectives and their attainment a matter of practical expediency. The process involves prudence, economy, and considered judgment, from case to case. The enterprise as a whole is conceived as a public trust, the exercise of which is vested in practitioners who are personally responsible for their decisions and actions (Bittner 1980, 47).

Bittner claims these two conceptions of the police role in the use of force are incompatible. The military prowess required by the former and the professional acumen dictated by the latter create a role conflict not easily negotiated by the law enforcement officer on the street faced with a situation where time to reflect is not available. For this reason the theoretical policy orientation of peacemaking or war on crime is important in determining if, how, and how much force will be used.

The Rodney King incident in Los Angeles serves as a good example of how the war on crime perspective with its military orientation reflects the use of force by the police (Fuller 1993). An amateur cameraman captures an 81-second beating by the police of a motorist who had led them on a high-speed chase for several miles. Rodney King was handcuffed and on the ground when several police officers who claimed he was resisting arrest beat him with clubs and flashlights and shocked him with a stun gun (Skolnick and Fyfe 1993). The tape was played and replayed on television news programs until it became a confirmation in the minds of many citizens of the excessive use of force by the police. Only by viewing Rodney King as the enemy, on whom extreme physical force could be used in the line of duty, could the police officers involved feel justified in their actions. A police officer with a peacemaking orientation would have employed Bittner's other conception of the use of police force, that of a professional invested with a public trust to use only the force necessary to bring the situation under control.

The use of force by the police is an important topic for our discussion of the war on crime and peacemaking perspectives because there is considerable variation in how citizens view this issue. Some citizens believe that criminals are treated too leniently and that the police should have their hands untied so they can get tough with criminals on the street. Other citizens think the police should exercise more restraint in how they deal with offenders because it is not the role of the police to mete out punishment. The job of the police is to arrest suspects and allow the courts to determine guilt and decide on an appropriate punishment or treatment based on the merits of the case and the harm done to society.

It is enlightening to note how the characteristics of individuals are related to how they view the proper role of police in the use of force. In a study by Arthur and Case (1994) it was hypothesized from a conflict perspective that those who were most disenfranchised from society would show little support for police use of force and those who were heavily invested in society in terms

From George Holliday 3 1991

Allegations of police brutality are common. (© Rob Crandall/Stock Boston.)

of social class would tend to support the police. Drawing on a long tradition of looking at how the police work to support the economic interests of the powerful, Arthur and Case (1994) examined how the race and social class of individuals is related to how much support they have for the use of force by the police. Additionally, they examined the theoretical perspective of cultural environment where ideas and symbols in which people live presumably shape their values, attitudes, and perspectives. Finally, they examined how those who have been victims of violence felt about the use of force by the police.

Arthur and Case (1994, 178) found that social status and privilege are related to how individuals feel about police violence. Women, African-Americans, and those with less cultural capital reflect attitudes that view the police as serving to protect the interests of the dominant groups. Also, "Those who see blacks, poor people, criminals and pornography users as different types of beings from themselves (violent, lazy, immoral) more likely favor police violence." Finally, those who have been victims of violence and those who feel the courts treat offenders too leniently are more likely to support the use of force by the police. While none of these findings is particularly surprising, they do serve to demonstrate that there is considerable difference of opinion as to how police use physical force.

When a significant proportion of the population loses trust in the police then the whole underpinning of the social contract that upholds a civilized society becomes vulnerable.

Police Riots

There may be legitimate differences of opinion as to whether too much police force was used in any given incident. People's perceptions vary according to how involved in the case they may be, how closely they can relate to the police officer or the suspect, and how familiar they are with actual police work as opposed to what they glean from watching television. While most people viewing the tapes of the Rodney King incident are convinced they are seeing a clear case of police brutality, there are those, including police officers, who will defend the behavior of the law enforcement officers involved as within the bounds of appropriate use of force. They will point to the high-speed chase that endangered the police and other citizens, the belief that Rodney King was under the influence of drugs, and the unwillingness of King to follow commands to stay on the ground. The point here is not to attempt to render a judgment as to whether this was an excessive use of force, but to point out that reasonable people can disagree even on the Rodney King case. So infused with passion is the issue about what constitutes the proper use of police force that a gulf exists between those who see the police engaged in a war against the criminal element and those who see the police as public servants.

One type of police problem where there is little disagreement over the proper role of the police is when the police get out of control and engage in what Rodney Stark (1972) terms a police riot. From time to time, police agencies overreact to situations on the street and immerse themselves in what sociologists would call a collective behavior situation where the command and control function break down and the police commit gross errors of judgment that can include acts of violence. In recent memory, the 1968 Democratic Convention saw the Chicago Police Department lose control of its officers and excessive police force was broadcast around the world.

The war on crime perspective is to blame for these unfortunate incidents where the police act as an unrestrained mob and attack citizens. The paramilitary nature of police organizations is not sufficient to deal with large crowds of people without resorting to force of a military nature. The central problem revolves around the differing nature of discretion needed for police work and the type of discretion needed for effective military operations. As previously mentioned, in police work the greatest discretion is found at the level of the individual officer on the street. No matter how hard the command structure tries to control decision-making, the street-level officers have the discretion to define behaviors as unlawful and the power to decide whether to invoke the criminal justice sanction. In fact, many if not most violations of the law are not processed by the police officer because she or he is expected to use professional judgment in deciding if the matter is serious enough to insert it into the criminal justice bureaucracy. The work of police chiefs, captains, and lieutenants is done in reaction to what is found by the street-level officer. It is not uncommon for the officer not to want to leave the street because that is "where the action is," meaning, to a large degree, where the discretion lies.

In the military, the flow of discretion lies in the opposite direction. The generals get to decide the big issues, such as what beach to invade. All the way down the chain of command discretion is exercised so that by the time it gets to the individual soldier, there is little to do other than follow very precise orders. The private ordered to charge a machine gun nest has little choice to make while the patrol officer has a wide range of discretion in deciding how to do her or his job.

The problem comes when we expect the police to operate like military units. Police officers are not trained to act as a unit but to use their own discretion. When collective behavior situations arise, police forces can be ineffective because they cannot respond in mass and they cannot function in a coordinated manner. One of the reasons the military or the National Guard is called out for urban riots or natural disasters is because these units function as a unit where each individual knows her or his role and there is adequate supervision to ensure a coordinated response. The police simply are not trained in this way and, when forced into situations where they are required to act as a unit, may degenerate into an unfocused group of individuals each pursuing what she or he believes to be correct police procedure.

The experience of the Los Angeles Police Department following the Rodney King verdict is a good example of how the police are ill-equipped in training and temperament to deal with collective behavior situations from a military standpoint. The LAPD made several tactical errors in predicting, preparing, and responding to the riots that resulted in not only a worse situation for their city but, because of the technology of instant communication, enabled the riots to spread to many other cities (Fuller 1993).

It is legitimate to ask as this point how the peacemaking perspective can better address the problem of **police riots** and, more specifically, how it could deal with collective behavior situations such as the 1968 Democratic Convention protests or the Rodney King verdict riots. The answer is quite simple and employs two complementary strategies. The first strategy would dictate how the police department routinely interacts with citizens. Residents in Chicago in 1968 and in Los Angeles in 1992 viewed their respective police departments as outsiders, akin to an invading army rather than as public servants. The peacemaking perspective would have developed a more friendly atmosphere based on community-building so that there would not be the animosity between the police and the citizens. Additionally, a peacemaking perspective could have been used with the leaders of the protesters in Chicago and allowed peaceful protest in a planned manner which allowed for the protesters to tactfully retreat. According to Stark (1972), the protesters were boxed in by the police and the only possible result was the violence that occurred.

In the Rodney King verdict riots the situation was even more problematic for the police. The police were the actual focus of the riots after four of their officers were acquitted of police brutality. The peacemaking solution would have trained officers in minority affairs and police-citizen interaction so that the incident (and others reportedly like it) would not have occurred. The minority communities in that city would not have been so alienated from the police force (Susta et al. 1995).

SWAT Teams

Perhaps the most visible military manifestation of police agencies is the Special Weapons and Tactics (SWAT) teams that are common is most large police agencies. These specially trained officers respond to dangerous situations such as hostage-taking or armed robberies. It is reasonable to train a few select experts to deal with these relatively rare occurrences and to try to ensure that only those fully equipped and rehearsed are exposed to danger. These situations are the closest the police come to actual military situations, and the special uniforms and high-powered rifles with scopes and night vision devices are useful when all other means of resolving the conflict have been exhausted.

A review of the curriculum of a SWAT training program illustrates the nature of the special instruction these officers receive and suggest the military nature of using these tactics. Barreto (1988, 38) enumerates the number of hours of training SWAT teams receive at the Miami Beach Police Department.

Course	*Hours*
Introduction and Orientation	2.0
Physical Conditioning	22.0
Team Movement Techniques and Knot Tying	3.5
Crisis Intervention/Conflict Management in Hostage Situations	3.0
SWAT Policies and Procedures	1.5
Organizing Special Equipment	1.0
Scouting, Sketching, and Briefing	1.5
Introduction to Chemical Agents and Protective Apparel	1.5
Explosive Devices, Cocaine Labs and Booby Traps	2.0
Introduction to Personal Survival Skills	5.5
Rappelling and Elevated Victim Rescue	14.0
Weapons Familiarization and Range Training	27.5
Introduction to Urban Terrorism	2.0
Introduction to Forcible Entry Tools	2.0
Introduction to Tactical Electronics	1.0
Organizing the Team Structure	1.5
Room and Building Search Tactics	11.5
Mobile Hostage Rescue	6.0
Testing and Evaluation	8.0
Team Tactical Problem	3.0

It is interesting to note that in the 120 hours of training for SWAT team members only the three-hour block devoted to Crisis Intervention/Conflict Management in Hostage Situations can be envisioned as something other than a war on crime tactic. While it may be unfair to look at SWAT team training in this way (because the peacemaking functions may be vested in other units like a hostage negotiation team), it does seem from this training plan that once a SWAT team is mobilized it is prepared to resolve the situation in only one way.

The types of situations where a SWAT team may be used include but are not limited to:

1. Protecting police officers engaged in crowd control from sniper attack
2. Providing high-ground and perimeter security for visiting dignitaries; rescuing hostages
3. Providing for the nonviolent apprehension of desperate barricaded suspects
4. Providing control-assault firepower in certain nonriot situations
5. Rescuing officers or citizens endangered by gunfire
6. Neutralizing guerrilla or terrorist operations against government personnel, property, or the general populace (Center for Research on Criminal Justice 1977, 94).

It makes sense to have officers specifically trained for these types of duties, as they occur so infrequently that it would be inefficient to require all officers to be trained in such a way. If time permits, it is better to have those with experience and training handle the potentially explosive situations and relieve other officers of incurring unnecessary risks. There is the added benefit of decreasing the danger to citizens when experts perform these tasks. However, there is a problem in the overuse and misuse of SWAT teams. When a child is given a hammer, all of a sudden he can find countless things around the house that need to be pounded. When a police agency invests time, resources, and personnel in a SWAT team, the tendency is to define situations as appropriate for SWAT intervention. Critics of the SWAT concept contend that, too often, these tactics predetermine a violent outcome for a touchy situation. In reviewing some of the SWAT activities during the 1960s in California, the Center for Research on Criminal Justice found:

> *The actual behavior of SWAT seems to contradict its avowed purpose of employing restraint in curbing incidents of urban violence. Quite the contrary, the net effect of SWAT's police-state tactics is to produce fear and outrage on the part of the community it purports to protect . . . The SWAT concept is an indication of the extent to which the police are willing and able to use the most brutally effective military tactics to ensure "order" at any cost in a time of social upheaval and mass discontent . . . No matter how much money and effort is poured into sophisticated programs aimed at*

> *improving police relations with the community, ultimately the basis of police power is the capacity to use force—and the emergence of SWAT shows how serious the police are about refining that capacity (1977, 97).*

The aim here is not to condemn the use of SWAT teams because there are some situations where they are the only way to save the lives of hostages, citizens, and law enforcement officers. At their best, they can surgically remove a threat with one well-placed sniper's bullet in the head of a rampaging mass murderer. At their worst, they can escalate a potentially violent situation into a full-scale tragedy where lives are lost. The incidents in Waco, Texas, with the Branch Davidians and Ruby Ridge, Idaho, with the Weaver family demonstrate the limitations of the war on crime perspective when it calls for military tactics on citizens who do not pose an immediate and substantial threat. It seems the federal government learned it lesson from these incidents, which became public relations disasters, and it took a much more conciliatory approach in dealing with the Freemen in Montana, where they waited patiently and were finally able to negotiate a peaceful solution.

There is not an inherent friction between being prepared to use force and working to resolve a situation peacefully. The goal should be to bring the incident to a close with as little violence as possible, but with the understanding that if force is the method of last resort it be used only as a last resort, and then as little force is used as necessary. The decision to use force is a judgment call that is more clear after the incident is over than at the height of the tension when the judgment has to be made. There are, however some steps that can be taken to help ensure that the decision to unleash the SWAT team is made in good faith after all attempts to conclude the incident peacefully have been exhausted. Karl Hansen (1988, 33), the Chief of Police for Racine, Wisconsin, reports how his department has institutionalized the coordination and cooperation of its SWAT team and its Negotiation Unit. In fact, the Negotiation Unit is available not only for hostage situations but also for the service of high-risk warrants, police-conducted raids, and risky-entry situations not involving hostages just in case they develop into a "barricaded subject" situation.

COMMUNITY POLICING

How would a peacemaking perspective be applied to the law enforcement function of the criminal justice system? Isn't policing inherently a war-like function that requires the use of force and the threat of force? Wouldn't the criminal element ignore or take advantage of a law enforcement agency that employed a peacemaking perspective? Would the street-level police officer support a peacemaking approach to law enforcement?

These are all reasonable questions to ask of the peacemaking perspective because of the important nature of the police mission. Certainly, we cannot experiment with half-baked, utopian ideas when the public safety is at stake. The peacemaking perspective had better have logical, effective, and testable ideas on how to make the streets, homes, and workplaces safe for citizens— and it does. The answers to all these questions can be encapsulated under the rubric of **community policing.**

A precise definition of community policing is difficult to find in the literature on law enforcement because scholars have used this term to refer to a variety of police practices (Skolnick and Bayley 1991). At its most basic level, however, most observers agreed that community policing involves enlisting citizens to help solve the law and order problems in their own communities (Mastrofski 1991). Community policing as a law enforcement strategy is an outgrowth of the failure of the professional model to solve the problems of making the streets safe. To be sure, the move to professionalize the police was needed and did allow for a greater efficiency of the law enforcement function, but it did so at a cost to the social fabric that needs to exist between the police and the citizens. When the police claimed a monopoly on being responsible for crime control, it resulted in the alienation of those who were supposed to be protected and served. Under community policing, the citizen is brought back into the picture and is viewed as an active participant in keeping the streets safe. Randolph Grinc describes the interaction between the police and the community as desirable but problematic.

> Community policing's emphasis on the role of the community as partner and co-producer of neighborhood safety is a key element distinguishing it from traditional or professional policing in which communities were given little, if any, formal role in policing their own neighborhoods. Indeed, professional or bureaucratic policing emphasized and encouraged the police officer's detachment from the community . . . In light of the failure of professional-era policing, police administrators and theorists of community policing, like the English statesman Disraeli, look out on the community as a vast, inchoate mass, and see in it an "angel in marble." Ordinary community residents represent a vast, untapped resources in the fight against crime, disorder, and fear. How to unleash the potential for effective organization lying dormant in our communities will prove itself to be the greatest challenge facing community policing (1994, 441).

By enlisting the citizens of the community in preventing and controlling crime, the police agency acknowledges that it along cannot control the streets. The active involvement of individuals and community organizations helps forge the sense of unity and connectedness not only between the police and the people but among the people themselves. If it is recognized that the police do not have the resources to be everywhere at once and that everyone is connected and impacted by the behavior of others, then the community members will take the responsibility for preventing crime and policing themselves in addition to being the eyes and ears of a cooperating police department.

But how does community policing actually work? Is it simply a public relations tool designed to co-op potential critics or does it represent a new paradigm of policing with potential to reduce crime and make citizens feel safe? The problem with answering these questions remains in the fuzzy definition of what constitutes community policing. The Officer Friendly who gives crime prevention talks at the local library or Kiwanis Club meetings represents a very narrow conception of community policing. Likewise, the Neighborhood Watch programs sponsored by many policing agencies do not fully encompass the range of community policing programs. It may not be possible to develop a comprehensive definition of community policing here, but a few examples can serve to demonstrate the diverse nature of these tactic centered around input and cooperation of the police officers and citizens. In an article published in the *American Journal of Police,* Bazemore and Cole (1994, 130–32) report several strategies used in a community policing program in Lawrence, Massachusetts.

- On one street drug dealers were escaping arrest because they hid their drugs under garbage barrels, inside fence post caps, and in mailboxes. Residents were armed with beepers and signaled police where the drugs were hidden. The police were able to find the drugs consistently, and asked if anyone wanted to claim them. No one did, and while the drug dealers were suspicious that there was a snitch, there were so many residents participating in the program that the dealers could not determine who was cooperating with the police.
- On another, street gangs opened fire hydrants on the pretext of keeping cool and used the diversion to rob passing motorists and sell drugs. The community police officers closed the street to all traffic except those who could prove they were residents and issued $35.00 citations to those with no apparent reason to be on the street, and thus, effectively shut down the drug trade.
- At another location, several neighborhood dealers sold drugs to individuals from outside the area. The police put up large signs saying "Warning—area under surveillance due to illegal sale of drugs—motor vehicle registration numbers being recorded by the police." Letters were then sent to the owners of these cars informing them of the cars' presence in that location. (Presumably many youths used their parent's cars). According to Bazemore and Cole, the traffic was reduced to a trickle in three weeks.
- After extensively patrolling a drug-infested area, community police officers wanted to ensure the neighborhood did not revert to its old patterns after the visible patrols ended. They invested $42.00 to disguise an old Police Special Operation truck that was headed to the junkyard to look like a surveillance van (tinting the windows and installing mirrors that were thought to be two-way mirrors). They then had uniformed officers deliver empty coffee cups and pizza boxes to give the impression the van was continuously occupied. This could be called a reverse Trojan Horse tactic.
- In one parking lot, youths would congregate to play loud music and handball. While most of the problems were nuisances such as littering

and graffiti, some of the youths were gang members and would rob passing motorists. The community police officers got the youth to agree to behave in order to be allowed to congregate and play handball. Residents of a nearby apartment building agreed to tolerate a certain level of noise in exchange for the elimination to the robbery, graffiti, and car break-ins.

While these successes are small and may result in crime displacement instead of real crime reduction, they did have other positive consequences for the community. Residents boarded up old buildings, cleaned up parks, and engaged in a variety of neighborhood problem-solving activities. Instead of being victims, the residents felt empowered to make changes in their neighborhood, and a sense of community was fostered.

These tactics demonstrate how crime can be addressed from a peacemaking perspective. Instead of employing widespread arrests of force, these problems were dealt with effectively by other means. The benefits to the community in terms of less crime and a reduced fear of crime, to the police force in terms of a safer working environment for its officers and improved public relations, and for offenders who are not stigmatized by the criminal justice system but have their behavior shaped in positive ways by the community are all difficult to measure but are significant attributes of the community policing concept.

It should be clear that one of the primary criticisms of the community peacemaking perspective, that it is soft on crime, is not borne out by community policing. By confronting problems in a creative way before they develop into extreme situations, the community policing concept enables people to avoid the serious unintended harm that is associated with the war on crime, get-tough approach. The sense of attachment in the community is strengthened rather than frayed when citizens begin to share responsibility with the police for the safety of their streets.

WHAT ARE THE LIMITATIONS OF THE COMMUNITY POLICING CONCEPT?

In some jurisdictions community policing is tough to sell to citizens, politicians, police administrators, and to the police themselves. Until there are demonstrable measures of success in reducing crime and making residents feel safer, community policing will continue to be looked upon as a public relations fad that will run its course and leave little lasting impact on the method of police work. Fortunately, it has been around long enough for studies to show that while it is not a panacea, it does have promise and should be given more resources and time to prove its efficacy. Bazemore and Cole (1994, 142) are cautiously optimistic in their evaluation of community policing.

Overall, the community policing initiative in Lawrence shows initial signs of at least partial success. Because law enforcement agencies are generally unaccustomed to operating in a community policing mode, a full transition from a bureaucratic, authoritarian, and service-call-focused methodology into a problem-oriented tactical approach can be expected to take time and extensive effort.

Perhaps the biggest problem in implementing the community policing concept is getting the cooperation of the citizens. Especially in areas where there is a history of strained relations between the police and the residents, simply announcing a new program does not guarantee immediate citizen input and involvement. The police must earn the trust of citizens and, according to Sadd and Grinc (1996), there may be some sound reasons why community residents may not want to get involved. These reasons include:

1. *Fear of retaliation.* Many residents fear that by helping the police they will become victims of retaliation by drug dealers and criminals. The police are unable to ensure the safety of those perceived as snitches, and only the most secure individuals are willing to stand up to the criminal element. Only if residents are unafraid can they assist in taking back the streets from the drunks, drug dealers, and muggers. In some low-income urban areas, the fear is deeply ingrained and only sustained and massive resources are going to convince a terrorized populace that the streets are truly safe again.

2. *The transitory nature of projects to assist disadvantaged neighborhoods.* There is a sad history of well-meaning efforts aimed at alleviating poverty conditions in disadvantaged neighborhoods in this country. Most of these efforts were short-lived and produced very little lasting impact. Residents are understandably reluctant to embrace new programs for fear they are more about style than about substance. The "here today, gone tomorrow" nature of past programs makes it difficult to convince residents that new community policing programs that require their support will receive the long-term commitment from politicians and police administrators. It thus becomes a vicious cycle of suspicion and mistrust where police officials wait to see of the community embraces their efforts and residents wait to see if the new strategy on the part of the police is ephemeral.

3. *Historically poor police-community relations.* Sadd and Grinc (1996) point out that one of the untested assumptions underlying community policing is that residents really want closer contact with the police and want to work with them to reduce crime. In surveying residents in eight communities where community police projects were implemented, they found a large number of residents who were hostile to the police based upon a historically negative relationship. The police, in turn, interpret the lack of involvement or hostility as meaning the residents do not care about reducing crime. All this points to the difficult task the police have in selling the community policing concept to the residents of disadvantaged neighborhoods.

4. *Lack of outreach by police.* There are two issues in the need for police to provide an outreach function. The first is to train the law enforcement offi-

cers in how to deal with the community. The training provided in police academies, for the most part, does not include sufficient emphasis for the specialized role of the community policing officer. The second issue that is important to the police outreach function is to train the community to become involved. Citizen councils, volunteers, and other inclusionary tactics require educating the residents in how they can become empowered to effect change by working with the police.

5. *The nature of the target neighborhoods.* Another reason residents of disadvantaged neighborhoods may be reluctant to become involved in community policing efforts is because there may be very little sense of community. Many of these urban areas are characterized by poverty, high unemployment, inadequate educational services, and tend to be highly disorganized. The police have the responsibility for helping develop the sense of community to complement their community policing efforts. If there were already strong community structures than there may not be a need for community policing. Sometimes the most stable and influential group in a disadvantaged urban area is a gang (Jacobs 1977).

6. *Intergroup conflict.* Not all the residents of a community will see problems in the same way and agree on how to solve them. Living in the same geographic location or sharing a racial or class background does not mean that individuals will have the same values. Conflicts that predate the introduction of community policing efforts may make those efforts highly problematic in terms of generating the support of the residents.

The reasons that residents may not fully embrace the community policing concept point to the need for a peacemaking perspective in the criminal justice system and in other institutions as well. Disenfranchised, alienated, and unconnected communities will have problems other than high crime rates. Without individuals engaging in mutual support and involvement the whole concept of meaningful democratic communities begins to unravel. Community policing can help restore the social fabric of neighborhoods torn apart by the fear of crime by getting residents to work together with the police to reduce the level of dangerousness in the public's space. The collateral benefits of community-building result in other problems being addressed.

While recognizing that community policing has not fully lived up to its promise and has demonstrated only limited success, we should look to redouble our efforts to develop and refine this peacemaking strategy because strong communities will eventually prove more worthwhile in combatting crime and other social programs than will disorganized and alienated communities.

COMMUNITY POLICING AND THE POLICE

One other dimension of the community policing concept that deserves mention is the reaction of the police to this style of law enforcement (Wilson and

Bennett 1994). There has always been a tension between the sometimes conflicting roles inherent in the police mission that requires both crime fighting
and social work. Community policing is looked upon by police officers as
leaning more toward the social work end of the continuum and has been
devalued in some police circles who consider making felony arrests as the core
of police work. Convincing the police to accept the community policing
model is sometimes difficult as pointed out by Lurigio and Skogan (1994,
315–330).

> *Hence the transition to community policing is frequently a battle for the*
> *hearts and minds of police officers. Community policing requires them to do*
> *many of their old jobs in innovative ways: it forces officers to attempt unfa-*
> *miliar and challenging tasks, to identify and solve a broad range of prob-*
> *lems, and to reach out to elements of the community who were previously*
> *outside their purview.*

The organizational climate of many police departments is predicated on
a war on crime model that makes instituting a community policing model difficult for officers to support. The status and rewards for effective community
policing are not as valued as those for waging war on criminals. Solving problems and preventing crime are not as visible to administrators or as easy to
measure as making arrests. The job of community policing can, however, offer
some intangible rewards not available in traditional law enforcement. Lurigio
and Skogan (1994, 328) reported that approximately half of the officers they
surveyed "reported that their jobs actually gave them opportunities for independence and control over how they did their job." Other measures were
mixed. Some officers were not especially excited about adopting new tactics
such as foot patrol or selling themselves to the public, and many were skep-
tical that the program would impact on the crime rate and their ability to
make arrests or improve their relations with racial minorities.

The job of police officer is very difficult. There are tremendous demands
on both the availability of police and how they do their job. Depending on
the neighborhood there may or may not be a great deal of community support. The popular image of the police officer is one that fits the war on crime
perspective. The police represent our "thin blue line" between order and
chaos on the street. The police wear uniforms, are called captain, sergeant, or
officer, and carry weapons. There is a tendency to think of the police as our
domestic military whose mission is to protect us from internal aggression.

The mission of law enforcement is much more complicated than that of
the military, and the war on crime perspective does not fully encompass the
nature of the profession. In fact, the peacemaking perspective, while not fully
implemented in police work, actually is the more appropriate model on
which to base the law enforcement component of the criminal justice system.
The strategies of community policing are more consistent with the peacemaking perspective and have demonstrated at least the potential of offering

significant social change in community-police relations and of helping to foster a sense of mutual regard and respect among residents. While the evidence of effectiveness of community policing is mixed, the peacemaking perspective proposes that it be continued and expanded because the war on crime model has clearly failed to provide safe streets and has actually aided in the deterioration of the social fabric in our cities.

CRITICAL THINKING QUESTIONS

1. Discuss how law enforcement agencies resemble military organizations. Talk about uniforms, ranks, discipline, and command structures. Also talk about the important ways the police and military are different.

2. In class, role-play situations where police are tempted to use force on citizens. What level of verbal abuse should police officers be expected to suffer before they resort to violence?

3. What lessons about the use of force by the police can we learn from the Rodney King case?

4. Discuss how community policing can be considered a desirable strategy by the peacemaking perspective. What elements of peacemaking are emphasized by community policing?

SUGGESTED READINGS

Arthur, John A., and Charles E. Case. 1994. "Race, Class and Support for Police Use of Force." *Crime, Law and Social Change* 21(2): 167–182.

Bazemore, Gordon, and Allen W. Cole. 1994. "Police in the 'Laboratory' of the Neighborhood: Evaluating Problem-Oriented Strategies in a Medium-Sized City." *American Journal of Police* 13(3): 119–147.

Bittner, Egon. 1980. *The Functions of the Police in Modern Society.* Cambridge, MA: Oelgeschlager, Gunn and Hain.

Lurigio, Arthur J., and Wesley G. Skogan. 1994. "Winning the Hearts and Minds of Police Officers: An Assessment of Staff Perceptions of Community Policing in Chicago." *Crime and Delinquency* 40(3): 315–330.

Stark, Rodney. 1972. *Police Riots: Collective Behavior and Law Enforcement.* Belmont, CA: Focus Books.

Skolnick, Jerome H., and David H. Bayley. 1991. "The New Blue Line," in Carl B. Klockers and Stephen D. Mastrofski, eds. *Thinking about Police: Contemporary Readings,* 2nd ed. New York: McGraw-Hill, pp. 494–504.

Skolnick, Jerome H., and James J. Fyfe. 1993. *Above the Law: Police and the Excessive Use of Force.* New York: The Free Press.

Wilson, James Q. 1972. *Varieties of Police Behavior: The Management of Law and Order in Eight Communities.* New York: Atheneum.

6

COURTS AND JUSTICE

Photograph by Richard Strauss, Smithsonian Institution. Courtesy of the Supreme Court of the U.S.

Learning Objectives

After reading this chapter, the student should be able to:

- Describe how the courts' major goal is to resolve disputes in a nonviolent manner.
- List the 12 steps in the court process.
- Describe the three types of discretion used by court officials.
- Discuss to what extent the courts have an adversarial process.
- Describe the relationships in the courtroom workgroup.
- Appreciate the extent and purposes of plea-bargaining in the courtroom.
- Explain the sources of sentence disparity.
- Describe the assumptions behind the indeterminate sentence.
- Explain the detrimental effects of the determinate sentence.
- Explain what Nils Christie means by "conflict as property."
- Discuss how the resolution of conflict without correcting social injustice is problematic from the peacemaking perspective.

Key Terms

Blood Feuds	*Nolo Contendere*
Arrest	Plea Bargaining
Initial Appearance	Pretrial Motions
Bail	Jury Trial
Release on Recognizance (ROR)	Sentence Disparity
Preliminary Hearing	Courtroom Workgroup
Defense Attorney	Adversarial Proceeding
Public Defender	Impression Management
Arraignment	"Conflicts as Property"

The courts are the pivotal component of the criminal justice system. Law enforcement is responsible for arresting suspects and correctional agencies are responsible for the treatment or punishment of those deemed to be offenders of the criminal law, but the courts are where the power resides in the criminal justice system. Not only do the courts decide on the guilt or innocence of defendants, and not only do they determine the sentence, but the courts also decide on how other criminal justice agencies conduct their business. The courts oversee the workings of a vast network of political and legal affairs. For the purposes of this book, the discussion of the courts will be confined to their impact on the criminal justice system, but the reader should be aware that much, if not most, of the work of the courts actually involves society's other institutions.

The criminal law has as its fundamental basis the prevention and handling of human conflict. In a sense, the courts employ the peacemaking perspective in that they are designed to minimize human conflict. In a democratic society where individuals are each freely pursuing their goals, the courts act as a mediating forum where differences can be aired and disinterested or neutral third parties can separate fact from fiction and make judgments. The law, as a body of rules specified before the conflict, prevents most conflict because people are able to conform their actions to expectations of appropriate behavior we have all agreed on (as represented in statutes, state or federal constitutions, administrative regulations, etc.). When conflict does arise the courts fulfill a second function of acting as a forum where they can be resolved.

The courts serve to satisfy the desire that justice be done. If there were no courts, individuals would be motivated to dispense justice in their own way. **Blood feuds** would wage for years between families seeking revenge for long-forgotten injuries but are fueled by a continuing cycle of combatants trying to "even the score." The court is able to bring closure to the dispute before it can escalate into a raging conflict that not only consumes the lives and resources of the contestants, but also before it disrupts the functioning of the rest of the community. The courts provide a vital service to the community by institutionalizing the conflict within an agreed-upon forum and set of procedures. By allowing an arena for the nonviolent resolution of conflict, the courts make meaningful communities possible. The underlying philosophy of the courts, justice through nonviolent conflict resolution, is a cornerstone of the peacemaking perspective.

In order for the courts to be successful in preventing and resolving disputes they need the confidence of the people. The courts need to be seen as applying the legal norms of society in an impartial and independent manner. The courts cannot be biased but must be viewed as working in the interests of an important but abstract conception of justice. By this we mean the courts cannot decide how justice is dispensed based on the social standing of the participants of a dispute but must give them all equal standing before the law. In order to secure the cooperation of the people the courts need to ensure an impartiality in their deliberations.

THE CRIMINAL COURT PROCESS

The most noticeable feature of the criminal court is the rate of attrition in the number of cases between the **arrest** and the final sentencing disposition. Only a percentage survive the process and end up penetrating the entire criminal court proceedings. According to Neubauer (1979), there are 12 steps to the criminal court process through which each defendant must pass. While each defendant may not go through all of the steps and the order for some might be changed, as a way of describing the criminal court process it is useful to review these 12 steps and consider how they help to sort out the cases into categories.

   1. *Arrest.* The criminal court process begins when a law enforcement officer presents a suspect to the court after an arrest. Taking a citizen into custody is done only when the police officer has amassed reasonable proof that the suspect has committed a crime. The number of people arrested represents only a fraction of the crimes committed because many times no suspect can be linked to a crime, and in others the police believe they know who is responsible but are unable to amass the necessary evidence. The decision to arrest is not made lightly by the law enforcement officer because in addition to damaging the prospects for bargaining the case, the law enforcement officer can be charged with false arrest if this decision is made capriciously. It is significant from a system's perspective that the courts have little control as to who is presented to them for insertion into the criminal justice system. The law enforcement component of the system makes this important judgment, and the courts must function with the cases presented to them by the police.
   2. *Decision to prosecute.* The link between the courts and law enforcement is the district attorney who provides the legal authority to continue pursuing the case. The district attorney exercises broad discretion in deciding whether to prosecute the case. A number of factors go into the district attorney's decision which may result in a judgment not to prosecute. The district attorney must first decide if there is sufficient evidence that a crime has been committed and if that evidence is adequately linked to the suspect presented by the law enforcement officer. Many cases are disposed at this stage because the district attorney disagrees with the law enforcement officer as to whether a crime has been committed, whether the suspect arrested committed the crime, and as to whether the evidence presented by the law enforcement officer is sufficient to secure a conviction. Sometimes the district attorney may file a less serious charge than initially requested by the law enforcement officer.
   3. *Initial appearance.* The arrested person must be brought before a judge in a reasonable period of time. In the United States suspects cannot be held indefinitely. The arrested person sees a judge within 48 hours for an **initial appearance** where notice of the charges is presented and the right to remain silent advised. Many misdemeanor cases are resolved at the initial appearance because the defendant pleads guilty and is sentenced immediately. For felony cases the initial appearance is a formality where no plea is taken and the defendant is advised to the right to **bail** and the right to an attorney.
   4. *Bail.* With the exception of capital cases (where the death penalty is possible) the law allows defendants to remain at liberty until the trial. The presumption of innocence requires that defendants be given the right to remain free unless there are compelling reasons to keep him or her incarcerated. However, the state must have some guarantee the defendant will appear for

further proceeding and so allows bail to be set. Bail is simply putting up money that will become the property of the state in case the defendant absconds. Defendants unable to secure the cash for bail may employ a bail bondsman who will charge 10 to 15 percent of the bond as a fee for exposing his or her resources to secure the defendant's liberty. This means that if the bail is set at $10,000 that is will cost the defendant $1,000 to remain out of jail until the trial. Some jurisdictions allow the defendant to sign a property bond that puts a state lien against their house or other property. If the defendant has strong ties to the community he or she may be **released on recognizance (ROR),** or their promise to return for further court proceedings. The bail or ROR function is to ensure the defendant continues to participate in the criminal court process. For those who are untrustworthy or are unable to make bail, the state is obliged to keep them in custody until the trial. This can be expensive for the taxpayer and contribute to jail overcrowding, but there are some individuals whose future appearance in court can only be assured by incarceration.

5. *Preliminary hearing.* While criminal court procedures vary across states, most have some sort of **preliminary hearing** function where a judge determines if there is probable cause to believe the defendant committed a felony. The strength of the evidence is reviewed, and if the judge decides there is insufficient evidence the defendant may be released from custody and the charges dismissed. It is important to keep in mind that the rules of evidence for determining probable cause are not as rigorous as those for a trial.

6. *Defense attorney.* Defendants in criminal proceedings are entitled by the sixth amendment to a **defense attorney** to help them prepare a defense to the charges brought by the state. The law is so complicated and the potential loss of freedom so critical that the law not only grants the right to an attorney but provides one for those who are unable to afford one on their own. In some states a member of the local bar is assigned to indigenous clients and in other states the tax-supported **public defender**'s office represents poor clients. While all defendants are entitled to a competent attorney, one should not believe that all attorneys are of equal skill or will devote equal time and resources to each case. There is a strong relationship between how much money a defendant has and the quality of legal representation.

7. *Grand jury.* The federal government and many of the states use the grand jury system to further protect against unwarranted prosecutions. Recognizing the tremendous discretion possessed by the prosecutor, the grand jury is a device designed to ensure it is not abused. The grand jury, which comprises citizens drawn from the voter eligibility lists, functions as an independent check on the prosecutor to ensure the nonpolitical nature of deciding who is charged with criminal violations. In reality, the grand jury does not live up to the ideals of independence. The ordinary citizens who make up the grand jury usually grant the wishes of the prosecutor. Most cases put before the grand jury involve a simple determination of whether there is enough probable cause for the case to proceed. The evidence requirements for the grand jury are less strict than for a trial, so the finding of probable cause is normally rou-

tine. Once in awhile a particular grand jury will demonstrate real independence and not grant the prosecutor the indictment, but a skillful prosecutor can present the evidence in such a way that the grand jury will almost always indict the defendant. In some jurisdictions the grand jury is also responsible for inspecting jails and other government facilities, and sometimes they can cause embarrassment to the local government by their findings.

8. *Arraignment on the indictment.* The **arraignment** is where the defendant in felony cases is first given the opportunity to enter a plea on the charge(s). In rare circumstances, the defendant will plead guilty at this stage of the criminal court process (unless, as often happens, it is part of a plea-bargaining agreement). Most often the plea will be not guilty or ***nolo contendere*** (no contest). With the *nolo* plea the defendant neither admits or denies guilt but agrees not to contest the case and this allows the case to go forward and is often taken into consideration during **plea bargaining.**

9. *Pretrial motions.* Often the judge is asked to make legal decisions on aspects of the case before the actual presentation of evidence begins. The defense attorney may request that some of the evidence not be allowed to be presented to the court because various procedural laws or regulations were not properly followed in gathering that evidence. The police may not have advised a suspect as to his or her rights, a confession may have been obtained by coercion, a wire tape may not have been authorized by a judge, or a host of other problems with the evidence may need a decision by the judge before the case can proceed. The prosecutor may also make **pretrial motions** where the defendant is asked to produce documents or submit a handwriting sample. This is an important stage of the criminal court process because it decides what tools the attorneys are going to be able to use in the trial. If the judge makes mistakes on the admissibility of key evidence the pretrial motions may later be used as grounds for appeal.

10. *Plea bargaining.* We will discuss plea bargaining in greater detail later in this chapter, but it is important to situate this practice in the criminal court process at this point. Plea bargaining involves an agreement among the defendant and his or her attorney and the prosecutor as to a disposition of the case. A plea bargain usually involves a compromise. In exchange for being charged with a less serious crime, for being granted a less severe sentence, or having some of the counts dismissed, the defendant agrees to plead guilty or *nolo contendere.* The defendant limits the forthcoming punishment by making a deal with the state. In cases where the defendant is guilty, and there is ample evidence to prove so (this situation involves the majority of criminal court cases), the defendant can escape the harshest sentence available to the court. The prosecutor benefits by being able to dispose of the case without having to expend further time or resources. As long as the sentence is sufficiently served to give the appearance of justice the prosecutor desires to move on to other cases. The simple truth of the matter is the prosecutor cannot take all cases to trial because there are too many of them. The negotiated plea is a way for the prosecutor to ensure that defendants pay something for their crimes and that all cases get considered. If all criminal defendants would get together and demand their right to a speedy trial the prosecutor could not accommodate them all. Some cases would have to be dismissed because there are not enough judges, courtrooms, and juries to provide a trial to all offenders. As taxpayers, citizens who complain about the practice of plea bargaining should consider how much tax money it would cost to provide the full extent of due process to every defendant accused of a criminal offense.

11. *Jury trials.* A **jury trial** is what most of us think of when we consider court proceedings. In actuality, jury trials are rare but they represent the full range of due process granted to the defendant. A chance to challenge the evidence presented against him or her, a chance to confront the accusers, and a chance to present evidence supporting his or her innocence are the rights enjoyed by those accused of crimes. The case can be decided by a jury or a judge sitting alone (*bench trial*). In either case, the burden of proof falls on the prosecutor to demonstrate a crime has been committed and that the defendant is the individual responsible.

12. *Sentencing.* The previous 11 steps of the criminal court process are devoted to determining the guilt or innocence of the defendant. Once that is established, the court has a further function of passing sentence. While we will discuss sentencing in greater detail later in this chapter, it is important to recognize at this point that the sentencing decision varies from state to state. In some jurisdictions the jury decides on the punishment, and in other jurisdictions the judge does so. Finding the appropriate sentence is difficult because each individual brings different ideas, values, and feelings to how they believe a defendant should be sentenced. Suffice it to say there is a tremendous amount of **sentence disparity** in the United States, and this causes intense debate on the criminal court process.

This brief overview of the criminal court process is not intended to represent the work of courts in all jurisdictions. It is simply a framework that provides the reader with an idea of the steps most cases go through as they wind their way through the court system. The most important point that can be made about the criminal court process is that many cases are disposed of in one way or another long before they complete the criminal court process. The reasons cases are dropped or settled before the criminal court process has run its course tell us a great deal about how justice is dispensed in this country. While we essentially have an open courtroom policy, much of what happens is of low visibility. The routine processing of cases involves the exercise of discretion in such a pervasive way that it becomes almost invisible because it is so conventional and ordinary.

DISCRETION IN THE COURTS

Discretion involves using one's own judgment in decision-making rather than relying on explicit rules and policies. In any profession there will be judgment calls where the doctor, professor, scientist, or judge must make distinctions that a colleague might decide in a different way. To appreciate how discretion is used in the court system, we need to look at these separate occasions where it is employed and understand that discretion is not a term that can be used to signify everything that cannot be otherwise explained. According to Neubauer (1979), the three types of discretion are:

1. *Legal judgments.* This type of discretion is what we pay professionals to do. There will always be cases where training and experience assist the prosecutor in deciding what course to take. If the police file a case where the defendant is clearly guilty, but they have botched the arrest by violating the defendant's rights, the prosecutor may drop the case. The discretion used here is the prosecutor's professional legal judgment that any more resources expended would be wasted. The prosecutor wants to pursue the case because the defendant deserves punishment, but he or she knows the case would certainly be dismissed by the judge or acquitted by the jury. The police officers may be upset with the prosecutor and not realize the benefit of the legal judgment at this early stage. On cross examination a good defense attorney would expose the shortcomings of the arrest procedure and embarrass the police officer.

2. *Policy priorities.* Prosecutors and judges are political animals to some extent. In many jurisdictions they are elected and in others they are appointed by officials who themselves are elected. When crime is a campaign issue, the election process specifies what types of criminal behavior will be vigorously pursued. In recent years, the war on drugs has enjoyed wide popular support, and court officials have responded by pushing these cases. In the 1960s drug use was considered less dangerous, and some police and court officials ignored or pressed these cases with less passion. The change in the way the drunk driver is treated by the court system is another good example of how policy priorities of the prosecution can result in the exercise of discretion. The criminal code is so broad that there is room for court officials to make judgments as to which types of cases they believe should be concentrated on in order to best reflect the sentiments of the community.

3. *Personal philosophies.* Some of the discretionary decisions made by court officials reflect their personal philosophies, whims, prejudices, and tastes. This is not to say that the defendant is being treated unfairly or that anyone's rights are being violated. It's just that there is room for judgment calls and, to some extent, the fate of the defendant is the result of the "luck of the draw" in terms of which prosecutor or judge is assigned to the case.

This review of the types of discretion found in the courtroom explains how the criminal court process can produce different results across jurisdictions and even within jurisdictions. There is a certain pattern of work that each court develops and this pattern guides how discretion is exercised. Neubauer (1979) describes how the courtroom work groups form a complex network of relationships between the judge, prosecutor, defense attorneys, court clerk, bailiff, court reporter, and, in some jurisdictions, even the bail bondsman. The relationships between these courtroom officials work to make the court efficient in processing the court calendar each day. Without the cooperation of all these courthouse regulars, the work of the court would become entangled in conflicts where each actor attempted to maximize his or her power.

Courtroom Workgroup

The courtroom work group is an interesting subject because in producing justice it does not work like other associations that can be studied from the organizational perspective. The courtroom work group is composed of individuals who all work for someone else. Thus, the system of rewards and punishments found in most traditional and hierarchical organizations is altered. At some level an adversary process is at work, but at the same time, the court officials are mutually dependent and must share in the decision-making. As cases are presented to the judge, many of the important decisions have already been structured by the prosecutor and the defense attorney. The norms of the **courtroom workgroup** have already decided the fate of many cases before the fact. Only in exceptional circumstances where the prosecutor and defense attorney disagree will the full criminal court processing take place. The courtroom work group must work together to dispose of the cases on the calendar and while it is recognized that each of the participants must account to their own agency, the courtroom workgroup decides most of the case outcomes.

The overall goal of the courtroom workgroup is to "do justice" (Neubauer 1979, 118), and this produces several difficulties for the workgroup, because participants bring their home agency's perspective to the courtroom. By doing justice it could mean punishing the guilty, rehabilitating the offender, protecting the public, respecting individual liberties, or deterring potential wrongdoers. It is impossible to do all of these things in any single case, so there is potential for conflict and disagreement. Because doing justice cannot be agreed upon and therefore not measured, other indicators of courtroom activity are used to evaluate the workgroup. The number of cases disposed of becomes a substitute for doing justice in the courtroom work group, and the needs of the organization become confused with the multiple overall goals of doing justice.

The Adversarial Nature of Courts

Given our discussion of the courtroom workgroup dynamics it may seem nonsensical to talk about the courtroom as an adversarial forum. There is a dimension to the criminal court process that involves **adversarial proceeding,** and it needs to be considered so that the reader does not mistake the courtroom workgroup for a harmonious and conflict-free environment. Certain cases become important to prosecutors and defense attorneys because of their sense of doing justice, but also because of their professional need to establish their legal reputations and to influence where the lines are drawn as to the norms of the courtroom workgroup. By selecting certain cases for their full professional attention, prosecutors and defense attorneys can structure how other cases are decided. There is a bit of the theater at work here that the sociologist Erving Goffman (1959) terms **impression management.** How others see us determines to a large extent how they treat us, so we all struggle to put forth a public facade designed to influence the impressions we give. The popular image of the prosecutor and the defense attorney are informed more by the popular media than by the actual functions they perform in the courthouse workgroup.

Because the courtroom workgroup, in establishing its norms, have already structured what is likely to happen in any individual case, the prosecutor and defense attorney must play their roles of adversaries to preserve the impression that the case is being seriously weighed on its merits. This is particularly important for the defense attorney who must justify his fee. This sounds extremely cynical to the outsider but it is well-known within the court workgroup. The eminent legal scholar Abraham Blumberg details this process in his classic article, "The Practice of Law as a Confidence Game: Organizational Cooptation of a Profession." In describing how the judge assists the defense attorney in collecting the fee from the client, Blumberg contends:

> *The judge will help an accused's lawyer in still another way. He will lend the official aura of his office and courtroom so that a lawyer can stage manage an impression of an "all out" performance for the accused in justification of his fee. The judge and other court personnel will serve as a backdrop for a scene charged with dramatic fire, in which the accused's lawyer makes a stirring appeal on his behalf. With a show of restrained passion, the lawyer will intone the virtues of the accused and recite the social deprivations which have reduced him to his present state. The speech varies somewhat, depending on whether the accused has been convicted after a trial or has pleaded guilty. In the main, however, the incongruity, superficiality, and ritualistic character of the total performance is underscored by a visibly impassive, almost bored reaction on the part of the judge and other members of the court retinue (Blumberg 1989, 263–64).*

As can be seen from this argument, the adversarial nature of the criminal court is largely a fiction. Blumberg goes so far as to say the defense attorney acts as a double-agent in representing the accused to the court. On one hand the defense attorney argues the merits of his client's case but on the other hand the defense attorney must convince the client that the deal offered by the court is the best that can be expected. In effect, the defense attorney must "cool out" the accused by persuading him or her that justice has been done. By contrast the prosecutor often has to do the same with the victim. In confidence game parlance, convincing the victim that the plea bargain was the best resolution of the case that was possible, the prosecutor "cools the mark."

It is distressing to some to realize that justice operates in such a mechanical, impassioned, and perfunctory way. The routinization of work in the courtroom robs the participants of their ability to be shocked or appalled by criminal behavior. The processing of cases becomes an organizational problem where the courtroom workgroup must efficiently dispose of cases while at the same time preserve the impression of outsiders that justice is being done.

PLEA BARGAINING AND JUSTICE

Plea bargaining in the criminal court process is considered by some as an essential feature of American justice. Because of the oppressive caseloads experienced by most criminal courts, the practice of plea bargaining is viewed as a necessary evil that has beneficial consequences for both the state and the offender. Nevertheless, plea bargaining is criticized as being unfair to both sides and calls for reform have been a constant theme of political rhetoric (Chilton 1991). Law enforcement officials and the public do not like plea bargaining because they view it as being soft on crime. Offenders are allowed to escape the full measure of the potential punishment by entering a:

1. *Vertical plea.* The offender pleads guilty or *nolo contendere* to a lesser-included charge. In the case of a homicide, the offender might be allowed to plea to manslaughter. The advantage to the offender is the manslaughter charge is not subject to the death penalty and carries a shorter potential prison term. Many felony drug charges are plead down to misdemeanors, which saves the offender from having a felony conviction on their record.

2. *Horizontal plea.* The offender pleads guilty or *nolo contendere* to some charges in exchange for other charges being dropped.

3. *Reduced-sentence plea.* In some jurisdictions, the prosecutor and defense attorney work out a suggested sentence as part of the plea negotiations. If the judge concurs, the deal results in a shorter prison sentence or probation. Some plea bargains will include division program placement or drug treatment. Additionally, restitution to the victim may be part of the deal, which allows the defendant to escape the full potential of the charges.

4. *Avoidance of stigma plea.* With the "habitual offenders" (three strikes and you're out) statutes in many jurisdictions, there is an incentive for an offender to plead the case out if it will not be officially counted toward his habitual offender record. In some jurisdictions, this may need to be accomplished by a vertical plea to a lesser charge, but the intent is to allow the defendant to escape the mandatory sentence that would be imposed under a habitual offender conviction. Additionally, defendants may plea to certain less-stigmatizing charges to escape being labeled a sex offender.

Plea bargaining is not concerned with determining guilt or innocence. Its purpose is to efficiently determine the amount of punishment the defendant will receive by giving up the due process right of a trial by one's peers. Critics of plea bargaining base their arguments from the war on crime perspective, which sees it as a way of softening the criminal law. Plea bargaining is also attacked from the peacemaking perspective, which sees it as a weapon in the hands of the prosecutor, which is wielded against defendants to circumvent their rights.

> *In practice, highly disparate results are obtained by plea bargaining. Individuals in similar circumstances receive widely varying punishments while the proportionality of punishment to offense becomes distorted by overcharging, draconian legislation, and political expediency. In practice, often there is no bargaining, because the prosecutor is in the position of the landlord with the only vacant apartment in town—"take my terms or forget it." Increasingly the prosecutor wields the sledgehammer with, for example, habitual offender laws carrying life terms for relatively minor offenses (Stitt and Chaires 1993, 72).*

Obviously, plea bargaining does not further the ends of justice. While some offenders may be able to reduce their punishment, they do so at the price of signing away their due process rights. Theoretically, because the defendant is represented by a defense attorney, this decision is made in his or her best interests. However, our discussion of the courtroom workgroup showed how the defense attorney has a conflict of interest between representing the client and adhering to the norms and demands of the courtroom participants. Remember, Abraham Blumberg identified at least three interests of the defense attorney: 1. represent the client, 2. maintain a good working relationship with the courtroom workgroup so as not to jeopardize future cases, and 3. collect the fee from the client. Blumberg is somewhat cynical about the defense attorney's priorities for these agendas in that he suggests that the third is paramount.

Any consideration of the U.S. criminal court system must include an evaluation of the ethical desirability of plea bargaining. Is it a necessity or is it the outgrowth of the unique organizational structure of a criminal justice system that is not really a system? The cynicism aimed at the criminal justice system because of the plea bargaining practice weakens the faith citizens have in their public institutions because they believe that the ideals of justice are being perverted.

> *. . . it is proposed that even if plea bargaining, as it currently exists, were to be an efficient and effective method of disposing of criminal cases, it is valueless because it does not meet any of the traditional objectives of criminal law and procedure. These objectives are retribution, deterrence, incapacitation, and rehabilitation. Finally, it is posited that plea bargaining, in its present uncontrolled form, cannot be justified as ethical or rational, or supported as practical, when it disproportionately and adversely impacts the poor and minorities (Stitt and Chaires 1993, 73).*

SENTENCING AND SENTENCE DISPARITY

Once the determination of guilt or innocence has been made in a criminal case, the judge must decide on an appropriate sentence. While plea bargaining may restrict the decision, there is still latitude or discretion exercised by the judge. In fact, the plea bargaining arrangement may only reflect how the prosecutor and defense attorney anticipate what the judge will decide. The sentencing decision is a product of a host of influences including the personal philosophy of the judge, the availability of prison space or treatment programs, the demeanor and remorsefulness of the defendant, and factors that should have no bearing on the sentence such as the defendant's age, race, sex, and economic status. Because of the discretion available to judges, it is a little like gambling for the defendant when she or he stands before the bench for sentencing. Depending on which state the court is in, which judge is assigned to the case, and even what kind of mood the judge is in that day, the sentence handed down can vary.

There are two ways of looking at the lack of uniformity in the way offenders are punished. One way is to condemn the disparity as unfair and insist that offenders with similar crimes be given comparable sentences. The other way of looking at the disparity of sentences is to embrace it by arguing that

The sentencing of an offender. (© Michael Newman/PhotoEdit.)

the punishment should fit the circumstances of the criminal rather than the crime. There has been a policy debate in the United States about which of these perspectives should determine how offenders are punished (Albanese 1984).

The Indeterminate Sentence

Is the judge always the best person to determine what the offender's sentence should be? Even in the case of plea bargaining, is the courtroom workgroup the appropriate body to make a sentencing decision that affects not only the offender, but also the agencies that have to carry out the sentence? Perhaps the prison is better able to decide which inmates deserve to be there and which are good probation or parole risks. Perhaps the trial, where passions are high and the details of the crime vivid, is not the time to decide how long a prisoner should be incarcerated. Perhaps society would be better served if the actual length of an offender's sentence would be determined on how well the offender adjusts to prison life and how safe society would be when the offender is released.

The indeterminate sentence takes these factors into consideration. Each offender is an individual with different circumstances and prospects, and the indeterminate sentence considers the uniqueness of each and patterns the sentence to fit the rehabilitation needs. In a hospital, each patient is treated according to a diagnosis of the medical problem. It is inconceivable to handle the patient with a broken leg in the same way as the patient who experienced a heart attack. The indeterminate sentence applies the medical analogy to the criminal offender. In viewing the unlawful behavior as a symptom of a social deficiency, the criminal justice system can prescribe a treatment. Vocational training, drug or alcohol treatment, or therapeutic counseling may be all that is necessary to correct the offender's problem and make him or her a productive member of society.

The indeterminate sentence is attractive if we make the assumption that criminal behavior is comparable to physical illness. We can prescribe individualized justice in the same way we do individualized medicine and develop a "cure" for the antisocial behavior of each offender. The time it takes to find this cure for each offender will be different, so the prison sentences should not be fixed but indefinite; that way the offender will not be released too soon. The professional prison staff will make the determination of when the offender should be released based on the success the inmate makes in rehabilitating himself or herself.

The indeterminate sentence, based on a medical model, enjoyed wide popularity in prison systems during the 1950s and 1960s. There was a progressive attitude that offenders should be and could be rehabilitated while in custody and that the criminal justice system would be more effective if the discretion for determining sentence length was shifted from the judge to the parole board. The indeterminate sentence was predicated on three assumptions:

1. The offender was sick and the prison staff could diagnose the problem.
2. The prison could provide the necessary treatment to correct the problem.

3. The prison staff could accurately determine whether the inmate was treated successfully and was ready to return to society.

It would have been wonderful if these assumptions had proven to be true. The scientific method used in medicine could have been used in the criminal justice system, and the messy problems of politics, racism, sexism, and social class bias could be forgotten. The problem of crime could be located in the social deficiencies of the individual offender and corrected while the offender stayed in prison. The problems of this philosophy will be discussed in greater detail in the next chapter, which deals with corrections. All we need to say at this point is that as a sentencing policy, the indeterminate sentence was jettisoned both because it was based on faulty assumptions and also because it resulted in widely disparate sentences. Individuals who had committed similar crimes ended up serving vastly different sentences based on the individualized justice concept that considered the prospects for rehabilitation.

This focus on rehabilitation was not lost in the inmate. If the prison sentence was to be determined by how well the inmate appeared to be rehabilitated, then it was in their best interests to play the game. The inmate developed a facade of success in order to convince prison officials that the treatment had worked and they were ready to be returned to society (Irwin, 1978). It was later decided that subsequent studies of recidivism rates revealed that the treatment efforts of correctional institutions did not affect the inmate's chances of staying away from a life of crime, and the discretion for deciding how long an inmate would serve in prison shifted from correctional officials to the legislature (Irwin and Austin 1994).

The Determinate Sentence

The perceived failure of the correctional system to change criminal behavior led to an attitude in the criminal justice system that rehabilitation, while a worthy goal, was not the foundation upon which sentencing practices should be based. As legislators heard stories about liberal judges and parole boards they decided to pass laws that would restrict the discretion criminal justice decision-makers could exercise in any individual case. Determinate or fixed sentences were developed by the various state legislatures whereby the length of time an inmate served would be determined not by a judge or a parole board but by the nature of the crime itself. Sentencing grids or guidelines were developed that allowed judges to consider a very limited range of time for each offender. At its most pure form, a determinate sentence would give a fixed term to each inmate depending on the crime for which they were convicted. For example, an armed robbery would call for a 30-year period. The judge would have no discretion to make it longer or shorter, no matter what the circumstances of the crime or the offender. Most determinate sentencing laws allow limited discretion for the judge to consider aggravating or mitigating circumstances but the range is very narrow. All the judge has to do is apply the guidelines to the case and the sentencing grid reveals what the sentence will be.

The perceived advantage of the determinate sentence is uniformity. Like cases are treated in the same manner and, theoretically, such factors as social class, race, and gender do not enter into the sentencing equation. These efforts to eliminate discretion from the criminal justice system have proved elusive. Determinate sentencing schemes have simply shifted the discretion from the judges and parole boards to the legislature and the prosecutor. This unanticipated consequence has resulted in two detrimental effects for the criminal justice system.

First, determinate sentencing has removed the power to make decisions from those closest to the case and in the best position to weigh the conflicting interests in the sentencing decision. Legislators who espouse a get-tough-on-crime policy are not always sensitive to the limitations of the criminal justice system to carry out the demands for long prison sentences for a vast number of inmates. The goal of the legislator is to get elected and reelected, and the making of effective criminal justice policy is a casualty of the demands of simplistic political expediency. Criminal justice resources are limited and legislators who restrict the discretion of criminal justice administrators to allocate those resources are the same legislators who do not provide sufficient resources in the first place. In many ways, correctional officials are left "holding the bag" in that they are given a workload by the legislature and neither the resources nor the discretion to effectively handle their duties within acceptable limits. Civil and human rights of inmates are infringed when prisons are overcrowded, but criminal justice system decision-makers such as judges and parole board members have little power to remedy the situation.

The second detrimental effect on the criminal justice system that has resulted from the determinate sentencing policy is the shifting of power from the judge to the prosecutor. By limiting the judge's discretion in imposing the sentence the determinate sentence increases the impact of the prosecutor's decision on what charges will be filed against the defendant. Defense attorneys unwilling to expose their clients to the long determinate sentences passed by the legislature are pressured to accept plea bargains for lesser-included crimes or in exchange for avoiding designation of drug or sex offense-related statutes. The mandatory minimum sentences for these types of offenses provide the prosecutor with tremendous leverage in extracting plea bargains from defendants and their attorneys. The hands of the judge and the parole board are tied by determinate sentencing, and this is unfortunate because they are in the best position to exercise discretion for both the interests of the inmate and the interests of the criminal justice system. Determinate sentencing reduces them to clerks without the power to apply justice to the individual case and offender.

PEACEMAKING IN THE COURT SYSTEM

The primary goals of the court are to resolve disputes and dispense justice. These goals are not mutually exclusive, which means that under some circumstances they can be achieved simultaneously. Because our courts have gotten so bureaucratic they have lost some of their ability to satisfy our desire to address each of these ambitions. The criminal court process all too often leaves victims, defendants, lawyers, judges, and the public all feeling as if justice has been only partially achieved. While everyone can see how the process ended up with the particular resolution, no one is happy with the process or the result. At a more abstract but equally important level, the criminal court process distances the behavior of the offenders from accountability to the victim and society. In a *British Journal of Criminology* article, entitled **"Conflicts as Property,"** Nils Christie details how the ability to confront the offender has been taken away from the victim and has been given to the more depersonalized Crown (state). Christie sees the conflict, and the right to engage in the conflict, as opportunities taken from the victim and given to the state, whose representatives, in the form of the police and the prosecutor, are not personally affected and cannot benefit to the same degree as the victim from the conflict. Furthermore, Christie sees society as suffering when the criminal courts place the case in its institutional control.

> *But the big loser is us—to the extent that society is us. This loss is first and foremost a loss in* opportunities for norm-clarification. *It is a loss of pedagogical possibilities. It is a loss of opportunities for a continuous discussion of what represents the law of the land. How wrong was the thief, or how right was the victim? Lawyers are, as we saw, trained into agreement on what is relevant in a case. But it means a trained incapacity in letting the parties decide what* they *think is relevant. It means that it is difficult to stage what we might call a political debate in the court. . . . Maybe decisions on relevance and on the weight of what is found relevant ought to be taken from the legal scholars, the chief ideologists of crime control systems, and brought back for free decisions in the courtrooms (Christie 1977, 8).*

In this argument for taking the conflict away from the professional criminal justice practitioners and returning it to the victim and the offender, Christie raises some interesting ideas. The concept that the criminal court with all its rules, procedures, safeguards, and policies actually serves the ends of justice begs the question: whose justice? Christie's concept of conflict as the property of the victim and the offender, and to a certain degree the public, suggests that handing the conflict over to the criminal justice systems cheats those most involved. This is a fascinating argument because keeping the conflict in the hands of the participants has the potential for using the energy of the conflict to allow its full dimensions to be realized. For example, in dealing with the offender, Christie contends:

It is not health control we are discussing. It is crime control. If criminals are shocked by the initial thought of close confrontation with the victim, preferably a confrontation in the very local neighbourhood of one of the parties, what then? I know from recent conversations on these matters that most people sentenced are shocked. After all, they prefer distance from the victim, from neighbours, from listeners and maybe also from their own court case through the vocabulary and the behavioural science experts who might happen to be present. They are perfectly willing to give away their property right to conflict. So the question is more: are we willing to let them give it away? Are we willing to give them this easy way out (Christie 1977, 9)?

Christie goes on to say that he is under no illusion that such accountability demanded of the offender will reduce recidivism. His argument is more fundamental. This conflict as the property of the parties involved and not the criminal justice system suggests the restoring of the sense of participatory community to the criminal justice process. From a peacemaking perspective, this involvement of the offender and the victims in the process can do much toward revitalizing the trust citizens have in their ability to govern themselves. When the victim and the offender are pawns in the games played by the courtroom workgroup they become disenfranchised. When mandatory sentences are decided by the legislature, the criminal justice system practitioners also become distanced and alienated from the process. In our rush to remove discretion from the criminal justice court system, we have also removed the attachment that bonds individuals to the process and to the outcomes. From a peacemaking perspective, what is needed is a way to bring people back into the system. Christie's concept of conflict as property provides a rationale for thinking of the criminal justice system as a mechanism that ought to serve individuals as opposed to an abstract society.

But there is a danger in simply shifting the responsibility of resolving disputes and dispensing justice from the formal mechanisms of the courts to more informal mechanisms of community mediation projects (Hall 1991). From a peacemaking perspective there is much to be said for empowering individuals to work out their differences without resorting to turning control and ownership of the dispute over to the criminal justice system (Keilitz et al. 1988). The trouble with the concept of community mediation is it can focus the blame on the interactions between the complaining parties when the problem might be more fundamental.

By locating the source of interpersonal disputing in the individual, community mediation is able to deflect attention away from the structural roots of such disputing and refocus it instead towards blaming the individual. Such an explanation for interpersonal disputing suggests that, if people want to rid themselves of such conflict, they have an obligation to change their habits, attitudes, and lifestyles. But such victim-blaming serves to depoliticize conflict and thereby (temporarily) maintain social stability by diverting attention from the need for collective rather than individual action. In this way order maintenance can be achieved, even at the expense of justice (Baskin 1988, 105).

Social justice must be the cornerstone of any attempts to empower individuals to solve their own disputes. Sexism and racism are deeply rooted in society. Defining disputes arising from these attitudes as simply qualities of the individual disputants misses the greater opportunity to address the endemic sources of future conflicts. The promise of the peacemaking perspective lies not only in its focus on resolving disputes in a peaceful way, but also in the comprehensive way it envisions the solution.

CRITICAL THINKING QUESTIONS

1. What is the courtroom workgroup? How does the workings of this group impact on the adversarial nature of the criminal court process?

2. Compare and contrast the indeterminate sentence with the determinate sentence. Which of these sentencing models is best for ensuring that justice is done in the courtroom?

3. Plea bargaining has been called a necessary evil. Debate whether it is either necessary or evil. What could plea bargaining be replaced with?

4. Should the criminal justice system allow the offender and victim to become more engaged in the resolution of criminal cases? What does Nils Christie mean when he refers to "conflict as property"?

SUGGESTED READINGS

Albanese, Jay S. 1984. "Concern about Variation in Criminal Sentences: A Cyclical History of Reform." *The Journal of Criminal Law and Criminology 75*(1): 260–271.

Blumberg, Abraham S. 1989. "The Practice of Law as a Confidence Game: Organizational Cooptation of a Profession," in Sheldon Goldman and Austin Sarat, eds. *American Court Systems: Readings in Judicial Behavior.* New York: Longman.

Chilton, Bradley S. 1991. "Reforming Plea Bargaining to Facilitate Ethical Discourse." *Criminal Justice Policy Review 5*(4): 322–334.

Christie, Nils. 1977. "Conflicts as Property." *The British Journal of Criminology 17*(1): 1–15.

Hall, Donald J. 1991. "Victims' Voices in Criminal Court: The Need for Restraint. *American Criminal Law Review 28*(233): 233–266.

Irwin, John, and James Austin. 1994. *It's about Time: America's Imprisonment Binge.* Belmont: Wadsworth.

Neubauer, David W. 1979. *America's Courts and the Criminal Justice System.* North Scituate, MA: Duxbury Press.

Stitt, B. Grant, and Robert H. Chaires. 1993. "Plea Bargaining: Ethical Issues and Emerging Perspectives." *The Justice Professional 7*(2): 69–91.

7

CORRECTIONS AND PEACEMAKING

© Bryce Flynn/Stock Boston.

Learning Objectives

After reading this chapter, the student should be able to:

- Explain how corrections is a multi-goal enterprise.
- Define and discuss the concept of deterrence.
- Explain the difference between general and specific deterrence.
- Describe what Bentham means when he refers to moral calculus.
- Define and discuss the concept of incapacitation.
- Define and discuss the concept of selective incapacitation.
- Define the difference between rehabilitation and habilitation.
- Define and discuss the concept of intermediate punishment.
- Discuss the concept of intensive supervision.
- Describe the practice and limitations of electronic monitoring.
- Describe and evaluate boot-camp prisons.
- Relate how prison overcrowding and token treatment are part of the contemporary prison.

Key Terms

Deterrence	Discipline
Specific Deterrence	"Gang Time"
General Deterrence	Intermediate Punishments
Moral Calculus	Intensive Supervision
Incapacitation	Electronic Monitoring
Selective Incapacitation	Boot-camp Prisons
Rehabilitation	Token Treatment
Habilitation	Electric Shock Therapy
Surveillance	Frontal Lobotomy

The corrections component of the criminal justice system is the most interesting for our discussion of the war on crime and peacemaking perspectives because it is here, after the offender is caught and sentenced, that there is so much controversy as to what should happen next. Some people feel society should do everything possible to make offenders "pay for their crimes," and that anything less than serving the full sentence given by the judge is coddling. Others think we should look at the "underlying causes" of the crime and provide treatment to the offender. Still others simply wish that the problem would go away as quickly and as cheaply as possible. They do not have a clear idea as to what should happen to the offender; they just operate on the "out of sight, out of mind" principle.

Corrections, then, is a multi-goaled enterprise with citizens, judges, politicians, and correctional officials pursuing different agendas. Based on one's personal experience, religious, ethnic, and social-class position, each individual has a philosophy about how to deal with the criminal offender. To further complicate matters, we each have inconsistent patterns of what behaviors we think are serious crimes and we each perform certain actions that we feel should not be crimes at all.

This is all by way of saying there is not uniform public consensus as to what the correctional system should do with offenders (Burton et al. 1993). Within the field of corrections itself we can find policies, strategies, and methods that have varied histories based on conflicting philosophies. Only by examining the diverse goals of the correctional system can we begin to appreciate why the system seems so disjointed and contradictory.

DETERRENCE

For many people, **deterrence** is the cornerstone of the criminal justice system. Deterrence is based on the idea that if people are held accountable for their crimes they will think twice about committing unlawful behavior (Gaylin 1974). Subsequently, they will be deterred or prevented from doing what they ought not do. There are two basic types of deterrence, specific and general. **Specific deterrence** (sometimes called individual deterrence) occurs when someone commits a crime and is caught and punished. The next time that person is in the position to break the law they abstain because they remember there are consequences to their actions. **General deterrence** is based on the idea that we see what happens to other people who violate the law so we do not commit those acts ourselves.

Of the two, general deterrence is more important to our development of meaningful communities. Think how chaotic the world would be if everybody had to commit each crime, be caught, and punished before they were deterred from committing them again. Obviously, general deterrence is extremely significant in the functioning of lawful society. Most of us are deterred from committing all kinds of behaviors because of the possible consequences resulting from detection and apprehension by the criminal justice authorities.

According to deterrence theory, we consider these factors when we decide whether or not to break the law. We consider the chances of getting caught (certainty), how quickly we might be detected and punished (celerity), and how drastic the consequences will be when we are brought to justice (severity) (Paternoster 1987). According to the English philosopher Jeremy Bentham, we each do a **"moral calculus"** whereby we weigh each of these factors against the benefits of getting away with the crime. That is why some people will invest a great deal of time and resources and take tremendous risks to break the law. They believe they have calculated the odds correctly and that the rewards of being successful at a crime outweigh the repercussions of getting caught and being held accountable (Huff 1996).

It should come as no surprise that many if not most of our criminals do not calculate these factors well. Our prisons are full of individuals who appear to have flunked even remedial math. They have committed crimes with serious penalties with little forethought or planning and with almost no chance to escape detection. It would be almost comic if it were not so tragic. The simple fact is many offenders in our prisons are ignorant. They have risked much for little possible gain, and they lost. It might be fair to say that our prisons are crowded with the incompetent criminals; the ones with real criminal skill are seldom apprehended.

Deterrence, then, is only partially successful. Most of us are prevented from committing numerous offenses because of the threat of the criminal sanction. However, many are not deterred either because they cannot fully appreciate the calculations necessary in determining if a crime is cost effective, or because for many, without resources or skills, crime may not be such a bad deal even given the consequences of getting caught. For some crimes like drug dealing, immense profit can be made with little chance of detection. This partially explains why the war on crime model has been embraced by law enforcement officials and politicians. They realize there is little that can be done in controlling the chance of catching most drug dealers, so they have increased the penalties for the ones who are caught as a way of trying to influence the moral calculus of potential offenders.

Unfortunately, this technique of increasing the criminal penalty for drug dealing and drug using may be having an unanticipated consequence of making drug law violation more attractive to the criminal. As penalties become more severe, the price of drugs go up and the potential profit of success makes the crime more attractive. Another unintended consequence of increased penalties is the impact on law enforcement (Manning and Redlinger 1986). Police are subject to increased temptation for corruption when drug profits get so exorbitant. Also, the drug dealer has more to lose when getting caught so that killing the law enforcement officer is entered into the equation. The taking of a life now appears to the offender as cost effective where it would have been unthinkable if the penalty for the crime remained less severe.

Deterrence is a complicated issue and one where there is real disagreement about just how constructive is it as a criminal justice policy (Anderson et al. 1977; Tittle 1980). Clearly deterrence is an important foundation for criminal law but efforts by politicians to change the behavior of criminals cannot be accomplished simply by increasing punishments.

INCAPACITATION

A more modest goal of the criminal justice system is **incapacitation.** By taking the offender out of the community and placing him or her in prison, the important function of protecting society is accomplished. Other methods of incapacitation include exile, cutting off the hands of thieves, or chemical castration of rapists. The idea is to hinder, inhibit, neutralize, or restrict the offender so future harm to society cannot be done. Incapacitation has limited goals that are concerned with addressing the public's perception of safety.

> *The 1980's was mainly an era of incapacitation and short-term behavior-control. This was corrections' chief response to the public's concern with safety now. It was a response which reflected a hope and belief that emerged in the mid-to-late 1970's, namely, that swift and certain punishment, by itself, could provide enough deterrence to produce high levels of immediate protection, and perhaps long-term safety as well. Furthermore, this response reflected a correctional philosophy called the justice model. This model, which began to dominate corrections by the mid 1970's, emphasized punishment and downplayed rehabilitation as well as alternatives to incarceration . . . (Palmer 1992, 62).*

If incapacitation is the goal, then one need not worry about the underlying causes of crime or even what the criminal is thinking in terms of weighing the cost-benefit factors of a particular crime. Incapacitation is atheoretical and has broad appeal to politicians who want criminals off the street. Prisons become warehouses where inmates "do time" with no real expectation that the prison experience will either deter them from future unlawful behavior or help them deal with the issues that led to their crime in the first place.

> *Yet, heavy or exclusive reliance on such a strategy can also have hidden (or not so hidden) costs, ones which are substantial and might include the following: Continued or increased institutional crowding, with its many attendant problems; absence of paucity of serious programming within and outside of lockup; little focus on long-term change in offenders even when some programming exists; and diversion of resources from broad activities such as delinquency prevention (Palmer 1992, 62).*

One of the ways incapacitation can be misused is to select offenses or characteristics of offenders for accelerated punishment. When the public decides certain offenses are particularly heinous they pass laws aimed at "nipping the problem in the bud" by invoking the criminal justice sanction quickly and intensely. The danger here is that individuals are subjected to increased attention by the criminal justice system for reasons having more to do with moral sensibilities rather than actual behavior. When an unlawful act is chosen for **selective incapacitation,** it may indicate more about the behavior of the criminal justice system than the offender. An example of this problem is the manner in which some career criminal statutes operate. Being convicted of three minor felonies is sufficient to get some offenders sentenced to extremely long periods behind bars. Each of these crimes would appear to be trivial by itself but taken together they are interpreted as demonstrating a pattern and are subject to an entirely different sentencing philosophy of selective incapacitation.

Protection of society is the main concern with the incapacitation philosophy, and it is readily embraced by politicians who desire to appear tough on crime. Getting criminals off the street is a popular election year slogan that the public supports but it also presents problems for a correctional system that must now manage an increased prison population.

REHABILITATION

The war on crime model of criminal justice policy does not embrace the **rehabilitation** philosophy. The peacemaking perspective, however, finds rehabilitation to be not only desirable but indispensable in accomplishing the duties and obligations of the criminal justice system. According to the peacemaking perspective, we as a society have a responsibility through our social institutions to provide for the needs of the citizens. It makes sense to those who believe in the peacemaking perspective that in addition to deterrence and incapacitation the public is served by changing the behavior patterns of offenders before they are released back to the streets. While there may be some argument as to how effective we are at changing the behavior of criminals (Andrews et al. 1990; Lab and Whitehead 1990; Logan and Gaes 1993), the rehabilitation philosophy remains one of the important concepts in the correctional component of the criminal justice system (Cullen and Gilbert 1982; Schichor 1992).

Rehabilitation is a word that may be misleading or inaccurate when talking about many criminal offenders. To rehabilitate means to return to a former condition, and for numerous offenders this does not apply because they never have led stable, productive, noncriminal lives. In his classic book, *The Felon* (1970), John Irwin talks about the state-raised youth who has been shuttled from detention center to foster home to juvenile court and back again and never learned the middle-class values espoused by our criminal justice system. To put it simply, the youth was never *habilitated*. Teaching offenders to live lawfully in the first place is a more realistic ambition than rehabilitating them. While this may appear to be a semantic argument to some, it is meaningful to make this distinction and recognize that for our purposes here we encompass the idea of **habilitation** when we use the word rehabilitation.

Rehabilitation is a concept whose time has come and gone in the criminal justice system. For roughly a 20-year period ending about 1970, rehabilitation was the expressed goal of the correctional system. Prisons became correctional institutions and guards were relabeled as correctional officers. A wide variety of treatment programs ranging from drug and alcohol rehabilitation treatment to vocational training to educational programs were established in prisons in many states. Correctional literature advocated the benefits and promise of rehabilitation as a correctional strategy. Unfortunately, the rehabilitation philosophy was abandoned before it had a genuine chance to demonstrate its promise (Cullen and Gilbert 1982). The resources required to give rehabilitation is fair hearing were never forthcoming from state governments and the rehabilitation philosophy was declared a failure. The country swung toward a more punitive mode of corrections aimed at a "just desserts" model where offenders were punished rather than treated (Von Hirsch 1976).

It now seems that the rush to jettison rehabilitation as a correctional philosophy was premature. Some individuals in some programs were successfully changed into productive citizens and some treatment strategies, when properly funded and evaluated, appeared to be fruitful models (Andrews et al. 1990). Some scholars contend rehabilitation was not given an objective examination. Rehabilitation became a victim of the war on crime model despite evidence that it was useful both in changing behavior and in giving hope and promise to offenders who had little reason to be optimistic they could make better lives for themselves.

The peacemaking perspective advocates a return to rehabilitation as a fundamental goal for the correctional system. Most inmates return to society, and it is in the best interests of all of us to attempt to rehabilitate them while we have them incarcerated. Too many offenders are coming out of prison angry, bitter, frustrated, and hopelessly ill-prepared for life in a fast-paced and ambiguous society.

Rehabilitation has been misused in the past. When parole decisions are based on inmates participating in programs, there is a potential for inmates to simply go through the motions and not sincerely participate. Irwin (1980) suggests that rehabilitation programs be available to inmates who wish to take advantage of them but that lack of participation not be used as evidence to deny parole.

Rehabilitation has also been misused by correctional authorities who relabeled punishment as treatment in an effort to circumvent the rights of offenders. Jacobs (1977) reports how the prison at Stateville used the Special Program Unit (SPU) as a tool to isolate gang members from the general population under the guise of treatment. The peacemaking perspective views this type of relabeling of punishment as treatment as an example of how rehabilitation has been not only misused but given a bad name by being linked with social control techniques. We will discuss how the concept of rehabilitation has been corrupted later in this chapter. For now it is sufficient to say that rehabilitation has been one of the major objectives of the criminal justice system and that it has fallen out of favor in recent times.

FOUCAULT AND SOCIAL CONTROL

It is easy to see why there is so much confusion as to what the criminal justice system should be doing when we examine the many, and sometimes conflicting, goals which different people attribute to it. Deterrence, incapacitation, punishment, and rehabilitation all suggest dissimilar correctional strategies and programs. Additionally there are some underlying goals of the criminal justice system that do not get articulated in most discussions of the functions of social control.

The French intellectual Michel Foucault wrote a startling history and social analysis of the prison entitled *Discipline and Punish: The Birth of the Prison.* Foucault argues that prison as a system of reform of the corporal punishment of mutilation has, in fact, become a more insidious attack on the human body. Through the use of **surveillance** and **discipline,** the government has increased its control over the lives of the inmate and, in a more general way, over all of us. Simply put, Foucault asserts we are all subject to forms of social control that we do not recognize as such. We internalize forms of discipline so that we behave in the prescribed manner even without the agents of the state there to ensure our conformity. Also, we are under constant surveillance by a variety of interests. In the case of the prisoner, all contact with the outside, and all interaction with both staff and other inmates, is subject to the routine and control of the state. To another degree, the staff itself is under the surveillance of the authorities, so very little authentic interaction occurs (Jacobs 1977).

Foucault believes the rehabilitative ideal is partially responsible for this intrusion of the social control method into the lives of citizens and inmates. He sees freedoms eroding in an imperceptible way. He might argue that regardless of what our stated goals are for the criminal justice system (rehabilitation, deterrence . . .) as a tool of social control, prisons dehumanize not only the inmates but also the staff and even to some degree all of us as well.

FORMS OF CORRECTIONS

To say we have a correctional system in the United States is to do violence to the word "system." System infers interconnected parts operating in unison, each working in a complementary way with the other parts. Even a cursory glance at corrections in this country reveals this is not the case. Because of the way corrections have developed, there is no system but only a number of entrenched policies aimed at various segments of perceived problems which do not operate according to any rational plan. Correctional history can be understood as a series of reforms stretching over the years where each new reform fails to completely convert the previous reforms so that what we are left with is a system whose parts were assembled for past problems which may or may not be of concern today. Therefore, our correctional system works against itself not only in its competing goals, but also in the very way it is structured.

Prisons

The foundation of the U.S. correctional system is the prison. The prison is the big stick held over the offender's head when the day of sentencing comes.

With the exception of the death penalty in very rare cases, the prison is the ultimate sanction at the disposal of the state. Much of our public impression of the prison is formed by movies and television. While there may be some truth in the media-provided image, there is a great deal of myth and misunderstanding also. To speak of the prison in the United States is really to refer to a wide range of institutions at the local, state, and federal levels. There are dramatic differences in prisons across jurisdictions, levels of security, and objectives. For the most part when we refer to the prison here, we will be talking about the maximum-security prison which is present in all prison systems. We focus on the maximum-security prison because that is where prison problems and concerns exist in their most critical and dangerous condition.

John Irwin (1980), a former prisoner and now a highly respected sociologist, asserts the maximum security prison has changed during the twentieth century. Until about 1950, prison was characterized by a strong inmate social code which specified roles and included a rigid social hierarchy based on commitment to criminal lifestyle and on the type of crime the offender specialized in. The pre-1950 prison was termed "big house" by Irwin, and while it was operated with litter interference from the outside, it violated many of the rights now provided to inmates. It had some beneficial aspects in that the prisoners did most of the prison work and many inmates developed vocational and social skills that helped them when they were released. Many of the big houses were dangerous and violent places, but some of them, like Illinois's Stateville, were highly ordered societies where the warden controlled everything that happened.

According to Irwin, the big house was replaced by the correctional institution between 1950 and 1970. The correctional institution as a prison type was characterized by the rehabilitative ideal. As mentioned previously, rehabilitation did not live up to its promise because of a lack of proper funding. Irwin says the rehabilitative ideal caused the prison structure to break down because it promised more than it could deliver.

Inmates were not given the type and quantity of assistance that would have enabled them to make significant changes in their lives, but they were forced to make-believe they had been transformed because parole was dependent on offenders taking advantage of the opportunities presented to them while they are in prison. This forced hypocrisy on the part of the inmate caused bitter resentment of the prison as an institution and upset the delicate balance of social roles that had developed. The result was a prison that became extremely dangerous and violent culminating in infamous riots at Attica, New York, and Santa Fe, New Mexico.

"Contemporary prison" is the term Irwin uses to describe the type of institution that evolved from the correctional institution. The contemporary prison does not pretend to rehabilitate the offender. Punishment and incapacitation are the philosophies that guide its policies. The contemporary prison is typified by rational decision-making processes, intervention by courts and other outside pressure groups, and by extreme overcrowding, all of which have greatly reduced the discretion prison administrators have in bringing about any rehabilitation. The problems of the contemporary prison have gotten even more acute in recent years, according to Irwin and his coauthor James Austin of the National Council on Crime and Delinquency. In their book *Its About Time: America's Imprisonment Binge* (1994), they argue we have greatly increased the number of people incarcerated and that many of these new inmates are petty criminal and drug offenders who do not pose a serious threat to society. Incarcerating these offenders diverts resources from social programs that could prevent many more individuals from committing crimes. Additionally, according to Irwin and Austin, the overuse of maximum security has a deleterious effect on inmates and results in the creation of "monsters" who are returned to society with very little chance of making a successful transition and a very large likelihood of hurting someone.

In many states, the most intractable problem in prison is the influence of gangs. In California, part of the prison intake process involves determining which gang an offender may be in so that a judicious classification decision can be made as to which prison and which cellblock the inmate is assigned. Sending a gang member to a prison controlled by a rival gang can result in violence. There is an insidious and ominous relationship between the street gangs of California and the prison gangs. Doing **"gang time"** is considered by inmates to be a badge of honor, and a social code revolving around gang membership makes efforts by prison authorities problematic. James Jacobs (1977) maintains that, at Stateville, membership in a gang limited how seriously an inmate could advocate prison reform. The gangs had their own agendas, and when making the prison better conflicted with making the gang more powerful, the inmate's loyalties always resided with his gang.

According to many peacemaking advocates, prison is part of the problem of our criminal justice system and should be abolished (Pepinsky 1994). For others who share the peace perspective, prisons are a necessary evil for there will always be offenders who should be withdrawn from the streets for the protection of society. Also, for some inmates, a period of respite to atone for their crimes can be beneficial (Irwin 1980). The problem with prisons in the United States is that they are overused. Alternatives to incarceration have long been advocated by those interested in reforming the criminal justice system, and a new class of sanctions is emerging to supplement traditional probation and parole. This new type of court disposition generally occurs between probation and prison and includes several different types of programs known as **intermediate punishments.**

Intermediate Punishments

One can almost capture the history of corrections under the term of diversion. When punishments were so harsh that minor offenders were being executed and mutilated, prisons were conceived as a human alternative. Probation and parole share similar histories as programs designed to prevent or diminish the impact of imprisonment.

The recent dramatic increase in prison populations has been equaled by an increase in probation and parole caseloads. It is no longer possible to give the individualized attention to cases, and the probation or parole experience has been watered down to the extent that offenders have very little contact with the probation or parole officer.

Many in the correctional community believe some offenders need more structure and surveillance than can be provided by probation and parole officers, and so have designed programs that place additional restrictions on clients released into the community. The major difference between these new programs and probation or parole as traditionally practiced is the emphasis on punishment rather than on rehabilitation.

Intensive Supervision

Both probation and parole agencies are overwhelmed with large caseloads and have sought innovative ways of handling particularly the serious offenders. One of these methods is the use of **intensive supervision** where officers are assigned caseloads far below the normal level (Byrne 1986). This, of course, means that other officers must take up the slack and supervise even larger numbers of minor offenders. This strategy is a form of triage as practiced in busy hospital emergency rooms: resources are devoted to the most serious cases where they can do the most good. Minor cases are required to wait until resources are available and those cases with only a slim chance of survival are allowed to die. In probation and parole departments, those who pose serious risks are supervised by experienced officers (sometimes with help by a team of supervision aides) and are required to report frequently, take drug tests, attend treatment sessions, pay fines or restitution, and maintain a curfew or other restrictive guidelines (Morris and Tonry 1990).

This increased surveillance is not designed to help the client stay out of trouble but is aimed at detecting deviant behavior which would have gone unnoticed had the offender been placed on a normally overcrowded caseload. With the increased surveillance and more technical conditions of probation, the offender finds it is more likely that the probation will be revoked, which will result in a return to prison (Blomberg 1980; Blomberg and Lucken 1994; Petersilia and Turner 1994). Irwin and Austin (1994) call this the "Tail 'em, Nail 'em, and Jail 'em" attitude on which intensive probation is based. It is a war on crime type of policy which does little to help the individual and places more stress on the criminal justice system because of the increase in offenders who end up behind bars.

Standard probation and parole practice has also gotten more punitive. Because of the excessive caseload size, very little rehabilitation is attempted. Probation and parole officers have become referral agents to other community resources for the treatment needs of their clients. Because there are no sufficient treatment programs in most communities, rehabilitation is not a priority for most probation and parole officers. At best, they can have infrequent contact with the majority of their clients and, for the most part, this face-to-face interaction takes place in the office. Getting out into the community and meeting clients where they work and live is a routine whose time has long passed. Older probation and parole officers remember with fond nostalgia when caseloads were smaller and they could get to know each offender and design and monitor individual treatment plans. Now they are stuck behind desks pushing paper and attempting to keep track of hundreds of cases.

Electronic Monitoring

Electronic monitoring is an attempt to use technology to solve a human problem (Corbett and Marx 1991). It is a form of Foucaultdian surveillance designed to keep an offender from having the freedom to get into trouble. While there are several types of electronic monitoring devices, they all function with much the same goal of maintaining a vigil over an offender without using human resources. A bracelet or anklet is affixed to an offender that signals an electronic device when the offender strays a proscribed distance from where the offender is supposed to be. Sometimes the electronic device uses a telephone or other signaling device, but the idea is the authorities will know automatically if the offender leaves home (Baumer et al. 1993; Schmidt 1994). It is a form of house arrest that has appeal because the guard is an electronic device instead of a person. A certain economy of scale comes into play if enough of these devices can be used whereby hundreds of probationers can be monitored by one person at a central location (Burns 1992).

There are notable limitations to what we can expect from electronic monitoring as a correctional tool (Maxfield and Baumer 1992). First, it can only be used on offenders who are considered safe to release into the community. By the time the authorities can respond to a signal, the offender has absconded and can be miles away and committing serious crimes. Only those who need not be behind bars in the first place can be placed in this type of program. For example, electronic monitoring has been used successfully with drunk drivers (Lilly et al. 1993).

Second, a technological device is subject to technological circumvention. If there are enough of these instruments in use, someone will find a way to circumvent the technology. We can see this in the area of drug testing; many individuals come up with techniques for masking drugs in their system. The ongoing battle between law enforcement's use of radar and companies manufacturing radar detectors is another example of how technology can be vulnerable to technological advancement. Many jurisdictions are afraid to spend thousands of dollars on equipment that could become obsolete and useless given a new discovery.

Finally, there is the concern of what happens to our humanity when we turn social control over to our technologies. This problem is illustrated by Corbett and Marx (1991, 412):

> In Kafka's short story The Penal Colony, *a correctional officer and his superior develop a complicated new machine capable of inflicting horrible moral punishment on inmates. In the end, the officer who argued so proudly for the new technology is horrifically consumed by it. We don't suggest anything like this will necessarily happen in corrections, but it is clear that*

innovations which are thought out carefully and offered honestly and mod-estly run the risk of doing great damage. So far we have seen little theoreti-cal or empirical support to justify the rush to EM.

Boot-Camp Prisons

Boot-camp prisons are a form of shock incarceration which have become very popular in local and state correctional systems around the country (Mackenzie 1990). They have a number of features which make them attractive to correctional authorities and politicians. Unfortunately, proven effectiveness in changing criminal behavior is not one of these features (Morash and Rucker 1990).

Boot-camp prisons are based on the military basic-training practice of stripping recruits of their civilian identities and remaking them as soldiers (Goffman 1961). This is a time-tested process used by armies all over the world designed to take basically good kids and turn them into interchangeable units who will follow orders without question and do things that their socialization has taught them not to do (Dyer 1985, 101–130). The theory behind boot-camp prisons is that this type of military training will instill a sense of discipline in the inmates, develop a sense of pride in inmates who are able to complete the program, give them a taste of incarceration, and help

Many states have adopted the boot-camp prison model with the idea that it teaches discipline. (© Sarah Putnam/The Picture Cube, Inc.)

them avoid future crime. Some politicians like Zell Miller, the governor of Georgia and a former Marine, have a romantic notion of how basic training turned them into men. They believe that this type of "kick in the butt" is all it takes to turn around some of these young offenders.

> *Corrections officials do not appear to be as delighted with shock incarceration programs as are judges, law enforcement officers, legislators, and prosecutors. Why is this? Perhaps the military emphasis makes them nervous. In one state the program was originally designed around programs of education, training, and the like. However, the director later became concerned that the military aspect has so much appeal that it became the rationale for the program,* not *providing emotional support, education, and job skills to these youngsters over the long term. It is further feared that the military style used by correctional officers may bring out their "dark side," or sadistic tendencies. There are possibilities for abuse of authority, especially since conventional disciplinary procedures are waived by inmates coming into these programs (Sechrest 1989, 18).*

There are some important and overlooked differences between military basic training and prison boot-camps. The purpose of military basic training is to change the mindset of the recruits so they will be willing to kill the enemy when ordered to do so. The military recruit is taught discipline, not self-discipline. They are trained to enter into a highly structured environment where they are not encouraged to think for themselves but to do everything the right way; that is, the army way. The boot-camp prison inmates are treated in the same manner but must enter an environment very much different than their military prototype. The boot-camp prison inmates must reenter an ambiguous world on the street where there is not someone to give them orders on acceptable behavior.

The boot-camp prison inmates should be taught how to think critically for themselves rather than blindly take orders from someone shouting at them. Some criminologists contend that all boot-camp prisons are good for is preparing young people to be drug dealers and gang members (Feeley and Simon 1992).

The peacemaking perspective considers the boot-camp prison experience to be the type of policy most likely to do emotional damage to the offender. Domination and humiliation are not the type of qualities the peacemaking perspective would promote in the prison setting. For many offenders from dysfunctional homes this is the model of behavior that caused them to become criminals in the first place. Boot-camp prisons are like graduate training in how to "get in someone's face." What the proponents of boot-camp prison fail to recognize is that they are dealing with a different type of individual from those in military basic training. The military attempts to select the best recruits possible, where the boot-camp prison gets the reverse. Some would argue we should be giving the inmates in boot-camp prison not lessons in humiliation but lessons in civility.

Another significant difference between military basic training and the boot-camp prison concept is that after military basic training the recruits are immersed in an environment that reinforces the culture of their indoctrination. They go on to further training where they are gradually given more responsibilities and more freedom, and step-by-step have their self-esteem rebuilt so that they can function in the military society. Military basic training as a total institution seeks to tear down the self of the recruits and then let the subsequent years of achieving rank and status build up their sense of worth. It is a time-proven concept that works very well in accomplishing its goal of creating soldiers who are prepared to follow orders (Morash and Rucker 1990).

In the boot-camp prison, there is no further training and culture to gradually resocialize inmates into respectable society. After several weeks of intense psychological and physical stress, the offenders are released onto the street with virtually no positive educational or vocational training to help them cope with the environment. They are in better physical shape and have been on the receiving end of constant intimidating behavior. Somehow the proponents of the boot-camp prison idea believe this will work to the benefit of the individual and society. If one thinks military basic training has benefits for changing behavior, then the offender should be encouraged to join the military where he or she has the opportunity to learn a trade and accomplish certain rite-of-passage rituals. The boot-camp prison experience is not an adequate substitute for military seasoning.

Given the problematic nature of what boot-camp prisons can accomplish for the offender, there are two reasons why correctional authorities and politicians have embraced this concept.

1. The first reason boot-camp prisons are so attractive is the cost. By limiting the program to only three months, four offenders can be run through each slot every year. This allows the authorities to greatly decrease the per-inmate expenditures of the state.

2. The second reason it looks attractive to those who administer the criminal justice system is because it represents a high-profile form of punishment. The media have devoted considerable attention to this form of prison and cameras have captured drill instructors yelling at inmates countless times. The public can look at these scenes and feel the offenders are not "getting off easy" but are being punished for their crimes. It should be easy to recognize that the boot-camp prison is part of the war on crime model of criminal justice policy.

The peacemaking perspective would take the boot-camp prison and transform it into a different kind of institutional culture. The punitive nature of the boot-camp prison could easily be changed into one of assistance designed to improve the chances of the inmate for successful reintegration into society. Intensive literacy programs would replace the military drill and the psychological anxiety that is now so purposefully inflicted on the offenders.

Accomplishments in areas that would assist inmates in staying out of trouble would replace the military veneer of the boot-camp prison. Classes in how to design a resume, interview for a job, and be a teammate in a work environment could all be accomplished in the short three-month period of incarceration and would do immeasurably more in preventing future crimes than the boot-camp atmosphere.

RESOURCES AND REHABILITATION

The trouble with the correctional system in the United States is not that we are failing to put money into changing the offenders' abilities to cope with the social environment. The real problem is how we are spending what money is allocated to corrections. Building more prisons dooms us to future operating costs for staff and upkeep, which soaks up resources that could be used for more promising programs. The "imprisonment binge," as Irwin and Austin (1994) call the increased reliance on incarceration that has become popular over the last two decades, has become a "national tragedy and disgrace." Placing more and more offenders in prison has stretched the limits of our ability to provide an atmosphere where we can keep them safe from each other while we are keeping ourselves safe from them. While many people contend we should not worry about inmates victimizing each other and that we should not spend money on making the prisons comfortable, the courts have intervened in many prison systems and dictated that more money be spent on bringing the living conditions up to minimum standards.

At the Georgia State Prison in Reidsville, Georgia, over 250 million dollars were spent transforming one of the most dangerous prisons in the country into one of the safest. This was done by a massive construction effort coupled with the slashing of the inmate population in half.

Overcrowding

The overcrowding of U.S. prisons frustrates all attempts of reforming both the institution and the individuals placed in its care. As more and more prisons are built we are forced to increase the size of the correctional staffs and spread experienced specialists over greater and greater areas. A prison culture is always in flux because, in addition to the normal turnover in such a stressful occupation, there is the constant difficulty of personnel transferring from one institution to another as opportunities to move into more important positions arise. While this may be good for the career prison worker, it is bad for the prison because of the lack of stability. It seems as if everyone is still in the learning phase of their jobs, and the inmates must await the learning curve of the prison administration and staff.

Overcrowding has the additional impact of stretching the abilities of the prison support services (Irwin and Austin 1994). The central offices of prison systems find the classification procedures get more cumbersome and problematic as more inmates and fewer options become obstacles to rational planning procedures. Administrators are spending time and resources either responding to lawsuits caused by overcrowding, or hastening to deal with problems before they become lawsuits. Consequently, overcrowding has an unseen impact on the resources of the prison in addition to the very visible impact of inmates squeezed into space designed for half their numbers.

Of course the primary problem with overcrowding is that the prison cannot provide for the security of both inmates and staff. As more and more inmates are jammed into institutions, the ability of prison administrators to separate members of rival gangs or isolate the violence-prone is greatly limited. Furthermore, as many state prison systems are under the scrutiny of the court, some offenders who might be considered a danger to society are placed on probation or granted an early parole. In short, overcrowding has a deleterious effect on inmates, staff, the prison system, and ultimately on society (Vaughn 1993).

Token Treatment

What has the overcrowding binge meant for the amount and quality of treatment given to inmates within the various prison systems around the country? Naturally, the answer to this question depends upon which prison system we are talking about. For some there has been little impact on rehabilitation activities because of overcrowding. The reason for this surprising statement is there were precious little rehabilitation efforts in many prisons before the overcrowding problem became so acute. Even during the heyday of the rehabilitative philosophy in the 1950s and 1960s, many prison systems allocated very little money for this prison function (Jacobs 1977). In other prisons, more robust efforts were made, but long, sustained, coordinated, and legislatively supported efforts were difficult to find in the prisons in the United States.

The idea of rehabilitation became a public relations facade in many prison systems. Inmates were assigned to various programs staffed by undertrained semiprofessional counselors who were themselves alienated from the prison. Treatment activities were not universally embraced by all segments of the prison community. At the Stateville prison in Illinois, an animosity developed between the custody staff and the college-educated treatment staff over how inmates were to be treated. According to Jacobs, the custody staff felt the treatment staff took the side of the inmate and were too trusting and lenient. The treatment people were assigned to do the "clean work" of advising, counseling, and helping the inmates while the custody staff were allocated the "dirty work" of making sure the inmates were secure and following the rules. The custody staff frustrated the efforts of the treatment staff by constantly claiming security issues prevented rehabilitative classes and programs from being implemented as the treatment people wished (Jacobs 1977).

To say that rehabilitation does not work based on the experience of prisons that appropriated insufficient resources and institutional support fails to give this important and potentially effective correctional philosophy a fair opportunity. Yet, rehabilitation in the criminal justice system has been the first casualty of the overpopulation crisis (Cullen and Gilbert 1982). The second casualty of this problem can be found throughout the criminal justice system in the form of eroding civil and human rights of citizens.

The apparent failure of the rehabilitative philosophy can be attributed to another feature of correctional reform: the indeterminate sentence. The rationale behind the indeterminate sentence rested on the belief that correctional officials had the ability to recognize when an inmate was rehabilitated and was safe to return to the community.

Offenders were sentenced to prison for an ambiguous length of time and could earn their release by undertaking various treatment programs and demonstrating to prison officials and parole boards that they had been successfully transformed. The problem with this doctrine, we now acknowledge, is that we really did not know when someone had been converted into a rehabilitated individual. The whole philosophy behind rehabilitation as the time demanded that the inmates acknowledge they were "sick" according to the diagnosis of the treatment staff and partake of the "cure" available in the prison. This pretense resulted in a dreadful charade where inmates "played the game" of rehabilitation because their release was dependent on their being able to convince the prison authorities and parole board that they had been transformed (Irwin 1980).

Many inmates did make dramatic changes in their personalities and abilities, but it is not clear if the rehabilitative efforts of the prison were responsible. John Irwin, who was himself an inmate for five years, talks about how reading became an escape for many inmates and how they devoured books in their hunger to learn. Many inmates undoubtedly also benefited from the rehabilitation programs but by linking the inmates' release to participation in whatever treatment programs the prison offered, the correctional system created a situation where the inmates had much to gain and little to lose by pretending they were being rehabilitated.

Treatment programs in prison have been dismissed as unproductive and deceitful because of the lack of resources and the linking of release dates to participation. These concerns have all but spelled the demise of treatment endeavors in the prison setting, but it is a big mistake to hastily conclude that rehabilitation cannot work. By making programs available on a voluntary basis to those who wish to gain skills or insight the problem of inmate deception is avoided. If offenders can seek help as they define it and participate for sincere reasons, treatment programs can be useful.

TREATMENT AS SOCIAL CONTROL

Before we leave the subject of rehabilitation it is vital to understand one additional abuse of this correctional philosophy if we are to appreciate its history and potential in constructing a criminal justice policy based on the peacemaking perspective. The rehabilitative ideal has been subverted by those who have used it as a form of social control. In both the criminal justice system and the mental health system, rehabilitation has been used as justification to increase the power of the government over inmates and clients and to conduct some truly inhumane procedures on them.

Electric shock therapy and **frontal lobotomies** are the most infamous examples of how rehabilitation has been used to do serious harm to people by seemingly well-intentioned professionals. There have been other less noticeable but equally damaging efforts to treat people for antisocial behavior. Drug therapy, chemical castration, some forms of corporal punishment, and some types of psychological counseling (behavior modification) have been associated with charges of abuse.

Prison officials have also used the rehabilitation label as a way of inflicting punishment on inmates. As a way of getting around the due process requirements, inmates at Stateville were assigned to a special programs unit (SPU), which was claimed to be a treatment facility but in fact functioned as solitary confinement. These types of abuses are not within the scope of the peacemaking perspective. The reduction of violence both by and to the offender are goals of the peacemaking perspective. By mistreating the inmate with coercion and brutality under the guise of treatment, we provide a faulty pattern of interaction that reduces the chances the inmate will experience positive change. Only by demonstrating compassion and justice as a correctional system can we expect the offenders to develop these qualities in themselves.

The reason, it is clear, that there is so little agreement as to what to do with the criminal offender is because there are several goals embodied in the correctional system. Deterrence, punishment, rehabilitation, and incapacitation each dictate policy which may, at times, overlap with one another and at other times directly conflict. This multiplicity of goals results in a seemingly irrational and illogical pattern of correctional dispositions. Offenders with long criminal records who commit serious crimes at times are given less severe sentences than those who do not appear to be a threat to society. The public is outraged and confused by the disparity in sentences and has moved, in the form of fixed sentences, to limit the discretion of judges and parole boards.

One way to make sense of the conflicting currents of crime policy is to view decisions through the war on crime and peacemaking paradigms. The war on crime model highlights punishment, incapacitation, and deterrence as its theoretical and policy foundations, while the peacemaking model emphasizes rehabilitation. The correctional system has seen many innovations in the past thirty years, including intensive supervision programs in probation and parole, electronic monitoring, and shock incarceration in the form of boot-camp prisons for young offenders. Each of these innovations has been met with a flurry of enthusiasm by judges and politicians while academic criminologists have questioned the effectiveness of such innovations and observed some unintended consequences (Blomberg et al. 1993). The rush of policymakers to "do something now" has prompted the introduction of correctional methods that may sound good to a public afraid of crime and demanding harsh punishments, but on reflection and evaluation, do little to address the underlying causes of crime or prepare the offender for successful reintegration into the community (Haney 1997).

CRITICAL THINKING QUESTIONS

1. Ask ten people to list three things a prison should do. Is there a difference in what individuals of different ages or gender say? Speculate on why there is a lack of consensus on the purpose of the prison.

2. Develop a plan for reducing prison overcrowding that does not cost the taxpayer more money and does not violate the rights of inmates. What rationale will you use in deciding which inmate to release?

3. Discuss the differences between military basic training and the boot-camp prison. Is the military model a viable approach to addressing criminal behavior?

4. "When you ain't got nothing, you ain't got nothing to lose." Discuss the implications this old saying has for deterrence theory. How can individuals who are not invested in society be expected to care about their social reputations?

SUGGESTED READINGS

Andrews, D. A., Ivan Zinger, Robert D. Hoge, James Bonta, Paul Gendreau, and Francis T. Cullen. 1990. "Does Correctional Treatment Work? A Clinically Relevant and Psychologically Informed Meta-Analysis." *Criminology* 28(3): 369–404.

Corbett, Ronald, and Gary T. Marx. 1991. "Critique: No Soul in the New Machine: Technofallacies in the Electronic Monitoring Movement." *Justice Quarterly* 8(3): 399–414.

Cullen, Francis T., and Karen B. Gilbert. 1982. *Reaffirming Rehabilitation.* Cincinnati: Anderson.

Foucault, Michel. 1979. *Discipline and Punish: The Birth of the Prison.* New York: Vintage.

Gaylin, Willard. 1974. *Partial Justice: A Study of Bias in Sentencing.* New York: Vintage.

Huff, C. Ronald. 1996. "Historical Explanations of Crime: From Demons to Politics," in Robert D. Crutchfield, George S. Bridges, and Joseph G. Weis, eds. *Crime.* Thousand Oaks, CA: Pine Force Press, pp. 12–23.

Irwin, John. 1980. *Prisons in Turmoil.* Boston: Little, Brown.

Jacobs, James B. 1977. *Stateville: The Penitentiary in Mass Society.* Chicago: The University of Chicago Press.

Lab, Steven P., and John T. Whitehead. 1990. From 'Nothing Works' to 'The Appropriate Works': The Latest Stop on the Search for the Secular Grail." *Criminology* 28(3): 405–418.

Palmer, Ted. 1992. "Growth-Centered Intervention: An Overview of Changes in Recent Decades." *Federal Probation* 56(1): 62–67.

Paternoster, Raymond. 1987. "The Deterrent Effect of Perceived Certainty and Severity of Punishment: A Review of the Evidence and Issues." *Justice Quarterly* 4(2): 174–217.

8

DRUGS

© Jean-Claude Lejeune/Stock Boston.

Learning Objectives

After reading this chapter, the student should be able to:

- Discuss the role of alcohol in colonial America and the role of the government in dealing with it.
- Discuss opium introduction into the United States.
- Trace the development of drug-control legislation.
- Describe the prevalence and problems of crack cocaine.
- Describe the emergence of the recent war on drugs.
- Discuss how the war on drugs has failed to curb drug use and the violence associated with the drug trade.
- Describe how the peacemaking perspective views the drug problem.
- Discuss the advantages and disadvantages of drug legalization.
- Discuss he problems of corruption in the criminal justice system as a result of the war on drugs.
- Discuss how drug treatment is not available to those who need it most.
- Discuss strategies that will make drug treatment more effective.
- Appreciate how a more sane drug policy requires a better understanding of drug abuse and of public policy.

Key Terms

Laissez-faire	Marijuana Tax Act
Whiskey Rebellion	Crack Cocaine
Patent Medicines	Drug Kingpins
Pure Food and Drugs Act of 1906	Drug Decriminalization
Harrison Act of 1914	Drug Legalization
Prohibition	Harm Reduction

Nowhere in the criminal justice system is there a wider divergence between policies of the war on crime and peacemaking perspectives than on the issue of drug use and abuse. Well-intentioned professionals can agree on the goal of reducing drug use in society and disagree on the most effective means. Additionally, there is considerable debate on whether the criminal justice system should be involved in regulating personal behavior at all.

The issue of drugs in society is a very complicated and complex issue that can only be touched on in this chapter. The history of drugs and drug regulation is presented to provide the student with an understanding of how our present drug laws reflect such an inconsistent and, at times, contradictory pattern. Only by understanding the development of the drug problems and society's response can we begin to appreciate how difficult it is now to achieve a consensus on what should be done today. Next, the war on drugs efforts are reviewed with the purpose of evaluating how effective these policies are in stemming drug use and also what other consequences arise because of this approach. Finally, policies favored by the peacemaking approach, including the legalization debate and treatment strategies, are discussed.

Throughout this discussion of the drug problem, it is important to keep in mind that the goals of providing for the public safety and empowering individuals to control their lives are of overriding concern. These goals may seem in conflict at times, but it is the balance of these ideals that determines how successful a democracy is in providing for the welfare of its people.

A HISTORY OF DRUG USE IN THE UNITED STATES

The use of drugs and alcohol has a long and fascinating history in this country. Individuals have altered their body chemistry by ingesting, injecting, and inhaling intoxicating substances from the beginning of time. Patterns of alcohol and drug use can be traced to the Old World cultures, but there has been a distinctive adaptation to the conditions and hardships of the emerging way of life in the New World.

If one looks closely at the drinking patterns of the early settlers of the United States, it is clear that alcohol was not only consumed in large quantities, but also that it presented serious social problems that the government was incapable of stemming. The early Americans integrated alcohol into their daily routine in such a way that most would be considered alcoholics by today's standards. In his book *The Alcoholic Republic: An American Tradition*, W. J. Rorabaugh examines how between 1790 and 1830 the United States was considered a nation of drunkards. Drinking patterns in this country shocked outside observers who found the drinking habits deplorable.

> *Alcohol was pervasive in American society; it crossed regional, sexual, racial, and class lines. Americans drank at home and abroad, alone and together, at work and at play, in fun and in earnest. They drank from the crack of dawn to the crack of dawn. At nights taverns were filled with boisterous, mirth-making tipplers. Americans drank before meals, with meals, and after meals. They drank while working in the fields and while travelling across half a continent. They drank in their youth, and, if they lived long enough, in their old age. They drank at formal events such as weddings, ministerial ordinations, and wakes, and on no occasion—by the fireside of an evening, on a hot afternoon, when the mood called (Rorabaugh 1979, 21).*

One interesting aspect of the use of alcohol in the early period of the country is how it was part of the daily lifestyle and routine of the people. It was not looked upon as quite the social problem that it is today. In fact, the use of distilled spirits was considered to be part of a healthy lifestyle. In addition to being considered nutritious, distilled spirits were believed to cure colds, fevers, snakebites, frosted toes, and broken legs (Rorabaugh 1979, 25).

While some religious groups like the Quakers felt this reliance on alcohol was harmful to individuals and to the fabric of society, most people saw the use of alcohol as a normal and desirable part of daily life. The government adopted a **laissez-faire** attitude toward the regulation of alcohol and drugs and intervened for only tax reasons as opposed to moral concerns. For example, in 1791, Congress passed an excise tax on whiskey that resulted in the first test of the federal government's ability to pass and enforce laws in the states. Farmers from west of the Appalachian Mountains refused to pay the tax and began what came to be known as the **Whiskey Rebellion.** Revenue agents who tried to enforce the law were tarred and feathered and, in 1794, George Washington was forced to call in the militia to establish the power of the government (Ray and Ksir 1993, 8).

The history of drug use and its regulation in the United States illustrates how ambivalent society has been toward intervening in what were considered to be personal matters. It is only after the widespread use of a drug is considered a social problem that the government is prodded to intervene. Drug use has often not been considered a social problem when it has been confined to marginal groups in society. It is only after it has spread to the middle and upper classes that it is deemed serious enough to provoke a government response.

The history of opium use is a good example of how drug laws have been developed to protect the interests of the powerful members of society. In the mid-1800s many British and U.S. merchants were engaged in the sale of opium to the Chinese. Many Chinese were brought to the United States to work on building the railroad system, and they brought their opium habit with them. It was not considered a serious problem worthy of societal reaction until it spread into the rest of society.

> *The practice spread rapidly and quietly among this class of gamblers and prostitutes until the later part of 1875, at which time authorities became cognizant of the fact and finding . . . that many women and young girls, as also young men of respectable family, were being induced to visit the dens, where they were ruined morally and otherwise, a city ordinance was passed forbidding the practice under penalty of a heavy fine or imprisonment or both (as quoted in Ray and Ksir 1990, 39).*

Laws were passed in many cities prohibiting opium dens and, in 1890, the federal government banned noncitizens from importing opium. The cost of opium on the black market increased dramatically and many addicts turned to other drugs that were less expensive and more readily available.

One drug that people had already discovered was morphine. The hypodermic syringe was invented in 1856 and, by the Civil War, morphine was used widely for both pain and dysentery. So many soldiers became addicted to morphine that it became known as the "army disease." One of the more popular treatments for morphine addiction was cocaine until it became clear that cocaine was also habit forming.

Even more widespread than the use of morphine and cocaine was **patent medicines.** Touted as therapeutic, many of these formulas contained high percentages of alcohol, cocaine, and other addictive drugs (Inciardi 1986). The unsuspecting public bought the patent medicines from traveling hucksters who were not qualified to diagnose medical problems or disease. A quick dose of alcohol or drugs would make people feel good temporarily and then as the effects wore off they sought more "medicine." Before long, the individual was addicted without knowing or understanding exactly what was in the patent medicine or how the process of addiction developed or should be treated.

Drug-Control Legislation

The twentieth century ushered in a steadily progressing set of laws aimed at curbing the unregulated abuse and use of drugs. In 1906 Upton Sinclair's muckraking book *The Jungle* shocked the nation with graphic descriptions of unsanitary conditions in the nation's meatpacking industry. Congress was so shocked at stories of rodents being routinely tossed into the nation's processed beef that they passed the **Pure Food and Drugs Act of 1906.** This law specified that ingredients of drugs and food had to be clearly labeled and that interstate transportation of misbranded or adulterated foods and drugs were prohibited. This law had the effect of crippling that patent medicine industry because now citizens could read what was in these products and make a more informed choice. Journalists alerted the public about the dangers of morphine, cocaine, opium, and heroin so the consumer could now see when the "cure" for one addicting drug was simply a replacement by another.

The important point to remember about the Pure Food and Drugs Act of 1906 is that it did not criminalize these drugs. It was still legal to sell and consume the drugs, they just had to be properly identified. The goal was not to protect people from themselves but to make sure that incompetent or unscrupulous merchants did not take advantage of unsuspecting individuals.

In 1914, Congress passed the **Harrison Act.** This was a law designed:

> *. . . to provide for the registration of, with collectors of internal revenue, and to impose a special tax upon all persons who produce, import, manufacture, compound, deal in, dispense, or give away opium or coca leaves, their salts, derivatives, or preparations, and for other purposes (Ray and Ksir 1996, 59).*

The intent of the act was not so much to prohibit people from using drugs but to make sure the federal government got its tax revenue. However, the law had the effect of beginning the criminalization of drug use and establishing a black market. While physicians could prescribe narcotics in the course of their medical practice, the U.S. Supreme Court in *Webb v. the United States and the United States v. Behrman* held that maintaining the comfort of an addicted person was not a legitimate medical purpose. In subsequent cases, the court reversed itself on this point but, by then, physicians decided not to treat addicts by maintaining their dependence on narcotics. This unintended consequence of the Harrison Act resulted in establishing the pattern for outlawing drug use.

If doctors could not prescribe drugs for the addict population, what was to be done with this population of at least 200,000 individuals dependent on drugs (Ray and Ksir 1993, 65)? By 1928, with one third of the inmates of federal prisons being drug violators, it became clear that our drug laws were expensive to maintain. Because drug violators were being repeatedly jailed a new tack was taken. Drug violators would be cured rather than punished for their addictions. The federal government established two narcotic farms for the treatment of persons addicted to habit-forming drugs. One farm in Lexington, Kentucky, opened in 1935 and served as a model of the type of treatment afforded drug violators. The farm operated as a total institution (Goffman 1961) where inmates/patients were isolated from society and had their addiction treated in a secure setting where they could not take advantage of the resources in the community nor commit further crimes.

The history of how marijuana use became a crime is another interesting chapter in the development of our attitudes toward drugs. With the end of **Prohibition** in 1933, we had a federal bureaucracy that needed a new foe. The Bureau of Narcotics in the Treasury Department, with Harry Anslinger at its head, adopted marijuana as its new cause. Anslinger began writing, speaking, testifying, and making films about the "devil drug," assassin of youth," and "weed of madness."

> *Here indeed is the unknown quantity among narcotics. No one knows, when he places a marijuana cigarette to his lips, whether he will become a philosopher, a joyous reveler in a musical heaven, a mad insensate, a calm philosopher, or a murderer.*
>
> *That youth has been selected by peddlers of this poison as an especially fertile field makes it a problem of serious concern to every man and woman in America (Anslinger and Cooper 1995/1937, 88).*

In 1937, the **Marijuana Tax Act** was passed, which placed it under the same type of legal control as cocaine and narcotics. Marijuana had a long history in the United States. In the early years, it was used to make many products, including rope. The growing of the marijuana hemp plant was popular with George Washington and Thomas Jefferson. The smoking of marijuana for recreational purposes was popular in South and Central America and first appeared in some Texas border towns and New Orleans. In Anslinger's campaign to villianize marijuana, the race of those who used the drug became an important factor. As the Chinese were seen as the suppliers of opium and a threat to the dominant white society, so too did marijuana and the Mexicans become stigmatized as dangerous.

The public's perception of drug use as a social problem remained one of little concern as long as drugs were thought to be an issue of the marginal classes in society. When only the poor and some immigrant groups suffered from drugs, politicians and the media were not motivated to see it as a pressing concern for the nation. The 1960s changed all that. Suddenly drugs were everywhere in the youth culture. Marijuana became as prevalent as beer on the college campus, and heroin and LSD became popular among many seeking new experiences and higher insights. Drug use in some parts of the youth culture was considered not just the experience of deviants, but what the best and the brightest did to expand their perceptions.

The 1960s were a significant decade in shaping not only the drug issues of the country but also the relationship between citizens and the government. For large segments of the middle- and upper-middle-class portions of the youth movement, the government became seen as an adversary. The civil rights movement and the opposition against the Vietnam War became arenas in which young people found themselves in opposition to the police, courts, mainstream press, and their parents. Defiance to authority was manifested in many varieties, not the least of which was the drug counterculture (Gitlin 1987, Jones 1980).

The 1960s were viewed as a new chemical age where new drugs arrived on the scene with such regularity it became hard to keep up with the drug parlance. Crafting and passing drug laws to keep up with the changing scene became even more problematic. Amphetamines, while not new drugs, found their way to the street. From "purple hearts" to "black beauties," youth were using uppers and downers to not only feel good but also to lose weight, stay up late to study for exams, and to relieve fatigue and depression.

One of the most interesting results of the drug revolution of the 1960s was the short-lived move to decriminalize or legalize some drugs. Marijuana offenders were subject to extreme penalties for possession of small amounts in many states. For instance, in Texas, possession of a marijuana cigarette was punishable by two years to life in the state prison system. Many states reduced possession of small amounts of marijuana from a felony to a misdemeanor. A few such as Alaska legalized growing marijuana for personal consumption (Schlaadt and Shannan 1986). These reforms were short lived, however. The move to liberalize drug use has been reversed in the 1980s, and the prospects for the legalization of marijuana (which many people thought was only a matter of time), are currently nonexistent.

Why did the drug revolution of the 1960s fail to make meaningful changes in how the nation deals with drug offenders? Part of the answer lies in the maturing of the youth generation. The 1960s ended with the withdrawal of troops from Vietnam and the oil embargo by the OPEC nations.

Suddenly, the focus of young people changed from transforming the country to transforming themselves. Without a war to protest, and marriages and careers to worry about, the politics of drug-law reform took a back seat to new and pressing personal issues. The solidarity of the youth movement disintegrated, and a new age of jogging and health concerns took precedent for a generation moving into its thirties and forties.

Today, drug-use patterns are very different from what they were in the 1960s. Marijuana and alcohol continue to be popular drugs, but the open and reckless public consumption of the flower-children years has been changed into a much more circumspect private affair. No longer are the rock concerts and public parks filled with dope-smoking and drinking young people. The war on drugs has had its biggest impact on changing the context of drug use. With law enforcement taking a more active stance in enforcing the drinking and driving laws, with penalties for illicit drug and alcohol use being more and more severe, and with schools and employers no longer willing to treat drug use as a private affair, the context in which drugs are used is greatly changed.

Perhaps the greatest difference on the contemporary drug scene is the problem of **crack cocaine.** Crack has replaced marijuana as the cheapest and most readily available drug on the street. With marijuana being worth its weight in gold (over $2,000 a pound), it is no longer the drug of choice for many users. Crack has become increasingly popular among inner-city drug users. Crime associated with the inner-city drug market has escalated to the point where street violence is viewed as one of the major concerns of society. Crack use can lead to a cycle of crime-drug use that is very hard to break.

> One major problem with the crack trade is that it facilitates crack addiction. Every single youth interviewed for this study who was involved in the crack business to even a minor degree was a crack user; of the crack dealers, over 70 percent used crack every day, while 15 percent used it less regularly. Furthermore, even though greater crack trade participation meant more crack earned directly, as payment for drug sales, it also meant heavier use patterns; so that crack dealers were paying an average of over $8,000 a year to purchase crack for personal use. The resemblance to the classic crime-drug interactive cycle seems clear: crack dealing finances crack use, crack use encourages more crack use, and more crack use requires more profit-making crimes of all sorts to support an ever-growing addictive use pattern (Inciardi and Pottieger 1995, 253).

THE WAR ON DRUGS

Today the abuse of drugs and the violence associated with the drug trade are considered to be the top public safety issues facing the nation (Akers 1992). Politicians, police, employers, and parents are waging a war on drugs that has many fronts. Many institutions and corporations have a zero-tolerance policy that actively discourages drug use and applies sanctions ranging from suspension, loss of pension rights, to loss of a job. Schools are drug testing athletes and other students, drug dogs are prowling the hallways and searching lockers and parking lots, and law enforcement officials are conducting hotlines where anonymous information is collected and acted upon. In short, the nature of drug use has changed into a high-risk, high-reward enterprise that has ramifications for all of society. The war on drugs has altered the relationship between police and the public in such a way that many feel our liberties are being eroded by a police state. How has this war on drugs happened, and what has been the impact on the way we live? More importantly, has the war on drugs been successful in solving the drug problems of the country or has it had the opposite effect? Elliott Currie (1993) summarizes the impact of the war on drugs in very negative terms.

> *Reasonable people may legitimately debate the details. But there is no denying the fundamental realities: the American drug problem continues to tower above those of the rest of the industrial world, and it does so despite a truly extraordinary experiment in punitive control. We have unleashed the criminal-justice system against drug users and dealers with unprecedented ferocity, but drugs continue to destroy lives and shatter communities outside the Third World. And now the drug war itself contributes to that destruction—first in the incarceration of vast numbers of the young in what should be the start of their most productive years; and again in the depletion of resources that could otherwise be used to deal with the deeper problems of devastated communities (Currie 1993, 33–34).*

In order to understand how the war on drugs has changed the patterns of drug use in the country, it is important to examine how this war has been waged and what weapons are being employed. The media and politicians have made productive use of the war on drugs to achieve their desired ends. One of the safest campaign issues today is to be opposed to drugs. Calling for increased penalties for drug use and for invasive measures to detect drug activity are standard fare for politicians. The more extreme the message, the more publicity the politician is likely to receive. One good example of how politicians have increased penalties for drug violations—which is aimed more at the voters than at any rational response to the drug problem—is the law that authorizes the imposition of the death penalty for drug-related homicides. This law, aimed at the **drug kingpins,** misses its mark, according to Tobolowsky (1992).

> *At the time of their enactment, proponents of the death penalty provisions hailed them as an essential part of the governmental attack on drug "kingpins." By including intentional killings by all those working "in furtherance of" a continuing drug-related criminal enterprise, however, the statute goes*

well beyond kingpins, and could reach all those with even a remote involve-
ment in a drug-related enterprise such as a lookout or messenger (69).

Voting for anything but the most stringent anti-drug bill makes politicians appear soft on crime. The result has been to increase the penalties for
drug sales and, in many cases, for drug use, to the point where the criminal
justice system is compelled to expend more and more of its limited resources
on drug offenders, leaving reduced capacity to deal with other types of serious crime.

The most telling criticism against the war on drugs is that it has been
largely ineffective in stemming the use of drugs, especially among the hard-core
users. According to one journalist writing about the war on drugs, "The dis-
couraging fact is that there has been no reduction in the 2.7 million hard-core
addicts who consume three-fourths of the street drugs and commit much of the
violent crime that devastates families and neighborhoods" (Malone 1995).

A second problem with how the war on crime has "upped the ante" for
participation in the drug trade is the reduction in the value of human life. The
war on drugs has increased the prevalence of guns on the street. Automatic
weapons have become standard for young drug dealers caught up in turf wars.
The police are often outgunned by teenagers, and the resulting shootouts
from the drug trade often take the lives of innocent bystanders. With long
prison sentences and, in some cases, the death penalty confronting a drug
offender, the prospect of killing rivals or law enforcement officers becomes
more likely. The violence associated with drugs is partially explained by how
severe the penalties have become.

A third problem that results from the war on drugs is the impact it has
had on undermining the integrity of public officials (Bertram et al. 1996). The
costs and profits associated with the drug trade have become so immense that
corruption of politicians and law enforcement officers is so commonplace it
no longer surprises us. With the millions of dollars involved in the drug trade
the price of bribing key law enforcement officers is simply a wise investment
associated with the cost of doing business. Corruption of criminal justice personnel can be found at every level. Prison guards supplement their income by
smuggling drugs to inmates, police officers take kickback money from drug
dealers, and politicians do business with corrupt governments involved in
drug trade in order to pursue national security agendas.

The war on drugs has changed the way in which law enforcement officials interact with the community. The style of policing that many law
enforcement agencies employ is a paramilitary model that not only alienates
many citizens but often borders on infringing on the rights of offenders.
Drug detection and enforcement is proactive, dangerous, and of questionable
effectiveness in the way it is practiced in many jurisdictions. The prospects
for inappropriate police use of force, destruction of property, and the tram-
pling of the rights of citizens are increased when law enforcement wages a
war on the citizen.

Anti-drug efforts are often said to violate civil liberties.
(© Jim Sulley/The Image Works.)

> *The clandestine nature of drug investigations and the enormous profits associated with illegal drugs inevitably lead to police corruption. Questionable, if not illegal, practices are characteristic of investigations of complaintless crimes. The use of low visibility tactics such as decoys, informants, bugging devices, wiretapping, and no-knock raids is commonplace in drug investigations, and it increases the opportunities for corruption (Johns 1992, 19).*

Johns goes on to list other problems with domestic enforcement of the drug laws. We get little in return for the money we invest in enforcement costs. The millions of dollars that are spent on enforcement could be better utilized on other crimes that are much more destructive to the social fabric. Environmental crime, white-collar crime, and corporate crime all are under-enforced because of the emphasis and resources expended on attempting to enforce the drug laws.

A critique of the war on drugs from a peacemaking perspective would argue that the cure is worse than the disease. In an effort to stop people from using drugs, the criminal justice system has made the drug problem much more dangerous for everyone and has done little to stem the use of drugs. It can be argued that the criminal justice system has increased the level of the drug problem because it has made the drug trade such a profitable enterprise.

PEACEMAKING AND THE WAR ON DRUGS

How does the peacemaking perspective deal with the drug problem? Given that drug abuse can be harmful to the body of the individual and bad for society as a whole if a large proportion of the population are addicts, how can the peacemaking perspective make our streets safe? Does the peacemaking perspective doom large numbers of people to a life of enslavement to drugs because it is soft on crime?

The peacemaking perspective begins by rejecting the war metaphor as an approach to dealing with drug use and abuse. The war metaphor is a faulty means for envisioning the nature of the drug problem and what we can reasonably do about it. The war on drugs, according to the peacemaking perspective, does more harm than good. The peacemaking perspective takes a radically different tack on addressing the drug problem, one that fundamentally changes our view of drugs and, just as importantly, one that greatly limits the role of the criminal justice system.

At the heart of the peacemaking perspective on drugs is the realization that drug use is of a voluntary nature. To this extent, drug use is a victimless crime. People choose to take drugs and can be held accountable for the effects drugs have on their bodies and on their behavior. If people under the influence of drugs commit a robbery or a murder, they should be brought before the criminal justice system to answer for their behavior. The drug use itself, however, should not, according to the peacemaking perspective, be of concern to the criminal justice system. Drug use would be **decriminalized** and/or **legalized** and problems of drug use would be dealt with by institutions other than the criminal justice system, most notably, the medical and mental health systems. The drug trade would presumably be greatly eliminated by the market forces driving the cost of drugs down past the point of being profitable for illicit dealers. The peacemaking perspective would still strive to keep drugs from minors and the criminal justice system would certainly be used to protect children from those who would provide them with drugs, but this type of regulation would be more similar to how we treat alcohol than the current methods of drug enforcement. Bertram et al. (1996) suggest a public health paradigm that would regulate drug-using behavior to protect society rather than enforce morality.

Drug Legalization

Is drug legalization a realistic alternative to the war on drugs? Would it lead to drug-infested anarchy? How can anyone in their right mind be in favor of more drug abuse? There are some important concerns to recognize when considering the peacemaking perspective's stance on drugs. The goal of the peacemaking perspective is to reduce the problems the prohibition on drugs has caused in this country. The goal of keeping people from abusing drugs is still paramount, yet the means of achieving that goal are different. Perhaps an analogy would help clarify the peacemaking perspective. People who are pro-choice in the abortion debate are not in favor of abortion. They are in favor of a woman having a choice in this very difficult issue. Pro-choice advocates encourage sex education, contraception, adoption, and help for mothers in caring for and educating their children. Pro-choice advocates, while working to keep abortion legal, would like also to make it unnecessary.

How would legalizing drugs help reduce the drug problem? There are a number of benefits that legalization would presumably entail.

1. The biggest problem with drugs is the collateral violence associated with the drug trade. Because there is so much money to be made in drug sales, individuals are willing to use deadly force to protect their economic interests. Legal drugs would be relatively cheap and readily available to adults so it can be assumed that with the vast profits taken out of the drug trade, the black market for drugs would shrink, and the violence associated with drug sales would almost disappear. The example of liquor law enforcement during Prohibition can illustrate this point. After Prohibition was repealed, the violence associated with organized crime disputes over territory vanishes. With liquor available at the corner store, the lack of money on the black market forced gangsters to turn to other endeavors. Individuals still provided alcohol to minors or tried to avoid paying taxes on what they bought, but the problems of enforcement of liquor laws are completely different, and less severe, than during Prohibition.

2. Criminal justice resources can be reallocated to other crimes. The money, time, and creative energy expended on the war on drugs by law enforcement officers, judges, prosecutors, prison officials, and other criminal justice personnel can be reallocated. The war on drugs has drained the criminal justice system of scarce resources that can be more productively utilized in dealing with other types of crimes and criminals. The reduction in the number of prison beds alone will go a long way toward making criminal justice more affordable.

3. Criminal justice system personnel will not be subjected to so much temptation for corruption under a peacemaking perspective as they are under a war on crime perspective. The big money of the black market drug trade will not be available to induce criminal justice personnel to compromise their ethics.

4. Drugs will be harder for juveniles to obtain. Today drugs are more available to youth than to adults. Because the juvenile justice laws are more lenient than the normal criminal justice system laws, drug dealers employ large numbers of juveniles in the drug trade. Because drugs are illegal, they have become one of the mainstays of the rebellious youth culture. Once the stigma of drug use is taken away by legislation, drugs will no longer be an act of rebellion to authority. Youths may still use drugs, but they will do so for different reasons.

5. The drugs available through legalization will be less dangerous than available through the black market. It will be possible to regulate the ingredients and potency of legal drugs in a manner now not possible. Depending on how drugs are made available to the public, such techniques as having the drugs dispensed from a pharmacy or government outlet will allow for assurances the drugs are properly labeled, pure, and have sufficient warning labels so consumers can make informed choices about what drugs they use.

6. Crimes such as burglary and robbery will be reduced in number and seriousness. Addicts will no longer need hundreds of dollars a day to support their drug habit. With drugs available legally, at a reasonable price, the potentially explosive predatory street crime of desperate drug users can be expected to decrease. There will still be burglars and robbers but they will be more predictable when they are not going through withdrawal pains and not needing so much money.

7. Respect for the law will be increased. Presently there are tens of millions of people who choose to violate the law in order to use drugs. The cynicism that is generated toward the law in general when so many otherwise law-abiding citizens willingly expose themselves to arrest and prosecution results in hostility and suspicion toward law enforcement officials (Nadelmann 1988, 20).

8. The economy of the country will be improved by the legalization of drugs. Currently the black market drug trade is a multibillion dollar enterprise for which the government gets no revenue. If the government would tax drugs at the rate it taxes alcohol and tobacco it would generate sufficient revenue to address prevention and treatment needs. The illegal money-laundering activities of big-time drug dealers rob the country's economy of much of its vitality and corrupts many individuals in the banking industry.

This list of benefits from the legalization of drugs suggests that the current drug prohibition policies need reevaluation. While it is impossible to tell how many, and to what degree, these benefits will be realized, it should be apparent that the current war on drugs has failed to achieve its goal and has produced destructive by-products that are destroying the social fabric of the country.

There is one nagging little question that keeps popping up in the legalization debate, which leads many to believe that allowing people assess to drugs will create legions of drug addicts who will become a financial and moral drain on the country. People have visions of hollow-eyed zombies rotting in every doorway, much like the clients of opium dens earlier in the century. This is a very legitimate concern, and if drug legalization resulted in multiplying the number of heavy drug users, as is feared, then it would not be advisable to explore this policy. However, there is reason to suggest these fears are exaggerated. There are three reasons why we can be optimistic that problems of drug use will not become a significantly more serious problem under a peacemaking perspective, such as legalization, than it is under the current war on drugs perspective.

1. The first reason why we can expect legalization of drugs to fail to cause the addict population to skyrocket is the simple fact that just about anyone who wants drugs now can get them. If we start with the assumption that there will only be a percentage of the population that desires to use drugs, there is every reason to believe this percentage has already (and at terrible cost to the country) been able to obtain their drugs. When Prohibition was repealed in 1933, the incidence of alcoholism did not skyrocket because, like the war on drugs, alcohol prohibition largely failed in depriving people of alcohol.

2. The second reason why legalization should not cause a substantial increase in problem drug users is because now the problem of drug use will be treated as a medical problem rather than a criminal justice problem. The strategies of drug treatment, drug prevention, and education on responsible drug consumption can be much more effective in altering drug-use patterns than the war on drugs crusade.

3. The third reason why there could be fewer drug users under legalization is because much of the romance will be taken out of the drug subculture. Now, drug use is a way to rebel against the dominant society. Under legalization, drug use will no longer be a signal of independence and risk-taking but will be considered simply a lifestyle choice, and its abuse will be considered a medical problem. It can be expected that risk-taking peer pressure would be reduced because drug use would be less deviant and attractive.

Drug Treatment

The history of drug treatment in the United States is not one of overwhelming success. The country has largely retreated from the idea that drug users can be rehabilitated and has systematically scaled back the support for treatment programs in favor of funding the interdiction and arrest programs of the war on drugs. In many jurisdictions, drug users find treatment programs either unavailable or with waiting lists which can delay admission for up to a year. Furthermore, those who need treatment the most—inner-city crack addicts—are least likely to find it. There is a growing private treatment industry that addresses those with financial resources or good health insurance, a good example being the Betty Ford Clinic in San Diego, California, the treatment center of choice for celebrities in the sports and film industries. But there is precious little help for those without the economic means.

> *To the degree that one driving force for this cycle is indeed crack use, one possibility for breaking the cycle is forced intervention into the addiction pattern. This requires that these youth be located, but the criminal justice system is, in fact, finding them: 92 percent of the total sample had been arrested at some time (true for almost 98 percent—199/204—of those with any crack business involvement at all). . . . Although these youths had been located, intervention has not occurred. Fewer than 4 percent of this extremely drug-involved sample had ever been in drug treatment. This reflects not only an overburdened juvenile court system, but also inadequate treatment resources for adolescents. Both problems are commonplace across the nation (Inciardi and Pottieger 1995, 253).*

In addition to the lack of availability of treatment programs, there are questions about the usefulness of drug treatment. Because there are so many types of modalities aimed at different populations and drugs, it is hard to make a blanket statement about just how successful drug treatment is. What we do know is that many individuals relapse and are continually in and out of treatment programs. According to Currie (1993), in addition to addressing the most serious drug users, we need to change our orientation and consider drug use as a social problem and not just a medical problem.

> *We should start by shifting the emphasis from curing disease to building capacities and increasing opportunities. As the Dutch specialist Govert van de Wijngaart puts it, "Treatment must be directed towards building up a new life." At the same time, even the best efforts to rebuild lives won't have much impact on the drug problem if only a minority of drug users ever make use of them. Accordingly, it's urgent that we make treatment both attractive and more accessible, and simultaneously develop more creative ways of reaching drug abusers—and those at risk of becoming abusers—in their natural surroundings, outside of formal treatment settings (241–242).*

The goal is not only to treat the drug user for psychological problems believed to be the cause of his or her drug abuse but also to deal with the social context within which the addict uses drugs. It makes little sense to treat someone outside their social environment and then toss them back in without addressing the skills they need to become functional in that environment. Currie details several principles of treatment which reflect the peacemaking perspective of viewing crime and criminals in a more holistic way.

1. *Taking treatment seriously.* There is a wide range of activities that fall under the rubric of drug treatment. Some are very successful and others are not worthy of being called treatment. Currie would fund treatment programs at a level where they can provide the quality of service required to be effective. Rigorous standards of accountability would ensure that what is being touted as treatment is evaluated and modified.

2. *Making treatment user-friendly.* Many programs regard addicts as criminals or dependent patients rather than normal human beings with a treatable problem. The punitive and negative atmosphere of many drug programs makes addicts reluctant to invest themselves in a treatment philosophy that can be confrontational and demands that they expose their feelings and vulnerabilities. There are treatment modalities that do not foster dependence and accept addicts as adults who are trying to regain empowerment.

3. *Linking treatment with **harm reduction**.* Because of the problems with AIDS, it is not reasonable to expect abstinence from drug use or sex among the addict population. Those entering treatment cannot be held accountable for the behavior expected after the treatment has been successful. Therefore, the goal for those entering treatment should be the reduction of harm to society that drug use entails. In order to be afforded treatment, the addict needs to agree to reduce the risk of transmitting AIDS and other diseases that spread as a result of dirty needles and unprotected sex. Kits to clean needles and syringes or new needles and syringes should be provided to the addict population to minimize the risk that the health problems associated with drug use are spread to the rest of society. Many may think that such a stance by the government condones drug use and gives the wrong message to our youth, but the AIDS epidemic makes such actions necessary to limit the spread of the disease. These steps are required to fight the problems rather than just bring moral condemnation on the victims of AIDS and, by doing so, continuing to allow its diffusion into the community.

4. *Making aftercare a priority.* Drug treatment is as much a process as it is an event. It can take a long time before a serious user gets addiction under control. Relapse is a common occurrence that could be better managed with good aftercare programs. Support groups for addicts are only part of the solution. Currie suggests that aftercare needs "a strong component of advocacy in order to help vulnerable ex-addicts negotiate the increasingly inhospitable housing and labor markets, as well as the criminal-justice system (253).

5. *Linking treatment with work.* There is a strong relationship between heavy drug use and unemployment. Many addicts have been out of the work force for a long time and lack not only the technical skills to do the job but also the social skills necessary to find a job, do well in a job interview, and interact with coworkers and supervisors once employed. Treatment programs can help provide the support and training that addicts need to develop a resume, locate job opportunities, learn proper working etiquette (showing up on time, talking in a respectful manner, dressing appropriately), and how to budget their earnings.

This reorientation of what treatment programs can do for drug users fits into the peacemaking perspective because it seeks to not only reduce the harm to society that addicts traditionally have caused, but also because this approach endeavors to address some of the intractable problems related to the addicts' use of drugs.

In order for treatment programs to work, however, there is a broader issue that needs to be considered. One of the features of the war on drugs that has been effective has been the demonizing of drug use and drug users. By placing such a negative stigma on drug use, the war on drugs has made it more difficult for drug users to admit their addiction problems and seek assistance. The zero-tolerance policies of schools and employers has further marginalized those who might otherwise seek drug treatment. If getting kicked out of school or losing your job is the reward for revealing drug use, then there is an incentive not to seek treatment until it is an absolute last resort, and by then the drug addiction may be extremely serious.

The peacemaking perspective would enlist schools and employers in the treatment process. Students and workers would be subject to sanctions for drug use only to the extent that it interferes with their work. Schools and employers would not attempt to monitor lifestyle but only maintain the standards of productivity that are applicable to everyone. Those who use drugs could seek treatment without fear of castigation or penalty. The war on crime perspective has co-oped the schools and employers to do what the criminal justice system has failed to do: eliminate drug use. The criminal justice system is hampered by the requirement of providing suspects with due process. Schools and employers have lower standards of granting rights to individuals and have successfully cast themselves as institutions of social control well beyond their traditional roles. The peacemaking perspective would restore the more benign relationship between individuals and schools and employers.

The benefits of such a peacemaking perspective in institutions other than the criminal justice system would be long term and positive. In an economy where employers are looking at the bottom line of profits and workers are no longer loyal, the peacemaking perspective can help restore the social fabric that held companies together. The adversarial nature of many work and school environments has caused a deterioration in the sense of community that holds society together. Something important is being lost by the antagonistic relationships between students and workers with their schools and employers. The war on drugs has made this relationship more unwholesome, and we are all the poorer for it. The contributions on the war on drugs to the alienation of individuals to their education and occupations can only be speculated on but it seems evident that asking schools and employers to impose lifestyle limitations is risky.

TOWARD A MORE SANE DRUG POLICY

Drug use and abuse is a social problem and has great implications for the criminal justice system. If the harm of drug abuse is going to be successfully addressed, it will take more than reforming how the criminal justice system responds to drug-related crime. While many individuals favor legalization of drugs, that does not seem to be a policy that is likely to occur in the foreseeable future. One trouble with the legalization concept is the tendency to lump all illegal drugs into the same category. If legalization were presented in a way that only some drugs were considered, there would most likely be greater support. For instance, marijuana has more support in the public arena than do drugs like cocaine and heroin. By considering all these drugs together, we are not able to differentiate the support that may exist for marijuana legalization. Additionally, the operational definition of legalization for different drugs would presumably be different. While some substances such as marijuana might be essentially unrestricted except for minors, other drugs such as heroin might be available only with a doctor's prescription.

The drug legalization debate has not evolved to the point where this level of distinction is being considered. It is stuck with the laws as they currently exist, and legalization is talked about in a simplistic "all or nothing" matter. The peacemaking perspective would argue that the legalization debate should aspire to find ways of reducing the harm done to individuals and society by not only drugs but also by drug laws. Clearly, these issues are much more involved and complicated than they are envisioned by the war on crime drug warriors or by the "legalize everything" drug advocates. Our discussion of drug policy in this chapter has not resolved the main issues, but hopefully we have framed them in such a way that further and more productive analysis can take place.

CRITICAL THINKING QUESTIONS

1. When was the first time you had to make a decision on whether to illegally use drugs or alcohol? What type of influence did your friends have in helping you to make this decision?

2. If you were to completely rewrite the laws concerning drugs and alcohol what changes would you make? What substances that are now legal would you make illegal and what substances that are now illegal would you make legal? Discuss your decisions with the class.

3. Does the government have a right to tell you what you can put in your body? How far should the government be allowed to go in terms of drug testing and searches in enforcing the drug laws?

4. The peacemaking perspective seeks to reduce the harm done to individuals and society by addressing the effects of drug use and the war on drugs. Can these two issues be dealt with simultaneously?

SUGGESTED READINGS

Akers, Ronald L. 1992. *Drugs, Alcohol, and Society: Social Structure, Process, and Policy.* Belmont: Wadsworth.

Alexander, Bruce K. 1990. "Alternatives to the War on Drugs." *The Journal of Drug Issues* 20(1): 1–27.

Anslinger, Harry Jr., and Courtney Ryley Cooper. 1995. "Marijuana: Assassin of Youth," in James A. Inciardi and Karen McElrath, eds. *The American Drug Scene: An Anthology.* Los Angeles: Roxbury, pp. 88–93.

Currie, Elliott. 1993. *Reckoning: Drugs, the Cities, and the American Future.* New York: Hill and Wang.

Gitlin, Todd. 1987. *The Sixties: Years of Hope, Days of Rage.* New York: Bantam Books.

Inciardi, James A. 1986. *The War on Drugs: Heroin, Cocaine, Crime, and Public Policy.* Palo Alto, CA: Mayfield.

Jones, Landon Y. 1980. *Great Expectations: America and the Baby Boom Generation.* New York: Coward, McCann & Geoghegan.

Ray, Oakley, and Charles Ksir. 1993. *Drugs, Society, and Human Behavior,* 6th ed. St. Louis: Mosby.

Rorabaugh, W. J. 1979. *The Alcohol Republic.* New York: Oxford University Press.

9

VIOLENCE

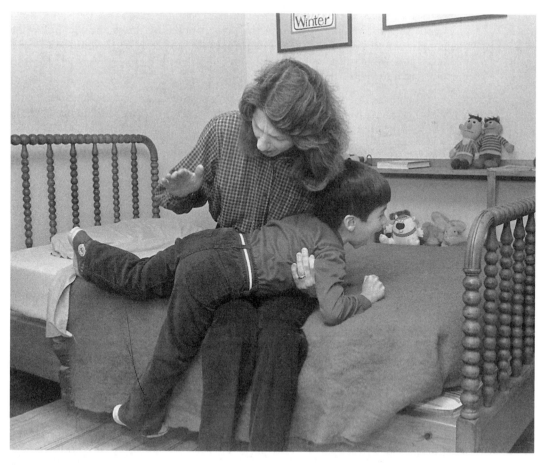

© Paul Fortin/Stock Boston.

Learning Objectives

After reading this chapter, the student should be able to:

- Describe the indicators of the fear of violence in society.
- Discuss the history of violence in the United States.
- Describe how youth are socialized into patterns of violence.
- Discuss the relationship between violence and masculinity.
- Describe the Southern culture of violence theory.
- Discuss the relationship of violence to corporal punishment.
- Discuss the limitations of deterrence in stemming the rate of violence.
- Discuss the relationship of gender to violence.
- Describe how the peacemaking perspective addresses the problem of violence.
- Discuss the strengths and weaknesses of the Broken Window thesis.
- Discuss the most extreme forms of criminal violence: the serial murderers and mass killers.

Key Terms

Interpersonal Violence	Southern Culture of Violence Theory
Institutional Violence	Domestic Terrorism
Drive-By Shootings	Vigilantism
Wilding	Broken Windows Theory
Masculinity	Mass Murder
Socialization	Serial Murderers

Americans have a strange relationship with violence. Even as our criminal justice system struggles to deal with the costly effects of a high rate of violent crime, the saturation of violence in the media through movies and television and the nightly news continues to numb us to the human suffering and pain that is the result. The number of violent acts seen by youngsters watching television numbers in the tens of thousands by the time they reach the age when they go out on the street by themselves and must deal with daily confrontations. Given the level of background violence in our culture, is it any wonder that the youth of America adopted violence as the response of first resort?

Perhaps nowhere has the criminal justice system failed to adequately address its mission as in the area of **interpersonal violence.** Even with an unprecedented percentage of our citizens in prison or under supervision of the criminal justice system, violence on the street continues to frighten Americans to the point where they are willing to go to extreme measures to protect themselves. One need only to look at the increase in the number of gated communities, private security firms, and people carrying guns to get an idea of how the fear of violence pervades our culture. Around the world, the United States has such a bad reputation for violence that cities like New York, Miami, and Los Angeles have worried about the perception of tourists of their cities as unsafe vacation destinations.

The most troubling aspect of the level of perceived violence in this country is the impact it has on our ability to engage in meaningful communities. As more and more individuals lock themselves away from danger, the streets are left to those who would prey on others. It becomes easy for the predator when good people abandon public places. The social fabric of the community is destroyed when people withdraw from interaction because of the fear of crime and violence, and this sets in motion a new cycle of alienation from neighbors, institutions, and society in general.

Where does all this violence come from? Is the United States a more violent country than other developed nations? What do the patterns of violence indicate about how we raise and educate our children? And finally, what can be done to prevent violent behavior, and how can we address the needs of violent offenders? These questions form the basis for the discussion in this chapter. The solutions to the problems of violence are not only beyond the scope of this chapter but have also eluded criminal justice scholars and practitioners for a very long time. This chapter does provide a peacemaking framework for rethinking the issues of violence and suggests the solutions require major changes in the way that not only the criminal justice system deals with violent criminals, but also on how our families, schools, workplaces, and overall society work to create, celebrate, and contribute to a culture of violence.

HISTORY OF VIOLENCE IN THE UNITED STATES

The United States has a particularly violent history (Gurr 1990). The willingness to use force, often deadly force, is deeply ingrained in the national character because of a history that rewarded accomplishment of desired ends over a concern for legitimate and humane means. It is not unfair to say that the willingness to use violence in the founding and settlement of this country has left a legacy of violent behavior that is now dysfunctional in the modern world. The record of the use of violence in the history of the United States is clear.

By now it is evident that historically, American life has been characterized by continuous and often intense violence. It is not merely that violence has accompanied such negative aspects of our history as criminal activity, polit-

ical assassination, and racial conflict. On the contrary, violence has formed a seamless web with some of the most positive events of U.S. history: Independence (revolutionary violence), the freeing of the slaves and the preservation of the union (Civil War violence), the occupation of the land (Indian wars), the stabilization of frontier society (vigilante violence), the elevation of the farmer and the laborer (agrarian and labor violence), the preservation of law and order (police violence). The patriot, the humanitarian, the nationalist, the pioneer, the landholder, the farmer, and the laborer (and capitalist) have used violence as a means to a higher end (Brown 1990, 14–15).

The violence celebrated by war has become a particularly ingrained feature of U.S. culture. Heroes of past wars are enshrined in the national psyche in such a predominant manner that the casual student of history would think that the military is the primary institution in American society. The accomplishments of women and men in other realms of endeavor such as education, commerce, religion, and the arts all pale by comparison to how our military leaders have been lionized. violence, particularly **institutional violence,** is learned by all Americans as a necessary part of our cultural history and a price we must all pay to maintain the legacy we believe is our birthright. The willingness of Americans to go to war, to support capital punishment, to discipline our children by spanking them, and to vicariously enjoy violence portrayed in the media all attest to a violent history that has unquestionably been interwoven into U.S. institutions.

. . . one can argue that the aggrieved in American history have been too quick to revolt, too hastily violent. We have resorted so often to violence that we have long since become a trigger-happy people. Violence is clearly rejected by us as a part of the American value system, but so great has been our involvement with violence over the long sweep of our history that violence has truly become part of our unacknowledged (or underground) value structure . . . (Brown 1990, 15).

How has this national characteristic of violence been translated into the behaviors of individuals? Is history destiny? Are Americans condemned to experience a level of violence of such a high degree that it overshadows all the other positive aspects of our national character? A look at how we are socialized into violence is a look into our future, and according to the prevailing child-rearing practices, we are in big trouble. While violence is certainly complex and multidimensional, it is clear that the United States is regenerating violent individuals with each new generation. As other institutions are failing to educate and care for a sizeable percentage of troubled youth, the criminal and juvenile justice systems are faced with offenders who have a multitude of problems which, if left untreated, will most likely be manifested in some form of emotional or physical violence.

SOCIALIZATION INTO VIOLENCE

Not all people are violent. Certainly we can observe a difference in the level and intensity of the violent behavior of males and females. Violence is also related to age where teenagers and young adults exhibit more than those in middle age and the elderly. Socioeconomic class and certain subcultural statuses also impact on the incidence of violence. What then is responsible for the homicides, rapes, assaults, **drive-by shootings, wilding** sprees, and other episodes of violence that Americans are subjected to on a daily basis?

One answer to this question concerns the dysfunctional American ideal of **masculinity.** To be considered a man in these times, it is necessary to adopt a pattern of behavior that alienates the individual from satisfactory relationships with others and causes critical self-examination and feelings of inferiority. In his book *American Manhood: Transformations in Masculinity from the Revolution to the Modern Era,* E. Anthony Rotundo observes how in the 1800s a "boy culture" developed where young men had a social existence separate from women, girls, and adult males. This boy culture had its own symbols and values that were in opposition to the dominant values of the time. Peer driven, these values emphasized violence and a predatory type of masculinity.

> *This environment existed in part because boy culture sanctioned certain kinds of impulses. Even as it curbed the expression of tender, vulnerable emotions, boy culture stimulated aggression and encouraged youngsters to vent their physical energy. The prevailing ethos of boys' world not only supported the expression of impulses such as dominance and aggression (which had evident social uses), but also allowed the release of hostile, violent feelings (whose social uses are less evident). By allowing free passage to so many angry and destructive emotions, boy culture sanctioned a good deal of intentional cruelty, like the physical torture of animals and the emotional violence of bullying (Rotundo 1993, 45).*

Contemporary manhood requires a set of responses to the culture that were tolerable in the nineteenth century but are inappropriate for the twenty-first century. The manner in which an adolescent proved his masculinity was through rites of passage that were developed for times in the past but which do not relate to current circumstances. Bernstein (1987) argues that there has been a decline in rites of passage in our culture that leaves men with inadequate ways to establish their masculinity. He further contends that as feminism has changed the way women think of themselves, the manner in which they relate to men has changed drastically and that men have been slow to adjust to this change.

> *The growing independence and assertiveness of women has put tremendous pressure on the male. This is evident in the labor market and, increasingly*

so, in the political arena. Most significantly, it has put psychological pressure on men to relate meaningfully with women. There can be little doubt that much of the "encroachment" by women into the masculine domain is resented by men. . . . Women are claiming their femininity, not as reflected by men, but as they experience it themselves (Bernstein 1987, 146).

Rites of passage in earlier times were clear indications of the transition from boyhood to manhood. They involved tests of endurance and courage that were designed to socialize the youth into the adult roles of hunter and warrior. Today, society does not need hunters or warriors in the same way that it once did and, clearly, the attributes desired in young men are different. Enduring physical hardships and displaying great courage are no longer required for routine jobs of insurance salesperson or computer analyst. In addressing this point, Raphael adds:

All this is true, yet many young males today still feel an urge, a yearning, a mysterious drive to prove themselves as men in more primitive terms. Even if traditional initiations no longer appear objectively necessary, the psychological function they once served is still very real. The psychic needs of contemporary males have not always been able to keep pace with sex-role liberation and a computerized economy and nuclear warfare, all of which contribute to the apparent obsolescence of traditional initiations. There is an obvious gap between our rapidly evolving social forms and our internalized, old-fashioned images of manhood (Raphael 1988, xii).

Young men are socialized into a masculinity that emphasizes violence by fathers, older brothers, peers, and by the media. When I was a boy, my older brother (by five years) provided what I now know to be male gender **socialization** by hitting me on the shoulder with his fist. He would hit me without warning, and I was expected to ignore the pain and pretend it didn't hurt. If I cried or whined (which I often did), he would threaten to beat me more severely. "Don't be a wimp," he would say. "Fuller boys don't cry. If you whine I'll give you something to really cry about." This way I learned to hide my pain and emotions and to "be tough." I have another brother who is four years younger than I, and I passed along the gender socialization I had received. I remember being quite satisfied with myself when I would hit him to teach him how to deal with pain and to be a man and not a wimp. I was taught and, in turn, I taught my younger brother that manhood was proven by adopting behaviors that denied pain and emotion and, most importantly, were not feminine. By suppressing feelings and emotions, I developed a traditionally masculine identity which, I now realize, delayed my full development as a human being. It is only in adulthood that I have come to understand the dysfunctional way boys are changed into men in our society.

With the changing nature of relations between men and women and the lack of clear and satisfying ways in which men can establish their masculinity,

Domestic violence is one of the most common reasons the police are called.
(© Richard Lord Ente/The Image Works.)

there is a tension in individuals and in society that all too often is manifested in some kind of violent behavior. Kaufman (1992) talks about the triad of men's violence where men commit violence against themselves, against other men, and against women. The price paid by men for the contemporary ideal of masculinity can be seen not only in self-destructive behaviors of alcoholism, drug abuse, and suicide or in the interpersonal violence between men, but also in the patriarchal violence against women and children. It is only recently that we have come to recognize that domestic violence is part of the dynamics of many families and relationships and that this violence is a result of our culturally-learned images of what it means to be masculine.

INSTITUTIONAL SUPPORT FOR VIOLENCE

Because violence is so pervasive in U.S. society when compared to other developed nations, it is useful to consider how our institutions contribute to the reliance on physical force to solve problems. With violence being a dominant motif of the culture, we can reasonably conclude that individual pathology is not the cause of the unreasonable levels of violent crime. That is, it is not just some "bad apples" giving us a negative reputation, but rather there is something about the cultural reinforcements provided by our institutions that engender violence. An example of this is the historically higher rates of violence in the south as compared to other parts of the country. A body of research has emerged debating the cultural and structural explanations of why the south has higher rates of homicide over most of the country. The evidence for this **Southern culture of violence** thesis is scrutinized by McCall, Land, and Cohen (1992), who find some support for it and point to the shift of high homicide rates to the western region of the country as in need of research to determine if these are factors that can add to a regional subcultural explanation.

At the heart of our institutions is the ideology of patriarchy. From the family to religion to education, the ideal of father-dominated and male-privileged cultural roles is translated into a reliance on discipline, control, and, ultimately, violence as unquestioned and seemingly natural products of our culture. There is an assumed pattern of relationships based on patriarchy which succeeds in ensuring a ready supply of violence-prone citizens in U.S. culture.

The family is the first arena where patriarchy can be seen molding the culture into a violent nature. The reliance on physical punishment of children is a contributing factor to the violence on our street. The axiom "spare the rod, and spoil the child" has attained the status of being a social law of behavior. Parents, particularly fathers, believe children need to be physically punished for their transgressions in order to be socialized into conforming adults. In some families this physical punishment is actually child abuse, but even the accepted spankings in most families teaches a standard of interpersonal violence that is internalized and later played out in unacceptable ways. Like light refracted through a prism, well-meaning violence learned at the hands of parents becomes manifested in distorted ways by children. Patriarchy provides the rationale and justification for physical punishment in the family, and it has only been in recent times that the government has intervened to limit how far parents can go in punishing their children. It is interesting to observe that the healthy discipline many people believe in actually borders on child abuse.

In my classes, I routinely ask my students if they plan to beat their children when they become parents (or, if they are already parents, if they presently beat their children), and they overwhelmingly reply they do not plan to beat their children, but they do plan on spanking them. Getting the students to define the line between beating and spanking is difficult. Some students consider spanking with a weapon such as a belt or brush to be perfectly acceptable, while others consider any use of a weapon as abusive. With few exceptions, the students planned to discipline their children in the same ways their parents disciplined them. It is clear that attitudes toward violence are first learned in the home and that children emulate their parents when deciding what forms of discipline they will use in their homes. Thus, we can witness a cycle of behavior that is supported by the institution of the family (Wallace 1996).

Other societal institutions support the ethic of violence in this country. Schools in the not-too-distant past routinely employed corporal punishment by spanking students with wooden paddles. One need only look at football, basketball, and certain aspects of baseball (the brush-back pitch, for example, when the pitcher throws directly at the batter on purpose) to see how contemporary sports teaches domination and violence. Additionally, many of our sports stars carry their violent proclivities off the basketball court or football field and into the streets or their homes where they victimize innocent people and loved ones. In writing about the seemingly increased incidence of athletes involved in cases of battering wives and girlfriends, Nack and Munson contend sports produce a desire to control and dominate.

> *An athlete cherishes nothing more than control over an opponent, and nothing lifts him higher that the sense that he has attained that control. For the pitcher whose hopping fastball intimidates a batter, for the lineman who muscles a foe to the turf, there is that sensation, the most sublime in sport, that they have established control. "I owned him after that," they all say, "He was all mine." The pursuit of dominance lies at the heart of all athletic contests, and it happens to be the animating force behind men who batter their women (1995, 69).*

The entire rationale behind the military is the institutionalization of violence. And finally, our criminal justice system, the institution responsible for dealing with violent individuals, employs the death penalty as its most visible form of violent punishment.

VIOLENCE AS A SOLUTION TO PROBLEMS

The history of violence in this country and the way violence is imbedded in our institutions and socialization suggests a disturbingly dark side to the American psyche. For a country that claims to love peace, the willingness to resort to violence on many levels indicates that force is viewed not only as an appropriate way to solve problems but also, in many cases, the preferred way. What is it about Americans (and other nationalities as well) that makes us "shoot first and ask questions later?"

The peacemaking perspective can be used to get an idea of why violence has been inappropriately used to solve problems of an interpersonal nature. When people are pitted against each other in the family, at the workplace, in almost all our recreational activities, and in civil life on the street, every transaction starts to become defined as zero-sum. Somebody wins and somebody loses in every interaction, and in a country where people take to heart the old axiom, "Winning isn't the most important thing, winning is everything," then losing becomes unacceptable to many people. The ultimate form of losing is to lose your life, so in important transactions violence becomes the final answer.

So heavy is the cultural emphasis on winning and not losing that deadly violence has become the solution to transactions which, in the past, were resolved by other means. One good example of this is the workplace violence that is all too prevalent these days where men (and it seems to be almost exclusively men) walk into a workplace and kill the wife or girlfriend or kill their boss who fired them. While love is a rocky road for many couples, there are some men who cannot handle the stress of divorce. While careers are important to us all, some men find that losing their job is so catastrophic that they are willing to kill supervisors and, often, themselves also.

Youth gang violence is another example of how violence is often the solution of first resort rather than last. Gangs engage in ritual violence for real or imagined slights from rival gangs. In the past, the violence was limited to less lethal weapons such as fists, knives, and brass knuckles. Today not only do youths use firearms, but they use the most deadly ones available. Shotguns, automatic weapons, and armor-piercing ammunition are employed to make sure that the force used is deadly force.

Finally, we are witnessing an arming of militia groups in this country that is especially alarming. Citizens who have not had interactions with the criminal justice system in the past are buying sophisticated weapons and making and using bombs (e.g., the federal building in Oklahoma City). These individuals are working out some deep-seated animosity against the police and society that most people find difficult to comprehend. In a country that allows for peaceful change via the ballot box, why do some advocate and engage in **domestic terrorism?**

Could it be that all these examples of violence are somehow related? That each is a manifestation of some more basic underlying problem with how individuals in our society have learned to deal with difficult problems? Clearly, if this is the case, the peacemaking perspective has implications for more than just the criminal justice system. Clearly, the peacemaking perspective can be applied to other settings and institutions to help individuals learn to manage problems in a way that is not only more effective but also less deleterious for all involved. The utilization of violence often signals a giving up on the finding of genuine solutions to problems.

RESPONDING TO VIOLENCE

Citizens expect the criminal justice system to respond to the threat of violence in a manner that not only protects against future violence but also projects a feeling of justice and fairness. This means the criminal justice system must appear sufficiently severe in its disposition to provide a sense of closure for the victim and society. Lacking the confidence that the criminal justice system will provide a response that will satisfy the public, individuals may be tempted to impose their own brand of justice on suspected criminals. This threat of **vigilantism** ensures that politicians, prosecutors, and judges attempt to reflect community standards in how violent offenders are treated by the criminal justice system.

We reserve our harshest penalties for those who commit violent crimes. Capital punishment is used almost exclusively for those who commit murder. Occasionally, at the federal level, treason can be a reason for capital punishment and, in the not-too-distant past, rapists were executed. Long prison sentences for drug sales and some "three strikes and you're out" statutes are beginning to crowd the prisons with individuals other than violent criminals but, for the most part, the public expects the dangerous offender to be dealt with the most severely by the criminal justice system. Criminologists, however, have long recognized that long prison sentences and the death penalty do not provide a sufficient deterrent to violent crime. The reasons are complex but at the most basic level it is understood that many violent acts are crimes of passion where the offender does not consider the nature of the sanction. No matter how harsh the sentence, the husband who catches his wife cheating might decide to kill her and her lover and accept the consequences. Pride, anger, and jealousy all provide reasons for individuals to let their passions override their fear of the criminal justice system's sanctions.

How then might the level of violence in society be reduced? If harsh penalties are ineffective then what can be done? The peacemaking perspective suggests that we look for alternatives to violence through prevention, conflict resolution, and treatment. No matter how much we express our outrage to the level of violence through long prison sentences and frequent executions, the level of violent crimes will continue. New criminals will replace those in prison unless the reasons are addressed as to why violence is such a distinguishing feature of this country.

PREVENTION OF HOMICIDE

In looking at why people kill others there are important distinctions that can help us understand the motivations. The relationship between the offender and the victim is one feature that researchers use to distinguish different types of homicides that can have implications for different types of prevention efforts. Zahn (1990) looks at homicides between family members, between friends and acquaintances, and between strangers and then identifies certain prevention strategies based on homicide theories which examine structural, cultural, interactional, or organizational features of society and its institutions. We will review each of these theoretical explanations for violence and Zahn's proscriptions for their prevention. Some of the prevention strategies are applicable to all offender-victim relationships and some are applicable to only one or two.

Structural Reasons and Prevention Strategies

At the structural level, Zahn identifies male dominance as a cultural value related to homicides. Additionally, poverty, the isolation of the nuclear family, institutional racism or racial segregation, relative economic deprivation, and urban density all are contributing factors to homicides. In terms of prevention, she suggests eliminating economic marginality for men and women, eliminating sexual inequality and notions of masculinity as requiring dominance, reducing the isolation of the nuclear family, reducing racial segregation and urban density, and reducing adolescent marginality.

It is clear that Zahn's structural prescriptions require fundamental change in many aspects of society. All of her structural suggestions fit into the peacemaking perspective and begin by advocating social justice in society as being important to addressing violence.

Cultural Reasons and Prevention Strategies

U.S. culture supports many beliefs that can be associated with violence, and changing these beliefs may go a long way in helping to reduce the level of homicide among family members, friends, and even strangers. Zahn identifies these cultural risk factors as sexism and the male belief in physical prowess. Here, men value toughness and control over the female. Alcohol and drug consumption and the availability of weapons, as well as the depiction of violence and support for the "bad guy" in the media, are other cultural risk factors. Additionally, the ethos of nonintervention by witnesses ("I don't want to get involved") and community support for the criminal way of life are factors in U.S. culture (particularly some segments of it) that encourage violence. Zahn's methods of preventing violence by addressing cultural risk factors include reducing alcohol and drug consumption, eliminating guns, increasing the individual's verbal ability and other means of problem solving, reducing media violence, increasing community and witness intolerance for violence, increasing empathy, providing swift and sure criminal justice detection and prosecution of robbery, special handling for those who injure someone, and providing new patterns of police surveillance.

Zahn's cultural prescriptions for violence reduction are, for the most part, within the peacemaking perspective, but she also advocates a war on crime approach for violent offenders by suggesting they be a special target of the criminal justice system. This is not completely incompatible with peacemaking in that it is necessary to ensure public safety. Removing violent predators does not violate what peacemaking perspective advocates would suggest; it is what is to be done with them that is important. The war on crime advocates would call for long prison sentences and the peacemaking advocates would advocate treatment and reintegration into responsible society.

Interactional Reasons and Prevention Strategies

Sometimes people kill others because they lack the skills to interact effectively. They get frustrated when they lose verbal arguments and employ violence to get their way. According to Zahn, particular interactional risk factors include the verbal-skills disparity between husband and wife or between friends, and the resistance of victims in crimes where the offender is a stranger. Prevention techniques identified by Zahn include the teaching of techniques of conflict resolution, including when to walk away from a disagreement, teaching anger control, providing victim education, encouraging witness cooperation and assistance, and increasing the construction of defensible space.

As with the previous structural and cultural risk factors, Zahn envisions interactional risk factors and prevention strategies in a predominantly peacemaking way. Most notable about the way she looks at the problems and solutions to violence is the lack of violent reaction on the part of society. She is not calling for citizens to arm themselves or for the police to kick down the doors of those suspected of violent behavior. Zahn's solutions do not include keeping violent offenders locked away for long periods of time to punish them and deter others.

Finally, Zahn includes an organizational dimension to preventing violence where it concerns spousal homicide. In this type of violent behavior, there may be some times where the criminal justice system and other social service agencies should intervene to help resolve domestic disputes. The dynamics of domestic assault are so explosive and ingrained in the idea that it is a private affair that it is becoming clear that spouses often need an aggressive law enforcement response. Simply responding to a domestic assault call and issuing a warning has sometimes made the situation worse and, nowadays, some states require the offending spouse to be removed from the home if there is evidence of physical harm.

Removing the violent spouse from the home is not incompatible with the peacemaking perspective. A police response does not always resolve the situation. Especially when alcohol is involved, the best response may be to separate the combatants until both are sober and can interact in a rational manner. The conditions for a peaceful settlement must exist before the police can feel confident in leaving a home experiencing domestic violence. The problem with this is that it is a matter of discretion, and the police are not always able to judge when the situation is defused enough to not intervene. Some states have solved this problem by taking the discretion away from the police and have developed a policy where the spouse leaves home and sometimes is taken into custody. It is viewed as better to err on the side of caution and inconvenience the spouse rather than to err on the other side and have the domestic situation flare up again, this time with deadly violence. There is considerable dispute in criminological circles as to the effectiveness and wisdom of this policy. In reviewing the results of one experiment in Minneapolis, Sherman and Berk (1990, 429–430) conclude:

> *Therefore, in jurisdictions that process domestic assault offenders in a manner similar to that employed in Minneapolis, we favor a presumption of arrest; an arrest should be made unless there are good, clear reasons why an arrest would be counterproductive. We do not, however, favor requiring*

arrests in all misdemeanor domestic assault cases. Even if our findings were replicated in a number of jurisdictions, there is a good chance that arrest works far better for some kinds of offenders than others and in some kinds of situations better than others. We feel it best to leave police a loophole to capitalize on that variation.

SAFE STREETS AND EMPTY STREETS

From a public policy perspective, there is an interesting proposal from James Q. Wilson and George L. Kelling (1983) commonly referred to as the **"broken windows"** theory. Wilson and Kelling observe that people develop a meaningful sense of community when they interact with one another and take pride in the ownership of their neighborhoods. When this meaningful sense of community exists, deviant behavior from vagrancy, panhandling, public drunkenness, and serious street crime are less evident than when residents are seen as less interested in the quality of the neighborhood. This is hardly surprising, but Wilson and Kelling see a thread of continuity running through the theory that violent street crime will emerge in neighborhoods where panhandlers and vagrants are allowed to congregate, and that these people will do so when it looks like the residents do not care about their community.

The broken windows thesis is predicated on some observations that if one broken window is left unfixed in a building it serves as a signal to people that no one cares about that building and soon all the windows end up broken. In one fascinating experiment, Zimbardo (Wilson and Kelly 1982) filmed what happened when he left cars abandoned on the street. In one disadvantaged neighborhood, the car was quickly vandalized and then completely stripped of all the parts that had value. In another more affluent neighborhood, his abandoned car remained untouched for days. Zimbardo finally smashed a window in the car and vandalism and theft of parts followed just like in the disadvantaged neighborhood. The broken window acts as a trigger to deviant and unlawful behavior.

From a social standpoint the public drunk, the panhandler, and the guy who wants a dollar to clean your windshield while you're parked at a red light all signify that the streets are up for grabs. When the criminals see that the police and public tolerate this type of nuisance behavior, they follow with drug dealing and mugging. This, in turn, drives more citizens off the street and behind barricaded doors, and soon the community resembles a war zone where only the predators dare to be on the streets.

Taking the streets back from the criminal element is difficult without the cooperation of the public, and the best way to get them to help is to foster a sense of community in the neighborhood. This, of course, becomes a case of circular reasoning unless public policies can be developed that would prevent the street culture from deteriorating. To this end, Wilson and Kelling suggest that the police fix the social broken windows before the citizens lose control of the streets. To do this, the public drunk, the panhandler, and the groups of juvenile loiterers have to be dispersed from the street. Then neighbors will use the parks, visit the shops, and engage in meaningful activities which will reinforce the impression that the neighborhood is going to contest the behavior of those who would commit crime.

The broken windows thesis has great appeal because it gives the streets back to the law-abiding citizens and helps create a civil society where neighbors once again care for each other and conduct affairs in public, enriching the urban scene. There are two issues concerning the broken windows policy that are not fully considered and need to be appraised. The first concerns the legal and moral authority of having the police disperse the public drunk, the panhandler, and the groups of juveniles who loiter on the street corners or in the park. If these undesirable "street people" are not breaking any laws, then what right do we have to instruct the police to make them leave public spaces? They are citizens also and, even though they may seem to be a nuisance and a threat, they have a right to be on the street. Giving the police discretion to remove people from the street simply because they are undesirable presents a problem in who decides what constitutes being undesirable. The police could easily abuse such broad discretion and violate the civil rights of young people, minorities, and lower-class individuals whose dress and automobiles do not match community standards.

There is a second concern with the broken windows thesis that has not been fully considered. If all of these undesirable people are chased from public places, where do they go? While it may be possible to make some areas more safe, dispersing the street people simply results in them moving to another street. Crime is not so much prevented as it is displaced. Some public places that enjoy a stepped-up police presence will certainly become safer, but the police do not have the resources to enforce a ban on undesirable street people throughout a large city, and the problems will simply be chased from one part of the city to another.

The broken window thesis can be scrutinized from a war on crime and a peacemaking perspective. It fits nicely into the war on crime perspective, which advocates getting tough on criminals and giving our public places back to the law-abiding citizens. The get-tough policy would rigorously enforce the broken windows thesis to the point of augmenting the police force and swelling the jails with misdemeanants swept up in the enforcement of the broken windows policy. It would be effective in reducing crime up to a point but would result in crime displacement and in violating the civil rights of people whose only offense is to be undesirable. There could be problems in the police abusing their discretion.

The broken window thesis can also be considered from a peacemaking perspective. It fits nicely with the peacemaking emphasis on community building and making public places safe for everyone. The problem the peacemaking perspective would have with the way Wilson and Kelling present their broken window thesis is in the reliance of law enforcement to solve the problem. The peacemaking perspective would address the undesirable people on the streets and public places not by chasing them off but by including them in the community and helping them to become integrated into the community in meaningful ways. Homeless shelters, job training programs, and youth recreation centers would provide better methods for dealing with the low-level deviants that are presumed by Wilson and Kelling to be the precursors to violent crime.

It is nonsense to believe that the conditions that breed crime can simply be chased away. The broken window thesis may be right in specifying that violent crime will flourish in neighborhoods where good people have abandoned the streets, but it is mistaken in its belief that law enforcement can remedy the situation. Community building will work in the long run only when everyone is made part of the community. Deviant people cannot be simply chased away or incarcerated. They must somehow become part of the solution.

SERIAL KILLERS AND MASS MURDERERS

Two types of violence that are comparatively rare but that capture the imagination of people and the media are the high-profile serial killing and **mass murder** cases. When the subject of violence is discussed, it is these extreme cases that are used as examples of the dangers on the street and the justification for public policy issues such as capital punishment and opposition to gun control. In considering how the peacemaking perspective might improve the criminal justice system, students will invariably ask, "Well, what about Ted Bundy or Jeffrey Dahmer? How can the peacemaking perspective help with people like that who are obviously insane?" Because most of us cannot conceive of committing these sensational behaviors, we are quick to label such people as insane and crazy. We are quick to use these examples of excessive violence to promote quick-fix solutions to more fundamental problems of social control. The mass murderer and serial killer phenomena are largely media creations that are burdened with myth and misconceptions.

The most level-headed book on the subject is Eric Wakem Hickey's (1997) *Serial Murderers and Their Victims*. In this influential survey of what we know and do not know about this type of violence, Hickey dispels the myths and debunks the stereotypes that surround *serial murderers*. What Hickey found is interesting because he concludes that what we do not know about serial killing is much greater than what we do know. The stereotypes and myths we use to advocate criminal justice policy are so flawed that we would do better to recognize that our strategies are based on emotion and bias rather than on any real appreciation of this type of violence. Hickey presents a fascinating array of profiles of serial killers and finds such a diversity of personalities that it is unproductive to attempt to identify individuals who might be serial killers before they actually commit these atrocious acts. Hickey interviewed the mother and brother of Jeffrey Dahmer, and they had absolutely no inkling of his deviant personality.

In terms of what can be done about serial killings, Hickey concludes that because we know so little about the causes, there is little we can do to prevent serial killings. Hickey is pragmatic about what we should do with these offenders.

> *We execute in the name of justice, for revenge, for punishment, for protection, to reduce recidivism, and a host of other often emotional reasons. These reasons seem to become clearer when we are faced with a case of multiple homicide. Aside from the moral and philosophical issues surrounding the death sentence, if American society is going to use capital punishment, then serial offenders, who are by far the most dangerous offenders, should be first to qualify for execution. If capital punishment is not to be used, then we must ensure that serial killers remain securely confined (Hickey 1997, 268).*

There are a number of suggestions that Hickey advances to enable us to develop a better appreciation of serial murder. With a little imagination we could alter and expand this list to include other types of violence. Regardless, Hickey's (1997, 273) list illustrates what it would take to even begin to understand how little we know about deviant behavior.

1. Increased interaction and involvement between academicians and law enforcement in the form of seminars and workshops
2. Increased cooperation between law enforcement agencies to improve the circulation of data regarding violent criminal offenders
3. Increased training of local and state law enforcement personnel in respect to serial murder and profiling
4. Increased empirical research into all facets of serial murder to further our understanding of the offenders and victims
5. To debunk and challenge many of the myths and stereotypes that surround serial murderers and their victims
6. To generate an acceptable operational definition of serial murder that will inevitably reduce confusion among governmental and private agencies
7. To explore improving methodological issues in data collection and analysis of multiple-homicide offenders
8. To examine prevention strategies using a team of experts, including law enforcement, social services, and medical, psychiatric, and academic personnel
9. To create public-awareness programs that filter information in a rational and responsible manner
10. To allow for greater accessibility to incarcerated serial killers through the establishment of special research programs and projects
11. To establish projects funded by the federal government specifically for the advancement of multiple-homicide research

There is a need for the greater understanding of violence and the steps Hickey espouses for studying serial killings is a useful beginning. While science has its limitations in dealing with issues of social behavior, we have not really funded the types of programs and research efforts that might be able to identify and predict violent behavior. There are a number of political, legal, and ethical issues that would have to be addressed, but as Hickey has shown us in his book, the poverty of our knowledge about violence and its prevention is considerable and the demand to do something about it is enormous.

CRITICAL THINKING QUESTIONS

1. When you have children will you discipline them in the same manner as your parents did with you? Where do you draw the line between healthy discipline and child abuse? Discuss these questions in class and determine to what extent you agree and disagree about the answers.

2. Are men more violent than women? Discuss the relationship between gender and violence and suggest reasons for your findings. Are there other sociological differences in patterns of violence such as race, class, or age?

3. If we accept the adage that violence begets more violence, what nonviolent policies can the government use to address deviant behavior?

4. If you were able to write one law that addressed the issue of interpersonal violence, what would you suggest? What types of resources and money would it take to fully enact your law?

SUGGESTED READINGS

Brown, Richard Maxwell. 1990. "Historical Patterns of American Violence," in Neil Alan Weiner, Margaret Zahn, and Rita J. Sagi, eds. *Violence: Patterns, Causes, and Public Policy.* San Diego: Harcourt Brace Jovanovich, pp. 4–14.

Gurr, Ted Robert. 1990. "Historical Trends in Violent Crime: A Critical Review of the Evidence," in Neil Alan Weiner, Margaret Zahn, and Rita J. Sagi, eds. *Violence: Patterns, Causes, and Public Policy.* San Diego: Harcourt Brace Jovanovich.

Hickey, Eric W. 1997. *Serial Murderers and Their Victims,* 2nd ed. Belmont, CA: Wadsworth.

McCall, Patricia L., Kenneth C. Land, and Lawrence E. Cohen. 1992. "Violent Criminal Behavior: Is There a General and Continuing Influence of the South?" *Social Science Research 21*(3): 286–310.

Rotundo, E. Anthony. 1993. *American Manhood: Transformations in Masculinity from the Revolution to the Modern Era.* New York: Basic Books.

Wallace, Harvey. 1996. *Family Violence: Legal, Medical, and Social Perspectives.* Boston: Allyn and Bacon.

Wilson, James Q., and George L. Kelling. 1993. "Broken Windows," in Roger G. Durham and Geoffrey P. Alpert, eds. *Critical Issues in Policing: Contemporary Issues,* 2nd ed. Prospect Heights: Waveland.

10

GUN CONTROL

© By Sygma.

Learning Objectives

After reading this chapter, the student should be able to:

- Discuss the second amendment of the Constitution.
- Discuss how the Supreme Court has interpreted the second amendment.
- Discuss arguments for gun control.
- Describe how police are often outgunned by criminals.
- Discuss the problems of gun accidents in the home.
- Discuss arguments against gun control.
- Discuss Gary Kleck's argument for defensive gun use.
- Discuss the provisions of the Brady Bill gun-control legislation.
- Discuss the limitations of the Brady Bill.
- Discuss the peacemaking perspective on gun control.
- Describe how the gun culture in the United States would need to change for gun-control legislation to be effective.

Key Terms

Well-Regulated Militia	Defensive Gun Use
Gun Control	Brady Bill
Militia Groups	Federally Licensed Gun Dealer

Sometimes when I'm driving down the highway and a car in front of me turns without signaling, brakes suddenly for no apparent reason, or simply goes too slow for my liking, I point my finger as if it were a pistol and, in my mind, "shoot" the car and make it disappear. This is a reaction many of us instinctively have when someone displeases us. One of the most recurrent gestures in child's play is to turn fingers into "pistols" to shoot their playmates. The mimicking of shooting a gun seems almost second nature to Americans, even to those who have never fired one. Problems are easy to solve when all you have to do is point your finger, whisper "bang" and wish people, if not dead, then at least out of your sight. The simulated shooting of those who annoy us is deeply ingrained in the American character, which has been conditioned by a long history of experience with guns and a more recent bombardment of media glorification of gun crime. One need only look at the play of young children to see how early in life a finger comes to represent a gun.

To say that guns are as American as apple pie is no doubt true, but in so saying it is important to remember that the problems linked to guns are also part of the culture. Additionally, it is important to consider just how destructive the gun culture is to the country and how the devastation caused by rampant gun use might be diminished.

The criminal justice system is forced to deal with the proliferation of gun violence without adequate safeguards for the control of guns and the protection of law enforcement officers and the public. The proponents of guns have created an atmosphere where the police are faced with massive firepower in the hands of children and criminals and are forced to use bulletproof vests as their primary means of protection. When the criminals and delinquents are so heavily armed it makes the streets less safe for all citizens. The contrasting war on crime and peacemaking perspectives each have something to say about the issue of gun violence. Not surprisingly, they come to different conclusions about how violent gun crime should be addressed. One idea of the war on crime perspective would require each citizen to have a gun in the home (this law has recently been passed but is not strictly enforced in Kennesaw, Georgia), while the peacemaking perspective would attempt to reduce the number of guns in society and strictly limit their availability to children, criminals, and the mentally ill. Before we examine just how the competing perspectives deal with guns, it is useful to consider just how ingrained gun ownership is in the history of the country.

THE LEGACY OF FIREARMS IN THE UNITED STATES

Any student of U.S. history is well acquainted with the role firearms played in the making of the country. From the earliest days of the colonies, the gun was used to procure food and for self-defense. Additionally, firearms were used as offensive weapons to wrest control of the frontier from Native Americans who found the encroachment on their lands by the colonists to be invasive to their way of life. It is hard to imagine how the country could have been taken from its original peoples without the use of guns. The advantage in warfare that the gun provided to the European colonizers allowed the conquest of desirable land all over the globe. The British, Dutch, French, Spanish, and, later, settlers and colonists throughout the world all used their superior technology to take land and resources from indigenous peoples. The historical legacy of firearms as part of the frontier is deeply ingrained in our conception of ourselves as a people. The fact that the frontier disappeared into shopping malls and tract housing has had little effect on the tradition of gun use in the country. Time and circumstances that once required guns have changed and some now argue that the wide availability of firearms now puts us all at risk rather than serving as protection.

A Well-Regulated Militia

Those who claim the individual has a right to possess a firearm cite the second amendment to the Constitution which says the government shall not infringe on the right of the state to have a **well-regulated militia.** After the heavy-handed rule of England, the colonists were weary of ceding to the federal government too much power. Each state sought to preserve the power to maintain its own militia in order to ensure its liberty, not only from foreign powers but also from the power of the federal government. In the United States of 1781, the joining of the colonies was a delicate task, and the framers of the Constitution tried to balance the requirements of the new country with the concerns citizens had with entering into an agreement that would limit their freedoms and expose them to government regulations they deemed unacceptable. The right to bear arms, given the historical circumstances, was intended in the second amendment, according to Halbrook (1986), not only for the state militia but also for the individual. Life in colonial times required weapons for supplying food and ensuring defense in remote areas where the government and neighbors were too far away to provide security. According to Spitzer (1995):

> *Settlers found it necessary to band together to provide for mutual defense from foreign armies and hostile Indians. This reliance on volunteer militias, instead of a regular, standing army was based on two facts of life. First, the emerging American nation did not possess the manpower or resources to raise, finance, supply, or maintain a professional army. Second, Americans shared a profound mistrust of standing armies. This suspicion stemmed from their knowledge of and experiences with standing armies in European history, where with depressing regularity professional armies had subverted or overthrown civilian governments and deprived people of basic rights (27).*

In the *Federalist Papers,* Alexander Hamilton and James Madison argued that the new country should maintain a standing army of 30,000 men which would not be a threat to the states whose militias totaled half a million. The aim of those debating the wording of the Constitution was to strike a balance between the power of the federal government and its standing army and the ability of the states to maintain their own militias. The balance was achieved by the second amendment, which reads, "A well regulated militia, being necessary to the security of a free State, the right of the people to keep and bear arms, shall not be infringed."

Absent from the discussion of the second amendment was any consideration of the right of the individual to bear arms for personal reasons, such as personal protection, hunting, or recreation. According to Spitzer (1995, 36), these freedoms were covered by eighteenth-century common law and were outside of the debate concerning the balance between the new federal government and its relationship to the states.

> *In sum, the possession of firearms referred to in the Second Amendment comes into play only at such time as (1) the unorganized militia is activated by a state or the federal government, a practice effectively abandoned before the Civil War; and (2) the government fails to provide weapons for that*

force. Thus the Second Amendment has been rendered essentially irrelevant to modern American life, as is the prospect of, say, National Guard troops from New York and Pennsylvania squaring off against each other, weapons at ready, along state borders (Spitzer 1995, 38).

The second amendment has provoked surprising little comment from the Supreme Court. It has been the subject of only five rulings:

United States v. Cruikshank, 92 U.S. 542 (1876), involved a case where the defendants were charged with depriving blacks of their constitutional rights, including the right to bear arms. The Court ruled that the second amendment pertain only to federal power and that Congress cannot infringe on the right to bear arms but the states can.

Presser v. Illinois, 116 U.S. 252 (1886), was a case where the defendant developed his own (armed) fringe group and paraded and drilled through the streets of Chicago. The court ruled the second amendment applied only to militias organized by the state or federal government and not to private armies. The right to bear arms is not extended to protect citizens' right to own weapons for their own purposes.

Miller v. Texas, 153 U.S. 535 (1894), and *Robertson v. Baldwin, 165 U.S. 275 (1897),* involved cases where states had passed laws prohibiting the carrying of dangerous weapons and the Court ruled the second amendment applied to Congress and not to the individual states. Therefore, states were free to pass gun-control legislation without fear of violating the individual's constitutional rights.

United States v. Miller, 307 U.S. 174 (1939), involved a case where the defendants carried an unregistered 12-gauge sawed-off shotgun across state lines, violating the National Firearms Act of 1934. The defendants claimed the second amendment protected their actions. The Court ruled that citizens could possess a constitutional right to bear arms only in connection with service in a militia and that the federal government and the states have the authority to regulate firearms. The defendants failed to demonstrate how their shotgun was related to any militia activity.

Clearly, the right of the individual citizen to bear arms is not protected by the second amendment of the constitution. Both the federal government and the states have the authority to pass limitations on the use of weapons. If the second amendment was interpreted the way opponents to **gun control** claim then we would each have the right to own tanks, guided missiles, and nuclear weapons. One fascinating aspect of this debate pertains to the emergence of local militias across the country. These groups are not part of the government and therefore are not protected by the second amendment. Furthermore, it would be hard to argue that these groups are well-regulated in that they often are no more than a rabble of men playing soldier.

ARGUMENTS FOR GUN CONTROL

Those who argue that we should do more to control firearms in this country contend that both the quantity and type of weapons available today are making the country an unsafe environment in which to live. The rate of firearm crime, accidents, and suicides convinces many that further steps need to be taken by the government to limit the number and kinds of weapons available to so many citizens. There are numerous proposals which cover a wide range of weapons to be controlled or banned and which have a variable level of support. There are legitimate concerns from parents, schools, police, and the public about public safety that are driving the demand that firearms be restricted.

Are the Police Outgunned?

The occupation of law enforcement officer has become more dangerous in the past generation because of the availability of automatic weapons. Despite advancements in communications and technology the police often find themselves at a tactical disadvantage when confronting criminals and drug dealers who possess sophisticated weapons which go beyond what we think of as necessary for hunting, recreation, or self-defense. The type of automatic weapons appearing on the street are more suited for the battlefield than for legitimate private use. Law enforcement officers are restricted in what weapons they can carry and are at a decided disadvantage when facing the criminal, gang member, or mentally deranged person carrying more firepower than a World War II infantry squad.

Automatic pistols and rifles are offensive weapons. They are of little use in hunting or sporting activities because what is gained in firepower is lost in accuracy. The term automatic means one has just to hold the trigger and bullets will continuously be fired at a very rapid rate. When we refer to machine guns we mean automatic weapons. The M-16 and AK-47, which became well known during the Vietnam War, are automatic weapons which gun enthusiasts like to collect. Semiautomatic means the trigger has to be pulled each time a bullet is shot. Many semiautomatic weapons can easily be converted to automatic with little trouble. The most important feature of automatic and semiautomatic weapons is the size of the clip available to hold the bullets. By having a ready supply of bullets available the weapon can dispense a vast amount of firepower without having to be reloaded. This gives a tremendous advantage in a gun fight over a more conventional revolver-type pistol.

Automatic weapons are useful in a military situation where firepower can suppress the movement of enemy troops. In a domestic situation automatic weapons mean innocent bystanders may be hurt or more victims killed by a disturbed person. For self-defense of the home there are other, more conventional weapons which are suitable.

Another issue that gun control advocates propose is a ban on the so-called cop-killer bullets. These are teflon-coated bullets that have amazing penetrating power. They are reportedly able to go through a bullet proof vest, which makes law enforcement officers at risk when they conduct raids on criminal establishments. Again, there is little legitimate need for these types of bullets as deer and other game animals do not wear bullet-proof garments. As law enforcement officers are prevented from using these types of bullets they are at a decided disadvantage when they must face a criminal element that has no such limitations.

Finally, there is the issue of plastic guns. These are weapons that do not have metal parts and therefore will not show up on X-rays or be discovered by metal detectors. Individuals with legitimate reasons for carrying a weapon do not need plastic guns. While they are lightweight their primary utility is escaping detection. When proposals are put forth to require gun manufacturers to place barium (a contrast medium which shows up in X-rays) in guns, they are opposed by the gun lobby. The legitimate concerns for safety among law enforcement officers suggests that limits placed on the availability of automatic weapons, cop-killer bullets, and plastic guns. The balance between the concerns of sportsmen and public safety surely lean towards the restriction of these devices.

Guns in the Home

Proponents of gun control question the usefulness of firearms in the home for self defense. They argue that the gun is more likely to cause harm to you or your family than it is to some would-be intruder. The incidents of accidents and suicides are far greater than the incidents of someone attacking your home with a firearm. Why then do so many people keep guns in their home for the purpose of protection? The answer is more closely related to people's fear of crime than the actual rates of crime itself. Many who keep guns in their homes live in areas that experience little or no crime. These individuals like the sense of security that having a firearm gives them even though the chances they will ever need to use it for self-defense is statistically remote. Conversely, many individuals who live in high-crime areas where a firearm may be needed to provide security do not possess one. Guns are not evenly distributed across the country and the patterns of who has them are not related to the potential for violence.

Using a firearm to protect the home is highly problematic. There are several scenarios that illustrate the possible consequences of firearms in the home.

1. You are awakened by a noise in your living room and you retrieve your pistol from the top drawer of your dresser and go to investigate. Upon flipping on your light switch you discover an armed intruder who fires at you and misses. You drop behind the couch and return fire, killing the intruder.

This is the scenario most people envision when they consider purchasing a firearm.

2. An unarmed intruder enters your home and you fail to wake up. In looking through your top dresser drawer the intruder finds your pistol and either uses it on you and your family, or takes it and fences it along with the other items stolen from your home.

3. Your five-year-old son and two playmates are exploring your bedroom when they discover your pistol in the top drawer of your dresser. Your son knows better than to touch the weapon but one of his playmates picks it up and it goes off, killing your son.

4. Your teenage son has just had a bad day. He is cut from the football team, dumped by his girlfriend, has flunked an algebra test, and wishes he could escape from all his problems. He remembers about the pistol in the top drawer of your dresser and uses it to kill himself.

5. You get into a heated argument with your spouse. One of you grabs the gun from the top drawer of the dresser and threatens the other. The one without the gun confidently proclaims "You don't have the guts to shoot me." The gun goes off.

These scenarios are provided to show that firearms have many uses, not all of which the owner intends. Proponents of gun control contend that the more firearms there are in the community the more violence that occurs. For instance, in the case of suicide the argument is that less guns would result in fewer suicide attempts and fewer successful attempts.

The key policy question is whether the availability of guns in and of itself enhances the likelihood of suicide. That is, if guns were not available, would individuals simply turn to other means (a phenomenon labeled "displacement")? This question takes on added importance when we note that from 1968 to 1985, firearms suicides increased 36 percent, whereas the suicide rate from other methods remained the same.

A growing list of studies have addressed this question. First, virtually all researchers agree that restricting gun availability does result in fewer gun suicides (Spitzer 1995, 72).

It may be that in the case of suicide limiting the availability of guns will do little good if people turn to other methods. While guns are more lethal, it is hazardous to contend those seriously contemplating killing themselves will not turn to other methods. Drugs are readily available, rivers, lakes and oceans nearby, and tall buildings or mountain cliffs accessible to nearly everyone. To restrict guns on the basis of their preponderance in cases of suicides most likely would be a policy that probably fails to adequately understand the dynamic of suicide. Guns certainly mean the attempt has a better chance of being successful and for impulsive individuals that may be significant, but banning guns will not solve the suicide problem in this country.

While there may be an association between firearms and violence it is not at all clear there is a direct causal relationship that shows more firearms equals more violence. The direction of the relationship may very well be in the opposite direction. As there is more and more violence in the community, individuals may be more likely to purchase a firearm for protection.

The war on crime perspective would support the proposition that people should protect themselves and that criminals are not the only ones who should have access to firearms. The war on crime perspective would ensure that law-abiding citizens are able to combat threatening behavior and by being armed with a firearm may deter aggression.

The peacemaking perspective on crime would argue that the fewer weapons there are in society the better off we will all be in terms of public safety. The possibility of alternative scenarios to what gun owners intend is always present and many of these scenarios (accidents, domestic violence, suicide) are common occurrences. Logically, from a peacemaking perspective, limiting the availability of firearms would reduce the level of death and injury in the community. Empirically, really observing this premise to be accurate is another matter. It is harder to demonstrate. Nevertheless, the argument that more guns would result in less violence is one that would be rejected by peacemaking criminologists.

ARGUMENTS AGAINST GUN CONTROL

Firearms hold a particular fascination for Americans. The freedom to own and bear arms is one of the most cherished beliefs among a wide variety of citizens who are not only law-abiding but in many cases represent law enforcement officers, teachers, store owners, and others who might wish to limit firearm availability. One of the arguments that anti-gun-control individuals espouse is that firearms cannot be held accountable for decisions that human beings make. The adage "Guns don't kill, people do," reflects the fact that violence is a problem of humans, not of technology. There was violence between people long before guns were invented and even in the absence of guns, those who wish to harm other individuals will find a way.

To take guns away from the vast majority of responsible owners in order to deprive the irresponsible or the criminal is not only unjust, according to gun proponents, but also ineffective. The disarming of America would be an impossible task and would likely result in the disarming only of those who use guns for legitimate means. The predatory criminal who would use a gun to rob and kill is unlikely to voluntarily surrender a firearm to authorities. The popular bumper sticker which reads, "If guns are outlawed, only outlaws will have guns," reflects a commonly held belief that effective gun control would not be possible and would leave the good citizen at the mercy of the criminal.

The logistics of disarming the population are staggering to consider. Given that those most likely to violate the law would be least likely to give up

The National Rifle Association is a powerful opponent of gun control proposals. (© AP/Wide World Photos.)

their guns, it would take a massively intrusive campaign of home searches, which is not either politically feasible nor socially desirable. When we consider the experience of alcohol prohibition we can imagine how attempting to take guns away from people would potentially result in violence and would certainly result in people viewing the government as an enemy rather than as having their best interests in mind.

There is another disturbing aspect to the popular opposition to gun control and that is the belief among a small number of people who see the government as threatening the liberty of citizens. These people want to keep their guns as protection against a government which they believe has over-stepped its authority and oppresses citizens. The incidents at the Branch Davidian complex in Waco, Texas, and at Ruby Ridge in Idaho, illustrates how alienated some people are from the government. The rise of local so-called militas further reflects the distrust some people have in the federal government especially, but also in state and local governments as well. These people see any form of gun control as a direct attempt to prevent them from defending themselves from what they consider to be a government that has strayed from the freedoms assured by the Constitution.

The most frightening aspect of these **militia groups** and their fringe supporters is not just the guns they stockpile but also the explosives. The bombing of the federal building in Oklahoma City may be an isolated incident by a few individuals but the antigovernment attitude is reflective of a growing number of groups that espouse opposition to big government and a position of resistance to any type of control on what weapons citizens are allowed to possess.

The most convincing argument against gun control is that in the United States it just will not work. Because of the long history of gun availability, it is reasoned, Americans will never be willing to give up their weapons and any attempt to make them do so is doomed to failure. The logistics of locating, much less confiscating the millions of guns owned by Americans is staggering. Furthermore, the guns we would most likely take off the street, those belonging to criminals and youth, are the ones we are least likely to be successful in procuring. If we take firearms away from responsible citizens are we making our communities less safe because the criminal will have little to fear when committing crimes? This issue is particularly sensitive when we talk about home safety. Opponents of gun control argue that criminals are deterred by the possibility of being confronted by a homeowner with a gun. Burglars are more likely to select vacant homes rather than occupied ones because of the risk of getting shot. Criminals have reported they are more concerned with confronting an armed resident than the chance occurrence the police will show up. Guns are viewed as a protection of last resort and are likely to be part of the discussion on public safety for a long time.

> *If predatory crime can be reduced, hopefully without sacrificing democratic values, the private resort to violence should decline. In the meanwhile, the widespread legal use of guns against criminals will persist as long as Americans believe crime is a serious threat and that they cannot rely completely on the police as effective guardians. Until then, scholars interested in gun control, crime deterrence, victimology, the routine activities approach to crime, and in social control in general need to consider more carefully the significance of millions of potential crime victims armed with deadly weapons (Kleck 1991, 142).*

One problem with Kleck's argument that guns in the home are an effective deterrent to crime is he ignores the fact that most burglars do not break into homes that appear to be occupied. Guns in homes that are not occupied not only fail to provide any deterrent effect but also become targets of theft. There is a sizeable black market for illegal guns which then find the in way into the hands of criminals. It is hazardous to conclude, as Kleck does, that the availability of legal firearms has a positive impact on crime. The line between legal and illegal is largely illusionary because firearms change hands easily and quickly and the weapon may have many owners and be used for a wide range of purposes.

It is hard to evaluate just how effective a firearm in the home is in proving safety because of the problem of accessibility. If a firearm is sufficiently protected by being hidden and locked up then the likelihood that it will be available when needed against an armed intruder is remote. Likewise, if it is readily accessible then the risk of accidents, especially if youngsters are in the home, is increased. Given the infrequent occasions when most individuals would need to protect their home with a gun, it is probable that most firearms are not within reach on those rare occurrences when one might be useful.

Outside the home the use of firearms takes on a different dimension that makes some of Kleck's arguments much harder to dismiss. Contending that criminologists have traditionally viewed street violence from a simplistic belief that it is usually a case of mutual combat between lower-class males where one is the victim and the luckier one the offender, Kleck and Gertz (1995) argue the point that a good deal of firearm violence is one-sided. In cases such as felony killings linked to armed robberies, burglaries, sexual assaults, contract killings, mass killings, and serial murders, it is the outlaw alone who has the gun and many of these incidents could end in a different result if citizens would have been able to use defensive force comparable to the firearm threat they faced.

The argument that defensive use of firearms has an important impact on protecting individuals from predators is worthy of consideration. Kleck and Gertz (1995) have done their homework and are able to provide not only a convincing rationale for their claims but also solid empirical support. They contend that **defensive gun use** has saved lives, thwarted rape attempts, driven off burglars, and helped victims retain their property. The law-abiding citizen is protected against predators by carrying a firearm and to pass restrictive gun control would likely mean the criminal would gain an advantage. The bumper sticker slogan *If guns are outlawed, only outlaws would have guns,* would have serious implications for the defensive gun-use thesis proposed by Kleck and Gertz.

> Since as many as 400,000 people a year use guns in situations where the defenders claim that they "almost certainly" saved a life by doing so, this result cannot be dismissed as trivial. If even one-tenth of these people are accurate in their stated perceptions, the total number of lives saved by victim use of guns would still exceed the total number of lives taken by guns. It is not possible to know how many lives are actually saved this way, for the simple reason that no one can be certain how crime incidents would have turned out had the participants acted differently than they actually did. But surely this is too serious a matter to simply assume that practically everyone who believes he saved a life by using a gun was wrong (Kleck and Gertz 1995, 180–181).

These conclusions reached by Kleck and Gertz are certainly important to the gun-control debate. While advocates of gun control are quick to detail how guns take lives, most opponents to gun control have argued that they have a constitutional right to bear arms regardless if criminals use guns to commit crimes. Kleck and Gertz give us an interesting twist to the gun-control debate by providing an empirical argument that guns actually save lives. One is tempted to try to find fault with the way Kleck and Gertz did their survey research. The renowned criminologist Marvin Wolfgang who asserts "I hate guns—ugly, nasty instruments designed to kill people," has given the Kleck and Gretz research a grudging endorsement.

> *What troubles me is the article by Gary Kleck and Marc Gertz. The reason I am troubled is that they have provided an almost clearcut case of method-ologically sound research in support of something I have theoretically opposed for years, namely the use of a gun in defense against a criminal per-petrator. Maybe Franklin Zimring and Philip Cook can help me find fault with the Kleck and Gertz research, but for now, I have to admit my admi-ration for the care and caution expressed in this article and this research (Wolfgang 1995, 188).*

An endorsement by Marvin Wolfgang should be all that is needed to vali-date criminological research. He is certainly one of the most respected schol-ars in criminology. Kleck and Gretz's research does, however, need to be closely subjected to follow-up efforts to determine if their results can be replicated. Additionally, their conclusions are based on only 213 cases with complete information. Although they used a sophisticated sampling method, this is still a relatively modest number of cases from which to draw conclusions. Can their 213 cases where they carefully gathered information be extrapolated to 400,000 incidents each year where guns have saved lives? One other method-ological issue which bears examination is the way they define defensive gun use. For Kleck and Gertz (1995, 162–63) in order for an incident to be consid-ered defensive gun use, it had to meet all of the following qualifications:

1. The incident involved defensive action against a human rather than an animal, but not in connection with police, military, or security-guard duties.
2. The incident involved actual contact with a person, rather than merely investigating suspicious circumstances, etc.
3. The defender could state a specific crime he thought was being commit-ted at the time of the incident.
4. The gun was actually used in some way—at a minimum it had to be used as part of a threat against a person, either by verbally referring to the gun (e.g., "get away—I've got a gun") or by pointing it at an adversary.

By defining defensive gun use as saying "get away—I got a gun" and then contending that a life has been saved or a rape attempt thwarted requires a leap of logic. It may be true, and certainly the respondent may believe it true, but the reader should pay attention to the qualifying language presented by Kleck and Gertz. With such a fuzzy definition of defensive gun use and only 213 cases, Kleck and Gertz have merely opened the debate rather than resolved it. Is gun availability more beneficial than harmful to society? The jury is still out on this question.

It is interesting to speculate on how firearm availability in the net effect either makes our society more dangerous or more safe. From a peacemaking perspective the fewer firearms in the hands of citizens, the less likely they will be used for crime. It can also be argued, from a war on crime perspective, that guns prevent as much sorrow as they cause. Kleck (1991) argues:

> *Much of social order in America may depend on the fact that millions of people are armed and dangerous to each other. The availability of deadly weapons to the violence-prone may well contribute to violence by increasing the probability of a fatal outcome of combat . . . However, it may also be that this very fact raises the stakes in disputes to the point where only the most incensed or intoxicated disputants resort to physical conflict, with the risks of armed retaliation deterring attack and coercing minimal courtesy among otherwise hostile parties (143).*

This type of argument may have some validity but from the peacemaking perspective it is doomed to make our streets less and less safe. If every home is an armed camp and every individual carrying deadly firearms it is easy to conclude that our society is more dangerous than alternative scenarios would provide. From a peacemaking perspective the goal should not be to arm to the teeth each citizen, but to disarm the criminals. The collateral violence that accompanies so many firearms can only have deleterious effects on the community.

REALISTIC GUN CONTROL

Much of the disagreement about proposals concerning gun control centers around what can be called "the camel's nose under the tent" problem. Those who are worried that the government's agenda is to completely disarm all citizens use this analogy to forestall any type of firearms restriction. Just as the rest of the camel will be in the tent if you allow him to stick his nose in, then any type of gun control will result in a total ban according to this line of thinking. By taking such an extreme point of view, gun-control opponents frame the debate in an all-or-nothing decision and are able to generate wide support from hunters, sportsmen, and those concerned about their safety. Urban mayors, law enforcement officials, and school administrators who are most affected by the proliferation of firearms are powerless to enact any meaningful reforms. What possible reason can responsible gun owners have for opposing curbs on assault rifles, cop-killer bullets, and plastic guns. While these items may not be involved in the majority of gun violence they are present in a proportion of it and, significantly, they can be banned without creating any meaningful limitations on legitimate and legal gun use. These items are important only to the criminal element and to a few collectors.

Gun control means very different things to different people. Some purists would say the second amendment of the Constitution prohibits any government interference of a citizen's right to bear arms. Taken to the extreme, this would mean citizens could own weapons normally associated with the military such as rockets, mines, tanks, fighter jets, etc. Clearly, there are limits on the types of arms citizens may own and carry and the gun-control debate centers around exactly where these limits are to be drawn. The war on crime and peacemaking perspectives draw the limits on gun availability at different ends of the spectrum. While the goal of each perspective is to reduce the level and harmful impact of crime, the means they would use are radically dissimilar and this can be seen in how they view the issue of gun control.

Where the war on crime perspective would say guns are needed by the good citizens to protect themselves from criminals, the peacemaking perspective would say if criminals did not have guns, the good people would not need such deadly protection. The prospects for a disarming of citizens are not good given the political climate and the fear of crime in this country. There are, however, some gun-control principles that the proponents of the war on crime and peacemaking perspectives can agree on and work together to craft legislation, educate citizens, and help law enforcement officers. Keeping firearms out of the hands of children, criminals, and the mentally ill should at the very least represent common ground for all concerned with lethal violence. The trick, of course, is how to keep firearms out of these hands while not restricting the right to bear arms of responsible citizens. This dilemma constitutes the battleground on which the gun-control debate is contested.

The Brady Bill

On March 30, 1981, John Hinkley attempted to assassinate president Ronald Reagan and in doing so severely injured several other individuals including Press Secretary James Brady. This led proponents for stricter handgun control to lobby for a federal law that would prevent criminals, the mentally disturbed, and other irresponsible or dangerous individuals from obtaining handguns. Over a period of years a fierce congressional battle was waged which saw the **Brady Bill** defeated three times before it finally passed by the 103d Congress on November 25, 1993, by a vote of 238 to 189 in the House of Representatives and 63 to 36 vote in the Senate (Jacobs and Potter 1995, 98).

The Brady Bill prohibits firearm dealers (federal firearm licensees, FFLs) from selling handguns to ex-felons, adjudicated mental defective, former mental patients, illegal drug users and addicts, juveniles, persons dishonorably discharged from the armed forces, persons who renounced U.S. citizenship, and illegal aliens. Furthermore, the Brady Bill requires a five-day "cooling-off period" in order for a background check to be carried out by the chief law enforcement officer in the jurisdiction where the dealer is located. The background investigation and waiting period apply only to handguns and do not limit sales of rifles or shotguns (Jacobs and Potter 1995, 95–96).

The intent of the Brady Bill is admirable but, according to Jacobs and Potter (1995), unworkable. They list several problems with the law, the most serious of which is the secondary market in handguns. The law applies to **federally licensed gun dealers** who may not represent the usual place that criminals obtain their weapons. Guns can be acquired from street dealers, friends, relatives, or a person advertising in the newspaper. This does not even take into consideration the large number of guns stolen each year. Consequently, a determined criminal can circumvent the Brady Bill by purchasing the handgun outside the legal channels but even more disturbing is that the Brady Bill has several gaps which would allow purchase from a licensed dealer.

According to Jacobs and Potter these gaps include

1. The federal licensing for gun dealers program is deeply flawed in many respects. One would think that only reputable gun shops could obtain such a license but in reality there are over 284,000 dealers and the majority of them do not operate legitimate businesses. It is easy to get a federal firearms dealers license through the mail and there is very little chance that the Bureau of Alcohol, Tobacco and Firearms will successfully be able to monitor whether an individual dealer is following the provisions of the Brady Bill.

2. Gun buyers are not required under the Brady Bill to provide fingerprints. Proof of identity is based on any identification document such as a driver's license. The gun dealer forwards the name, address, and eligibility information contained in the Brady Form to the chief law enforcement officer in the jurisdiction and waits five days for a background check to be done before selling the firearm. One need only look at the fake identification minors use to buy alcohol to see how vulnerable this system is.

3. The gun buyer can use a straw man to purchase the weapon. A fellow gang member, friend, or relative can buy the gun and hand it over to the felon or mentally disturbed individual that the Brady Bill is designed to address.

4. There is a large responsibility placed on the chief law enforcement officer (usually the county sheriff's office) to determine in five days whether gun buyers are eligible under the Brady law. There is no currently existing database that can be checked to determine if the would-be gun buyer is a felon, drug user or addict, former mental health center client, alien, or has been dishonorably discharged from the military. While some reasonable effort could be made to determine if the potential gun buyer fits into some of these categories (a record check of the NCIC could determine a criminal conviction), there is no single place to check all of these categories. Additionally, some records such as mental health center and drug programs are frequently deemed confidential. Determining if someone is dishonorably discharged from the military can take months and there are no records anywhere that can identify illegal aliens.

These are just some of the logistical problems that plague gun-control efforts under the modest goals of the Brady Bill. Some gun-control advocates want to include the secondary gun market to the same restrictions (Cook, Molliconi, and Cole 1995). The secondary market would have to be addressed if the overall goals of the Brady Bill are to be realized. Youth, criminals, and the mentally ill are unlikely to obtain weapons through legitimate dealers if gun-control advocates could address all the gaps in the Brady Bill. Keeping handguns from those who are determined to use weapons for unlawful purposes cannot be done with the Brady Bill and probably will fail even if the Brady Bill is expanded to the secondary market. The wide availability of guns makes it extremely difficult to limit their distribution to selected categories of people through legislation.

Is the Brady Bill then doomed to failure because of all the ways it can be circumvented and because it does not cover the private sale of handguns? Not necessarily. It makes a certain amount of sense to put obstacles in the way of purchasing guns. Certainly, there are requirements for a person to get a driver's or marriage license in this country, so why not at least attempt to restrict handguns to those who are competent and law-abiding? If fewer guns are sold because individuals do not want to go through the hassle of filling out the Brady form and wait five days for a background check, then those individuals do not want or really need a handgun in the first place. It seems reasonable to some people that a certain "cooling off" period can prevent impulsive handgun use. If in a dispute one party need only go to the nearest strip mall to purchase a handgun within 10 minutes, it is easy to conceive how hot tempers and inflamed passions could lead to violence that would be prevented by the Brady Bill. Of course, the truly determined will find a gun sooner or wait the five days, but for many, simply sobering up and cooling down will allow the crisis to pass. If fewer handguns are sold it is conceivable there will be fewer accidents and children's tragedies as a result. While this is a difficult empirical argument to prove, there is a certain logic that suggests the fewer guns in society the fewer times they will be used inappropriately.

PEACEMAKING AND GUNS

Gun control is a controversial topic and one where criminologists can legitimately disagree. Respected scholars like Gary Kleck contend that citizens should be allowed to own guns for defensive purposes. The streets can be dangerous and the police cannot be everywhere and protect everyone. The possibility that a citizen may have a gun presumably deters the criminal from mugging, raping, or breaking into a home. If all guns were taken from citizens (which would be almost impossible) then criminals could act with impunity in victimizing the rest of us. Guns, in the hands of the right people, would presumably make society safer.

The peacemaking perspective views the prevalence of guns in a much different light. Certainly, under present circumstances, there is some legitimate defensive gun use, and certainly there are major gaps in the Brady law which allow handguns to get into the wrong hands, but there are still compelling reasons to consider limiting the number and types of weapons available to the public. From a peacemaking perspective, guns are part of the crime problem, not part of the solution. The fight-fire-with-fire theory taken to its logical extreme ends up with the whole world being burned to the ground.

The gun-control controversy has been around long enough for a body of empirical evidence to accumulate. The issue, however, is still in dispute because there are only two empirical findings that have wide support. The first is the relationship between firearms and violence. According to Zimring (1995, 8), the serious assault rate in the United States is 30 percent greater than in England, while the homicide rate is 530 percent greater. That firearms are an important part of the problem of lethal violence in the United States is not in question.

The second conclusion that can be drawn from the empirical literature is that "relatively low cost interventions that do not interfere with the general availability of guns can probably have only a limited impact on the death rate from violence" (Zimring, 1995). From a public-policy point of view we have not devised interventions that can keep guns out of the wrong hands while preserving the ability for others to be hunters, collectors, or to carry guns for defensive purposes. The bottom line remains: guns cause death, and gun control in the United States has not been successful in preventing deaths.

From a peacemaking perspective the solution to gun violence in the United States is simply to eliminate guns. Certainly other countries have a much lower rate of lethal violence that can be attributed to the lack of availability of guns. The long history and fascination with guns in the country has prevented many from considering the radical step of disarming the public. Second amendment arguments can be solved by simply amending the Constitution. After all, the founders of the country realized that times would change and made provisions for amendments. The frontier is gone and the reasons for firearms have changed. Hunting for subsistence is no longer required for survival and the major reason to have a firearm today is because everybody else has one. By taking guns from all citizens, then none of us would need one. Will there be objections to this radical policy? Certainly, and they can be seen on the bumper stickers of cars and trucks.

1. *When guns are outlawed, only outlaws will have guns.* The goal would be to get the guns out of the hands of the outlaws. They have guns now because guns are so readily available. By making guns impossible to buy the supply will eventually dry up. With the projected drop in homicides there may actually be room in prison for those who violate the strict gun prohibition.

2. *They can have my gun when they ply it from my cold dead fingers.* Gun culture is so entrenched in this country that many individuals will not be willing to give up their weapons. They will see gun prohibition as either a communist plot designed to disarm the citizenry so an invasion can occur (since

the fall of the Soviet Union from where the invasion would come is not clear) or as an internal power move on the part of liberals.

It is of course unfair to attribute bumper-sticker logic to the many sincere and clear-thinking individuals who oppose gun control for legitimate reasons. It is a complex theoretical and logistical issue and opponents of gun control are also opponents of violence. The means of reducing violence are what are in question. This brings us to the most popular of all the gun-control bumper stickers.

3. *Guns don't kill people, people kill people.* This is true, but in the United States too many people use guns to kill other people. Many times the mere availability of a firearm results in an accident, suicide, or homicide that was only meant to be a bluff but got out of hand.

Can there be a way of reducing the violence associated with firearms that does not include gun control? From a peacemaking perspective the answer is yes, but gun control would still be desirable. The peacemaking perspective concentrates on nonviolent conflict resolution and guns do not provide the basis for settling arguments peacefully. The peace-through-strength logic is unworkable in society when everyone is armed. We each will have a different threshold of when gun use is necessary, and as we can already see from the prevalence of gun violence, that threshold for many of us is ridiculously low.

The peacemaking perspective argues that we find other ways of solving conflicts that do not require firearms. The transforming of the culture of violence in the United States will need to be contested at many levels and will require individuals to change their reliance on force as a solution to problems. While it is true that the modest programs of gun control have not worked in the past, the issue should still be at the forefront of any discussion of making our society safer. It may require challenging some long-held and cherished beliefs about our national heritage, but gun control may prove more effective if we tried more of it.

CRITICAL THINKING QUESTIONS

1. Debate the language of the second amendment to the Constitution. What does it say about the right of the people to own firearms? What has the Supreme Court had to say about this issue?

2. Compare and contrast the arguments for and against gun control. Define where the issues are ones of evidence and facts and where the issues are ones of ideology.

3. How can the Brady Bill be made more effective in combating gun violence? Is the Brady Bill a minor inconvenience or is it significantly intrusive into the rights of legitimate gun owners?

4. Critique Kleck's defensive gun-use argument using the peacemaking perspective. Is there any common ground shared by these widely divergent perspectives?

SUGGESTED READINGS

Cook, Philip J., Stephanie Molliconi, and Thomas B. Cole. 1995. "Regulating Gun Markets." *The Journal of Criminal Law and Criminology 86*(1): 59–92.

Halbrook, Stephen P. 1986. "What the Framers Intended: A Linguistic Analysis of the Right to Bear Arms." *Law and Contemporary Problems 49*(1): 151–162.

Jacobs, James A., and Kimberly A. Potter. 1995. "Keeping Guns Out of the Wrong Hands: The Brady Law and the Limits of Regulation." *The Journal of Criminal Law and Criminology 86*(1): 93–120.

Kleck, Gary. 1991. *Point Blank: Guns and Violence in America*. New York: Aldine de Gruyter.

Kleck, Gary, and E. Britt Patterson. 1993. "The Impact of Gun Control and Gun Ownership Levels on Violence Rates." *Journal of Quantitative Criminology 9*(3): 249–287.

Kleck, Gary, and Marc Gertz. 1995. "Armed Resistance To Crime: The Prevalence and Nature of Self-Defense with a Gun." *The Journal of Criminal Law and Criminology 86*(1): 150–187.

Spitzer, Robert J. 1995. *The Politics of Gun Control*. Chatham, NJ: Chatham House Publishers.

Zimring, Franklin E. 1995. "Reflections on Firearms and the Criminal Law." *The Journal of Criminal Law and Criminology 86*(1): 1–9.

11

CAPITAL PUNISHMENT

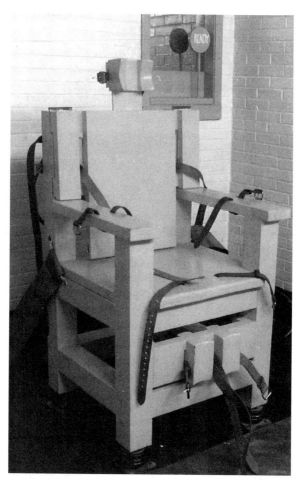

© Ap/Wide World Photos.

Learning Objectives

After reading this chapter, the student should be able to:

- Put the death penalty in historical perspective.
- Trace the changing attitudes about the death penalty in the United States.
- Discuss the impact of the *Furman* case.
- Describe the five methods used in the United States to execute offenders.
- List and discuss the argument for capital punishment.
- Discuss the deterrence argument for capital punishment.
- Discuss the just-desserts argument for capital punishment.
- Discuss the cruel-and-unusual argument against capital punishment.
- Discuss the dehumanization process of capital punishment on offenders and correctional officers.
- Discuss the racial and social-class bias in the implementation of capital punishment.
- Discuss the financial cost of capital punishment.
- Describe the peacemaking perspective on capital punishment.

Key Terms

Mutilation

Furman v. Georgia

Lethal Injection

Cruel and Unusual Punishment

Just Desserts

Racial and Class Bias

The killing of another human being is an awesome act that is condoned in only special circumstances by society. Certainly, war is one of these special times when killing is not only allowed but rewarded. The soldier operating under the conventions of war is expected to use his or her training to eliminate the enemy. But even in war there are some limits on who can be killed and how it is done.

One is also allowed to kill in self-defense. If someone presents a credible threat to ourselves or to some other innocent person then it may be necessary and permissible to take their life. This is certainly a judgment call, but the law recognizes and allows for killing under circumstances of self-defense.

The law also allows the state to take the life of an individual who has been convicted of a capital offense such as murder or treason. Capital punishment is a very different type of action than killing in time of war or in self-defense.

Capital punishment raises all kinds of moral, ethical, and practical questions that have made it the subject of passionate debate for over 200 years in the United States. There is little consensus as to whether the death penalty provides any worthwhile function in our system of law or whether it serves to brutalize us as citizens and human beings and perpetuate the deadly violence that is such a part of the American landscape. On one level, capital punishment satisfies a desire for societal revenge and, on another level, it sickens many individuals who equate it with premeditated murder.

One justification for capital punishment is that it serves a greater good. By executing individuals who commit the most serious crimes we send a message to others that society will react with the most extreme measures possible to certain types of crime. Theoretically, people will think twice before committing these crimes because their lives may be at stake. Deterrence theory argues that we are all held in constraint because we see the consequences of behavior that society deems most undesirable.

There are two levels at which deterrence theory is questioned by opponents of the death penalty. First, on a logical level, the question is asked, "Why do we kill people to teach people that killing people is wrong?" By providing a model of killing behavior it is, according to the opponents of the death penalty, unreasonable to expect the behavior to be deterred (Keve 1992). Deterrence theory is also questioned from an empirical position. Opponents contend that there is insufficient evidence to support the position that capital punishment makes society safer because potential killers weigh the benefits of committing crime against the possible punishment if they are caught. Deterrence is an important reason for support of the death penalty and will be dealt with later in the chapter, but it is necessary at this point to understand that it has been accepted as a common-sense principle by society for a very long time.

This chapter attempts to put the death penalty in historical perspective and link it to other types of punishments that have been employed by the criminal justice system. Arguments for and against capital punishment are reviewed and finally capital punishment is connected to the war on crime and peacemaking perspectives.

HISTORY OF CAPITAL PUNISHMENT

Death is a common form of punishment when viewed in a historical perspective. However, it should be kept in mind that there are many factors associated with when and how capital punishment is used. At some points in history, human life was considered too valuable to the society for the state to use the death penalty very much.

> *The Germans, as described by Tacitus, sixty years after the death of Christ, considered only treachery, desertion, cowardice and sexual perversion to be*

crimes serious enough to be punished by death. In a society where every fighting man was a valuable asset, execution and mutilation could not reasonably be considered suitable punishments for lesser offenses, such as murder and theft; and so, Tacitus discovered, the German murderer or thief when convicted paid a fine 'in a stated number of oxen or cattle. Half of the fine was paid to the King, half to the person for whom justice was being obtained or to his relatives' (Hibbert 1963, 3).

A century and a half later there was not such a premium on human life, and the death penalty was employed frequently. In addition, torture and **mutilation** were included in what became public spectacle designed not only to deter but also to amuse the citizens.

In 1666 at Auvergne, 276 criminals were hanged, forty-four were beheaded, thirty-two were broken on the wheel, twenty-eight were sent to the galleys and three were burned. A man who made an attempt on the life of Louis XV had his hand burned off, molten lead and boiling oil was poured into the stump and four horses were set to drag him apart. As the strength of the horses proved inadequate for this task the executioner loosened his joints with a knife. In Germany, men sentenced to death were nipped on their way to the place of execution with red hot pincers which were used to tear out the tongues of blasphemers (Hibbert 1963, 34).

In many societies, both in the western world and in Africa and Asia, the death penalty was used for a wide variety of offenses with our without the benefit of any sort of due process in how the crime was investigated and how the trial was conducted. Confessions that were extracted by torture were often followed by executions of the most painful and humiliating types. Stoning at a pillory, being drawn and quartered by horses, and hangings or beheadings in the public square were all witnessed by villagers who often jeered and threw things at the accused. By the standards of the way the death penalty used to be carried out, the procedures used today look very humane. Many reforms have been instituted in the criminal justice system concerning the death penalty and the public of today is not confronted with the brutal methods of yesterday.

Capital Punishment in the United States

The first person executed in the United States was Daniel Frank in 1622 (obviously it was not called the United States then) in the colony of Virginia. His crime was theft. In more than three and a half centuries since, an estimated 18,000 to 20,000 individuals have been lawfully put to death with 15,759 being confirmed (Espy 1989, 48). In seventeenth-century Massachusetts, a person could be put to death for idolatry, witchcraft, blasphemy, murder, manslaughter, poisoning, bestiality, sodomy, adultery, man-stealing, false witness in a capital trial, and rebellion (including attempts and conspiracies).

The justification for the death penalty for these offenses came from the Old Testament of the Bible. Before long, other crimes without Biblical underpinnings were added to the list of behaviors that could result in death. Rape, arson, and treason were added before 1700 and, by the time of the War of Independence, most colonies had adopted a similar range of offenses which included murder, treason, piracy, arson, rape, robbery, burglary, sodomy, and, from time to time, counterfeiting, horse-theft, and slave rebellion.

Compared with today, the list of offenses carrying capital punishment was long and the imposition of sentences was both supported by the community and used frequently by judges. It was not until 1787 that public executions came under attack in this country. Dr. Benjamin Rush delivered an address on "The Effects of Public Punishments Upon Criminals and Upon Society," which helped change the attitudes toward how the criminal justice system dealt with offenders. Three years later, the Walnut Street Jail was built and incarceration started to become an alternative to hangings.

In the early 1800s, several states started to question the wisdom of the death penalty. In 1847, the Territory of Michigan became the first English-speaking jurisdiction to abolish hanging and replace it with life imprisonment. Several other states including Wisconsin, Maine, Iowa, and Rhode Island did likewise in the next thirty years. Early in the twentieth century, nine more states followed suit but there followed a period during the roaring twenties when many states restored it (Bedau 1994, 22).

The most significant development in the legal status of the death penalty did not happen in the state legislatures but in the federal courts. In 1972, the Supreme Court handed down its decision in ***Furman v. Georgia,*** which found the way the death penalty was administered in the United States to be "cruel and unusual punishment in violation of the Eighth and Fourteenth Amendments" (Bedau 1994, 249). The *Furman* decision concluded the death penalty had been inflicted in a "wanton" and "freakish" manner and was used most consistently for poor people and unpopular groups.

The *Furman* decision was a great victory for groups opposed to capital punishment. It effectively halted all executions in the United States and permanently removed all those waiting on death rows from the threat of having their sentences carried out. Many state legislatures were shocked by the Court's decision and quickly rewrote their death penalty statutes in accordance with the constitutional questions that had been raised. By 1976, 35 states had enacted new laws and 500 people were under death sentences (Scheidegger 1987). Table 11.1 shows how many prisoners were executed in each state both before the *Furman* decision and after. In examining this table see if you can discern any pattern in terms of which regions of the country execute the most and the fewest number of offenders.

TABLE 11.1 Prisoners Executed (By Jurisdiction, 1930–Dec. 31, 1993 (aggregate))

Jurisdiction	Number Executed	
	Since 1930	Since 1977[a]
United States, total	4,085	226
Georgia	383	17
Texas	368	71
New York[b]	329	0
California	294	2
North Carolina	268	5
Florida	202	32
Ohio	172	0
South Carolina	166	4
Mississippi	158	4
Louisiana	154	21
Pennsylvania	152	0
Alabama	145	10
Arkansas	122	4
Virginia	114	22
Kentucky	103	0
Tennessee	93	0
Illinois	91	1
New Jersey	74	0
Missouri	73	11
Maryland	68	0
Oklahoma	63	3
Washington	48	1
Colorado	47	0
Indiana	43	2
Arizona	41	3
West Virginia[b]	40	0
District of Columbia[b]	40	0
Nevada	34	5
Federal system	33	0
Massachusetts[b]	27	0
Connecticut	21	0
Oregon	19	0
Iowa[b]	18	0
Utah	17	4
Kansas[b]	15	0
Delaware	15	3
New Mexico	8	0
Wyoming	8	1
Montana	6	0
Vermont[b]	4	0
Nebraska	4	0
Idaho	3	0
South Dakota	1	0

Continued

TABLE 11.1 *Continued*

Jurisdiction	Number Executed	
	Since 1930	Since 1977[a]
New Hampshire	1	0
Wisconsin[b]	0	0
Rhode Island[b]	0	0
North Dakota[b]	0	0
Minnesota[b]	0	0
Michigan[b]	0	0
Maine[b]	0	0
Hawaii[b]	0	0
Alaska[b]	0	0

Source: U.S. Department of Justice, Bureau of Justice Statistics, *Capital Punishment 1993*. Bulletin NCJ-150042 (Washington, DC: U.S. Department of Justice, December 1994), p. 11, Table 10. Table adapted by SOURCEBOOK staff.
Source: Maquile, Kathleen, and Ann L. Pastore, eds. 1995. *Sourcebook of Criminal Justice Statistics 1994*. U.S. Department of Justice, Bureau of Justice Statistics. Washington, DC: USGPO, p. 596.
[a]The Supreme Court reinstated the death penalty in 1976.
[b]State not authorizing the death penalty as of Dec. 31, 1993.

In a number of new cases (*Gregg v. Georgia, Jurek v. Texas,* and *Proffitt v. Florida*), the Supreme Court held that capital punishment was not unconstitutional as long as the states provide:

1. An opportunity to put before the court information about the defendant to assist it in reaching the sentencing decision
2. A special emphasis on any mitigating factors that affect the defendant's blameworthiness
3. Common standards to guide trial courts in their sentencing decision
4. A review of every death sentence by a state appellate court

The primary issue in the *Furman* case and related cases had to do with how the death penalty was imposed by the states and not with the morality or efficacy of the practice. These statues dealt with the *how* and not with the *should*. Opponents to the death penalty found their victory short-lived. They were able to stop the state from executing people for a time, but the state legislatures were able to redraft their laws so that the procedural constitutional questions were satisfied. In 1977, Gary Gilmore was shot by a firing squad in Utah and capital punishment was once more alive and well in the United States.

The method of execution varies across the states that execute offenders. The five methods used in the United States are **lethal injection,** electrocution, lethal gas, hanging, and the firing squad (see Table 11.2). There is considerable debate as to which method is preferable. Some people want the offender to suffer as much as possible while others consider it **cruel and unusual punishment** to make the offender suffer (Miller and Davis 1989).

TABLE 11.2   Methods of Execution in States Authorizing the Death Penalty (By State, 1993)

Lethal Injection	Electrocution	Lethal Gas	Hanging	Firing Squad
Arizona[a,b]	Alabama	Arizona[a]	Montana[a]	Idaho[a]
Arkansas[a,c]	Arkansas[a,c]	California[a]	New Hampshire[a,d]	Utah[a]
California[a]	Connecticut	Colorado[a,e]	Washington[a]	
Colorado[a,e]	Florida	Maryland		
Delaware	Georgia	Mississippi[a,f]		
Idaho[a]	Indiana	Missouri[a]		
Illinois	Kentucky	North Carolina[a]		
Louisiana	Nebraska	Wyoming[a,g]		
Mississippi[a,f]	Ohio[a]			
Missouri[a]	South Carolina			
Montana[a]	Tennessee			
Nevada	Virginia			
New Hampshire[a,d]				
New Jersey				
New Mexico				
North Carolina[a]				
Ohio[a]				
Oklahoma[a,g]				
Oregon				
Pennsylvania				
South Dakota				
Texas				
Utah[a]				
Washington[a]				
Wyoming[a,g]				

Source: U.S. Department of Justice, Bureau of Justice Statistics, *Capital Punishment 1993,* Bulletin NCJ-150042 (Washington, DC: U.S. Department of Justice, December 1994), p. 6, Table 2.
Source: Maquire, Kathleen, and Ann L. Pastore, eds. 1995. *Sourcebook of Criminal Justice Statistics 1994.* U.S. Department of Justice, Bureau of Justice Statistics. Washington, DC: USGPO, p. 599.
Note: Federal executions are to be carried out according to the method of the State in which the inmate was sentenced.
[a]Authorizes two methods of execution.
[b]Arizona authorizes lethal injection for persons whose capital sentence was received after Nov. 15, 1992; for those who were sentenced before that date, the condemned prisoner may select lethal injection or lethal gas.
[c]Arkansas authorizes lethal injection for those whose capital offense occurred after July 4, 1983; for those whose offense occurred before that date, the condemned prisoner may select lethal injection or electrocution.
[d]New Hampshire authorizes hanging only if lethal injection cannot be given.
[e]Colorado authorizes lethal gas for those whose crimes occurred before July 1, 1988 and lethal injection for those whose crimes occurred on or after July 1, 1988.
[f]Mississippi authorizes lethal injection for those convicted after July 1, 1984; execution of those convicted prior to that date is to be carried out with lethal gas.
[g]Wyoming authorizes lethal gas, if lethal injection is ever held unconstitutional.

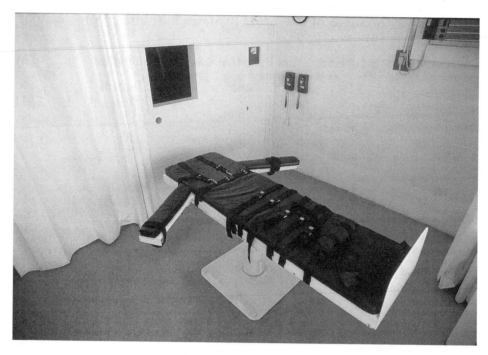

The lethal injection method of capitol punishment is thought by some people to be more humane than other forms of execution. (© Brooks Kraft/Sygma.)

Many states are switching to lethal injection either to limit the suffering of the individual or to make the policy of capital punishment more palatable to the public. To opponents of capital punishment, lethal injection is as objectionable as other forms of execution and is viewed as a devious attempt on the part of the state to make an immoral policy less politically unpopular.

ARGUMENTS FOR CAPITAL PUNISHMENT

The death penalty is a popular policy in the United States. Poll after poll demonstrates that Americans are solidly in favor of executing criminals who commit not only murder but other serious crimes. Many individuals view the death penalty as society's ultimate defense against a criminal element that to them seems to be threatening the very fabric of society. Those who favor the death penalty adopt the war on crime perspective. They see benefits for the community arising not only from the elimination of an undesirable individual but also, in a wider context, in the strengthening of the ties that bind society together. When rules are enforced, everyone is more likely to obey them and when the death penalty is meted out then we should be able to expect less serious crime. That is the line of reasoning of the supporters of the death penalty, and it is worth examining just how useful this philosophy is in making society safer (Miller and Davis 1989).

Deterrence

There are two types of deterrence that proponents of the death penalty claim as a justification for their position. The first, specific deterrence, contends that if the offender is punished for a crime then the offender is less likely to repeat that crime. In terms of the death penalty, this line of reasoning is difficult to argue with. If someone is executed, then the chances of recidivism are nil. Dead people tell no lies and do not commit additional crimes. Proponents of capital punishment argue that offenders may commit crimes in prison, escape and commit crimes, or be released on parole and commit more crimes. There is no way to be certain the offender will no longer pose a threat to society other than to remove him completely from interaction with others. The death penalty does this and, for some people, this alone justifies its use.

The second and more pervasive deterrence argument involves general deterrence. The philosophy of general deterrence is that by punishing the criminal, the rest of us will see that there are consequences to our actions and will be deterred from committing crimes. General deterrence is fundamental to the maintenance of meaningful communities. Think of how chaotic our society would be if, in order to learn how society will react to a crime, each of use has to commit the crime, get caught, and be punished. If we learn only from direct experience with the criminal justice system then each of us who are tempted to rob, rape, steal, or murder would commit these crimes until we are specifically brought under control by the police. Fortunately, the vast majority of us do not commit these crimes even though there may be times when we may be tempted. We understand by seeing others punished that we will be held accountable for our behavior.

When examining general deterrence, there are several issues that make it hard to determine whether the death penalty operates in this way.

1. Does the death penalty deter criminals the same way it deters the rest of us? In order for deterrence to be effective we each must weigh the risks of getting caught and punished against the benefits of successfully committing the crime. For most citizens there are very few circumstances where we would risk our lives, fortunes, and reputations for the possible benefits derived from crime. In short, general deterrence works very well on those who have something to lose. It may not be so effective on those who have little invested in the status quo. To think that drug dealers who stand to gain thousands of dollars, professional assassins, youth gang members, and jealous spouses rationally calculate the prospects of the death penalty is not something of which we can be assured.

2. Does the death penalty deter better than other forms of punishment? Is it unreasonable to believe that someone contemplating murder would conclude that getting caught and sentenced to life imprisonment (even though we all understand that release is possible) is an acceptable risk? If someone is going to be deterred by the death penalty, then they will, in all likelihood, be deterred by other sanctions.

3. Many murders are crimes of passion where deterrence may not enter into the case at all. The intent to kill is often absent in domestic violence, which escalates into homicide. The death penalty is not a factor taken into consideration in a heated argument between loved ones.

4. There is little empirical evidence that deterrence theory works. Granted, it is hard to measure something that does not happen, in this case murder, but studies done of comparable states do not demonstrate that those with capital punishment have fewer homicides than those without. Deterrence is a common-sense philosophy without observable confirmation as to if it actually operates in practice.

Given these concerns about the deterrent effect of the death penalty we may conclude that this theory is insufficient to continue executing offenders (Pugsley 1981; Stevens 1992). To be fair to those who support capital punishment, we must recognize that while we cannot demonstrate that it does have a deterrent effect, so too can we not demonstrate that it does not prevent serious crime. In order for a law to deter, it must be widely known and consistently enforced (Stack 1993). When we consider the vast numbers of murders that are committed each year and the very few offenders who are executed, it is reasonable to conclude that individuals are not overly concerned with the probability of capital punishment.

If deterrence theory is to be effective, we must do more than raise the severity of the punishment. Swiftness and certainty of punishment are also factors that criminals supposedly take into account when contemplating their crimes. In the case of the death penalty, neither certainty nor swiftness are significant concerns. Most executions occur 10 or more years after the crime has been committed. Given the restrictive way statutes are written, plea bargaining, and the reluctance of some judges or juries to impose the death sentence, then we can honestly say that, under present conditions, deterrence theory has not had a fair opportunity to demonstrate its potential.

Those who favor the war on crime perspective call for reforms that would make the death penalty quicker and more certain. The limiting of the defendant's appeals and laws that make capital punishment mandatory are some of the ways in which those who propose a get-touch-on-crime approach would employ the death penalty. They argue that if we executed a large number of offenders in a swift and certain manner then capital punishment laws would be perceived as having some teeth and could provide a deterrence function that would make our society safer.

Just Desserts

Proponents of the death penalty cite other reasons for embracing capital punishment. In order to demonstrate how seriously society values human life, killing someone should be grounds for the offender to sacrifice his or her life. In short, murderers *deserve* to be executed for their crime. According to this perspective, there are two rationales why capital punishment satisfies a societal need. First, for some people, justice would not be complete if murderers were not subjected to a punishment that is proportionate with their crime. In the case of murderers (and for some people, rapists and drug dealers), nothing short of execution satiates society's need for retribution. Secondly, and related to the need for retribution, is the fear that if citizens do not feel that the criminal justice system responds to serious crime in a serious way, then it is up to the individual to see that justice is done. In order to have meaningful communities, citizens must have faith that the law will protect them and dispense the kind and level of justice they demand. Lacking confidence in government, citizens take the law into their own hands and become judge, jury, and executioner. Law by vigilantism represents the fear of those who have lost confidence in the ability of the law to protect them and promote the goals of justice.

Finally, proponents of capital punishment point to one other consideration when defending their position. The cost of incarceration for offenders grows each year, and the prospect of life without parole sentences promises to cost the taxpayers a great deal of money. As offenders grow old in prison they require more medical attention, and there are those who think it foolish to house a prisoner for the remainder of his or her life and incur the costs maintaining a life that is doomed to die in prison. It may be more humane (and certainly cheaper) in the view of some individuals to execute the criminal instead of warehousing him or her in prison. We will deal with this argument in more detail later in this chapter as there is considerable debate on which course is actually less expensive.

ARGUMENTS AGAINST CAPITAL PUNISHMENT

Those who oppose capital punishment do so for a variety of reasons. Some individuals believe that the government does not have the moral right to take the life of a human being. Even though capital punishment is allowed by the law, it is looked upon as being legal homicide by people who believe that only God has the right to make such a judgment. Others believe that capital punishment is unjustified on scientific grounds because its deterrence effects have not been adequately demonstrated by research. To continue to execute offenders based on the assumption that it does a greater good by preventing crime is a flawed assumption and not an acceptable reason to support this policy.

Still other individuals question the fairness with which the death penalty is imposed. They contend that social class and race are variables that demonstrate a discriminatory pattern in who lives and who dies at the hands of the state.

As we discuss each of these objections to capital punishment we will relate them to the peacemaking perspective. Because killing a criminal offender is an act of violence in itself, regardless of the reasoning, the peacemaking perspective is in opposition to this policy. The premeditated taking of a life, even, or maybe especially, by the state is a violation of the basic tenets of the peacemaking perspective and continues to find opposition in many parts of society (Havlena 1987).

Cruel and (Un)usual Punishment

Given the history of capital punishment both in this country and in an historical perspective it would be hard to suggest that it is unusual. In fact, many of the reforms of criminal justice (including the penitentiary) throughout history have been instituted as alternatives to capital punishment. It can be argued that the death penalty is cruel and, because of the way it is carried out (that is, in a high bureaucratic and routinized manner), it is also highly unusual.

> *The modern death penalty involves nothing less than a slow death by psychological torture, which no offender deserves. Today's condemned prisoner is literally and often completely dehumanized. He is reduced to the status of an object—a body and not a person—then put to death following an impersonal bureaucratic routine. His executioners are dehumanized as well, though only partially and symbolically, in the specific context of carrying out executions. This dehumanization allows prison officials to function as bureaucrats of violence while remaining largely unaffected in their personal lives (Johnson 1990, 4).*

Under the phrase "cruel and unusual punishment," opponents of the death penalty would also include the impact of capital punishment on the rest of society. It dehumanizes everyone when a human life is systematically destroyed by the state in the name of the people. This makes everyone in society an accomplice to the state's killing. It models a form of behavior that the state reserves for itself but which everyone is aware of and may imitate.

Cesare di Beccaria (1761/1963) articulated one of the earliest rationales about the brutalizing effects of the death penalty:

> *The death penalty cannot be useful, because of the example of barbarity it gives men. If the passions or the necessities of war have taught the shedding of human blood, the laws, moderators of the conduct of men, should not extend the beastly example, which becomes more pernicious since the*

inflicting of legal death is attended with much study and formality. It seems to me absurd that the laws, which are an expression of the public will, which detest and punish homicide, should themselves commit it, and that to deter citizens from murder, they order a public one (50).

Is it possible for the state to execute offenders in a way that is not cruel and unusual? Is there any form of the death penalty that would satisfy the critics who see it as barbarous and vicious? Given the manner in which the execution protocol in the United States has evolved, is it possible to legally execute an offender without causing intense psychological suffering?

In his influential book, *Deathwork: A Study of the Modern Execution Process,* Robert Johnson (1990) answers these questions in the negative. He likens the execution process to torture that has ramifications not only for the condemned prisoners but also for the prison guards who must participate.

The underlying function of death row confinement, then, is to facilitate executions by dehumanizing both the prisoners and, to a lesser degree, their executioners, making it easier for both to play their roles in the execution process. The confinement that produces these results is a form of torture. Indeed, the essence of torture is the death of a person—that is, his conversion into a subhuman object, a nonperson. Persons whose consciences have been muted by the official authorizations and routines that shape their work as well as by the dehumanization they too have sustained can then, without guilt, commit violence against that nonperson. Stated differently, the death penalty is simply a form of bureaucratically administered violence, a bureaucratization of death in which death row is an integral component (136).

Johnson is uncompromising in his condemnation of the brutalizing effects of the way the death penalty is carried out in this country. He contends that the emotional and psychological trauma that occurs on death row results in a moral death of the condemned person that makes it possible for the prison officials and guards to conduct the physical death. A humane death row, according to Johnson (1990, 137), would "operate as a kind of high security hospice with the objective of preparing full-blooded human beings for a dignified death . . ." Even if we can reform the execution process, Johnson contends that the suffering caused by the death penalty is not worth its continued use. Imprisonment as a form of civil death can accomplish some of society's needs of norm clarification without visiting inhumane suffering on the prisoner and reducing prison officials to killers themselves.

Whatever dehumanizing aspects there are to capital punishment, we can discern a trend to make it less objectionable to the public. One means of making the death penalty more palatable is removing it from view. Public executions were considered beneficial to society because of the presumed deterrent effect. By executing criminals with fanfare and ceremony, it was assumed that others predisposed toward serious crime would be prevented from carrying out their desires by fear of this extreme punishment. Some today argue that we should bring back public executions (halftime at the Superbowl is the extreme) so that the full impact of their deterrence effect can be realized. This is unlikely to happen because of the anti-death penalty furor that such public displays of state violence would certainly cause. It is easier to support capital punishment when the killing is done behind prison walls and away from the eye of the camera. The real question about the concept of public executions is which has the more brutalizing effect on society: low-visibility killings where the public has little knowledge of the details of the execution, or high-visibility public executions where people can witness the criminal justice system carrying out the law in all its final dimensions?

Another trend in the practice of capital punishment which seems aimed at reducing the charge that it is cruel and unusual is the method in which the death penalty is carried out. We have come a long way from the public torture and brutal execution of the past to the seemingly civilized process of lethal injection utilized by many states today. It is a fascinating thought to consider how we have reformed the procedures of capital punishment so that we kill without hurting. The electric chair was looked upon as a great advance in humane lifetaking. As an alternative to hanging and the firing squad, the electric chair was thought to kill the brain instantly and allow the offender to escape pain. Whether this happens or not is subject to controversy as those in the best position to provide input are, of course, dead. The important issue to remember is society has made an effort to be more humane in executing people. Lethal injection is the final reform states have adopted in their attempts to spare the suffering of the offender and to spare themselves (perhaps we should say ourselves as the state executes in the name of all of us) the emotional and psychological consequences of systematically killing a fellow human being.

The cruel and unusual prescription of the eighth amendment is still a very hotly debated topic in the capital punishment discussion. Aside from the obvious impact the death penalty has on the offender, it also extracts something from society. Given that the United States is one of the very few countries in the western world to use capital punishment, it should be recognized that there are other dimensions to the ethical stance upon which the death-penalty reasoning rests (Nathanson 1987).

Racial and Class Bias

Perhaps the most damaging argument against capital punishment in the United States is the charge that it is carried out in a discriminatory fashion (see Table 11.3). Race and social class have been found to be highly related in the decision on who to charge with capital offenses and, once charged, on whom to impose the death penalty. In southern states, where most executions are carried out, African-Americans receive a disproportionate share of

TABLE 11.3 Prisoners under Sentence of Death (By Race, Ethnicity, and Jurisdiction, on Apr. 30, 1995)

| Jurisdiction | Total | Race, Ethnicity | | | | | |
		White	Black	Hispanic	Native American	Asian	Unknown
United States[a]	3,009	1,455	1,217	233	52	22	30
Federal statutes	6	2	3	1	0	0	0
U.S. military	8	1	6	0	0	1	0
Alabama	135	74	57	1	0	1	2
Arizona	122	81	15	21	4	0	1
Arkansas	39	20	17	1	1	0	0
California	407	172	151	60	13	6	5
Colorado	3	2	0	1	0	0	0
Connecticut	5	3	2	0	0	0	0
Delaware	14	6	7	0	0	0	1
Florida	342	184	121	35	1	1	0
Georgia	104	59	45	0	0	0	0
Idaho	20	19	0	1	0	0	0
Illinois	161	53	100	8	0	0	0
Indiana	50	31	18	1	0	0	0
Kansas	0	X	X	X	X	X	X
Kentucky	27	21	6	0	0	0	0
Louisiana	45	12	27	4	0	0	2
Maryland	13	2	11	0	0	0	0
Mississippi	55	21	34	0	0	0	0
Missouri	92	49	36	3	1	1	2
Montana	8	6	0	0	2	0	0
Nebraska	11	8	2	0	1	0	0
Nevada	72	38	25	8	0	1	0
New Hampshire	0	X	X	X	X	X	X
New Jersey	9	3	5	1	0	0	0
New Mexico	3	1	0	2	0	0	0
New York[b]	0	X	X	X	X	X	X
North Carolina	155	80	67	2	4	0	2
Ohio	142	61	71	4	2	0	4
Oklahoma	128	74	35	2	14	3	0
Oregon	14	12	0	1	1	0	0
Pennsylvania	186	63	112	9	0	2	0
South Carolina	59	29	29	0	1	0	0

Continued

TABLE 11.3 *Continued*

Jurisdiction	Total	White	Black	Hispanic	Native American	Asian	Unknown
					Race, Ethnicity		
South Dakota	2	2	0	0	0	0	0
Tennessee	102	66	32	1	2	1	0
Texas	398	161	155	64	5	4	9
Utah	11	8	2	1	0	0	0
Virginia	56	26	27	1	0	0	2
Washington	13	10	2	0	0	1	0
Wyoming	0	X	X	X	X	X	X

Source: Table constructed by SOURCEBOOK staff from the data provided by the NAACP Legal Defense and Educational Fund, Inc.
Source: Maquire, Kathleen, and Ann L. Pastore, eds. 1995. *Sourcebook of Criminal Justice Statistics 1994*. U.S. Department of Justice, Bureau of Justice Statistics. Washington, DC: USGPO, p. 587.
Note: The NAACP Legal Defense and Educational Fund, Inc. periodically collects data on persons on death row. As of April 30, 1995, 38 States, the Federal Government, and the United States military had capital punishment laws; 34 States, the Federal Government, and the United States military had at least 1 prisoner under sentence of death. Between Jan. 1, 1973 and Apr. 30, 1995, an estimated 1,458 convictions or sentences have been reversed or vacated on grounds other than constitutional. Between Jan. 1, 1973 and May 30, 1990, an estimated 558 death sentences have been vacated as unconstitutional.
[a]Detail will not add to total because prisoners sentenced to death in more than one State are listed in the respective State totals, but each is counted only once at the national level.
[b]Recently passed death penalty legislation will take effect Sep. 1, 1995.

death sentences even when other important legal variables such as prior record and aggravating circumstances are taken into account (Baldus et al. 1983; Radelet and Pierce 1985; Bower 1983).

When looking at the racial dimension of who is executed in this country, it is not enough to consider only the race of the offender. Just as important to understanding how race is related to the death penalty is the race of the victim (Bohm 1994). Here, the patterns show us the criminal justice system puts more value on the life of a white victim than on a black victim. Prosecutors were more likely to seek the death penalty, and judges and juries more likely to impose it, if the victim was white and especially if the white victim was killed by a black offender. One study (Gross and Mauro 1984), found that even after taking into account five legally relevant variables (felony circumstances, victim/offender relationship, number of victims, sex of victim, and type of weapon) that, in Georgia, killers of whites had a seventimes greater likelihood of receiving a death sentence than killers of blacks. Another study (Paternoster and Kazyada 1988) found that in South Carolina the race of the victim had a significant impact on the sentencing decision but an even greater influence on whether the prosecutor charged the offender with a capital crime. This decision is less visible than the sentencing decision and more important to the concept of evenhanded justice. If the discretion of the prosecutor is not subject to review, then discrimination in the way the death penalty is decided upon cannot be subjected to the kinds of scrutiny required if its patterns of imposition are to be accurately examined.

If the evidence demonstrates that race is a significant factor in who gets the death penalty, then how does the Supreme Court continue to let this practice remain a mainstay of the criminal justice system? According to Ellsworth (1988, 188–189), the court simply ignores evidence of racial discrimination in the death penalty than in other types of cases it would consider.

> *Once again it is clear that the majority Justices (five of them, in* McClesky*) value the death penalty so highly that they are willing to ignore the inescapable implications of the social science research and to undermine fundamental constitutional guarantees. The majority admitted that the system for deciding who lives and who dies is imperfect, and conceded that the evidence of discrimination found in the Baldus study would have been persuasive if the case had involved discrimination in jury selection or employment. Traditionally, the Court has assumed the decision to impose the death penalty should be safeguarded with higher standards of fairness than other sorts of cases. In* McClesky, *the Court reversed this traditional attitude. Empirical evidence that would be sufficient to protect McClesky's job was not considered sufficient to save his life.*

In addition to race being a factor in capital punishment cases, social class also appears to be related. While not as directly connected as race, it has been suggested that those with the financial means are better able to protect themselves from the imposition of the death penalty than the poor. The money and justice relationship pervades the entire criminal justice system but in the case of the death penalty the costs and consequences are much greater. Public defenders simply do not have the time and resources to put up the type of spirited defense that well-heeled offenders are able to buy from private attorneys. The costs of depositions, expert witnesses, jury selection advisers, and the many hours of case preparation make it prohibitive for overworked public defenders or attorneys for offenders with limited means to compete with the state.

The evidence on the discriminatory manner in which the death penalty is administered suffers much the same fate as the evidence indicating the lack of a deterrent effect. It is largely ignored and dismissed because there is such popular support for capital punishment from the public. Additionally, it is apparent that as this century draws to a close that politicians are finding the get-touch-on-crime approach to be immensely popular with voters. Capital punishment is being touted as a solution for more and more crimes, especially those related to drug smuggling and drug dealing. In the war on crime, the death penalty is a weapon that may be ineffective in deterring criminals but is very useful in electing politicians for higher office. President Clinton proudly pointed to the fact that he signed several death warrants when he was governor of Arkansas, which helped allay fears during his campaign that he might be soft on crime.

Big Mistakes: Capital Punishment and the Innocent

There is one aspect of capital punishment that opponents continually bring up which is difficult to address. Because of the finality of the sentence, there is the possibility of grave injustice being done if the offender is later found to be innocent of the crime. If the offender was imprisoned the error could be partially corrected by lettering him or her out. If the offender was executed, however, there is no chance for the criminal justice system to rectify the mistake. The fact that this is likely to happen infrequently is of little solace to the offender and the offender's family.

COSTS OF CAPITAL PUNISHMENT

It may seem ridiculous to some but often the argument is heard that violent criminals should be executed rather than spend the rest of their lives in prison because it would cost society less money. To base the reason to take a human life on economics is objectionable to many individuals who believe the criminal justice system is already biased against poor people. However, there are those who would say a life spent in prison is pretty much a wasted life anyway so in making the choice between incarceration and execution it is legitimate to ask questions concerning how much the public will have to pay.

Regardless of how one feels about the morality of deciding on a policy of capital punishment based on economics it is important that this argument be based on an accurate assessment of what the costs actually are. While one might think it would be cheaper to execute an offender rather than to keep that person in prison for the rest of his or her life, there are some hidden costs that seem to suggest that the economic argument is fallacious. When one considers the differences between capital and noncapital cases at each point in the criminal justice process, it becomes clear that the death penalty costs an exorbitant amount to society in strictly financial terms. Whatever other arguments can be made for or against capital punishment, the dollar cost is one argument that can be decided on grounds that do not include ideology but simple accounting. The ultimate question of how much should be spent on taking a human life or incarcerating the offender needs to be made on actual figures and not on supposition.

It is enlightening to observe how the costs of incarceration and execution in this country compare. Spangerberg and Walsh (1989) attempt to estimate the different in costs by looking at the pretrial, trial, postconviction, and corrections costs of capital cases. The money starts to add up fast when one considers how much high-paid expertise goes into a capital case.

Service	Cost
Investigators	$500–$1,500 per day
Psychiatric experts	$500–$1,000 per day or $100–150 per hour
Medical examiner	$700–$1,000 per day
Polygraph expert	$200–$300 for courtroom testimony or $150–$250 for polygraph examination
Expert witness concerning eyewitness identification	$500 per day

Spangerberg and Walsh (1989, 50) report that, "in California during the fiscal year 1984–85, the average per case allotment for defense experts' preparation for trial was $12,000." The number of pretrial motions from both the prosecution and defense tend to be more numerous, longer, and more complex in capital cases. This means that not only the defense but the prosecution and the court personnel (judges, bailiffs, clerks, etc.) all experience increased costs. Plea bargaining is not used as often in death penalty cases so more of them are likely to go to trial, according to the authors of this study who contend, ". . . capital cases may result in jury trials ten times more often than in noncapital cases."

The costs also mount during the trial level which Spangerberg and Walsh point out includes the guilt phase, the penalty phase, and the appeal phase. At each phase the process is more involved and more complex for capital cases. By way of example, Spangerberg and Walsh (1989, 53) write:

The estimates of the guilt and sentencing phases vary greatly from state to state. New York has estimated that if the death penalty were reinstated there, trial costs including attorney fees, investigators, and experts would be $176,350, and the costs for the prosecution would be $845,400. Further, New York also estimated court costs at $300,000, exclusive of corrections costs. Appeals have been calculated to cost another $320,000.

When the costs of corrections, which include the expense of death row where the average inmate spends about eight years, are calculated into the equation the cost of capital punishment outweighs the cost of incarceration for life. Again, Spangerberg and Walsh conclude:

A New York study compares a $1.4 million cost figure for each death penalty trial with $602,000 for the cost of life imprisonment for forty years in noncapital cases. Florida has estimated that the cost of each execution is approximately six times what it would cost to keep that person in prison for the rest of his or her natural life (58).

Where is all the money that goes into these calculations coming from? Why do capital cases cost so much more than noncapital cases? The big difference is because capital cases require greater amounts of due process than other criminal cases. In cases that decide the difference between life and death, the courts need to be particularly sensitive that every safeguard has been observed. Not only must the court guard against convicting an innocent person unjustly, but it must also guard against convicting a guilty person without adequate due process because the case could get overturned on appeal.

In another study done on a single case in Kentucky (Blakely 1990), the costs of execution were estimated to be even higher once appeals, new trials, and other problems associated with the case were still being contested 10 years after the death of the victim. Blakely's total estimate of how much it is costing Kentucky to get this defendant sentenced, convicted, and through all 10 levels of appeal is between $2,618,000 and $7,345,000. While this may be an extraordinary case, it does demonstrate how any capital case can be dragged out and contested until the costs get so exorbitant that a reasonable person would conclude that change is needed. While the defense attorneys will probably not realize the income such cases could produce if the defendant had the financial resources to actually pay, the costs to the prosecution and the state are all too real. This is not just paper money, but salaries, security, expert witnesses, and a host of other costs to the taxpayers. Blakely (1990) concludes his study be saying:

> *If moral considerations and the humane aspects of abolishing the death penalty are not sufficient, the cost alone should be enough to lead the informed public to reject the death penalty. Public opinion has already begun to shift toward alternatives to capital punishment where such alternatives are clearly understood.*
>
> *The death penalty has outlasted its utility. For more than moral reasons, it is time to abolish this costly, irreversible anachronism before the Commonwealth reaches bankruptcy (79).*

The purpose of this section has been to present the evidence that capital punishment is an expensive proposition. One of the arguments in favor of the death penalty that is often voiced is that life imprisonment is too costly to society. The studies reviewed here show that capital punishment has costs of its own that far outweigh what it would cost to keep someone in prison for the rest of his or her life. There is little reason to believe the cost of capital punishment can be reduced. According to Blakely (1990) the Supreme Court has demonstrated in a pattern of decisions that legal shortcuts are not to be allowed when the death penalty is at stake. Many conservative politicians campaign on the issue of limiting the appeals process for capital cases, but it may make more sense to eliminate the death penalty because of the cumbersome requirements of due process (Powell 1989).

PEACEMAKING AND CAPITAL PUNISHMENT

It should come as no surprise to the reader that the peacemaking perspective rejects capital punishment as inconsistent with the objectives of resolving disputes through nonviolent means. The death penalty is inherently violent and sends the wrong message to society regarding the desired way of dealing with deviant behavior (Cobb 1989). If the state can morally kill someone, then it is a short leap of logic for individuals to conclude they also can have legitimate reasons for taking someone's life (Cochran et al. 1994).

Because of the inconsistent way the death penalty is applied in the United States, the peacemaking perspective rejects it on the grounds of social justice. Social status, race, and gender are all factors that make it more likely that some will be executed while others who are equally guilty will be spared. In the case of capital punishment, Lady Justice is lifting her blindfold and peeking at the defendant. The punishment of death is not handed out impartially but is administered arbitrarily on grounds that many people find objectionable and that do not, in the long run, add to the prospects of making society more civilized and less crime-ridden. The deterrence effects of capital punishment are questionable and are quite likely conterproductive. Additionally, there seems to be little hope that the death penalty can be applied without causing dehumanization of both the condemned person and those vested with the responsibility of doing the killing for the rest of us.

How, one might ask, would the peacemaking perspective address the serious crime that capital punishment is concerned with? Shouldn't those guilty of brutal murder be punished with the ultimate sanction? Proponents of the peacemaking perspective would contend that using the death penalty is equivalent to closing the barn door after the horse has already escaped. In order to prevent the types of violent crimes that those on death row have committed it would be more useful to understand the causes and conditions that led to those crimes rather than killing the guilty. Capital punishment, from a peacemaking perspective, is a barren policy that has little relevance to making our society safer (Tifft 1982). It is simply a salve to the public to make them believe that the state can address violent crime without addressing the fundamental issues of poverty, racism, poor education, firearms availability, and the many other factors that may lead to homicide.

CRITICAL THINKING QUESTIONS

1. Discuss the issue of cruel and unusual punishment. Given the level of violence in our society and in our media, can the killing of an individual be considered unusual?

2. Debate the argument that capital punishment provides general deterrence to the commission of other serious crimes. What logical flaws are possible within the deterrence theory?

3. One of the arguments in this chapter is that the death penalty dehumanizes both the offender and the people who must carry out the execution. What is the basis for this argument and is it possible to make executions more human?

4. What is the peacemaking perspective position on capital punishment?

SUGGESTED READINGS

Bedau, Hugo Adam. 1994. "American Populism and the Death Penalty: Witnesses at an Execution." *The Howard Journal of Criminal Justice 33*(4): 289–303.

Bohm, Robert M. 1994. "Capital Punishment in Two Judicial Circuits in Georgia." *Law and Human Behavior 18*(3): 319–338.

Johnson, Robert. 1990. *Deathwork: A Study of the Modern Execution Process.* Monterey, CA: Brooks/Cole.

Keve, Paul W. 1992. "The Costliest Punishment— A Corrections Administrator Contemplates the Death Penalty." *Federal Probation 56*(1): 11–15.

Miller, Kent S., and Betty Davis Miller. 1989. *To Kill and Be Killed: Case Studies from Florida's Death Row.* Pasadena: Hope Publishing House.

Spangenberg, Robert L., and Elizabeth R. Walsh. 1989. "Capital Punishment or Life Imprisonment? Some Cost Considerations." *Loyola of Los Angeles Law Review 23* (November): 45–58.

Tifft, Larry. 1982. "Capital Punishment Research, Policy, and Ethics: Defining Murder and Placing Murderers." *Crime and Social Justice* (Summer): 61–68.

12

YOUTH AND GANGS

© A. Ramey/Stock Boston.

Learning Objectives

After reading this chapter, the student should be able to:

- Describe the youth culture in the United States.
- Discuss the relationship of masculinity socialization in sports to crime.
- Explain what behaviors are considered status offenses.
- Discuss how vandalism and graffiti are often means for youth to establish their identity.
- Describe how larceny and shoplifting are often status rituals.
- Discuss how fights between rival high schools are an enduring quality of U.S. culture.
- Describe what is meant by the code of the street.
- Appreciate the complexities of the urban gang problem.
- Discuss the difficulties in redefining the youth culture.
- Discuss the ways in which the peacemaking perspective can be used as a model to address the problems of youth crime.

Key Terms

Status Offenses	Status Rituals
Youth Culture	Code of the Street
MTV Generation	Aggression Replacement Training
Graffiti	Peer Counseling
Hate Crimes	Throwaway Children

Crime is a young person's game. The involvement of youth in unlawful behavior is a problem that has afflicted society since the time of the early Greeks. Channeling the exuberance, energy, and frustration of young people is an age-old problem which has become even more acute in the United States as we approach the twenty-first century. The amount of deviant behavior and criminal acts that occur in contemporary society can only be partially explained by the "kids will be kids" axiom. Crimes of young people today not only are increasing, but they are becoming more serious and often deadly. The rise in violent, predatory youth gangs who engage in drug sales, drive-by shooting, and contract murder signals a modern urban nightmare in which schools, parents, and law enforcement seem unable to stem.

    The increase in youth crime is not limited to the inner city. Suburban and rural areas also have been inflicted with an expansion of youth crime and violence which has made the whole country concerned and frightened about the lack of conformity exhibited by the younger generation (Hagedorn 1988; Wooden 1995). To an extent, this uneasiness is a function of generational succession; one need only look to the flower children of the 1960s to understand this. The increase in violence, however, marks the present generation as a distinctive problem that has perplexed parents and inspired politicians and law enforcement authorities to "get tough on youth crime."

Are young people of today really different than past generations? Is there cause for concern over how children are being prepared for the future? Are policies aimed at curbing deviant behavior in young people having the desired effect? These are all questions that lack a consensus as to what is the correct answer. The problem in conceptualizing youth crime is that most people view it in a simplistic way. Behavior that is considered juvenile delinquency ranges from **status offenses** such as underage drinking to serious felonies such as rap and murder. There is no simple solution to youth crime any more than there is to crime in general. In fact, there are some unique factors operating on young people which may make their deviant behavior more difficult to handle.

In this chapter, we will look at the phenomena of the **youth culture** in the United States and see how current crime-control strategies may need rethinking if we are to effectively address this serious problem. Perhaps nowhere in the criminal justice system can the differences in the war on crime and the peacemaking perspectives be seen more clearly and have greater potential for disparate results than in the area of youth crime policy.

YOUTH CULTURE IN THE UNITED STATES

Let us begin the discussion of youth culture by admitting that some of us understand it better than others. An argot, or special language, develops around the music, sports, activities, clothes, and folk heroes of each generation. What is the insider's joke to one generation may seem like sacrilegious drivel to another. One need only observe adults' reaction to the style of language in the movie *Wayne's World* or their lack of comprehension of rap music to witness a generation gap. Generational fashions and tastes change quickly and necessarily as each new cohort of youth attempts to define itself by its opposition to what has come before. It is almost as if youth are saying, "I oppose therefore I am."

The youth culture of today is influenced by a variety of factors that make it extremely difficult to discuss what motivates, influences, or arouses their behavior. Race, ethnicity, social-economic status, region of country, quality of school, and a host of other ingredients each function to create different types of youth environments. From the surfer cultures of the coasts to the hip-hop scene of the inner-city, there is constant variation in the categories of youth spectacle. At the center of all these cultures, however, are some core values or ideas that are present and that serve to give meaning and significance to the lives of young people (Wooden 1995). It is these core values and ideas that we will examine in this chapter to see how, while vastly different, each of these youth cultures provides the same functions of inclusion, meaningfulness, and identity for adolescents. Only by understanding what the cultural icons and symbols mean to the participants of the youth culture can we hope to develop public policies aimed at alleviating the problems and obstacles that result in so much undesired behavior.

The MTV Generation

One can get a glimpse at just how negative and seemingly malicious the youth culture is by watching what is considered juvenile entertainment: the music video. With a technology not available to their parents the youth of today are tuned in to a megabuck entertainment and advertising industry that caters to a national audience of young people with limited experiences in authentic activities. The institutions that molded and shaped their parents have either disappeared or have been so radically changed they bear little resemblance to our ideal of child-serving agencies. Public parks can no longer afford the insurance rates to sponsor little league football and baseball programs. Many of the traditional youth sports activities are available to only a small percentage of those who would like to participate. While there are certainly many excellent programs for youth across the country, a closer inspection reveals that many of them are privately sponsored and accessible only to the affluent. Music lessons, gymnastic classes, supervised summer camps, and many other activities that communities used to offer to youth are now so limited or restricted that they can no longer be assumed to be part of the life experiences for a vast number of children.

In place of the adult-managed activities, we now find that adolescents are left to their own devices in providing entertainment, learning activities, and role models. At the center of the youth-oriented subculture of the contemporary teenager is music television which portrays a popular culture filled with sex, violence, and hedonism which conditions adolescents to avoid socially approved patterns of living in favor of a dissenter image.

In addition to the music video, television has other negative influences on the youth culture. From Bart Simpson to Beavis and Butt-head, television presents youth with a cynical and sarcastic model of behavior designed to appeal to young people and drive parents and teachers to despair. At one level, these television characters can be amusing and to some extent they reflect the concerns and style of youngsters, but for some youths, these images do not reflect their pattern of living but dictate it. Ridicule of achievement, disdain for anyone different, insincerity in dealing with other people, especially adults, are all part of the pattern of behavior instilled by many youth-oriented television programs so popular today. It is little wonder the generation gap is not being bridged by parents and children.

So how do we deal with the issues of mass media indoctrination of young people? Do we censor what music they can listen to and the television programs they watch? While these tactics may be appropriate for very young children, they are not desirable or realistic for teenagers. The culture is out there and any attempt to censor it can have unintended effects. If the child has been instilled with a critical mind and a decent set of values she or he will see the hollowness of the popular culture for what it is and pay attention to it for its entertainment value only. If the child does not have a critical mind and a decent set of values, she or he will find the music and television programs anyway and any attempt at censorship will only make these amusements more alluring.

The most effective method of combating these artificial experiences is to offer youngsters authentic encounters with interesting and stimulating activities. MTV and Beavis and Butt-head appeal to the bored and unimaginative youth who is all-too-little involved in his or her own life. Decent schools, artistic and recreational activities, and alternative learning experiences can all deliver kids from the popular culture wasteland of the mass market-dominated media.

Masculinity and Sports

One of the most enduring myths of U.S. culture is the tremendous benefits that can be accrued from participation in organized sports. Self-discipline, character, perseverance, unselfishness, and many other qualities have been attributed to sports as a builder of healthy citizens (Bissinger 1990). Sports programs in high schools and universities are allocated enormous sums of money and immense prestige because of the presumed values they have for young people. Doubtlessly there are individuals who can point to their involvement in sports as a positive influence in their development. There are also many individuals who did not derive such wonderful benefits from sports, and, in fact, may have been better off if they had never set foot on a basketball court or scored the winning touchdown in the homecoming game of their senior year (Bissinger 1990; Coakley 1993; Foley 1993). Many others might have been better off if they had not been the captain of the cheerleading squad or gotten the athletic scholarship to the state university.

Contemporary sports in the United States has undergone a transformation from an institution providing healthy exercise and entertainment to one of big business and corporate greed (Weisman 1993). The values transmitted by sports today with its player work stoppage by millionaires, in-your-face trash talking by superstars, and sport specialization beginning at the middle-grade level have robbed sports of the positive influence it may have had to enhance the development of young people. Now sports promotes the values of the dog-eat-dog paradigm of the corporate state and cheats young people out of the healthy, growth-promoting experiences it is supposed to provide. Once thought to be a good method to release aggression in individuals, it

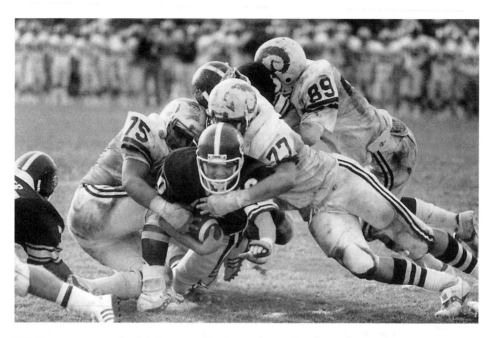

While many people think organized sports are a release for aggression others think they promote competitive values that can result in aggressive behavior. (© Dean Abramson/Stock Boston.)

now appears that violent sports, through a social learning process, may actually increase the level of violence in a society.

> *Modification of behavior—individual or social—is difficult at best. If we wish to take on this task, though, my research would indicate that aggressive behavior is best reduced by eliminating combative or conflict-type sports. Attempting to siphon off aggressive tension by promulgating the observation of or participation in aggressive sports is more than a futile effort; to the degree it has any effect at all, it most likely would raise the level of aggression in other social and individual behavior patterns (Sipes 1993, 84).*

Of most interest to the student of crime and delinquency is the type of masculine behavior promoted by coaches and players today. The prototype athlete produced by sports organizations from little league to the pros is a patriarchal, domineering, insensitive, and hostile individual (Messner 1992). The win-at-all-costs mentality that pervades sports is exacting an exorbitant cost on the personalities of many young athletes. Coaches teach players to injure their opponents, cheat, abuse their own bodies, and hold women in contempt or as sex objects. What passes for locker-room humor are sexist, oppressive, and brutal efforts to maintain and enhance a gender hierarchy (Neimark 1993). Sports is touted as providing healthy values for youth but, in many cases, it only reiterates a dubious model of manhood that is being corrected more rapidly in other segments of society (Foley 1993).

One of the features of modern sports that is the most to blame for perverse values being promoted is the paramilitary style of coaching. Coaches used to be teachers (and many still are), but the pressure to win has prompted many to attempt to gain control over not only what their players do on the field but over their entire life, from how they dress, to where they live, to who their friends are. In a manner reminiscent of Foucault (1977), coaches have instituted a model of surveillance and discipline designed to capture the soul of the athlete every bit as much as the modern prison attempts to cage the soul of the inmate. Instead of teaching leadership, many coaches demand their players follow all orders without question. Instead of teaching self-discipline, many coaches punish players for slight infractions of ridiculous and trivial rules. Instead of teaching sportsmanship, many coaches teach humiliation and hatred of opponents (Eitzen 1989).

Perhaps there is a place for this paramilitary model of coaching in professional sports where players are handsomely compensated for their services and have achieved a level of self-esteem that can withstand this type of treatment. There is a real problem, however, when this paramilitary model of coaching is employed at the high school level and below, where youngsters are in their formative years and can be emotionally scarred from the fierce and ruthless treatment of overzealous coaches (Lombardo 1986). Only a small fraction of young athletes will play at the college level, and even fewer will make it into the pros, yet the paramilitary model of coaching pervades youth sports and indoctrinates kids with a value system not suitable for operating in a complex and ambiguous society. The link between domination in sport and domination in relationships between men and women has been asserted by several observers. The misogynistic viewpoint taught to young men by the sports culture facilitates attitudes toward women that consider spouse abuse, rape, and sexual exploitation to be excusable behavior. The intimate relationships of sports stars such as O. J. Simpson, Wayne Boggs, Wilt Chamberlain, Jim Brown, and Andre Rison all suggest that success in sports may be insufficient training for success in establishing meaningful relationships.

Organized sports as practiced in North America is problematic. Beyond the myth of healthy competition is a social structure that generates a sometimes sexist (Messner et al. 1993), often racist (Edwards 1989), predominantly patriarchal (Messner and Sabo 1990), and increasingly homophobic (Griffin and Genasci 1990; Pronger 1990) pattern of values that undermine the development of emotionally well-adjusted women and men.

YOUTH CRIME

Young people are subject to numerous pressures from parents, teachers, coaches, and peers to establish an identity that distinguishes them as unique individuals. This is difficult to accomplish when we consider how routinized the lifestyles and opportunities for young people have become. There are precious few ways for a juvenile to individualize himself in today's society. Breaking the law is one method for a young person to confirm his identity. The juvenile justice system treats numerous kids who engage in mildly deviant behavior because of boredom and lack of alternative activities to fill their time. Some youth also engage in such serious criminal behavior that many feel they should be dealt with by the criminal justice system as adults. Juvenile delinquency covers a broad range of behavior and is fascinating to consider because there is so little consensus as to what should be done with young law breakers, and at what point we should intervene in their lives.

Status Offenses

There is a category of behaviors that are against the law only if the offender is below a certain age (Schur 1973). An adult performing identical actions would not be subject to criminal sanction. In effect, these *status offenses* treat individuals for who they are rather than for what they did. Underage drinking, running away from home, truancy, being incorrigible, and, in some jurisdictions, violating a curfew can bring a youth before a juvenile court judge, while his or her older brother would not be vulnerable to the authorities. These status offenses were established to help the parent(s) handle children engaging in unwanted behaviors (Platt 1969). The juvenile court and associated youth-serving agencies can act in the child's best interests to force him or her to stay in school, stay off drugs, stay away from bad company, or generally stay out of trouble until he or she is old enough to make suitable decisions for himself (Fuller and Norton 1993). Not all parents are equally competent to supervise their children and the juvenile court has the responsibility to provide a safety net and catch the children who are in danger of becoming delinquent or are in danger of becoming victims of incapable or unfit parents. While some may argue that juveniles should not be subjected to laws simply because of their age, the intent of the law is to protect the youth, not make life more difficult. We can all agree there has to be some line drawn as to where one has the freedom to drive a car, enter into a legally binding agreement, drink alcoholic beverages, or quit school. What we differ upon is exactly where that line should be drawn.

Vandalism and Graffiti

The quest to establish identity is a recurrent theme in the literature on adolescent development. The desire to leave one's mark on society is something that we all possess but are not all able to accomplish in socially accepted ways. Vandalism and **graffiti** are two related methods that young people have long employed to make their mark on the community (Klofas and Cutshall 1985; Wooden 1995). At one point in time it was considered great fun for youngsters to sneak out at night and tip over their neighbors' outhouses.

Setting fire to vacant buildings or desecrating the town's cemetery were other methods of vandalism which enjoyed a long history in the United States. However, contemporary styles of vandalism can take more sinister forms. Racist and homophobic statements are made by young people as political declarations of disenchantment with the manner in which society is sharing power with previously marginal groups and becoming more tolerant of alternative lifestyles. Some youngsters are using the public media of vandalism and graffiti to register opposition and hate toward peoples they feel are threatening their place on the social ladder. So prevalent has such behaviors become, a new type of crime has been added to the lexicon. **"Hate crime"** is the term used to describe acts that victimize individuals because of race, religion, or sexual orientation.

A current form of art has also emerged from the graffiti form of vandalism where public buildings, buses, and subway cars are defaced by some rather elaborate and, to some eyes, beautiful artwork. Often in the form of cartoon characters, graffiti makes humorous or political statements, but the real appeal and motivation is to have the work seen by as many people as possible.

Graffiti as deviant behavior has another dimension in large urban areas. Graffiti is used by gangs to mark their territory (Shaw 1973). A squiggly shaped symbol seen in big cities on street signs, mailboxes, and walls of buildings signifies the lines of demarcation between one gang's territory and the next. When the turf is in dispute, the symbols are marked over or crossed out. The stability of gang relations can be witnessed by looking at the contest nature of the graffiti markings.

Larceny and Shoplifting as Status Rituals

Another form of youth crime that bears examination is the influx in shoplifting that is plaguing retail establishments. The mall culture has spawned a curiosity known as the mall rat (Wooden 1995). These teen and preteen youngsters often spend entire days hanging out at air-conditioned malls often in game rooms and fast food restaurants that cater to their business. The other stores in the mall have found that groups of roving adolescents can present a big problem, both in establishing an atmosphere where shoppers feel comfortable and in protecting merchandise from youthful shoplifters. Given the tremendous pressures on adolescents to consume material goods, especially brand-name clothing, it comes as no surprise that stealing from mall stores has become both an art form and a rite of passage in the suburban landscape. The extensive target-hardening procedures employed by stores, particularly music and clothing outlets, provide evidence of just how serious the shoplifting problem has become. While it may be unfair to attribute all of this issue to teenagers, there is a facet of the youth culture that is centered around the shopping mall and includes ritualistic deviant behavior in the form of shoplifting, intimidating store employees and shoppers, display of peculiar clothes, hairstyles, tatoos, and jewelry piercing various body parts. As malls have become the new downtown for many communities, the problems of main street have been transported to the video arcade (Wooden 1995, 27):

> *According to police officials, suburban malls—though not as crime-ridden as inner cities—are not as safe as one would expect. Besides being convenient for consumers, they also entice the criminal element as well, including muggers, rapists, car thieves, and shoplifters. Crime, it appears, is occurring more frequently in "nice places, like suburban malls."*

YOUTH VIOLENCE

If the experience of adolescents is different for contemporary youngsters than it was for past generations, the most notable characteristic of the dissimilarity is the level and lethality of violence. The willingness to use violence to settle disputes or organize the social hierarchy has always been a trait of American society, but the manner in which violence has become part of the youth culture has developed into a basis of great apprehension among parents in both the inner-city and suburban neighborhoods. The incidence of children carrying guns to school even at the elementary level has prompted some school districts to install metal detectors similar to those found at airports. The efforts of keeping nonstudents off high school campuses consumes resources in the form of security officers and detracts from more educational ways to allocate this money. Violence among youth is a grave problem and it comes in several guises.

The Great High School Fight

The pressure to win in high school is not felt only by the athletes. A great deal of the "us-versus-them" mentality is whipped up in conjunction with high school sports, and intense rivalries are championed by coaches, teachers, and administrators. Neighboring schools are villainized for the purposes of creating unity for the football team on Friday night. Unfortunately this intense loathing of the rivals cannot be turned off as easily as it has been turned on. The malice spreads to more than just the game, and an unofficial contest takes on premiere importance as young men (and, in some cases, young women) engage in the after-game ritual of the high school fight (Foley 1995).

Each school has long histories of these fights, and parents and uncles will tell teenagers about the classic battles from their own high school experiences. On one level these fights seem like a normal rite of passage where the honor of the school must be protected, and the teenagers establish themselves as local heros not unlike the football players. But on the other hand, the high school fight has escalated in some localities to a deadly game of gunfire and severe beatings. The concern here is that in the name of good healthy competition between schools on the athletic field, a spillover effect happens, and some of the students in the school (and some ex-students or nonstudent hanger-ons) battle the rival school in more fatal competitions. Casting the opponent in the role of enemy gets taken to an extreme by some students, and the war metaphor becomes a shocking reality.

The Code of the Streets

Because of the threat of violence, much of the civility expressed in everyday life is disappearing into a grim "leave me alone" demeanor which deprives everyone from enjoying social interaction in public places. The differences in street behavior between urban areas and small towns has been long recognized. Today street behavior is not so much about civility as about survival. In the inner city a rigid **code of the street** has developed, which must be adhered to if one is to successfully negotiate even the most everyday tasks of going to the store or walking the dog. Elijah Anderson explains how youngsters from inner-city families committed to middle-class values must adopt the oppositional culture of "the streets" in order to survive.

> *The operating assumption is that a man, especially a real man, knows what other men know—the code of the street. And if one is not a real man, one is somehow diminished as a person, and there are certain valued things one simply does not deserve. There is thus believed to be a certain justice to the code, since it is considered that everyone has the opportunity to know it. Implicit in this is that everyone is held responsible for being familiar with the code. If the victim of a mugging, for example, does not know the code and so responds "wrong," the perpetrator may feel justified even in killing him and may feel no remorse. He may think, "Too bad, but it's his fault. He should have known better" (Anderson 1994, 89).*

Anderson goes on to explain how the issue of manhood is demonstrated by having nerve. "Nerve is shown when one takes another person's possessions (the more valuable the better), 'messes with' someone's woman, throws the first punch, 'gets in someone's face,' or pulls the trigger." One must show a lack of fear, even of dying, in order to display the appropriate demeanor of someone who can take care of himself on the street. According to Anderson, this behavior is useful in the contested environment of the street, but some youth have a difficult time changing into a more appropriate manner of behavior when they interact with teachers or employers. Thus, his identity being wrapped up in the presentation of manhood becomes problematic and it begins to control him.

Young men are not alone in having to develop a special method of behaving on the street. Young women also need to cultivate a deportment of themselves which fixes their identity and wards off predatory behavior.

> *A major cause of conflicts among girls is "he say, she say," This practice begins in the early school years and continues through high school. It occurs*

when "people," particularly girls, talk about others, thus putting their "business in the streets." Usually one girl will say something negative about another in the group, most often behind the person's back. The remark will get back to the person talked about. She may retaliate or her friends may feel required to "take up for" her. In essence this is a form of group gossiping in which individuals are negatively assessed and evaluated. As with much gossip, the things said may or may not be true, but the point is that imputations can cast aspersions on a person's good name. The accused is required to defend herself against the slander, which can result in arguments or fights, often over little or real substance. Here again is the problem of low self-esteem, which encourages youngsters to be highly sensitive to slights and to be vulnerable to feeling easily "dissed." To avenge a dissing, a fight is usually necessary (Anderson 1994, 92).

While girls used to turn to male relatives to do their fighting for them, they are increasingly engaging in violence themselves. According to Anderson, they have a brother or uncle teach them to fight and even form gangs to attack other girls. Because they do not use guns like boys, their fights are not the life-or-death struggles where "manhood" is defended to the ultimate extreme.

The code of the street was developed in the inner city but variants of it can be seen in public places in many different locales. The running gun battles on the freeways in many cities show how respect and honor are stressed to ridiculous limits as the civility and courtesy that once characterized public behavior has become lost in the alienated spheres of communal living.

Gangs, Drugs, and Drive-By Shootings

Nowhere is the problem of youth violence more serious than in the gang-related problems of our large cities. The media routinely documents the carnage of killings by youngsters disputing territory, drug markets, and real or imagined insults.

Gangs in the United States have a long and sometimes romantic history, but the deadliness of many gang activities today has captured the public's fascination and evoked a new sense of fear that chases many people off the streets, especially at night. Entire neighborhoods are taken over by the gangs who dictate the quality of life and intimidate anyone who tries to stand up to them. While gangs used to kill each other over control of territory, they now also insist on overseeing the drug markets and other vices such as gambling and prostitution (Skolnick 1995).

Not all cities have the problem of gang-related drug sales. It seems that as each city develops its own response to problems of crime that the type and level of gang activity varies (Maxson 1995; Meehan and O'Carroll 1995). For example, in Miami, where there is a significant problem with drug use and serious delinquent behavior, very little of it can be attributed to the activities of gangs. Miami's gang structure developed only so far and does not resemble the gangs found in California or the major cities of the east coast.

In south central Los Angeles, the Bloods and the Crips are two major gangs which best exemplify the type of gang problem that concerns so many law enforcement officials and school administrators. The Crips and Bloods are actually supergangs that have annexed smaller groups into their structure. While there are several layers to gang membership, the important point is being aligned with one or the other of the organizations. Being able to "throw your sign" signifies just how much other youths can hassle a person. Having access to the resources of the gang, especially the willingness to use violence in defending honor or assets, means others will not elect to give the gang member a hard time. In addition to this security function, the gang also gives its members a sense of belonging and togetherness. Many of the gang members come from broken or dysfunctional families, and the gang represents the most stable and dependable entity in their lives.

The drive-by shooting has become the assassination method of choice by the gang culture. This is easy to understand when the nature of the geography, availability of automatic weapons, and role of the automobile in California is considered (Sanders 1995).

Los Angeles is a city that has spread out rather than grown up. The territory controlled by gangs can be measured in square miles rather that in square blocks. Cars give gang members mobility extending beyond the neighborhoods they claim as their own. Members of segments of different gangs come into contact with each other at various disputed places which may be miles from the home base of either group. The car has extended the battlefield and is instrumental in structuring the interactions between gang members. As the freeway system allows for easy access in and out of neighborhoods it is convenient and relatively safe for gangs to attack rivals in hit-and-run maneuvers of drive-by shootings. This is further facilitated by the widespread use of automatic assault weapons. Accurate shooting is not required when a streetcorner or parking lot can be sprayed with round after round of automatic gunfire.

The killing of innocent bystanders is a by-product of the drive-by shooting tactic, and not one that causes gang members to feel remorse. Gang warfare recognizes no such luxury as innocent bystanders. If they are standing around the intended target then they were not considered innocent.

Combating gang violence is something law enforcement agencies have a particularly difficult time accomplishing (Klein 1995). Gangs based on race, ethnicity, and neighborhood affiliation have proved extremely hard to infiltrate. Outsiders are seldom allowed access to information that would help police in identifying gang members who engage in homicide. Elaborate initiation rites are required of anyone attempting to become part of the gang, and the solidarity of established gangs is difficult to penetrate. Using the war metaphor as a policy model for confronting gangs has met with mixed results at best.

The questions as to why gangs emerge and what functions they provide for youth are seldom asked because the policy implications of addressing these questions would require more than just a law enforcement response by the community. Dealing with the underlying issues of poverty, racism, and school systems that are not equipped to deal with a multicultural student body require more resources than many politicians are willing to ask of their constituents (Miller 1996). In addition to addressing these community issues, there are some promising strategies for dealing with the gang members themselves.

A technique that has proved effective in one location is **aggression replacement training.** According to Goldstein and Glick (1994), there are some positive qualities about gangs that can be channeled by training in self-control to produce prosocial behavior. It is this type of skill-building that offers more potential for reclaiming wayward youth than does the war-type strategies of police gang task forces.

PEACEMAKING FOR YOUTH

The solutions for the many problems associated with youth crime are neither simple or politically popular. The money necessary for the criminal justice system to remedy the failures of families, schools, and child welfare agencies is not forthcoming from state legislatures. The commitment of society to attempt new and innovative programs which deal with problem youth is lacking in many parts of the country, particularly in the inner city. The optimism necessary to view each adolescent as still having a chance to be rescued from a life of crime has been beaten down by harsh experience. Finally, the vision that young people themselves often hold the answer for these ills is seldom pictured.

The curious element in the whole failure of American society to provide a healthy environment for children is that it is so simple to conceptualize what should be done. Instead of asking why some kids go bad, we should be asking why most kids are good. What is it in a child's surroundings that causes him or her to accept a conforming lifestyle? Once we answer that question it becomes obvious what should be done to provide the same type of background for children who are likely to get into trouble. This response, however, demands a more comprehensive reaction from society than is available from the criminal justice system. In order to address the requirements for producing emotionally healthy and economically secure children, we need to intervene much earlier in their development. After 14 years of neglect and abuse, the criminal justice system cannot be expected to rehabilitate or even deter a youngster who is illiterate, embittered, hostile to authority, and guilty of some heinous crime. Why wait until so much harm has been done to the child, and he or she has done so much harm to society before his or her problems are treated?

Redefining Youth Culture

There has always been an element of rebelliousness in youth and attempts by adults to influence how kids think are often met with cynicism, distrust, and ridicule. The simplistic and naive message of Nancy Reagan's "just say no" drug prevention campaign did little to quell the drug crisis in the country. It was a public-relations campaign that did more to satisfy the parents than it did to actually alter how children dealt with their problems. In some ways it was not a bad idea in that the program reached down into the elementary school level with its message; however, the message was indoctrination, not actually education. Children were not told what they needed to know in order to make informed decisions about drug use. They were told only that drugs are bad, and if anyone tries to get you to use drugs you should tell them no thank-you. For many youngsters drugs are already a part of their families, peer groups, and neighborhoods. Drug use for them is not a simple yes-no decision but one that requires them to distinguish between types of drugs and dose levels. Scare tactics of the "just say no" campaign do not provide the skills and education that many youth need to deal with actual decisions. They have seen their friends and family members use drugs on a social basis, and they have not seen the drastic consequences that were predicted. The all-or-nothing message to children backfires when their experiences conflict with what they have been told. Streetwise adolescents cannot be brainwashed by simplistic slogans. The elementary school children of the Reagan years are now at the peak drug-using period in their lives and there seems to be little evidence that the high profile and expensive "just say no" campaign has had any lasting effect.

Attempts to censor what children read, listen to, and watch also do little good in altering the youth culture. Conservative groups periodically undertake bids to remove books from the shelves of school libraries or ban records that contain references to sex and violence. These attempts underestimate the ability of youngsters to find these materials on their own and serve only to increase the interest on the part of the child for the proscribed material.

Changing the culture of the youngster's world requires reforming it. The reason there is so much distrust and bitterness on the part of children is because they are powerless to affect their destinies in socially allowed means. They turn to deviant behavior to obtain the rewards denied them by the conventional society. Decent schools, accessible recreation programs, and training for useful occupation is part of what it takes to make the society meaningful to adolescents. Something else kids need, which we seldom acknowledge, is the power to make decisions which are important to them. Too many times all the consequential decisions are made for children so they get the impression that things are done to them rather than feeling they are doing.

Participatory democracy is a vital experience that is lacking in youth culture. Children are told what to do by countless authority figures and never get the opportunities to learn to settle disputes between themselves. They learn the tactics of domination and exploitation from watching their parents, teachers, and television, but they seldom get the chance to work on meaningful issues in their lives and negotiate the outcomes. The only place they can get power is on the street and power there is always physical and at the expense of someone else.

The empowerment of children is a promising method of preparing them to make effective decisions and deal with the ambiguities of life which too often seem to lead to deviant behavior. It is easier for most parents and schools to dictate what is to be done rather than teaching youth how to accomplish tasks. When the youth finally gets into a decision-making situation, he or she looks to others for a clue as to what to do and, too often, the clue leads to crime or other socially destructive behavior.

There are several programs around the country that recognize this problem and are designed to give youths the types of experiences that will teach them how to think for themselves. Some of the more notable programs include **peer counseling** and conflict mediation.

The idea behind the peer-counseling type of program is that youth are much more likely to listen to someone closer to their own age and someone who faces the same contingencies in life as they do. Getting yelled at by adults is viewed by children as something that contains no message worth hearing. Talking to someone your own age where there is a give and take of important ideas is viewed as being worth engagement. Conflict-mediation programs are even more useful in that they give youth experience in reaching resolutions to problems in peaceful and satisfying ways.

One method of teaching conflict resolution is to allow children to role-play a situation in which they are likely to confront. This gives them an opportunity to explore alternative styles of working out the problem (Goldstein and Glick 1994). They can see where they fail to achieve their desired outcomes in a trial situation and prepare themselves for the real conflicts to come. Sometimes in a role-playing situation the facilitator will reverse the roles of the participants. By having to act out the part of a parent explaining why his or her child should not use drugs, the youth may gain some insight or empathy for his or her parent's position.

Conflict resolution programs may also teach such techniques as anger control, alterative stress-relieving procedures, or insights into one's communication style. The goal of all these strategies is to redefine how youngsters deal with their problems by reforming not only their culture, but their ability to interact with others. Too often, kids simply follow the patterns they learned from their parents and their peers on the street and the cycle is continued until they are in jail or dead.

Education and School Safety

Schools provide a pivotal opportunity to intervene in children's lives. Schools are the principal institution outside the family that have responsibility for shaping the lives of children. For the most part, schools do a good job of meeting the needs of youth. When one considers the awesome task of providing universal education for such a large number of children, one can began to appreciate just how effective schools are. However, some schools are better than others. Some schools have the resources and teachers to provide not only a good education but also an atmosphere that encourages the student to maximize her or his potential.

The deciding factor in how good a school or school system is turns out to be the economic situation of the local community. Because school financing is based on local property taxes, the schools in the affluent communities are superior to schools in poverty areas (Kozol 1991). Additionally, control of most features of public schools rests with the local school board so schools whose parents are politically powerful and who are able to secure grants and other outside funding are able to provide a very high level of education. Schools whose parents are unsophisticated and politically impotent find they are unable to give an adequate education even though the teachers may be extremely dedicated and hard-working. While money cannot solve all problems, it is a vital ingredient in the quality of schools (Kohl 1967; Kozol 1967).

Recognizing that the disparity between the quality of schools is based essentially on the resources on hand to finance teaching efforts and recreational activities, it is easy to see that resources are also related to the ability of the school to provide a safe learning environment. The same schools that have inadequate money to furnish competent education also cannot maintain the safety of the school. Drugs and weapons are problems that afflict many schools and that interfere with the educational mission by creating an environment of anxiety and fear. The first obligation of a school system is to provide a setting where learning can occur without the worry of physical violence.

What can be done to ensure school safety short of ameliorating all the problems of poverty from the surrounding community? Not much. The school reflects the culture of the neighborhood and as a social institution should provide outreach programs and services aimed at helping families manage the conflicting demands of raising their kids in a violent world while trying to provide material support in an economically depressed area. Schools can best help protect themselves from violence not by walling themselves off from the community with metal detectors, drug tests for students, and quick expulsion for troublemakers, but by becoming an integral part of the community by offering after-school learning and recreational activities, classes and support groups concerned with effective patenting, and efforts to involve local businesses and community groups in making the school the nucleus of the social structure of the surrounding area. In this way, everyone begins to take an interest in what happens at the school and vandalism, violence, and drug activity are addressed by the citizens and not just the school officials.

Reclaiming Throwaway Children

If all the students who are supposed to be in school ever showed up on the same day there would not be enough desks for all of them. High schools have a very high dropout rate and in the work force of today those lacking a high school diploma are excluded from many opportunities for employment. The issue of school dropouts is important to the understanding of youth crime.

Education does more than simply provide the student with skills that make them more employable. Educational institutions can also provide a sense of belonging and identity to young people. Involvement in extracurricular activities can promote feelings of belonging and increased self-esteem, which can compensate to a degree the feelings of hopelessness and unconnectedness which many youth from disadvantaged backgrounds experience. Using the juvenile justice system as a dumping ground for these youths is a policy fraught with unattractive consequences. Yet, this is the policy emerging in local justice systems.

> *We are changing our society. We are retreating from working with youth in the school and working more with them in corrections. If we do not change that pattern of shifting emphasis, we will no doubt shift the youth to where the emphasis is and find ourselves working with more and more youth in corrections and fewer and fewer youth in schools. We will turn our society into a treacherous divider of youth, relaxing both the degradation and support provided by schooling, rewarding those who succeed in this new freedom, banishing to a correctional archipelago those who fail (Miller and Ohlin 1985, 183).*

The peacemaking perspective would transform the juvenile justice system to do what the family, school, and church have not been able to accomplish in the past few generations. The integration of the youth into a meaningful community should be the objective of child-serving agencies. On one level, this would mean making our communities more meaningful in ways that foster a perception of belonging among the members. In many cities and towns this feeling of belonging is noticeably absent for large segments of the population.

The second requirement for the integration of deviant youth would be a dismantling of much of the juvenile justice empire (Schur 1973). The concept of community corrections has been distorted by recent policies of placing maximum security institutions in communities without developing the linkages necessary to capitalize on the advantages of the other social institutions available. Isolating youth behind walls and sharp wire still means they are in prison even if the prison is located in a neighborhood. Community corrections entails linking the schools, churches, youth groups, and recreational activities to the correctional institution. The answer to the problems of youth corrections is to deinstitutionalize and integrate the offender into the community, not to further isolate.

The war on crime perspective is most destructive in the area of juvenile delinquency. Unless one is willing to concede that certain youth are so far socialized into crime by the time they are 15 years old that they cannot be reclaimed, then it is incumbent on society to address both the individual's needs as well as reform the social structures that produced the offending behavior. A war on crime is literally a war on our children. After failing as parents and as social institutions to provide for the physical and social welfare of youth, we label them as the enemy and use considerably more resources to arrest, incarcerate and demonize the victims of our neglect. Perhaps if we used the vast sums of money we now use for the correctional system for ensuring that all youth are provided an adequate education, decent health care, nutritious food, and safe shelter, we would find our problems of crime to be greatly diminished.

The peacemaking perspective requires that the needs of children be dealt with before they engage in serious delinquency. Gang involvement, vandalism, drug abuse, and other forms of deviant behavior occur in a context that is subject to change and modification. By confronting the social and moral environment with peacemaking principles, it will be possible to influence the conditions that influence young people to seek out and engage in crime.

CRITICAL THINKING QUESTIONS

1. Make a list of all the unlawful behaviors you committed as a juvenile (drinking underage, shoplifting, assault). How many of these behaviors would have been crimes if you had been an adult?

2. Discuss in class how the youth culture of today is different from that of the 1960s and 1970s. Is it harder to be a teenager today than it was back then?

3. Write a page or two recounting an experience of gender socialization from your youth. Include who did the socializing and what your feelings were at the time. Would you react differently to that situation if you knew then what you know today?

4. If you were given a million-dollar grant to study the problems caused by urban gangs, what would you do with it? What recommendations can you now make on what to do about the problems of gangs?

SUGGESTED READINGS

Anderson, Elijah. 1994. "The Code of the Streets." *The Atlantic Monthly* (May): 89–94.

Bissinger, H. G. 1993 (1990). "High School Football and Academics," in D. Stanley Eitzen, ed. *Sport in Contemporary Society,* 4th ed. New York: St. Martin's Press, pp. 66–76.

Edwards, Harry. 1989 (1984). "The Black 'Dumb Jock': An American Sports Tragedy," in D. Stanley Eitzen, ed. *Sport in Contemporary Society,* 3rd ed. New York: St. Martin's Press, pp. 158–166.

Foley, Douglas E. 1993. "The Great American Football Ritual: Reproducing Race, Class, and Gender Inequality," in D. Stanley Eitzen, ed. *Sport in Contemporary Society: An Anthology,* 4th ed. New York: St. Martin's Press, pp. 326–354.

Hagedorn, John, and Perry Macon. 1988. *People and Folks: Gangs, Crime and the Underclass in a Rustbelt City.* Chicago: Lakeview.

Maxson, Cheryl L. 1995. "Street Gangs and Drug Sales in Two Suburban Cities." *National Institute of Justice* (September): 1–14.

Messner, Michael A., and Donald F. Sabo. 1990. "Toward a Critical Feminist Reappraisal of Sport, Men, and the Gender Order," in Michael A. Messner and Donald F. Sabo, eds. *Sport, Men, and the Gender Order: Critical Feminist Perspectives.* Champaign: Human Kinetics Press, pp. 1–15.

Messner, Michael. 1992. "Boyhood, Organized Sports, and the Construction of Masculinity," in Michael S. Kimmel and Michael A. Messner, eds. *Men's Lives,* 2nd ed. New York: MacMillan, pp. 161–175.

Neimark, Jill. 1993. "Out of Bounds: The Truth About Athletes and Rape," in D. Stanley Eitzen, ed. *Sport in Contemporary Society: An Anthology,* 4th ed. New York: St. Martin's Press, pp. 130–137.

Wooden, Wayne S. 1995. *Renegade Kids, Suburban Outlaws: From Youth Culture to Delinquency.* Belmont: Wadsworth.

13

CRIME FROM A GLOBAL PERSPECTIVE

© Tony Savino/The Image Works.

Learning Objectives

After reading this chapter, the student should be able to:

- Appreciate how ethnocentrism plays a role in how we evaluate other cultures.
- Discuss how religion acts as a form of social control in Saudi Arabia.
- Describe the division of behaviors covered under Islamic law.
- Trace the three historic traditions that contribute to the culture in African nations.
- Describe how ancient tribalism continues to be a divisive force in contemporary South Africa.
- Describe how organized crime has become a serious problem in Russia.
- Discuss how neighborhood committees contribute to the rehabilitation of offenders and the resolving of disputes in China.
- Discuss how the goals of the criminal justice system differ in China and the United States.
- Discuss how prostitution in developing countries has turned into an international sex tourism trade.
- Describe how the peacemaking perspective views the sex tourism trade.

Key Terms

Ethnocentrism
Hudud Crimes
Qisas Crimes
Ta'zir Crimes
Colonialism

Post-Colonial
Apartheid
Bang-jiao
Tiao-jie

The problems and issues of criminal justice as an institution are not confined to the United States. Every country struggles with controlling the antisocial behavior of its people. What is fascinating and informative to the student of criminal justice is the vast variability in how other nations define crime and deal with the violator. By looking at how different countries administer their criminal law, we can develop a deeper appreciation for our own criminal justice system.

This chapter is not meant to be an exhaustive survey of comparative criminal justice systems around the globe. That task would require more space than is available for our purposes here. Many university criminal justice programs have advanced-level classes on international or global crime, and it is there the student will receive a comprehensive and integrated introduction to this massive topic. Our purposes in this chapter are much more limited. Here we can only introduce some criminal justice issues in some countries. This incomplete picture of crime on a global basis is meant merely to hint at the extensive diversity in the method of maintaining social control that exists in other countries.

There are two principles that guide the selection of criminal justice issues and countries. The first is comparison to the United States. Countries with different cultures that have contrasting ways of dispensing justice are reviewed. While some western industrialized democracies are mentioned, the bulk of the chapter is devoted to developing and third-world countries that have very different criminal justice problems and resources than the United States. The aim here is to develop a viewpoint that acknowledges the diverse nature of crime around the world.

The second guiding principle in selecting which issues and cultures are addressed is their relevance to the war on crime and peacemaking perspectives. By using these orienting perspectives, we can better compare and contrast the respective criminal justice issues and systems. Many countries use peacemaking techniques in their cultures that can be emulated by the United States. Of course, we must keep in mind that many practices are cultural-specific and translating them from another part of the world to the United States can be problematic. Nevertheless, this chapter looks at how other peoples sometimes employ the peacemaking perspective to address criminal justice issues. If we are to develop this perspective in greater detail in the United States, we need all the help and ideas we can get.

A NOTE ON ETHNOCENTRISM

There is a danger that in looking at other cultures we judge them against our own. The term **ethnocentrism** means that we think of our own cultural patterns as the right way, God's way, or the only way to do things. Anthropologists apply the term "cultural shock" to someone who visits another culture and finds that the approved ways of thinking and doing things are different. It takes a deep understanding and appreciation of another culture before their norms and values make sense to the outsider. In this chapter, we will never be able to develop this deep understanding and appreciation of the countries we visit as we skip around the globe, briefly considering the many faces of crime and the different methods of social control. Therefore, we should not be judgmental but, instead, remember that there are other, perhaps better, ways to address crime. The rate and seriousness of crime in the United States does not allow us to be elitists when looking at how other countries deal with their social problems.

CRIME AND JUSTICE IN SAUDI ARABIA

Saudi Arabia is the first country we look at in comparison to the United States because it is such a drastically different culture that dictates a method of criminal justice that most outsiders find difficult to comprehend. In order to appreciate the practices of the criminal justice system in Saudi Arabia, one must understand how religion is an all-encompassing institution that governs every aspect of public and private life.

While most Moslem Arab countries have adopted secular constitutions and penal codes (Egypt, Iraq, Jordan, Kuwait, Syria, and Tunisia), Saudi Arabia has adopted sacred scripture (the Quran) as its constitution and Islamic legislation for its penal law (Ali 1985). Saudi Arabia is therefore considered a theocracy, where the church and state are one in the same. In a country with a homogenous population like Saudi Arabia, where virtually everyone is a practicing Moslem, this type of criminal justice system is functional. Obviously, those who are not Moslems are constrained by the law and must accommodate their beliefs and behaviors to conform to the law of the land. Deviance from the dominant culture has unpleasant consequences.

The blending of church and state gives Saudi Arabia a system of social control that is more encompassing than western nations. The emphasis is on prevention of crime through deterrence and building a moral foundation in the individual. According to Sanad (1991):

1. It constantly seeks to reform the individual and purify his conscience and soul with sublime Islamic ideals and lofty morals.

2. It adequately warns people against committing offenses and admonishes the offender with dreadful punishment in this world and the hereafter.

3. It commands Moslems to assist one another on the path of righteousness and piety by offering counsel, moral support, and the exchange of religious teaching.

4. It prevents crime by blocking the path to its commission; for example, by prohibiting the use of intoxicants.

5. It protects Moslems, in recognition of man's fallibility, by urging marriage at a young age and requiring the rich to contribute to the needs of the less fortunate in accordance with the concept of *zakat* (alms giving) (49–50).

Islamic penal law divides crimes into three categories according to a complex criteria that is quite different from western ways of judging seriousness of crimes. The three Islamic categories are ***hudud* crimes, *qisas* crimes,** and ***ta'zir* crimes.** It is useful to examine how these categories of crimes are conceived in terms of seriousness and the punishments that can be applied to their offenders.

Hudud *Crimes*

1. *Adultery (zena).* Adultery in Islamic law is different than in western law. Islamic law defines it as voluntary intercourse with anyone other than one's spouse. If neither of the individuals are married it is still considered adultery under Islamic law. The Islamic faith considers clear and honorable bloodlines to be particularly important, so adultery is a very serious offense. If either of the participants are married the penalty can be death by stoning. For unmarried persons the penalty is 100 lashes.

2. *Theft (sariga).* There are various levels of theft under Islamic law, and the most serious is when the thief breaks into a private place and takes property. Theft in a public place or where there is some dispute over ownership is not considered as serious a crime. Punishment for theft is amputation of the hand(s), which is done in public places to serve as a deterrent.

3. *Banditry (haraba).* Banditry can be compared to armed robbery in the United States. It is considered more serious than theft and the penalties can range from execution to crucifixion to exile.

4. *Defamation (gadhf).* Defamation under Islamic law occurs when someone unjustly accuses a woman of being unchaste. In order to not be punished as a defamer or slanderer, the accuser must produce four witnesses. The penalty for defamation is 80 lashes.

5. *Transgression (baghi).* Transgression is the rebellion by use of force against the legitimate *imam* (local religious ruler). Under Islamic law, believers are permitted to revolt against an unjust and vicious ruler, but this is a judgment call and those found to rebel without adequate justification are subject to punishment.

6. *Drinking alcohol (shorb al-khamr).* The prohibition against the drinking of alcohol extends to all substances that "befog the mind and make a person lose his sense and conscience, no matter what these intoxicants are (wine, cocaine, opium, hashish, marijuana, etc.)" (Sanad 1991, 55). The penalty for using these substances can be 80 lashes or 40 lashes, depending on which legal or religious authority is invoked.

7. *Apostasy (ridda).* Apostasy is the renouncing of the Islamic faith after having adhered to it.

It should be evident that the penalties for violating these *hudud* crimes are usually a form of corporal punishment. In the western view, this is considered inhumane. Sanad (1991) contends this western way of looking at pain inflicted on the offender's body is actually not inhumane when the culture of the Arab world and the dictates of the Islamic religion are taken into consideration. Furthermore, when the pain of corporal punishment is contrasted with the psychological stress of imprisonment, it is debatable which is more inhumane. One western scholar, Graham Newman (1983), has made a case for corporal punishment in the United States without resorting to justification from the Islamic religion. The infliction of corporal punishment must take place in public so that the goal of prevention can be accomplished.

Qisas *Crimes*

In contrast to Western criminal justice, "crimes against person" such as murder or intentional physical injury are not considered as serious as the *hudud* crimes already mentioned. These *qisas* crimes have as their penalty a retaliation by the victim or his or her male blood relative. The retaliation can be only to the extent that the victim was harmed which, of course, means that in the case of murder the victim's family has the right to kill the offender. In cases of unintentional harm, *diyya* (blood money) is paid to the victim or his or her family. It is interesting from a western view to see how men and women are valued in monetary terms under Islamic law.

> *Muslim scholars agree that the amount of* diyya *required for a female is equivalent to half that for a male. This is justified by the fact that in Islamic* shari'a *men are the economic foundation of the society. They are the breadwinners of the family. They are the only ones responsible for earning the family living. Women carry no responsibility in this regard even if they have their own income and are more wealthy than the men (Sanad 1991, 62).*

Ta'zir *Crimes*

The least serious category of crimes under Islamic law are those "based on *ijma* consensus regarding the Moslem state's right to criminalize and punish all inappropriate behaviors that cause any physical, social, political, financial, or moral damages to an individual or to the community as a whole" (Sanad 1991, 63). Under these laws are such acts as rape, homosexuality, lesbianism, eating pork, tampering with measurements and lengths, usury, and traffic violation. These crimes are not all considered the same in terms of seriousness, and the penalties can exhibit a wide range. While the death penalty is usually reserved for *hudad* and *qisas* crimes, *ta'zir* crimes can be handled by such punishments as flagellation, imprisonment, and fines.

It should be clear that Islamic law differs greatly from the criminal justice system in the United States. Some interesting legal and moral questions are raised when we compare how other cultures exert social control. Laws and procedures that are considered discriminatory in the United States are encoded not only into the law but into the religious foundation of the law in countries like Saudi Arabia. For instance, Jones (1992) contends the two major weaknesses of the Saudi system are its treatment of women and non-Islamic minorities who are accorded second-class citizenship rights. How fair is it to judge their law by our standards? Is our cultural pattern an adequate basis to evaluate another culture's long-standing and deeply ingrained practices? We will keep these questions in mind and deal with them later in this chapter after we have considered examples of criminal justice procedures from other cultures.

CRIME IN AFRICA

It is very difficult to make any generalizations about crime on the African continent because it represents a vast area of multiple countries, numerous cultures, and at least three historical traditions from which its criminal justice practices are drawn. In northern Africa, there is a strong Islamic tradition that influences most of the secular governments. Throughout the continent are the remnants of European colonialization that have left a legacy of Western concepts of law and justice. Finally, there are the indigenous cultures that encompass a heritage of tribal relationships, territorial disputes, and bitter animosity between groups of people who find themselves fellow citizens in nation-states that have been arbitrarily established as a result of historical circumstance.

Any generalization about crime in Africa is further frustrated by the vast disparity in the level of social and economic development and the political instability that spans the continent. For example, Mushanga (1992) asserts:

> The political and economic situation in most African states, makes it impossible for any government to be organized in such a way that it can gather criminal data. Consider the fighting that has been going on in Chad; in Angola between the MPLA and UNITA; in Mozambique between the RENAMO and the FRELIMO; in Uganda between the northern Nilitics and the southern Bantu; in northern Nigeria between Moslems and Christians; in the Sudan between northern Arabs and southern Africans; in Somalia between rival clans after the overthrow of President Siad Barre; in Liberia between contending factions; also between opposed groups in Sierra Leone; in Ethiopia between the Oromos, the Eritreans and others; in Rwanda between the minority Tutsi and the majority Bahutu; in Kenya between the Kalenjin and their neighbouring Luyia, Kikuyu, and Luo; in Burundi between the ruling elites and the Bahutu people on one hand and blacks and whites on the other hand, making the future of that country difficult to predict with any degree of accuracy, and this goes for almost all the nations in Africa south of the Sahara (iv).

The abrupt social change that many of these countries are experiencing makes it difficult to differentiate behaviors that are the results of crime from those that are the results of war. As governments change and soldiers go from being rebels to police forces it is hazardous to speculate on what is legitimate crime-fighting strategy and what are war crimes and human-rights violations. As these countries change from preliterate and agricultural societies to urbanized, semiliterate nation-states there is not only an increase in crime but entirely new types of crime. Counterfeiting, bank robbery, and drug trafficking are all crimes brought on by economic development of societies that had never had to face these types of problems. There is a lack of established norms on how to sanction these behaviors and a problem of a creation in the desire for wealth and the inability of the economy to supply individuals with the goods and services they discover are available elsewhere.

Criminal justice systems in African countries are of interest to criminologists because they illustrate the problems of introducing innovation and social change into the institution of society. Because of the demise of **colonialism** across the continent after World War II, Africa presents a vivid experiment in nation-building where social institutions have to be reinvented to reflect the new political order. Thus, the study of how institutions evolved from traditional to colonial to present-day criminal justice systems represents not only underlying principles of law and justice in Africa but also useful comparative lessons for Western societies. A case study of this transition in social control in what today is the country of Tanzania is particularly illustrative of how forms of government transform the nature of how social conflict is resolved.

In precolonial times, communities were stateless in that conflicts were considered interfamily, interclan, or intertribe. As far as communal property was concerned, it was pointless to sanction someone within the clan because of the indivisibility of the family's property interest. Treason to the clan or witchcraft could be punishable by death but, otherwise, expulsion from the clan was the preferred method of sanction (Shaidi 1992).

In disputes between clans, a collective responsibility was enforced so that blood money (cattle and goats) was paid by all of the offender's clan and was divided up by the victim's clan. The concept of individual responsibility for crime and personal harm were not as developed as they are in **post-colonial** times.

> Collective responsibility which prevailed in pre-colonial African societies was also very significant in social control. It was the responsibility of every adult in the village to play mother or father roles in scolding, instructing, advising, or rewarding children (Shaidi 1992, 4).

The reputation one had in the clan was of prime importance. One's manners and good name were treasured parts of one's identity and helped to ensure social conformity. Public opinion during this time truly reflected what the community acting as a whole thought and did not represent the interests of the dominant class as it did later in colonial times when social control was enforced by laws, politics, new religions, and educational systems.

The criminal justice system in African countries during the colonial period can be characterized as a facade designed to justify the interests of the Europeans. During the early period of colonialization, the courts were operated by the administrators of the colony as opposed to an independent judiciary. Consequently, the concept of separation of powers was absent, and the criminal justice system was just another tool to keep the indigenous peoples under control. There was clearly a racist element to the administration of justice where whites were the only ones trained in the law and the only ones who served as judges. For some minor crimes, there were courts made up of indigenous peoples, but these tribunals were a fraud in that they represented the interests of the whites. The traditions of African law were not utilized and, instead, a confusing and alien form of European law was imposed.

> *The judicial system of colonial Tanganyika was clearly racist in character. The most favored people were the Europeans followed by Asians, and the most disadvantaged were the Africans. For example, juries were solely for Europeans, and legal representation, except in capital crimes, could only be afforded by the propertied classes (mainly Europeans and Asians); while Africans were placed under native courts of administrative officers without any safeguards. . . . With English as the official language of the subordinate courts, and many people speaking their ethnic language other than Swahili, interpretations sometimes involved three languages . . . Coupled with the technicalities of both procedural and substantive law, and without any legal representation, the conviction rate of the local people had to be high. Things were definitely much worse where the complainant or prosecutor was a European versus a black accused (Shaidi 1992, 9).*

The post-colonial period of criminal law in Africa is still developing. Many nations have yet to achieve the stability required for criminal justice agencies to mature. One of the problems is that Europeans did not adequately train the African peoples to administer the law during the colonial period. For example, when Tanganyika attained independence in 1961, only one in 100 lawyers was not white. Also, when Zimbabwe gained independence in 1980, there was not a single qualified judge (Shaidi 1992, 13). Colonialization destroyed traditional forms of justice and imposed its own courts to keep native peoples under social control. When the Europeans left or were driven out of Africa they had failed to instill criminal justice systems as well as other social and economic institutions that could maintain order and justice. Post-colonial Africa is still suffering from a colonial heritage based on racist and exploitive criminal justice administration.

This imperfect transition from pre-colonial to post-colonial institutions is nowhere better illustrated than in South Africa. The hegemony of the white Afrikaners is being dismantled with the demise of the race-based **apartheid** system, and the type of society that will eventually be installed is still being contested. In many ways it is hazardous to predict what will happen in South Africa, but it is useful to examine some of the present-day issues to see how this country is experiencing the stresses and strains of modernity as have already transpired in other African countries.

As apartheid loses its grip on the mechanisms of social control, it is being replaced by a powerful form of tribalism that threatens to prevent peaceful relations among blacks. Bill Berkeley describes South African tribalism as:

South Africa's system of apartheid in some ways typified African's most self-destructive tendency. It was tribalism codified. By "tribalism" I mean not an exotic habit of hatred but rather a method, as common elsewhere in the world, from Bosnia to Lebanon to India, as it is in Africa: a cynical means of acquiring or retaining power by exploiting or exacerbating ethnic differences (1994, 85).

In South Africa, the black-on-black crime, which has tribalistic political parties at its root, threatens to destroy the prospects for an orderly transition from white to black power. According to Berkeley, the strife between the African National Congress (ANC) headed by Nelson Mandela and the Inkatha Freedom Party headed by Mangosuthu Gatsha Buthelezi is responsible for the deaths of over 15,000 black South Africans since 1985. The complicity of whites in allowing or encouraging this violence is deeply embedded in the apartheid system.

The failure of the police derives from a number of factors. Apart from the partisanship of many police officers, to whom the ANC has always been a murderous and—until four years ago—illegal organization, there is outright racism among many white and Indian officers, who imagine that blacks killing blacks is the natural order of things. There is also severe understaffing and pervasive incompetence in investigative work. Under South Africa's draconian security laws and extended states of emergency, the police never had the legal incentive to develop evidence beyond what could be beaten out of a subject with no lawyer, no right to remain silent, and no limit on how long he could be detained without charges (Berkeley 1994, 88).

The violence in South Africa is in part caused by the failure of whites to allow blacks participation in the government. With the criminal justice system being used historically to suppress the population, it is little wonder that citizens do not turn to the criminal justice system to protect them. As blacks take over control of the institutions of society, they use those institutions to further their own tribal agendas. The criminal justice system becomes a mere tool for those with power to wield over those without power. When the criminal justice system fails to protect people from violence, as in South Africa, they will turn to other protectors such as political parties which are part tribal enforcers and part organized criminal gangs. Throughout the continent, the prevalence of violence is an indicator of the criminal justice system's inability to protect and defend citizens from anarchy or a sign that the mechanisms of social control have been co-opted for political purposes. The legacy of colonialism is still being felt in Africa where, in many countries, the problems of criminal justice are caused by the strains of nation-building.

ORGANIZED CRIME IN RUSSIA

As we saw in Africa the rapid pace of social change can be unsettling to institutions of social control. As old systems are dismantled and new ones attempt to establish their legitimacy and power, crime, like water seeping through cupped hands, spills out into society. In the former Soviet Union the rate of social change has been revolutionary, and countries such as Russia are struggling to develop democratic institutions that can replace the centrally controlled economy of the Soviet regime. For criminologists, one absolutely fascinating aspect of this transition has been the development of organized crime in Russia.

Because of the inefficiencies of the Soviet economic system, especially for domestic consumption, there is a long history in Russia of organized circumvention of the dominant economy.

> *Over time, factory workers and managers developed methods for manipulating the system, diverting raw materials into private workshops on factory grounds to produce high quality goods while fulfilling its quota of low quality goods for the state. This gave rise to significant underground "private business" anathema to the principles of the communist world. This, in turn, provided a window through which organized crime developed (Serio 1992, 132–33).*

The structure of organized crime is complex and resembles a pyramid with street criminals at the bottom and elites (some of whom are former Soviet officials) at the top. The street criminals include pickpockets, porno brokers, prostitutes, burglars, confidence men and swindlers, black marketeers, and drug dealers. While they prey on Russian citizens they also target foreigners, "to, literally 'iron the firm' (utiuzhit' firmu). In street jargon, all foreigners are considered members of one giant corporation or 'firm' that needs to be ironed, flattened, or straightened—in American slang, 'to be ripped off' " (Serio 1992, 136).

The street criminals become associated with more organized groups because of the protection and resources that are afforded to them. Additionally, the street criminals share their ill-gotten booty with their bosses for the right to exclusive territories. Above the street criminals is a rank of enforcers who act as a buffer between those who take the risks of crime and the elites. The enforcers will help the families of imprisoned criminals and will provide a publicity function where they romanticize criminal life to attract young people into their organization. Some of the members of this group are former athletes who have reached the end of their competing career and now turn to organized crime as a way of maintaining an affluent lifestyle while having no other marketable skills. At the top of the crime organizations are the elites who do not commit illegal acts themselves and have no direct contact with

As social control attempts to establish legitimacy in the former Soviet Union, crime has emerged into society. (© BETTMANN.)

criminals. They are often outside the reach of the criminal law and use their money, prestige, and connections to frustrate the criminal justice system.

The extent of influence that organized crime is able to exert in Russia is staggering. According to the Department of Energy's Office of Threat Assessment the "Russian Mafia" has over 4,000 organized crime groups or gangs operating inside Russia. These groups have penetrated not only private businesses but the government as well, according to the study. Hersh (1994) summarizes the DOE report as finding:

1. One quarter of the organized-crime groups are believed to have ties to similar criminal groups abroad or in former Soviet republics. A significant number of the groups have merged some or all activities with corrupt government and police officials.

2. Forty percent of private businesses and 60 percent of state-owned companies have been corrupted by organized crime.

3. The Russian mafia may own half the nation's commercial banks and 50 to 80 percent of the shops, hotels, warehouses, depots, and service industries in Moscow. A substantial portion of the commercial district in St. Petersburg is similarly in the control of criminal elements, with businessmen being forced to pay 15 percent of their income for protection.

4. Corruption of the Russian army is widespread . . . Russian defense officials announced that they planned to discipline 3,000 officers for questionable business practices and that 46 general officers faced court-martial proceedings on corruption charges . . .

5. Organized crime now uses high-tech communications equipment, including fax machines, shortwave radios, and cellular phones, far more sophisticated than anything used by Russian law-enforcement officials (67–68).

By far the most disturbing feature of organized crime in Russia, however, is the likelihood that it is engaged in the export of former Soviet Union defense materials, including nuclear weapons. There is a problem with lack of adequate security of nuclear weapons today because Russia's police forces are not as efficient as those of the Soviets. According to Hersh (1994), the Soviet Union did not worry so much about internal security because everyone was afraid of the KGB. Now Russian weapons-storage areas are relatively unsecured, and the fear is that there are elements of organized crime who can gain access to the weapons and export them out of Russia to the highest bidder. The whole point of nuclear security has been the lack of proliferation to unstable political countries or groups. State-sponsored terrorism is a difficult problem to deal with, but the danger of the future may be when organized crime sells nuclear weapons to freelance extremists who will be willing to use them to advance their political or criminal agendas. It is reasonable to expect that when Russia and other former Soviet bloc countries develop their democratic institutions that they will be able to better control the organized crime groups that presently are unfettered. Until then, not only do these organized crime gangs pose domestic threats, but they are of serious concern to anyone interested in international terrorism.

CRIME CONTROL IN CHINA

Culture plays a tremendous influence on how social behavior is evaluated. In our examination of Saudi Arabia, Africa, and Russia we have seen how religion, colonialism, and political instability have fashioned criminal justice systems that are unique to their countries' historical circumstances and cultures. As we look at China, we see an even more profound effect of how culture affects how behavior is judged.

One difference between the criminal justice systems in the United States and China is the role that formal and informal rules play in guiding individual behavior. One of the cornerstones of social control in the United States is deterrence, where people weigh the risks of getting caught and the level of punishment against the benefits of succeeding at a crime. The reason we have proportionality in sentencing (murders get the death penalty or life imprisonment while burglars get probation) is to help criminals decide not to commit serious offenses. With determinant sentencing we specify very clearly exactly what penalties will be applied to what crimes.

The assumptions underlying the social control effect of deterrence are very different in China:

> *Because the boundary and punishment are not clearly defined, it makes the testing and challenging of the boundary more difficult. Meanwhile, Chinese society has a more uniform system of moral values. Challenging or testing the boundary is not an attractive or heroic model. Because the punishment is not clearly defined, one cannot calculate the cost and benefit of a violation. But, it there is anyone who attempts to make such a calculation, the strategy of the society is to make the individual overestimate the punishment to derive the deterrent effect. There are two ways to do this: (1) The law enforcement agencies have a wide range of discretionary power. When they see fit, they can even give an offender with high social status a very harsh punishment. That is, when this particular offender and his violation are highly visible, his punishment can be used to set an example to impress the general public. (2) Enforcement agencies can create an impression, however false, that no violation can escape punishment. Because the news media are controlled by the government, this can be done by reporting only solved cases (Jan 1983, 198).*

This broad discretionary power present in China's criminal justice system has additional benefits in ensuring social control. Because individuals do not know where the boundaries of illegal behavior are drawn, and they also do not know what is likely to happen to them if they should venture over those boundaries, they tend to give themselves a wide margin of error. That is, unlike in the United States where staying just inside the law is culturally rewarded (for example look at the behavior of Americans concerning the income tax or speeding laws), in China, people attempt to conform to the norm as closely as possible because flirting with violating the law can be so injurious.

The prisons in China are unlike those found in the United States. Because of the differences in cultures it is hazardous to make direct comparisons between prison philosophies. In China, the assumptions that guide behavior are "based largely on Confucian philosophy, assumes human nature is basically good, there is no original sin, individuals are willing to perfect themselves, and that they can be taught or led to virtue (Jan 1983). Given this optimistic conception of the potential for individual reform it should come as little surprise that the prisons in China emphasize rehabilitation. John Klofas reports:

> *The process of rehabilitation in Chinese prisons involves classes and study sessions that focus on Chinese history and society. Families are encouraged to visit, as are ex-prisoners, who can demonstrate the value of conformity after release. Model prisoners are also used as tutors to assist inmates in*

understanding why they commit crimes and to help them "remold" themselves. Prisoners are continually given opportunities for self-criticism and confession as part of the reformative process (1991, 177).

One must keep in mind the differences in the role of conformity between the United States and China in order to understand why rehabilitation in Chinese prisons is emphasized so much. In order to be confident that the released prisoners will not commit additional crimes, the Chinese are concerned that they impact the mind and soul of the inmate and not just the body. In the United States, we care little about what an offender may think or feel, we just insist that his or her behavior not harm other people. In China, the concern for social control goes much deeper.

This moral definition is heavily socialized into each individual either by Confucius' method using ritual and other techniques, or by the Communist method of brainwashing. Once this definition is internalized, control is internal. One can escape the external control of the law but such internal control is hard to escape (Jan 1983, 199).

This is not to say that there are no external controls on behavior in China. By some standards it can be considered a very repressive criminal justice system. The use of the death penalty is a good example of how the Chinese criminal justice system can be more oppressive than our own. There are as many as 50 different crimes punishable by death in China (Klofas 1991), with most executions carried out on murderers, rapists, and robbers. Other offenses such as hooliganism and counterrevolutionary activities also are punishable by death and at times the Chinese government can accelerate the execution process. Klofas (1991, 181) quotes one journalist as reporting that during a clean-up before the Asian Games in Beijing in 1990 that "the pace of justice is often dizzying: it is possible in China to be arrested, tried, convicted, sentenced to death, have an appeal rejected and finally executed in a single week."

The safeguards of due process that are enjoyed in the United States are not as pronounced in China. The system is by nature informal and nonadversarial so the due process requirements are not appropriate in this context. The reason China's system is so fascinating is because given its population (1.2 billion as opposed to 0.28 billion in the United States) it would be impossible to control the populace if there were not a highly structured culture of conformity. The rugged individualism that makes up the ideological culture of the United States would result in chaos in China. Yet there are reasons to believe (Tiananmen Square Protest) that, in the future, China may be faced with western-style challenges to its system of social control. In the meantime, it is instructive to examine how China is able to maintain social control of its enormous population without the formal mechanisms of the criminal justice systems found in the United States.

Confucian thought continues to be the cornerstone of informal social control in China throughout its traditional, republican, and communist eras. Zhang et al. (1996, 203–204) identify three philosophical underpinnings of a community-based system of social control that are influenced by Confucian thought:

1. People are guided more by moral example and persuasion than by rigid codes and severe punishment. The informal rule of moral codes, rites, and customary law instills a sense of shame in offenders that is useful in mediation and conciliation tribunals handled at the clan and village level.
2. There is an emphasis on early intervention before situations become too serious or offenders become too immersed in criminal careers. "Nipping crime in the bud" is a contemporary Chinese phrase that illustrates the philosophy that there is a developmental connection between minor infractions and serious crime.
3. Confucian philosophy believes that everyone's behavior is changeable and through proper education and instruction that individuals can be guided away from bad thoughts and bad behaviors.

What is important about the philosophical foundations of the Chinese criminal justice system is the way they are integrated into the informal social control mechanisms of crime prevention. Zhang et al. identify two processes that can be considered community-based crime prevention efforts that reflect China's unique cultural context. **Bang-jiao** is a program where neighborhood committees are used to help young offenders become reintegrated into the community. What is especially unique in these programs is the level of involvement and equality that is afforded to the offender. The youth is treated as a member of the community and does not suffer discrimination but instead is given love and emotional support. The goal is to get the deviant to engage in genuine repentance and to want to become an integrated member of the community again.

The *bang-jiao* can be considered a peacemaking perspective approach to crime control because it emphasizes the inclusionary nature of social justice. The neighborhood committee, made up of the delinquent's parent, local police officer, work supervisor, and school supervisor all work on equal footing with the deviant youth to convince him or her of the benefits of lawful and harmonious behavior. The goal is not to scare the youth into conformity by deterrence, but to address the causes of the behavior by rehabilitating the offender and allowing him or her to make peace with the community through mediation and reconciliation.

A second community-based crime prevention program used in China is called **tiao-jie.** There are neighborhood committees that resolve disputes in both criminal and noncriminal cases. Such noncriminal problems such as housing problems, marital disputes, and uncollected debts as well as minor criminal cases such as property damage and personal injury are heard by these committees in order to resolve the issues without having to resort to formal criminal processing. While there is wide variation in the extent of how these programs are implemented across the large and diverse Chinese landscape, these programs represent an informal way to resolve many of the problems that arise in any society. Perhaps because of its acute population problems, China has had to find informal ways of dealing with the mass of low-level conflicts in its society, but this would not have been possible without the underlying cultural ethic of conformity attributable to China's Confucian heritage.

There are clear differences in the social contexts in China and the United States which makes comparisons of criminal justice programs risky. We know precious little about how well the community-based programs in China actually work (Zhang et al. 1996), and transposing these mechanisms here would involve both legal and social obstacles. The due process safeguards of Americans must be preserved, and the willingness of people to serve on neighborhood committees to help troubled youth cannot be assumed. There is, however, from a peacemaking perspective something to be learned by the Chinese example.

1. The assumptions made about human behavior dictate the method of correction. The Chinese have an optimistic view of human nature that says people can change through moral guidance and rehabilitation. They believe that people are basically good and because they are concerned with their place in the community that shame is a powerful tool in changing criminal behavior.

2. Informal social control is more powerful than the criminal justice system. Used properly, that is, early in the criminalization process, intervention by parents, teachers, employers, and neighbors can prevent criminal tendencies from reaching their maturation. Young people can be reeducated into more socially acceptable behavior through the caring and emotional support of significant others. The responsibility for preventing or changing criminal behavior is not ceded to distant authorities but is vested in neighborhood committees which include, interestingly enough, the offender.

SEX TOURISM

The world's oldest profession has developed some structural features that make it a concern for criminologists who adopt the peacemaking perspective. While it may be unfair to judge another culture by our Western standards, the case of prostitution in Thailand and other countries has become such an injustice that groups like Human Rights Watch and Amnesty International have produced reports detailing the abuses of women and girls. Of particular interest in this chapter is the sex-tourism trade where men from Western countries and affluent Asian countries like Japan go to Thailand, the Philippines, and other third-world nations to engage in sex holidays with young girls and boys.

Thailand is not the only country to offer its youth for sale on the international sex market, but it is interesting because of the way the sex trade has been almost institutionalized and the reliance of the country's economy on commercial sex. According to the Human Rights Watch *Global Report on Women's Human Rights* (1995, 207), the tourist industry is a $3 billion-a-year concern, and the sex trade is an important subsector that caters to men from many different countries. One of the distinguishing features of the prostitution in Thailand is the relationship between the women and girls and their employers. Many of the prostitutes (800,000 of the estimated two million) are children under the age of 16 and are sold into an indentured form of slavery by their impoverished parents. The girls have no skills or education and are not aware of even how much money they need to save in order to buy their freedom.

Other countries that have flourishing or developing child sex trades include the Philippines and Sri Lanka (Baker 1995), India, China, Nepal, Cambodia, Hong Kong, South Korea (Hodgson 1994), Cuba (McClintock 1992), Indonesia (Ford et al. 1995), Egypt (el-Gawhary 1995), and even some Eastern European nations. What all these countries have in common is a level of poverty that results in the selling of the virtue of their children. While there is a considerable local demand for prostitution in these places, it is the international tourist that fuels the industry. Men, both straight and gay, flock to third-world nations to engage in sex with young people that would be forbidden in their home country. Some of these men try to rationalize their behavior as being beneficial:

> *Many Western sex tourists are convinced that, in indulging their fantasies, they are helping the young girls at the same time. "The Asian boys who sleep with tourists are markedly more exuberant, happy and healthy than the hundreds of millions of poor children who are slowly withering away or being crippled by back-breaking labor," writes Dutch observer, Edward Brongersma.*
>
> *"To try and solve the terrible dilemma of Third World poverty by suggesting that a few children will be happier as temporary sex objects for wealthy foreigners is the kind of flippant solution which makes a mockery of human suffering," replies Ron O'Grady, who claims that tourists almost always end up with a distorted view of the reality under which a majority of child prostitutes live (Baker 1995, 13).*

The power of the Western dollar (or yen) makes sex tourism an attractive way for men (and some women) to go overseas to indulge in fantasies they would not contemplate at home. It seems that the farther away one can get from his or her own culture, the weaker the cultural bonds that constrain their behavior. The erotic potentials of exotic places allow individuals to drop their moral training and take economic and sexual advantage of young people caught in a seamy sex industry.

American servicemen have long romanticized the lures of foreign ports of call and have engaged in supporting the prostitution industry to the point where it is almost institutionalized. Every military base, both foreign and domestic, has to contend with servicepeople seeking sexual services. What is new about the sex-tourism industry is not only its growth but the declining age of the children whose services are for sale and the way the industry can harm the victimized population. The incidence of AIDS and other sexually transmitted diseases is extremely high in Thailand where the problems have been imported by the sex-tourist industry. Many sex tourists are now going to countries that have been relatively unaffected by AIDS, such as former Soviet bloc nations like Romania, and bringing with them the AIDS problem.

From a peacemaking perspective, the sex-tourism industry represents a violation of moral dictates to not harm other people. The sexual exploitation of children and the economic dependence of countries on the sex-tourist industry represents a cultural hegemony that is scandalous. Those who engage in such behavior cannot be controlled by the countries that have a monetary stake or by the unenforced U.S. laws:

> *In sum, the U.S. law is similar in scope and severity to other consumer countries' laws. On its face, the U.S. amendment imposes serious penalties against sex offenses abroad. However, the law has yet to be implemented and will consequently have little effect if the penalties are not imposed. Establishing extraterritorial jurisdiction and meeting evidentiary standards are two concerns that have impeded the prosecution of sexual offenders in other consumer countries. These issues will likely influence the effectiveness of implementing this new U.S. law (Li 1995, 521).*

It will not be enough to use the law to deter the predatory behavior of the sex tourist. Education and prevention are two methods for convincing these individuals that they cannot leave their morality at home when they visit overseas ports of call. People have to be held to the same moral standards no matter where they are or how much more money they have than the indigenous population. From a peacemaking perspective, the sex-tourist industry commits a form of sexual and economic violence on women and children who have little choice in the matter.

Our review of criminal justice issues from other cultures has shown us that we are not unique in having seemingly intractable problems of crime and justice. This review was not intended to be comprehensive and it was not aimed at finding countries that have solved the crime problem. Rather, it was intended to simply show the diversity of confounding and perplexing factors that can be linked to crime and justice from around the world. It has also shown how the peacemaking perspective can be used to examine crime from a moral point of view.

CRITICAL THINKING QUESTIONS

1. In addition to the examples in this chapter, think of countries where there may
   be a cultural gap with the United States. What problems might these cultural gaps
   cause in the criminal justice system?

2. What peacemaking lessons can be learned from looking at how other cultures deal
   with issues of crime and justice? Is the criminal justice system in the United States
   a peacemaking model when compared to the criminal justice systems of other
   nations?

3. Compare and contrast the systems of criminal justice in Saudi Arabia and China.
   Which criminal justice system would you rather live under?

4. What should be done about the sex-tourism industry? Is it fair to judge how other
   countries treat women and children by our standards? What role should the concept of international human rights have in evaluating how underdeveloped countries engage in the sex-tourism trade?

SUGGESTED READINGS

Ali, Badr-el-Din. 1985. "Islamic Law and Crime:
The Case of Saudi Arabia." *International
Journal of Comparative and Applied Criminal
Justice* 9(2): 45–56.

Baker, Christopher P. 1996. "Child Chattel Lure
Tourists for Sex Beneath the Palms." *Insight*
11(11): 11–13.

Berkeley, Bill. 1994. "The Warlords of Natal."
The Atlantic Monthly (March): 85–100.

Hersh, Seymour M. 1995. "The Wild East." *The
Atlantic Monthly* (June): 61–86.

Hodgson, Douglas. 1994. "Sex Tourism and
Child Prostitution in Asia: Legal Responses
and Strategies." *Melbourne University Law
Review* 19(3): 512–544.

Jan, Lee Jan. 1983. "Deterrence and Social Control in the United States and China." *International Journal of Comparative and Applied
Criminal Justice* 7(2): 195–200.

Jones, Mark. 1992. "Islamic Law in Saudi Arabia: A Responsive View." *International Journal of Comparative and Applied Criminal Justice* 16(1): 43–56.

Klofas, John M. 1991. "Considering Prison in
Context: The Case of the People's Republic
of China." *International Journal of Comparative and Applied Criminal Justice* 15(2):
175–186.

Li, Vickie F. 1995. "Child Sex Tourism to Thai-
land: The Role of the United States as a
Consumer Country." *Pacific Rim Law and
Policy Journal* 4(2): 505–542.

Sanad, Nagaty. 1991. *The Theory of Crime and
Criminal Responsibility in Islamic Law:
Sharia'*. Chicago: The University of Illinois
at Chicago.

Serio, Joseph. 1992. "Organized Crime in the
Soviet Union and Beyond." *Low Intensity
Conflict and Law Enforcement* 1(2): 127–151.

Shaidi, Leonard P. 1992. "Traditional, Colonial
and Present Day Administration of Justice," in Tibamanza mwene Mushanga, ed.
Criminology in Africa. Rome: United
Nations.

14

GIVE PEACE A CHANCE

© Bob Daemmrich/Stock Boston.

Learning Objectives

After reading this chapter, the student should be able to:

- Understand how the war on crime and peacemaking perspective compete to explain how the criminal justice system operates.
- Appreciate how the National Criminal Justice Commission's recommendations to shift the crime policies of the United States are compatible with the peacemaking perspective.

There are two primary reasons why criminal justice is such a fascinating field of study. The first is because it represents real-life problems that are of vital importance to society. Along with medicine and education, the application of criminal justice is an essential institution that is required for the maintenance of meaningful communities. The student who decides on a career in the field of criminal justice is answering a call to service for something greater than simply making a living. Criminal justice entails benefits to the whole of society.

The second reason that criminal justice is such a fascinating field of study is because there is so little agreement on which goals should have priority, which policies best achieve the goals we can agree upon, and which policy makers should get to decide these important issues. Criminal justice is a contested terrain and by its nature will remain so. The ebb and flow of debates concerning gun control, capital punishment, drug use, and police discretion have not been settled by our explorations in this book. We have only introduced these and other contemporary issues, not resolved them. It has been the ambition of this book, however, to introduce the field of criminal justice in such a way that the student becomes excited about the vitality and promise of this discipline as a site where she or he can explore some of the great issues that can enrich one's educational experience.

The field of criminal justice is vast, complex, and sometimes daunting. It is impossible in this book to cover all its aspects in adequate depth. More advanced, upper-division courses will explore in greater detail issues whose surface we've only been able to scratch. By framing our discussions in a war on crime versus peacemaking perspectives we have greatly simplified the multifarious and complex nature of criminal justice debate. This was necessary to provide a context in which the issues of criminal justice could be considered, but there is also a danger in adopting the war on crime versus peacemaking perspectives in that not all the important questions or concerns of criminal justice can be adequately addressed in this way. It is legitimate to contend that the peacemaking versus war on crime contexts employed in this book present a false dichotomy, in that many issues cannot be neatly placed in one category or the other. The war on crime versus peacemaking perspectives are not always mutually exclusive and certainly are not exhaustive. Some issues would not fit into either category.

With these limitations in mind, the war on crime versus peacemaking perspectives are used as orienting perspectives because they do illustrate the diversity of opinions, knowledge, and research applicable to criminal justice. The boundaries of the old liberal versus conservative perspectives have become so blurred that they are no longer useful ways to envision crime control policies (Walker 1994). The war on crime versus peacemaking perspectives are also worthwhile perspectives to employ because they can readily be modified to look at other institutions. The debate about child abuse versus healthy discipline can be envisioned along a continuum very similar to the war on crime versus peacemaking concepts. At the international level, the conflicts between nation-states are the best example of the war and peacemaking perspectives.

Throughout this book, the two perspectives have been compared and contrasted in terms of how well they can be applied to criminal justice programs, policies, and problems. It has been demonstrated that although the war on crime perspective is a popular metaphor for criminal justice policy, many criminal justice practitioners use peacemaking tactics both in the United States and in other countries. The urging of further development of the peacemaking perspective is not to ask for revolutionary change so much as to ask for recognition of what is already common practice in many jurisdictions. While the war on crime is trotted out for election year posturing by political candidates, the peacemaking perspective is quietly and productively being used in criminal justice jurisdictions around the country.

The war on crime perspective is rejected by our analysis in this book for several reasons. The most basic of which is because war is a metaphor that is inappropriate and misleading when discussing the domestic crime situation. To wage war internally invites a form of self-mutilation that has disastrous consequences. In the case of the war on crime in the United States, the war metaphor has caused increased violence associated with the drug trade, an increase in the proportion of people under social control (especially prison) without a corresponding increase in the level of crime, criminal justice personnel being subjected to corruption because of the exorbitant profits in drug trafficking, and a reduction in trust given to criminal justice officials by poor and minority groups who are most often the targets of the war on crime. Our ability to form meaningful communities has been so undermined by a criminal justice system intent on sanctioning behaviors that there is considerable disagreement on their criminal harmfulness. Drug use, prostitution, and gambling are all crimes that lack consensus. In some states gambling is illegal and in other states it is a form of major revenue. The war on crime would be better used to fight violence as opposed to moral differences among citizens.

The National Criminal Justice Commission (1996) has recently developed a set of policy guidelines that specify what steps can be taken to reform the criminal justice system. These guidelines correspond to the principles of the peacemaking perspective and are useful tools in constructing a responsible response to crime.

National Criminal Justice Commission

Ten recommendations to shift the fundamental direction of U.S. crime policy

1. Decrease the reliance on prisons as the primary response to criminal behavior. Impose a three-year moratorium on new prison construction until a systematic assessment of prison needs can be completed. Replace many prison sanctions with alternative programs that are less expensive and often more effective at reducing crime.

2. Replace the war on drugs with a policy of harm reduction where the police work with public health professionals to stem illegal drug use. Drug addiction should be treated as a public health challenge rather than a criminal justice problem.

3. Balance criminal justice spending with resources spent on other civic activities. Stop doing what doesn't work, and invest resources in proven prevention programs and other crime fighting alternatives.

4. Restore the internal balance of the criminal justice system so that judges have more discretion at sentencing and victims of crime receive better treatment by the court system.

5. Commission an independent clearinghouse to gather and report criminal justice information to the public. The clearinghouse should be separate from the Department of Justice.

6. At all levels of government create crime councils to develop a coordinated anti-crime strategy. This council should be created at the city, county, state, and national level. They should include representatives of law enforcement, prosecutors, social service professionals, public health specialists, child welfare officials, crime victims, and representatives of other government agencies concerned with crime prevention.

7. Reduce violence by using innovative approaches developed in the field of public health; and reduce the harmful effects of violence by passing gun control legislation at the federal level.

8. Commit ourselves to reducing poverty in order to prevent street crime. Funds should be provided so that each child can enter an early childhood development program.

9. Eliminate racial bias and reduce racial disparity with the criminal justice system.

10. Shift ourselves from an agenda of "war" to an agenda of "peace." Wars against American citizens are wars that nobody can win.

These policies are aimed at improving the criminal justice system by reforming the way it approaches the problem of criminal behavior. It represents a shift from deterrence and punishment models to an emphasis on prevention and treatment models. In some ways it does not adopt some of the more extreme policies that some peacemaking advocates put forth, such as policies like the legalization of drugs. But these recommendations do reject the war on drugs and urge treatment as a method of reducing the harm of addiction.

The ultimate goal of the peacemaking perspective is to reduce the suffering of victims, offenders, law enforcement officers, and everyone else associated with the workings of the criminal justice system. In order for the peacemaking perspective to work to its full potential it has to become an accepted approach not only for the criminal justice system but for other institutions in society. The peacemaking perspective is not a quick-fix tactic aimed at minor tinkering with the status quo but is, instead, a fundamental change in the way criminal behavior is defined and controlled. The peacemaking perspective can best be envisioned as a process as opposed to a result. How the society goes about dispensing justice is as important as the actual sentence handed down by a judge. A sense of fairness and participation is essential to securing the support and cooperation of the citizens in a democratic society. Unlike totalitarian regimes where force and coercion can cower the population, democracies require their institutions to serve the interests of the people and not just the interests of the state.

The focus of this book has been to compare and contrast the war on crime and peacemaking perspectives to allow us to examine a range of issues that make the field of criminal justice such an exciting area of study. While not all the important issues in criminal justice could be addressed, the intent was to point out some of the diversity, contradictions, dilemmas, and problems that criminal justice scholars and practitioners must contend with in attempting to ensure a society based on order through the rule of law. To the extent we have been effective in highlighting and explaining the issues through the war on crime and peacemaking perspectives, this book has been successful. If the book has raised more questions than it has provided answers, it has also been successful. The field of criminal justice is a contested terrain and there are not simple, complete, satisfying, and provable solutions to its problems. If you require such finality in your scholarly endeavors, go to the mathematics department.

The wonderful challenge that the study of criminal justice provides is not so much in finding the ultimate solution to the problem of crime and justice but in participating in developing the solutions to many problems of crime and justice that are related to how all of our institutions and our culture structure our lives. In spite of all the complexity of human interaction there is one little nugget of truth we can leave with you and that is:

Make peace, not war.

CRITICAL THINKING QUESTIONS

1. What are the limitations of envisioning the field of criminal justice through the war on crime versus peacemaking perspectives? What are the strengths of using these perspectives?

2. Discuss what suggestions made by the National Criminal Justice Commission are compatible with the peacemaking perspective.

3. Discuss what is meant when we say that the peacemaking perspective is more of a process than a result.

4. Suggest what other ideas, philosophies, theories, or orientations might be usefully employed by the peacemaking perspectives.

APPENDIX A

CRIMINAL JUSTICE AS A CAREER

Gandhi said, "All work has dignity." This is certainly true for the work of the criminal justice system. As one of society's essential institutions, the criminal justice system provides services needed for the creation and maintenance of meaningful communities. There are many occupations in advertising, professional sports, or entertainment that, while being extremely lucrative, are not required by a healthy society. Many of these occupations could be eliminated tomorrow and society would not be the poorer. If there were no criminal justice system, however, we would have to invent one. Or at least the work done by the criminal justice system would have to be absorbed by other institutions as it was centuries ago. The work of social control in modern societies is essential to revolving disputes, protecting life and property, and demarcating the boundaries of conventional norms and laws.

In some respects, it seems as if the dignity of the occupation is inversely related to its monetary remuneration. Like other worthwhile professions such as nurses, teachers, and firefighters, the salaries in the criminal justice system are moderate at best. While the business of crime is good, it is the criminal (who takes the really big risks) who makes the big money. But this is true only for the successful criminal. The ones who get caught lose more than an investment of time, money, or other resources, they often lose their freedom and autonomy. But from a Gandhian perspective, whether they get caught or not, the difference between the criminal and the criminal justice practitioner is not the money they amass but the honor of their name and the service they provide to society. In discussing careers in the criminal justice system, we will not limit ourselves to the details of which jobs require what kinds of training, but will talk more extensively about the responsibility and integrity that is needed in those who serve society by becoming law enforcement officers, judges or lawyers, probation and parole officers, or correctional officials.

Ultimately, the work of the criminal justice practitioner is cast in the peacemaking perspective. While many may go into the job with a war on crime attitude, this is not always the mindset needed for a long and productive career. Catching the bad guys is only a small part of what the criminal justice system must do. Being of service to everyone, while not as high-profile or exciting as catching and punishing crooks, is important and demanding work. The person who makes a career out of criminal justice needs to be aware that the work is sometimes frustrating and boring. The image of criminal justice portrayed in the movies and on television is skewed toward its exciting and dangerous aspects and glosses over the routine nature inherent in not only criminal justice, but also in just about all occupations. Many young people do not have an appreciation for what qualities of perseverance are needed to work at the same job day after day. The burnout rate of criminal justice practitioners can be high when people go into the occupation with unrealistic expectations and little knowledge of what working life is all about.

NATURE OF WORK

Working in the criminal justice system present challenges, temptations, and problems not faced in other work environments. The opportunities for work-related deviance dictate that criminal justice practitioners be held to the highest standards of ethical conduct. After all, the damage one can do in a fast-food restaurant by skimming from the till or giving free food to friends is limited. The damage an unethical law enforcement officer or prison guard can do, however, could be a matter of life or death. The level of competence at which one performs his or her duties is also of importance. A police officer who is careless in searching a suspect may overlook a weapon that results in the injury or death of a colleague. A dispatcher who transposes the numbers on a street address may direct officers to the wrong house and permit a domestic disturbance to turn fatal. The criminal justice system cannot afford to employ the sloppy or dishonest worker. The student of criminal justice should evaluate his or her motivations and aptitudes before applying for a career in this field.

The first question someone should ask themselves about a career has to do with their philosophy of work. Some people approach every task with the attitude that they will do their very best and get the job done. Other people look for ways to get other people to do the job but still want to take credit for it. Others seem to procrastinate, hoping the job will simply go away. At different periods of my life I have been guilty of all three of these strategies. You'd be surprised at how much work proves unnecessary if you just stall and wait for those in power to get tired of asking you to perform a task. Sometimes they get so frustrated with you, they do the task themselves. I do not advise that you employ this strategy often as it does not lead to job stability. The point I'm attempting to get across is that there are several ways to approach work and the way you do it will have consequences. When holding a position of public trust in the criminal justice system, it will be noticed if you do not perform your duties. Pay raises, promotions, and special assignments will go to those who prove to be ethical, competent, and industrious.

There is another dimension to work that needs to be recognized, and this has to do with the area of interpersonal relations. While good, honest workers will always be valued, those that can become part of a team will find even greater rewards. Some occupations can tolerate those who cannot get along with others, but for the most part, work in the criminal justice system requires cooperation with people in your agency as well as with those who work in related agencies. One's ability to achieve the goals of the organization is more valued than simply working toward personal goals. Obviously, each job in the criminal justice system will require different competencies and dispositions, so those contemplating such careers should answer the following questions.

1. *What type of work do you enjoy?* Some people cannot sit at a desk and must be on the move while others sit all day. Some law enforcement officers love to be in the squad car but hate to be inside the station doing the paperwork.

2. *What level of interaction with other people do you enjoy?* Serving the public can be very difficult. Some criminal justice practitioners are skilled at interacting with citizens and others get frustrated and angry.

3. *How much physical risk are you willing to take?* I have had students complete a four-year criminal justice degree program and then decide they did not want to work with criminals because of the possibility of getting hurt. While not all jobs in the criminal justice system entail the same level of risk, those who pursue this career should be aware of the potential dangers.

4. *Are you going into a criminal justice career for the right reasons?* Criminal justice agencies attempt to screen out applicants who have inappropriate motivations. Some individuals who desire to go into law enforcement have an excessively authoritarian personality. They tend to treat all citizens as suspects and are quick to define situations as needing criminal justice intervention, are quick to use excessive force, and tend to make conflicts more volatile rather than helping get them resolved. Law enforcement agencies need clear-thinking problem solvers as opposed to emotional and confrontational athletes.

5. *Do you have realistic expectations about the career path you are choosing?* Whenever we have an orientation day at my university, I have numerous high school seniors (mostly male) come to my criminal justice display and announce they plan to be an FBI, CIA, or Secret Service agent and want to know if I have any contacts with these agencies and can get them a job when they graduate. I patiently explain that while graduates of our institution are working for each of these agencies that the chances of anyone actually becoming an FBI agent are slim. The FBI and other federal agencies can draw from a nationwide pool of applicants and the competition for the few slots open in any year is intense. The vast majority of the graduates from our program (and from any social science programs) will go to work for local criminal justice agencies. The road to the higher-paying and more glamorous federal jobs is by way of demonstrated successful criminal justice experience and advanced education. The law of supply and demand allows the FBI and the Secret Service to fill their ranks with highly qualified and experienced individuals. While I never actively discourage young students from aspiring to these agencies I counsel them on the necessity of getting excellent grades, applying for internships or our co-op program, and on the advisability of starting at the state or local level and proving themselves before expecting to be hired by the agency they have dreamed of working for. Once some of these students understand what is involved in working for a criminal justice agency they are content to work at the local level. They find out they do not really want to work in other states but want to be an FBI agent in their hometown where they can be with friends and family and play on their church softball team. Given the way federal agencies place people where they need them it is not very likely that someone will be able to pursue this criminal justice career in their hometown.

6. *Have you maintained a clean criminal record and established a reputation of honor?* While everyone certainly makes mistakes in their life, those who wish to pursue a career in criminal justice will be evaluated on their past as well as their academic qualifications.

One of the best predictors of behaviors is the pattern of past behavior. Those with records of drug use and violence will not be judged good candidates for criminal justice positions. While minor transgressions may not be fatal to your application process, they will put you at a disadvantage. Similarly, when you go to your professors to ask for letters of recommendation, it helps if you have not only earned good grades but also have been prepared for class. A number of years ago I had a student who had plagiarized a paper and had been caught cheating on a test who later came to me asking for a letter of recommendation to a sheriff's office. I told the student that based on his dishonesty in my class that I could not in good conscience write a letter that would help him get the job. I felt so strongly about this student's blatant cheating I considered writing a negative letter.

These are all questions that students should consider early in their college careers. They will help in deciding what discipline to pick as a major and what type of classes to take to be eligible for the job they would like when they graduate. Many people do not know exactly what they want to do with their lives, and it is important to keep an open mind and not force a decision. I never really had a plan for my career, so I just kept taking the next challenge that looked interesting and one day found myself to be a university professor. There were many opportunities to pursue other areas of the criminal justice vocation but my love of reading and arguing kept leading me back to the classroom. Sometimes when I reflect on my career I wish

I had developed a better idea about what I wanted to do and had sought out more advice from my professor and colleagues. Who knows where I might be today if I had chosen law school instead of a graduate program in criminology? I fantasize about sitting on the Supreme Court or playing quarterback for the Dallas Cowboys. A little more encouragement from this person, or a different decision at that point, and who knows what alternative career paths I could have pursued. Each person should consider what type of work they would like to do and begin to do early what is necessary to prepare themselves.

CRIMINAL JUSTICE CAREERS

Many students major in criminal justice because they see it as a path to a good job. One thing I tell my students is that there are several academic disciplines that will enable you to work in the criminal justice field and that each discipline should be considered. Political science, sociology, history, economics, social work, and many other behavioral science and humanities programs can prepare the student with the academic tools needed for a career in criminal justice. What most criminal justice programs around the country attempt to do is provide a sufficiently broad liberal arts education so that their graduates can step into any work environment and quickly learn the skills necessary to be proficient in that job. University-level criminal justice programs are aimed at providing an education, not specific job training. Most criminal justice agencies desire candidates who can absorb their training programs and become productive members of their agencies and do not expect the candidates to already have the job-specific training.

It is unfortunate for society but good for those whose wish is to pursue a career in criminal justice that the business of crime is good. Criminal justice is a growth industry as more and more prisons are being built and law enforcement agencies have a continual need for good applicants. Depending on what aspect of the criminal justice system one goes into, there are varying levels of opportunities, but many people find that once they have established a good work history in a criminal justice agency that transfer to another agency is often possible. Police officers become parole officers and youth workers go to law school and become lawyers and judges. It is a mistake to believe that your first job in the criminal justice system will be your last and only job. By taking advantage of in-service training programs, getting an advanced degree or specialized instruction, it is possible to carve out your own career path to a position that can best utilize your skills. The trick at this early stage of your education is to realize the vastness of the criminal justice system and the many different levels and specialties that exist. What follows is an incomplete guide to the opportunities the student may wish to investigate.

LAW ENFORCEMENT

A law enforcement career is the most visible in the criminal justice system and one that many students aspire toward. Every community is protected by some law enforcement agency whether it be its own police force of the county sheriff's office. Additionally, private security agencies employ hundreds of thousands of individuals to protect everything from warehouses to shopping malls to banks. One way to envision the myriad of law enforcement agencies is to categorize them according to the level of government they serve. According to Harr and Hess (1992) the federal agencies that employ law enforcement officers include: the Federal Bureau of Investigation (FBI), the Federal Drug Enforcement Administration (DEA), U.S. Marshals, the Immigration and Naturalization Services (INS), the Bureau of Customs, the Internal Revenue Service (IRS), the Secret Service, the Bureau of Alcohol, Tobacco and Firearms Tax (BATF), Postal Inspector, and the military services.

At the state level of law enforcement there are several opportunities for employment depending on the resources of each particular state. These opportunities, according to Harr and Hess (1992), include the State Bureau of Investigation and Apprehension, State Fire Marshal Division, State Department of Natural Resources (Fish, Game, and Watercraft), Driver and Vehicle Services Division, Department of Human Rights, and the State Police and State Highway Patrol.

At the local level, there is the county sheriff, the coroner or medical examiner's office, and municipal police. It's at this level where the greatest number of law enforcement officers are employed.

COURTS

There are many opportunities in the court system for employment. The highest paying and most prestigious require a degree in law. Prosecutors, defense attorneys, and judges occupy the positions of influence and power in the courts. Criminal justice graduates must compete with those from other academic disciplines to get into law school. Requirements include not only a high grade point average (GPA) but also good scores on the Law School Aptitude Test (LSAT). Therefore, it is important to get good grades early in your academic career if you aspire to go to law school. Many students don't get serious about preparing themselves for their career until their senior year in college, and, for many, the lower grades from their first three years cannot be overcome. It also helps to study for the LSAT. There are many good programs around the country that offer night or weekend short courses that claim they can improve a student's performance on this important test.

There are several other types of occupations associated with the courts that are available to the criminal justice graduate. One of the more interesting and rewarding is in the area of victim support services. Whether it involves victim/offender reconciliation programs or sexual assault counseling, these programs require individuals who have an understanding of the criminal justice process as well as good interpersonal skills. Other opportunities include legal research as a paralegal. Some university programs offer specialized legal research education, while many criminal justice graduates find programs in the private sector that provide this type of training. While paralegal work can be rewarding I always tell my best students to take a shot at law school if legal research is what they want to do.

CORRECTIONS

Depending on the jurisdiction, corrections and court job opportunities can overlap. Juvenile case workers and probation officers can be employed by either the court or a local or state correctional agency. These jobs commonly require a college degree in a behavioral science such as law enforcement. Probation and parole officers can be found at the federal as well as the local level and their exact duties will vary according to their jurisdiction. For example, in some states parole officers are required to carry a firearm and to arrest their clients whose parole has been revoked. In other jurisdictions, parole officers are forbidden to carry firearms and are instructed to call a law enforcement officer if they need to have their client arrested. The study should carefully explore the dimensions of each criminal justice position for which they apply to ensure that they are going to be comfortable with the work.

Of course the most obvious agency for those interested in corrections is the prison. Prisons and jails can be found at every level of government and represent a real growth sector of the criminal justice system. University graduates will find a variety of jobs associated with the prison and should look very closely at the career tracks available. It is not unusual to find bright former students enter a state prison system and move up the hierarchy quickly by being flexible enough to move from one prison to another, pursuing positions of ever-increasing responsibility. Along the way, the student should consider an advanced degree in criminal justice, public administration, or some other field that will allow them to move into management positions.

Like private security in the law enforcement sector, there are growing opportunities for employment in private correctional agencies. Some jurisdictions enter into a contract agreement with private prisons or probation programs to confine and punish law violations. While this is not a very big field at the present time, there does seem to be a movement to privatize many government functions, and jails and prisons are likely candidates. Students should not only be open to these employment opportunities but they might also think in terms of getting some experience in the field and starting their own private correctional agencies. While some people might question the moral and legal positions of the "punishment for profit" business, it does represent a fertile area for job opportunities for the criminal justice graduate.

These are only a portion of the job opportunities in the criminal justice system. For the student who is confident that this is the type of career he or she wants to pursue it is never too early to start preparing. Most colleges and universities have some type of internship and/or co-op program where the student can get a taste of the real-life criminal justice system before graduation. These programs are very useful for gaining experience, making contacts, and establishing your reputation as an individual who can be trusted with responsibility. In a competitive job environment, the deciding factor between otherwise equally qualified candidates can be internship or co-op experience.

THE PUBLIC TRUST

Regardless of which criminal justice career path the student chooses, there will be opportunities to help people and opportunities to harm people. There will be an inherent role conflict between protecting society and aiding the law violators in coping with life. It is best to recognize this conflict and remember that the best criminal justice practitioners have been able to reconcile the often conflicting demands on their loyalties. Discretionary judgment is the art and science of criminal justice work. Use it wisely and you can help humanity. Use it unwisely, abuse it, or don't use it at all, and you will find criminal justice to be frustrating and unrewarding. The war on crime and peacemaking perspectives illustrate ways of envisioning the underlying assumptions inherent in criminal justice occupations. As your career progresses it will be useful to continually reexamine the way you think and feel about these perspectives. To that end you will want to keep this book in your personal library and resist the temptation to sell it back to the bookstore for the measly fraction of what it is worth.

APPENDIX B

CRIME AND JUSTICE ON THE WORLD WIDE WEB

Liberty Activists' List
ftp://ftp.zeta.org.au/home/aldis/liberty-activists-list
The Liberty Activists' List is a Frequently Asked Questions (FAQ) file that is regularly posted to a number of Usenet newsgroups, alt.activism and talk.politics.drugs. Here, visitors will find a list of over 200 international and U.S. organizations that support drug law reform.

Marijuana and the War on Drugs
http://www.calyx.net/marijuana.html
Here, find information about the medicinal uses of marijuana, including its use by AIDS patients. Other links include a list of activist groups, a wide variety of marijuana-related reading and, amusingly, some links to anti-marijuana "rhetoric."

ABOLITION NOW!!!
http://www.abolition-now.com/
Albert Camus wrote, "An execution is not simply death. It is just as different from the privation of life as a concentration camp is from prison." Abolition Now! offers a great deal of anti-death penalty-related information, including news, links to Texas and California coalitions, articles, facts and figures, and activist resources.

Aware
http://www.aware.org/
At the Aware site, women and men can learn more about how to deal with violence, both stranger-related and domestic. Features include a self-defense quiz, a list of courses, a reading list and much more.

National Campaign to Reduce Youth Violence
http://.wnet.org/aav/index.html
The National Campaign to Reduce Youth Violence is a public broadcasting project that provides telecommunications tools and works with community and national groups to reduce and prevent youth violence. The site provides in-depth information about the program, including a list of publications, videos, and television programming.

Center for Peacemaking and Conflict Studies
http://www.fresno.edu/pacs/
The Center for Peacemaking and Conflict Studies at Fresno Pacific College maintains this page with details about the center's courses and faculty, as well as a calendar of special events. The center, whose philosophy is based on the Hebrew/Christian understanding of peace,

specializes in constructive conflict management and dispute resolution.

Federal Bureau of Investigation
http://www.fbi.gov/

Not necessarily a peacemaking site, but an important criminal justice site, nevertheless. Find out who the ten most wanted fugitives are, see a list of recent kidnappings and check up on the bureau's most recent investigations. Such details as an "FBI Fact Sheet" and the location of field offices are also provided.

ACLU Freedom Network
http://www.aclu.org

The American Civil Liberties Union (ACLU) maintains its Freedom Network site with information and updates on its current causes and key issues, its activity in the courts, and details about the organization itself. Site visitors can also find out how to join.

Family Violence Awareness Page
http://www.iquest.net/~gtemp/famvi.htm

The Family Violence Awareness Page provides a number of resources, including domestic violence myths and facts, lists of hotlines, information about reconstructive surgery for victims, and contact information for a number of U.S. and international organizations.

Ethics Updates
http://www.acusd.edu/ethics/

From the University of San Diego, Ethics Updates provides links to articles, Internet resources, essays, and discussion and term paper topic suggestions for a number of morally and ethically controversial issues. The variety of sections includes abortion, animal rights, poverty and welfare, and the death penalty.

Gunfree
http://www.gunfree.inter.net/

The Gunfree site is a collection of resources from a number of antigun, antiviolence organizations, including the Coalition to Stop Gun Violence, the Educational Fund to End Handgun Violence, and the

Violence Policy Center. Also, learn more about upcoming conferences and activities.

Police on the Web
http://www.suntimes.com/arc/oct/thu/12thsee.html

Courtesy of the Chicago Sun-Times, Police on the Web features a number of links to the home pages of national and international police organizations. Learn more about Scotland Yard, the Chicago Alternative Policing Strategy, and Royal Canadian Mounted Police, Alcatraz Island, and the Metro-Dade Police Department Crime Lab.

National Organization for Victim Assistance
http://www.access.digex.net/~nova/

The National Organization of Victim Assistance (NOVA) is a private group working for crime and disaster victims. At the organization's site, read an overview of victim's rights and find information about training, conferences, and other organizations.

Justice Center
http://www.statesattorney.org/main/button03.htm

Maintained by the Cook County, Illinois, State's Attorney office, the Justice Center features a guide to the criminal courts, information about hate crimes and juvenile justice, law enforcement resources, and links to a number of criminal justice Web sites.

National Archive of Criminal Justice Data
http://www.icpsr.umich.edu/NACJD/home.html

The National Archive of Criminal Justice Data page provides access to over five hundred criminal justice data collections, including those concerning community studies, corrections, crime and delinquency, and victimization. The archive provides the most recent studies possible and is searchable.

Police Resource List
http://police.sas.ab.ca/prl/index.html

The Police Resource List, based in Canada, features links to international criminal justice agencies, as well as information about crime prevention, electronic crime, forensics, missing persons, and much more. The links here include both Canadian and U.S. resources.

Criminal Justice Links

http://www.stpt.usf.edu/~greek/cj.html

Here, a University of South Florida criminology professor maintains a comprehensive page of criminal justice links. Links are categorized by almost every aspect of criminal justice imaginable, and include photographs and links concerning the most popular and current issues in the public arena. Sections include federal agencies, the media, international resources and law sites.

UN Charter and Universal Declaration of Human Rights

http://www.library.yale.edu/un/un3a1.htm

Here, you'll find the United Nations charter and preamble, a bibliography of the charter, and the Universal Declaration of Human Rights, adopted in 1948. The full text of these documents is provided here

by the Yale University Library and Social Science Statistical Laboratory.

The University of Minnesota Human Rights Library

http://www.umn.edu/humanrts/

The University of Minnesota Human Rights Library features a large and varied collection of documents and resources related to international human rights. Here, you'll find treaties, links to organizations and committees, U.N. resolutions, and much more. Help in using and searching this site is also provided.

Amnesty International

http://www.igc.apc.org/amnesty/

Amnesty International (AI) is an activist organization dedicated to, among other issues, abolition of the death penalty. At the organization's U.S. site, find news, general AI information, details about its programs and campaigns, and a catalog of AI publications.

GLOSSARY

Adversarial Proceedings The model of court structure where the prosecution and defense are pitted against each other in a contest of law. Adversarial proceedings are the norm in adult courts but not in the juvenile court where the judge, prosecutor, defense, and caseworkers all attempt to decide what is best for the child.

Ageism The idea that one is treated differently because of one's age. Ageism is a form of discrimination that can be aimed at the young or the old. The age at which individuals are given rights and responsibilities or have them taken away varies across societies.

Aggression Replacement Training The idea that aggression is learned and can also be unlearned. Aggression replacement training teaches individuals to deal with problems and frustrations in socially constructive ways.

Apartheid A system of law formerly practiced in South Africa where one's legal status was contingent on race. Apartheid is an example of highly structured institutional racism.

Arraignment A formal court proceeding where an accused individual is told the charges and given an opportunity to enter a plea. The arraignment is the first of what can become many court appearances before the case is disposed of.

Arrest The taking of an accused person into physical custody prior to a court proceeding.

Ascertainable Criteria The idea that the evidence, data, rationale, and testimony that criminal justice decisions are based upon is available and understood by all parties.

Bail An amount of money posted by an accused person as a guarantee that they will appear at a future court proceeding. Bail is useful to the criminal justice system because it relieves jail overcrowding and is useful to the accused because she or he can remain at liberty until their guilt or innocence is determined. Bail is theoretically used only for those offenders who are safe to release into the community until their cases can be heard.

Bang-jiao A form of community-based justice practiced in China whereby the accused is allowed to participate in the proceedings.

Bill of Rights   First ten amendments to the Constitution of the United States whereby the rights of citizens are defined. The Bill of Rights is important to the criminal justice system because they limit the power of the state in many areas.

Blood Feuds   The idea that families will take matters into their own hands when dealing with issues of justice. In some societies people are honor-bound to avenge real or imagined transgressions to members of their family. The famous feud of the Hatfields and McCoys is a good example. The modern criminal justice system has replaced the blood feud as a mechanism for dispensing justice.

Boot-Camp Prisons   A form of shock incarceration where offenders are subjected to a harsh physical and emotional regimen fashioned after military basic training. This short-term sentence is designed to develop respect for authority and discipline in young offenders.

Brady Bill   A federal law restricting the availability of handguns. Named after the Press Secretary wounded in an assassination attempt on President Ronald Reagan, the Brady Bill requires the chief law enforcement officer in each jurisdiction to check to see if any person trying to buy a handgun has a criminal record or a history of mental illness.

Broken Windows Theory   The idea developed by criminologists James Q. Wilson and George Kelling that physical deterioration of a neighborhood invites undesirable individuals and crime. By keeping up appearances it shows that people care about the neighborhood and it is easier to develop a sense of community.

Career Criminals   Offenders who make their living from crime. These repeat offenders may specialize in one type of crime or may commit a variety of offenses. In some jurisdictions they are targeted for special prosecution.

Categorical Imperative   The philosophical principle of Kant that says one's actions should be able to be applied to more than the immediate circumstances.

Civil Rights Movement   A form of collective social protest designed to change the patterns of racial discrimination in the United States. Predominately identified with Martin Luther King, Jr., the Civil Rights Movement has prompted the repeal of laws and practices which have disenfranchised African-American citizens.

Code of the Street   A rigid pattern of social etiquette practiced on the streets of many cities where individuals do not engage in polite behavior. People do not make eye contact and reframe from acknowledging each other because of the threat of violence. The code illustrates just how dysfunctional the sense of community has become in the inner-cities.

Collective Violence   Violent behavior committed by a group of individuals. Riots, lynching, and stampedes are examples. Scholars of collective behavior believe individuals may engage in behavior as part of a group that they would not perform as a individual.

Colonialism   The annexation of a people's property and resources by another people. The conquering of the new world by European powers has had long-lasting effects on the development of social and economic structures that still influence the world order. Inner colonialism refers to patterns within a country where one group of people exploits another.

Community Policing   A strategy of law enforcement that encourages the police to become more engaged in the community. While community policing is used to refer to a broad range of practices, it is usually meant to signify a progressive method of getting the police officers out of their patrol cars and involved with the citizens.

"Conflicts as Property"   The idea of Nils Christie that the criminal justice system takes conflicts away from individuals and deprives them of achieving satisfactory closure. Crimes against individuals are redefined as crimes against the collective and the state takes responsibility for handling the case.

Correct Means   A Gandhian concept that says the end must be achieved by means that embody moral principles. A righteous end cannot justify corrupt means.

Courtroom Workgroup   The judge, prosecutor, defense attorney, bailiff, and other regular participants of the courtroom. These individuals routinize their work and recast it in ways that achieve efficiency. The public's sense of immediacy and truth-finding is transformed into routine case-flow management and plea bargaining.

Crack Cocaine   A form of cocaine that can be smoked. It provides an intense high and is alleged to be highly addictive. It is relatively inexpensive and has become the drug of choice in many disadvantaged neighborhoods. Some jurisdictions have targeted crack cocaine with more harsh sentences than for powder cocaine. Crack babies is a new term that refers to infants who are addicted to crack because their mothers used the drug during pregnancy.

Crime Clock   An illustration used by the Uniform Crime Reports to demonstrate the prevalence of crime. The frequency of the seven index crimes are shown for the nation.

Criminal Justice System   The agencies that are responsible for the detection and administration of the criminal law. These agencies work together to process cases but are functionally independent. The term system does not accurately reflect the relationship between law enforcement, courts, corrections, and the other agencies that make up the criminal justice system.

Crisis Intervention   A practice of social and criminal justice agencies where individuals experiencing stressful situations are given help and/or protection.

Critical Traditions   One of the three (religious and feminist) intellectual traditions that informs peacemaking criminology. Critical traditions examine the economic and power structures that are the underpinnings of capitalist society.

Cruel and Unusual Punishment   A phrase from the eighth amendment of the Constitution that prohibits the government from using barbaric methods such as torture. This is still a contested principle as certain forms of the death penalty such as the electric chair are questioned.

Dark Figure of Crime   The difference between the number of crimes committed and the number of crimes reported to the police. We know there are many more unlawful acts committed but have no way of measuring just how much crime really happens.

Defense Attorney   Part of the courtroom workgroup. The defense attorney may be a private attorney or may be a public defender. The job of the defense attorney is to represent the accused in the adversarial criminal proceedings.

Defensive Gun Use   The use of firearms to prevent crime. Criminologist Gary Kleck contends that defensive gun use is a good reason to question much gun-control legislation. Defensive gun use envisions good citizens protecting themselves and others from criminals.

Determinate Sentence   Sometimes called a fixed sentence, this type of sentencing model limits the discretion of the judge in determining how long the offender will spend in prison. The fixed sentence is set by the legislature or a sentencing commission and is intended to limit sentencing disparity.

Deterrence   One of the underlying philosophies of the criminal justice system. Deterrence is based on the fear of getting caught and punished for committing crimes.

Discipline   According to Foucault the internalization of rules and patterns of behavior. Also is the application of punishment for rulebreaking behavior.

Domestic Terrorism   Terrorism is violence with a political motive. Often we associate it with people from other countries. In the United States there have been several incidents of American citizens committing terrorist acts with political motives against individuals, corporations, or the government.

Drive-By Shootings   A form of armed assault associated with gang violence. Individuals fire weapons from an automobile as it drives by the target. Often automatic weapons or shotguns are used and bystanders are wounded or killed.

Drug Legalization   Removing penalties and punishments for the sale and possession of drugs. Proponents of legalization claim that the violence associated with the drug trade would be greatly diminished if drugs were made legal. Depending on how the legislature crafted the laws it could be possible for drugs such as marijuana, cocaine, or heroin to be available at a drugstore or even a supermarket.

Drug Decriminalization   Unlike legalization the drugs would not be legal but the penalties for drug violations would be greatly reduced. A number of states decriminalized marijuana in the 1960s but have since recriminalized it.

Drug Kingpin   Major drug dealer. A drug kingpin is head of a network of drug sales and/or drug manufacturing, smuggling, or cultivation. Some states have enacted legislation aimed at providing harsh penalties for drug kingpins.

Due Process   Constitutional guarantee of fair treatment in the criminal justice process. Due process rights include the right to a trial, a right to cross examine hostile witnesses, a right to present witnesses or evidence on your own behalf, and a right to an attorney.

Electric Shock Therapy   A form of therapy used decades ago and seldom used today. It consisted of applying electronic shock to the brains of individuals with mental illness with the goal of curing them. This was a very controversial and painful treatment that has not been continued because of the lack of positive results.

Electronic Monitoring   A form of intermediate punishment where an offender is allowed to remain in the community but must wear a bracelet or anklet that allows the authorities to monitor his or her whereabouts. There are several types of monitoring devices and all are technological aids to help keep track of offenders. The advantages to this alternative to incarceration are low cost and allowing the offenders to remain a productive citizen in the community.

Ethnocentrism   The feeling that one's own culture is a model from which to judge other cultures. Differences in customs, rituals, institutions, and fashions are judged to be deviant where they are simply culturally relative alternatives.

False Consciousness   A term used by Karl Marx to refer to the belief of the workers that capitalism was a system of economics that allowed them to achieve their fair worth for their labor. False consciousness is similar to brainwashing in that people become responsible for their own subjugation through their incorrect beliefs.

Federally Licensed Gun Dealer   Under the Brady Bill new guns are allowed to be sold only by a Federally Licensed Gun Dealer. Almost anyone can become one and the Brady Bill does not address the secondary market of used guns. This stipulation is a form of gun control aimed at keeping guns out of the hands of juveniles, criminals, and individuals suffering from mental illness.

Feminist Traditions   Peacemaking criminology draws much of its inspiration from the feminist movement. The ideas of equal opportunity, equal rights, cooperation, and the struggle against patriarchy are all contributions the women's movement has made to the peacemaking perspective.

Forfeiture Laws   Some states have passed laws allowing the police to confiscate money and property used in the commission of felonies, particularly the drug trade. There is a great deal of criticism about these laws because they allow the government wide discretion in determining if the money or property are related to criminal activity. Reportedly, innocent people have had large sums of cash confiscated based on the judgment of law enforcement officers that it was used in the drug trade.

Frontal Lobotomy   A form of treatment for mental illness where the two sides of the brain are surgically separated. Lobotomies caused the patient to become very docile in behavior but unable to function normally. It was an extreme form of treatment that has been discontinued in the medical profession because it reduced the quality of life to a point where the patient was completely dependent on other people.

Furman v. Georgia   A case decided by the Supreme Court that declared the way in which Georgia administered the death penalty was racially discriminatory and therefore violated the fourteenth amendment in that it was cruel and unusual. Its practical effect was to cause states to rewrite their death penalty laws.

"Gang Time"   The idea that gang members serving time in prison are political prisoners and are being punished for their gang membership more than for the crimes they have committed. Some gang members will have tatoos which illustrate how many years of "gang time" they have served.

General Deterrence   A form of deterrence which says that individuals will be prevented from committing crimes when they see what happens to other people who are punished for criminal activity. General deterrence is an important rationale for the philosophy of the criminal justice system which aims at preventing crime.

Graffiti   The physical defacing of a surface by some medium. In the criminal justice context it is a form of vandalism where individuals paint pictures or write slogans or symbols on public or private property. Some graffiti has the quality of art while other graffiti is simply vandalism. Some gangs use graffiti to mark the boundaries of their territory.

Gun Control   Includes a wide range of proposals which limit the accessibility of firearms. There is considerable debate about the rights and desirability of allowing individuals to own and carry firearms.

Habilitation   A term used in relation to rehabilitation. Some individuals have never been fully socialized into society so to rehabilitate, or return them to a former state, makes little

sense. Habilitation means to teach them the socially approved patterns of behavior for the first time.

Harm Reduction   A goal of drug-control policy that recognizes that the war on drugs has unintended consequences of increasing the level of violence and making the drug trade economically attractive. Harm reduction strategies would substitute drug treatment for the drug war and seek to limit the overall harm done to society by drugs.

Harrison Act of 1914   A law designed to make sure the federal government received taxes on the production, sale, importation, and dispensing of opium and coca leaves.

Hegemony   Dominance of one ideology over others in a society.

Hudud Crimes   Forms of serious crimes under Islamic law that include adultery, theft, banditry, defamation, and the drinking of alcohol. Often the penalty for this type of crime is some form of corporal punishment.

Humanist Traditions   Based on philosophical ideas of nonviolence and harmony, humanist traditions inform the peacemaking perspective. In conjunction with religious traditions they seek to limit the violence between peoples.

Impression Management   A term used by sociologist Erving Goffman to refer to how individuals adopt purposeful patterns of behavior and alter their appearance when appearing in public. Everyone has a public and a private self and impression management is how the public self is presented.

Incapacitation   The idea that individuals can be incapacitated from committing future crimes by incarceration. Also, pickpockets can be prevented from plying their trade if their hands are cut off. Incapacitation does not aim at rehabilitation but simply at structuring the conditions so the offender is not in a position to commit crimes.

Indeterminate Sentence   A sentence imposed by the judge that gives a range of time between when parole can be granted. This shifts the discretion for determining when the offender will be released from the judge to the parole board. The idea behind the indeterminate sentence is that the parole board will be able to tell when the offender has been rehabilitated and is safe to return to society.

Index Crimes   Eight crimes measured by the Uniform Crimes Reports to give a comparative picture of the level of serious crime in the United States.

Initial Appearance   A formal step in criminal court processing where the suspect is brought before a judge and advised of his or her rights and the opportunity to post bail.

Institutional Violence   Violence supported or ingrained in institutions. War is a form of institutional violence. Domestic assault, while a form of interpersonal violence, can also be a form of institutional violence when family patterns are based on patriarchy or male dominance.

Intensive Supervision   A form of intermediate punishment where parole of probation supervision is more intense that the norm. Some parole and probation departments have intensive supervision teams which visit the offender at the home or job on a frequent basis.

Intermediate Punishments   A range of punishments between traditional probation and incarceration. They

may include such features as electronic monitoring, drug testing, or more frequent supervision.

Interpersonal Violence   Violence between individuals.

Jurisdiction   The geographic or political boundaries giving a court or law enforcement agency the responsibility for administering the law.

Jury Trial   A trial before one's peers as opposed to before a judge where guilt or innocence is determined.

Just Desserts   A model of corrections based on the idea that the punishment should be proportional to the crime.

Juvenile Delinquency   The committing of a crime by a juvenile. There are some behaviors such as drinking under age and curfew violations which are considered crimes based on the status of being a juvenile that are not applicable to adults.

Laissez-faire   A term from economics which refers to the "hands-off" approach the government takes when regulating the marketplace. In the criminal justice system it is used most often to refer to the way the government did not interfere with the manufacturing and distributions of drugs in the early part of the country's history.

Laws   Rules of conduct enacted by a legitimate authority for a specific jurisdiction.

Legalistic Style   A style of policing specified by James Q. Wilson where the law enforcement agency adheres to a strict interpretation of the law and their mandate. The legalistic style is contrasted with the service style and the watchman style primarily in terms of the discretion each officer is allowed to exercise.

Lethal Injection   A form of capital punishment where a lethal drug is injected into the condemned. Lethal injections are thought to be painless and are considered by some people to be a humane way to execute a human being. Opponents of the death penalty contend there is no way to humanely kill someone and that the lethal injection is simply a way to make the capital punishment more palatable to the public.

Mala Prohibita   Behavior that is a crime because it has been written into law but where there can be a lack of agreement. Laws on drugs and gambling can vary over time and across jurisdictions.

Male In Se   Illegal acts that are inherently wrong and about which there is little disagreement. Crimes such as murder and rape.

Marijuana Tax Act   A law passed in 1937 that placed marijuana under the same type of legal control as cocaine and narcotics.

Masculinity   A culturally prescribed pattern of behavior for males in a society. In the United States masculinity is taught through the institutions of the family, sports, and the military and has been criticized by feminists as producing males who are emotionally impacted.

Mass Killers   Someone who kills several people in one incident. Mass killers are distinguished from serial killers who kill several people in separate incidents over a period of time.

Metaphor   A linguistic device that compares one thing to another. In the criminal justice system the war on crime perspective is a metaphor which compares crime-control policies to military warfare. This is a misleading metaphor because of the distinct differences between war and crime control.

Militarization of Civil Society   Part of the war on crime perspective where society adopts aspects of the military culture or strategies. The use of military planes in drug interdiction efforts or the dress and tactics of SWAT teams are examples of how civilian law enforcement has adopted military overtones.

Militia Groups   Self-appointed quasi-military groups of individuals who organize for the purpose of protecting themselves from what they perceive as internal or external threats to their freedom. They range from relatively innocuous men who play war games in the woods to domestic terrorists who see the state and federal governments as the enemy.

Moral Calculus   The idea that criminals think about and weigh the benefits of successfully committing a crime with the costs of getting caught and punished. Our sentencing system of graduated punishments is based on this idea that serious crimes should be punished by serious penalties as a way of deterring individuals.

MTV Generation   Name given to the youth culture which emphasizes materialism, rejection of authority, and hedonism. An MTV-generation youth is a stereotype for the wasted potential of young people in the same way the term hippie was used a generation ago. The stereotype is based only partly in the truth.

Nolo Contendere   A plea of no contest to a criminal charge made in lieu of a guilty or not guilty plea. Often part of a plea bargain where if the offender successfully completes a diversion program there is no conviction put on the permanent court record.

Nonviolent Social Protest   Demonstrations, sit-ins, marches, or other ways of protesting against the authorities. Popularized by Gandhi and Dr. Martin Luther King, Jr., nonviolent social protests have been used by civil rights proponents, antiwar demonstrators, and students as methods for highlighting what they consider to be injustices on the part of the government or other institutions.

Norms   The accepted patterns of behavior in a society. Norms can be relative in time and place.

Parentis Parens   "In place of Country" is the authority of the juvenile court to look out for the welfare of the child. Rather than punishment, the traditional philosophy of the juvenile court has been to seek to help the youth adjust to the rules and laws of society.

Patent Medicines   Unregulated medicine popular a century ago that promised to cure a variety of ailments. Commonly loaded with alcohol or drugs these "medicines" led to the regulation of food and drugs.

Patriarchy   A society, community, or country based on the idea that males hold supreme power, knowledge, and authority.

Peacemaking Pyramid Paradigm (P³) A model of the philosophies that contribute to the peacemaking perspective. The model is designed to demonstrate how certain elements such as nonviolence and social justice are the foundation for solutions to criminal justice problems and that other elements such as correct means and inclusion are integral parts.

Peacemaking Perspective   A philosophy of criminal justice policy that rejects the war on crime perspective and advocates the elimination of suffering for all those involved in criminal activity.

Peer Counseling   The idea that youth will accept advice from people their own age as opposed to adults. Peer counseling is also used in drug and alcohol treatment programs because some individuals believe that only those who have faced the same problems of addiction can truly understand what the offender is going through.

Personal Advocacy   In some victim/witness assistance programs staff members will accompany the victim through the criminal justice process and advocate on their behalf. Some victims or witnesses need help in understanding and dealing with criminal justice proceedings.

Plea Bargaining   The negotiation in court proceedings between the prosecutor and the defense attorney that results in the defendant pleading guilty or *nola contendere* in lieu of a reduced sentence. Plea bargaining saves the state the time and expense of providing a jury trial and the defendant benefits from a reduction in the possible punishment.

Police Use of Force   The legitimate use of physical force used by police to control a situation. There are times when police can use excessive force such as in the Rodney King incident.

Police Discretion   The latitude of decision-making used by the police in deciding whether to invoke the criminal justice sanction or to use physical force.

Police Riots   The misconduct of the police when their commanders lose control in a collective behavior incident. The 1968 Democratic Convention in Chicago, where the police beat the protestors, is used by some people as an example of a police riot.

Political Crime   Acts against the security of the state. Political crimes include treason, espionage, and sedition.

Post-Colonialism   The period of time after the demise of colonial authority. Many times the post-colonial period in a country is characterized by violence and uncertainty as the political landscape is contested by opposing factions.

Preliminary Hearing   Hearing held in front of a judge to determine whether there is enough probable cause to hold the suspect for a trial. The preliminary hearing does not determine guilt or innocence.

Pretrial Motions   A range of motions made by the prosecution or defense to set the limits on what will be allowed in the trial. Some pretrial motions seek to limit or exclude evidence that may be illegally gathered or considered discriminatory.

Procedural Law   Rules that specify how criminal justice agents may implement the substantive law.

Prohibition   The period between 1919 and 1933 when alcohol was illegal in the United States. The prohibition experience is often used by those who wish to legalize drugs as an example of the ineffectiveness of outlawing something the people really want to have.

Public Defender   A defense attorney appointed by the state for someone who cannot afford one of his or her own. In some jurisdictions the public defender is an employee of the state and in other jurisdictions the public

defender is a private attorney who is paid by the state for a specific case.

Pure Food and Drugs Act of 1906   Specified that the ingredients of foods and drugs had to be clearly labeled so citizens could make an informed choice as to what they put in their bodies. The intent was not to make drugs illegal but to make them safe.

Qisas Crimes   Part of Islamic law that roughly corresponds to the crimes against persons in western law.

Quasi-Military Bureaucracies   The nature of law enforcement agencies that adopt qualities of the military. Uniforms, ranks, and tactics all serve to make the police resemble military services. There are important differences, however, especially in the nature of their mandate and the amount of discretion vested in those at the lowest level of the bureaucracy.

Racial and Class Bias   Forms of discrimination found in the imposition of the criminal justice sanction. Especially found in how the death penalty is allocated in the United States.

Racism   Form of discrimination based on one's race.

Rehabilitation   The correctional practice of attempting to change the behavior of criminals so they can lead productive lives in normal society. One of the goals of the criminal justice system.

Release on Recognizance (ROR)   Allowing a defendant to remain at liberty until future court proceedings based on his or her promise to appear when requested. In lieu of a cash bond.

Religious Traditions   One of the inspirational source of the peacemaking perspective. Many of the world's most popular religions have tenets that inspire the peacemaking perspective, such as nonviolence and social justice for all citizens.

Representational Democracy A form of government where citizens select other citizens to represent their interests in the makings of laws. The United States is a representational democracy as opposed to a pure democracy where every citizen would vote on every policy issue under consideration.

Satyagraha A strategy for confronting injustice developed by Gandhi where one attempts conquest over an adversary by suffering in one's own person. As a form of nonviolent social protest this strategy often shined the light of public attention on an unjust situation and embarrassed the authorities into doing the right thing.

Selective Incapacitation The correctional practice of incarcerating certain offenders who are felt that because of their crimes or backgrounds are likely to commit more crimes. Individuals targeted for selective incapacitation may receive relatively long prison sentences.

Self-Reported Crime Studies A type of study done by criminologists to determine the extent and level of crime in society. Self-reported studies ask individuals to answer questions about how many and what type of crimes they have committed. While self-report studies have some limitation, they are a useful alternative measure to official reports of crime such as the Uniform Crime Reports.

Sentence Disparity The differences in punishments given to offenders who are convicted of similar crimes and have similar backgrounds. Sentence disparity is one of the byproducts of allowing judges discretion in how they sentence. Determinate sentencing is designed to limit sentence disparity and treat like criminals in the same manner.

Sentencing Patterns The overall pattern of sentences given by a judge or judges in a jurisdiction.

Serial Murderers Offenders who commit a series of similar crimes over a period of time. Serial murderers are contrasted with mass murderers who kill several people in one incident.

Service Style One of the styles of policing used by James Q. Wilson in his typology of how police do their work. The service style is characterized by the helpful attitude the police have toward the members of the community.

Sexism The discrimination or prejudice against someone based on their sex.

Sky Marshals A proposal in the early 1970s to put armed guards on every airliner to prevent skyjacking. This proposal was not adopted because of the unattractive prospect of having gun battles at high altitudes where a bullet piercing the skin of the airplane would cause rapid decompression and endanger all those on board.

Skyjacking The crime of taking control of an airplane by the threat of violence that was common in the early 1970s and occurs today in some countries. The skyjacking problem prompted the government to require everyone wishing to board a commercial airplane to undergo an electronic search and to have their baggage x-rayed.

Socialization Process   The passing on of culture from one generation to the next.

Southern Culture of Violence Theory   The idea that violence is more prevalent in the south than in other regions of the country and that the reason has to do with cultural variables including a history of firearm use and of chivalry as practices in the old south.

Specific Deterrence   A form of deterrence where one is deterred from committing crimes because he or she was caught and punished in the past.

Status Ritual   A behavior used to demonstrate one's status in a group. Primitive societies had elaborate status rituals to demarcate passage from one stage of life to another. In modern society there are few rituals for a young male to signal his passage into manhood.

Status Offenses   Behaviors considered crimes based on the status of the offenders. For example, young people are subjected to a range of laws such as curfews and drinking under age that adults are not subjected to.

Substantive Law   The body of law that defines what behaviors are proscribed. Procedural law defines how violations of substantive law will be handled.

Supreme Court   A court in the federal government that oversees all other courts and acts as a court of last resort. Few cases make it to the Supreme Court but their decisions are used as a basis for interpreting the law. Each state also has a Supreme Court that acts as a court.

Surveillance   The visual or electronic monitoring of an area or an offender's behavior. Surveillance or the threat of surveillance acts to deter individuals from committing crimes and helps in their apprehension when they do commit crimes.

SWAT   Special Weapons and Tactics teams used in many law enforcement agencies to deal with potentially violent situation. Usually includes individuals trained as snipers.

Ta'zir Crimes   The least serious offenses under Islamic law but some offenses such as rape would be considered serious under western law.

Throwaway Children   The idea that many children in society do not receive the love, attention, and resources required to give them the self-concept and physical and mental health necessary to grow into productive citizens. Many children are left to the care of incompetent parents and when the state does not step in to take control of their care and education, the children can grow to be wards of the state.

Tiao-jie   Neighborhood committees in China that resolve disputes in criminal and noncriminal cases.

Token Treatment   The reality that rehabilitation programs in many prison systems are under-funded and provide services for only a fraction of the inmates who need them.

Victim and Witness Assistance Programs   Many jurisdictions have established agencies which help victims and witnesses of crime deal with the criminal justice system.

Victimization Studies   Studies done by criminologists which ask individuals what crimes they have been a victim of in the recent past. An alternative way of measuring crime that in conjunction with official measures gives us a better picture of the nature and extent of crime in society.

Victimless Crime The idea that there are some behaviors such as gambling, prostitution, and drug use where individuals freely choose to participate and therefore cannot be considered a victim.

Vigilantism The taking of the law into one's own hands to apprehend or punish criminals.

War on Crime Perspective The model of criminal justice policy that likens crime control to war. The war on drugs is another example of the inappropriate metaphor of using war to model crime-control policies.

Watchman Style One of the styles of policing used by James Q. Wilson in his topology of how police do their work. The Watchman style involved the wide use of discretion by the police officer.

Well-Regulated Militia Language from the second amendment of the Constitution used by gun proponents to claim they have a right to own weapons.

Whiskey Rebellion A revolt by farmers against attempts by the federal government to collect an excise tax on whiskey.

White-Collar Crime Crimes such as embezzlement committed in otherwise lawful endeavors usually committed by people in high social and economic standing.

Youth Culture The social environment of young people that may encourage rebellion toward authority and escapism through music, alcohol, and drugs. Efforts to deal with young people need to be cognizant of the pressures and strains of the youth culture.

Zero Tolerance The policy that gives no second chances to those who violate the law. As part of the war on crime model the zero tolerance policy has been used in drug cases where minimal amounts of an illegal substance have been enough to have property confiscated.

BIBLIOGRAPHY

Agopian, Michael W. 1989. "Targeting Juvenile Gang Offenders for Community Service." *Community Alternatives 1*(1): 99–108.

Akers, Ronald L. 1992. *Drugs, Alcohol, and Society: Social Structure, Process, and Policy.* Belmont: Wadsworth.

Albanese, Jay S. 1984. "Concern about Variation in Criminal Sentences: A Cyclical History of Reform." *The Journal of Criminal Law and Criminology 75*(1): 260–271.

Aldrich, Michael R. 1990. "Legalize the Lesser to Minimize the Greater: Modern Applications of Ancient Wisdom." *The Journal of Drug Issues 20*(4): 543–553.

Alexander, Bruce K. 1990. "Alternatives to the War on Drugs." *The Journal of Drug Issues 20*(1): 1–27.

Alexander, Bruce K., and Patricia L. Holborn. 1990. "Introduction: A Time for Change." *The Journal of Drug Issues 20*(4): 509–513.

Ali, Badr-el-Din. 1985. "Islamic Law and Crime: The Case of Saudi Arabia." *International Journal of Comparative and Applied Criminal Justice 9*(2): 45–56.

Anderson, Elijah. 1994. "The Code of the Streets." *The Atlantic Monthly* (May): 89–94.

Anderson, Kevin. 1991. "Radical Criminology and the Overcoming of Alienation: Perspectives from Marxian and Gandhian Humanism," in Harold E. Pepinsky and Richard Quinney, eds. *Criminology as Peacemaking.* Bloomington, IN: Indiana University Press, pp. 14–29.

Anderson, Linda S., Ted Chiriros, and Gordon P. Waldo. 1977. "Formal and Informal Sanctions: A Comparison of Deterrent Effects." *Social Problems 25*(October): 103–114.

Andrews, D. A., Ivan Zinger, Robert D. Hoge, James Bonta, Paul Gendreau, and Francis T. Cullen. 1990. "Does Correctional Treatment Work? A Clinically Relevant and Psychologically Informed Meta-Analysis." *Criminology 28*(3): 369–404.

Anslinger, Harry Jr., and Courtney Ryley Cooper. 1995. "Marijuana: Assassin of Youth," in James A. Inciardi and Karen McElrath, eds. *The American Drug Scene: An Anthology.* Los Angeles: Roxbury, pp. 88–93.

Arthur, John A., and Charles E. Case. 1994. "Race, Class and Support for Police Use of Force." *Crime, Law and Social Change 21*(2): 167–182.

Associated Press, The. 1990. "Guests Get Handcuffs at 'Wedding'." *The Atlanta Journal/ The Atlanta Constitution,* September 23.

Bailey, William C. and Ruth D. Peterson. 1990. "Capital Punishment and Non-Capital Crimes: A Test of Deterrence, General

Prevention, and System-Overload Arguments." *Albany Law Review 54*: 681–707.

Baker, Christopher P. 1996. "Child Chattel Lure Tourists for Sex Beneath the Palms." *Insight 11*(11): 11–13.

_____. 1995. "Kiddy Sex—Luring the Tourist for Love Beneath the Palms." *The World and I 10*(2): 360–369.

Baldus, David C., Charles Pulaski, and George Woodworth. 1983. "Comparative Review of Death Sentences: an Empirical Study of the Georgia Experience." *Journal of Criminal Law and Criminology 74*: 661–753.

Bard, Morton, and Dawn Sangrey. 1986. *The Crime Victim's Book,* 2nd ed. New York: Brunner-Mazel.

Barreto, Richard R. 1988. "The Making of a SWAT School." *The Police Chief* (February): 35–41.

Bartollas, Clemens, and Michael Braswell. 1993. "Correctional Treatment, Peacemaking, and the New Age Movement." *Journal of Crime and Justice 16*(2): 43–58.

Baskin, Deborah. 1988. "Community Mediation and the Public/Private Problem." *Social Justice 15*(1): 98–115.

Baugh, Dennis G. 1992. "ACA Gang Survey Examines National Control Strategies." *Corrections Today* (July): 82.

Baumer, Terry L., Michael G. Maxfield, and Robert I. Mendelsohn. 1993. "A Comparative Analysis of Three Electronically Monitored Home Detention Programs." *Justice Quarterly 10*(1): 121–142.

Bazemore, Gordon, and Allen W. Cole. 1994. "Police in the 'Laboratory' of the Neighborhood: Evaluating Problem-Oriented Strategies in a Medium-Sized City." *American Journal of Police 13*(3): 119–147.

Beccaria, Cesare. 1963 (1761). *On Crimes and Punishments.* New York: Macmillan.

Bedau, Hugo Adam. 1994. "American Populism and the Death Penalty: Witnesses at an Execution." *The Howard Journal of Criminal Justice 33*(4): 289–303.

Berkeley, Bill. 1994. "The Warlords of Natal." *The Atlantic Monthly* (March): 85–100.

Bernstein, Jerome S. 1987. "The Decline of Masculine Rites of Passage In Our Culture: The Impact on Masculine Individuation," in Louise Carus Mahdi, Steven Foster, and Meredith Little, eds. *Betwixt and Between: Patterns of Masculine and Feminine Initiation.* La Salle, IL: Open Count.

Bertram, Eva, Morris Blackman, Kenneth Sharpe, and Peter Andreas. 1996. *Drug War Politics: The Price of Denial.* Berkeley: University of California Press.

Bissinger, H. G. 1993(1990). "High School Football and Academics," in D. Stanley Eitzen, ed. *Sport in Contemporary Society,* 4th ed. New York: St. Martin's Press, pp. 66–76.

Bittner, Egon. 1980. *The Functions of the Police in Modern Society.* Cambridge, MA: Oelgeschlager, Gunn and Hain.

Blakely, Alan F. 1990. "The Cost of Killing Criminals." *Northern Kentucky Law Review* 18: 61–79.

Blomberg, Thomas G. 1980. "Widening the Net: An Anomaly in the Evaluation of Diversion Programs," in Malcolm W. Klein and Katherine S. Teilmann, eds. *Handbook of Criminal Justice Evaluation.* Beverly Hills: Sage, pp. 571–592.

Blomberg, Thomas G., William Bales, and Karen Reed. 1993. "Intermediate Punishment: Redistributing or Extending Social Control?" *Crime, Law and Social Change 19*: 187–201.

Blomberg, Thomas, and Karol Lucken. 1994. "Stacking the Deck by Piling Up Sanctions: Is Intermediate Punishment Destined to Fail?" *The Howard Journal of Criminal Justice 33*(1): 62–80.

Blumberg, Abraham S. 1989. "The Practice of Law as a Confidence Game: Organizational Cooptation of a Profession," in Sheldon Goldman and Austin Sarat, eds. *American Court Systems: Readings in Judicial Behavior.* New York: Longman.

Blumstein, Alfred. 1993. "Making Rationality Relevant—The American Society of

Criminology 1992 Presidential Address."
Criminology 31(1): 1–16.

Bohm, Robert M. 1994. "Capital Punishment in Two Judicial Circuits in Georgia." *Law and Human Behavior 18*(3): 138–319.

Bright, Stephen. 1994. "Time for Georgians to Face Facts: State's Death Penalty Discriminates." *The Atlanta Journal/The Atlanta Constitution,* May 24, p. A11.

Brilliant, Eleanor L. 1986. "Community Planning and Community Problem Solving: Past, Present, and Future." *Social Service Review* (December): 568–589.

Brooks, Laure Weber. 1993. "Police Discretionary Behavior: A Study of Style," in Roger G. Dunham and Geoffrey P. Alport, eds. *Critical Issues in Policing: Contemporary Readings,* 2nd ed. Prospect Heights, IL: Waveland, pp. 140–164.

Brown Richard Maxwell. 1990. "Historical Patterns of American Violence," in Neil Alan Weiner, Margaret Zahn, and Rita J. Sagi, eds. *Violence: Patterns, Causes, and Public Policy.* San Diego: Harcourt Brace Jovanovich, pp. 4–14.

Buckley, William F., Jr. 1996. "The War On Drugs is Lost." *National Review 48*(2): 35–38.

Buentello, Salvador. 1992. "Combatting Gangs in Texas." *Corrections Today* (July): 58–60.

_____. 1992. "Profiles of the Seven Major Gangs." *Corrections Today* (July): 59.

Bullington, Bruce. 1995. "War and Peace: Drug Policy in the United States and the Netherlands." *Crime, Law and Social Change 22:* 213–238.

Burns, Mark E. 1992. "Electronic Home Detention: New Sentencing Alternative Demands Uniform Standards." *Journal of Contemporary Law 18*(1): 75–105.

Burton, Velmer S., Jr., R. Gregory Dunaway, and Renee Kapache. 1993. "To Punish or Rehabilitate? A Research Note Assessing the Purpose of State Correctional Departments as Defined by State Legal Codes." *Journal of Crime and Justice 16*(1): 177–188.

Byrne, James M. 1986. "The Control Controversy: A Preliminary Examination of Intensive Probation Supervision Programs in the United States." *Federal Probation 50*(2): 4–16.

Calathes, William. 1990. "Gun Control in a Developing Nation: The Gun Court Act of Jamaica." *International Journal of Comparative and Applied Criminal Justice 14*(1): 317–344.

Campbell, Jacquelyn C. 1985. "Beating of Wives: A Cross-Cultural Perspective." *Victimology 10*(1–4): 174–185.

Castellano, Thomas C., and Edmund F. McGarrell. 1991. "The Politics of Law and Order: Case Study Evidence for a Conflict Model of the Criminal Law Formation Process." *Journal of Research in Crime and Delinquency 28*(3): 304–329.

Caulfield, Mina Davis. 1993. "Imperialism, the Family, and Cultures of Resistance," in Alison M. Jaggar and Paula S. Rothenberg, eds. *Feminist Frameworks: Alternative Theoretical Accounts of the Relations Between Women and Men,* 3rd ed. New York: McGraw-Hill.

Cederblom, Jerry, and Cassia Spohn. 1991. "A Model for Teaching Criminal Justice Ethics." *Journal of Criminal Justice Education 2*(2): 201–217.

Center for Research on Criminal Justice. 1977. *The Iron Fist and the Velvet Glove: an Analysis of the U.S. Police.* Berkeley, CA: Center for Research on Criminal Justice.

Chambliss, William J. 1995 (1973). "The Saints and the Roughnecks," in James M. Henslin, ed. *Down to Earth Sociology,* 8th ed. New York: The Free Press, pp. 254–267.

Chilton, Bradley S. 1991. "Reforming Plea Bargaining to Facilitate Ethical Discourse." *Criminal Justice Policy Review 5*(4): 322–334.

Christie, Nils. 1977. "Conflicts as Property." *The British Journal of Criminology 17*(1): 1–15.

Coakley, Jay. 1993. "Play Group Versus Organized Competitive Team: A Comparison," in D. Stanley Eitzen, ed. *Sport in Contemporary Society: An Anthology,* 4th ed. New York: St. Martin's Press, pp. 48–57.

Cobb, Paul Whitlock, Jr. 1989. "Reviving Mercy in the Structure of Capital Punishment." *The Yale Law Journal 99:* 389–409.

Cochran, John K., Mitchell B. Chamlin, and Mark Seth. 1994. "Deterrence or Brutalization? An Impact Assessment of Oklahoma's Return to Capital Punishment." *Criminology 32*(1): 107–134.

Conquergood, Dwight. 1994(1991). "For the Nation! How Street Gangs Problematize Patriotism," in Herbert W. Simons and Michael Billig, eds. *After Postmodernism: Reconstructing Ideology Critique.* London: Sage, pp. 200–221.

Cook, Philip J., Stephanie Molliconi, and Thomas B. Cole. 1995. "Regulating Gun Markets." *The Journal of Criminal Law and Criminology 86*(1): 59–92.

Cook, Rhonda. 1995. "Back to Hard Labor." *The Atlanta Journal/The Atlanta Constitution* August 20, p. D4.

Cooprider, Keith W. 1992. "Pretrial Bond Supervision: An Empirical Analysis with Policy Implications." *Federal Probation 56*(3): 41–49.

Corbett, Ronald, and Gary T. Marx. 1991. "Critique: No Soul in the New Machine: Technofallacies in the Electronic Monitoring Movement." *Justice Quarterly 8*(3): 399–414.

Cullen, Francis T., and Karen E. Gilbert. 1982. *Reaffirming Rehabilitation.* Cincinnati: Anderson.

Cullen, Francis T., Edward J. Latessa, Velmer S. Burton, Jr., and Lucien X. Lombardo. 1993. "The Correctional Orientation of Prison Wardens: Is the Rehabilitative Ideal Supported?" *Criminology 31*(1): 69–92.

Cummings, Jeanne. 1994. "Death Penalty Rules: 'Quotas' or Fairness?" *The Atlanta Journal/The Atlanta Constitution* May 27, p. A7.

Currie, Dawn H., and Brian D. MacLean. 1995. "Critical Reflections on the Peace Process in Northern Ireland: Implications for 'Peacethinking Criminology'." *Humanity and Society 19*(3): 99–108.

Currie, Elliott, 1989. "Confronting Crime: Looking Toward the Twenty-First Century." *Justice Quarterly 6*(1): 5–25.

Currie, Elliott, 1993. *Reckoning: Drugs, the Cities, and the American Future.* New York: Hill and Wang.

Currie, Elliot and Jerome H. Skolnick. 1997. *America's Problems: Social Issues and Public Policy,* 3rd ed. New York: Longman.

Czajkoski, Eugene H. 1990. "Drugs and the Warlike Administration of Justice." *The Journal of Drug Issues 20*(1): 125–129.

Dagger, Richard. 1991. "Restitution: Pure or Punitive?" *Criminal Justice Ethics 10*(2): 29–39.

Decker, Scott H., and Barbara Salert. 1987. "Selective Incapacitation: A Note on its Impact on Minorities." *Journal of Criminal Justice 15*(4): 287–299.

DiCristina, Bruce. 1995. *Method In Criminology: A Philosophical Primer.* New York: Harrow and Heston.

Doerin, Dennis D. 1988(1980). "A Case Study of the Misuse of Social Science in Capital Punishment Cases," in Kenneth C. Haas and James A. Inciardi, eds. *Challenging Capital Punishment: Legal and Social Science Approaches.* Thousand Oaks: Sage, pp. 213–244.

Doerner, William, and Steven Lab. 1995. *Victimology.* Cincinnati: Anderson Publishing.

Duke, Steven B. 1996. "The War on Drugs Is Lost." *National Review 48*(2): 47–48.

Dyer, Gwynne. 1985. *War.* New York: Crown.

Edwards, Harry. 1989(1984). "The Black 'Dumb Jock': An American Sports Tragedy," in D. Stanley Eitzen, ed. *Sport in Contemporary Society,* 3rd ed. New York: St. Martin's Press, pp. 158–166.

Eitzen, D. Stanley. 1989. "The Dark Side of Coaching and the Building of Character," in D. Stanley Eitzen, ed. *Sport In Contemporary Society,* 3rd ed. New York: St. Martin's Press, pp. 133–136.

Ellsworth, Phoebe. 1988. "Unpleasant Facts: The Supreme Court's Response to Empirical Research on Capital Punishment." in Kenneth Haas and James A. Inciardi, eds. *Challenging Capital Punishment: Legal and Social Science Approaches.* Newbury Park, CA: Sage, pp. 177–211.

el-Gawhary, Karim. 1995. "Sex Tourism in Cairo." *Middle East Report 25*(196): 26–27.

Erlanger, Howard S. 1979. "Estrangement, Machismo and Gang Violence." *Social Science Quarterly 60*(2): 235–248.

Espy, Watt. 1989. "Facing the Death Penalty" in Michael L. Radeletm, ed. *Facing the Death Penalty: Essasys on a Cruel and Unusual Punishment.* Philadelphia: Temple University Press, pp. 27–37.

Etzioni, Amitai. 1993. *The Spirit of Community: The Reinvention of American Society.* New York: Touchstone.

Falco, Mathea. 1992. "Foreign Drugs, Foreign Wars." *Daedalus 121*(3): 1–14.

Fears, Darryl. 1994. "So Long Dirty Harry." *The Atlanta Journal/ The Atlanta Constitution,* March 27, pp. F1, F2.

Feeley, Malcolm, and Jonathan Simon. 1992. "The New Penology: Notes on the Emerging Strategy of Corrections and Its Implications." *Criminology 30*(4): 449–474.

Finn, Peter. 1988. "Dealing with Street People: The Social Service System Can Help." *The Police Chief* (February): 47–51.

_____. 1995. "The Manhattan District Attorney's Narcotics Eviction Program." *National Institute of Justice* (May): 1–12.

Fischer, Louis. 1950. *The Life of Mahatma Gandhi.* New York: Harper and Brothers.

Flanagan, Timothy J., Edmund F. McGarrell, and Alan J. Lizotte. 1989. "Ideology and Crime Control Policy Positions in a State Legislature." *Journal of Criminal Justice 17*(2): 87–101.

Foley, Douglas E. 1993. "The Great American Football Ritual: Reproducing Race, Class, and Gender Inequality," in D. Stanley Eitzen, ed. *Sport in Contemporary Society: An Anthology,* 4th ed. New York: St. Martin's Press, pp. 326–354.

Foley, Douglas F. 1995. "The Great American Football Ritual," in James M. Henslin, ed. *Down to Earth Sociology,* 8th ed. New York: The Free Press, pp. 406–419.

Ford, Kathleen, Dewa Nyoman Wirawan, Peter Fajans, and Lorna Thorpe. 1995. "AIDS Knowledge, Risk Behaviors, and Factors Related to Condom Use among Male Commercial Sex Workers and Male Tourist Clients in Bali, Indonesia." *AIDS 9*(7): 751–759.

Foucault, Michel. 1979. *Discipline and Punish: The Birth of the Prison.* New York: Vintage.

Franke, Herman. 1990. "Dutch Tolerance: Facts and Fables." *The British Journal of Criminology 30*(1): 81–93.

Frazier, Patricia A. 1993. "A Comparative Study of Male and Female Rape Victims Seen at a Hospital-Based Rape Crisis Program." *Journal of Interpersonal Violence 8*(1): 64–76.

French, Laurence Armand. 1994. "Early Trauma, Substance Abuse and Crime: A Clinical Look at Violence and the Death Sentence." *Journal of Police and Criminal Psychology 10*(2): 64–67.

Friedman, Robert. 1994. "'Super Agency' is Key to Community Policing." *The Atlanta Journal/The Atlanta Constitution* (March 27), pp. F1, F2.

Fuller, John R. 1993. "The Rodney King Verdict and Urban Riots: A Value-Added Theory Perspective." *Journal of Police and Criminal Psychology 9*(2) 42–45.

Fuller, John R., and William N. Norton. 1993. "Juvenile Diversion: The Impact of Program Philosophy on Net Widening." *Journal of Crime and Justice 16*(1): 29–45.

Gardiner, Gareth S., and Richard N. McKinney. 1991. "The Great American War on Drugs: Another Failure of Tough-Guy Management." *The Journal of Drug Issues 21*(3): 605–616.

Gaylin, Willard. 1974. *Partial Justice: A Study of Bias in Sentencing.* New York: Vintage.

Gitlin, Todd. 1987. *The Sixties: Years of Hope, Days of Rage.* New York: Bantam Books.

Glick, Barry. 1992. "Governor's Task Force Tackles Growing Juvenile Gang Problem." *Corrections Today* (July): 92–97.

Goffman, Erving. 1959. *The Presentation of Self in Everyday Life.* New York: Doubleday.

Goffman, Erving. 1961. *Asylums: Essays on the Social Situation of Mental Patients and Other Inmates.* New York: Anchor Books.

Goldstein, Arnold P., and Barry Glick. 1994. *The Prosocial Gang: Implementing Aggression Replacement Training.* Thousand Oaks, CA: Sage.

Goode, Erich. 1993. *Drugs in American Society,* 4th ed. New York: McGraw-Hill.

Gottfredson, Michael, and Travis Hirschi. 1989. "War on Drugs Attacks Problem From Wrong Angle." *The Atlanta Journal/The Atlanta Constitution* (September 24), p. D3.

Greene, Jack R., and Carl B. Klockers. 1991. "What Police Do," in Carl B. Klockers and Stephen D. Mastrofski, eds. *Thinking About Police: Contemporary Readings,* 2nd ed. New York: McGraw-Hill, pp. 273–284.

Griffin, Pat, and James Genasci. 1990. "Addressing Homophobia in Physical Education: Responsibilities for Teachers and Researchers," in Michael A. Messner and Donald F. Sabo, eds. *Sport, Men, and the Gender Order: Critical Feminist Perspectives.* Champaign: Human Kinetics Press, pp. 211–221.

Grinc, Randolph M. 1994. "'Angels in Marble': Problems in Stimulating Community Involvement in Community Policing." *Crime and Delinquency* 40(3): 437–468.

Gross, Samuel R., and Robert Mauro. 1984. "Patterns of Death: An Analysis of Racial Disparities in Capital Sentencing and Homicide Investigation." *Stanford Law Review* 37(1): 27–153.

Gurr, Ted Robert. 1990. "Historical Trends in Violent Crime: A Critical Review of the Evidence," in Neil Alan Weiner, Margaret Zahn, and Rita J. Sagi, eds. *Violence: Patterns, Causes, and Public Policy.* San Diego: Harcourt Brace Jovanovich.

Guydish, Joseph, George Clark, Delia Garcia, and Jesus Bucardo. 1995. "Evaluation of Needle Exchange Using Street-Based Survey ethods." *Journal of Drug Issues* 25(1): 33–41.

Hagedorn, John, and Perry Macon. 1988. *People and Folks: Gangs, Crime and the Underclass in a Rustbelt City.* Chicago: Lakeview.

Halbrook, Stephen P. 1986. "What the Framers Intended: A Linguistic Analysis of the Right to Bear Arms." *Law and Contemporary Problems* 49(1): 151–162.

Hall, Donald J. 1991. "Victims' Voices in Criminal Court: The Need for Restraint." *American Criminal Law Review* 28(233): 233–266.

Haney, Craig. 1997. "Infamous Punishment: The Psychological Consequences of Punishment," in James W. Marquart and Jonathan R. Sorensen, eds. *Correctional Contexts: Contemporary and Classical Readings.* Los Angeles: Roxbury, pp. 428 437.

Hansen, Karl A. 1988. "A Successful Composition of SWAT/Hostage Teams for Medium to Small Cities." *The Police Chief* (February): 32–33.

Hearn, Wayne. 1995. "Track Record: Needle Exchange Programs Related to HIV Infection Statistics." *American Medical News* 38(15): 12.

Havlena, Thomas. 1987. "Abolishing the Death Penalty— Why? How? When?" *Western State University Law Review* 15: 127–177.

Henslin, James M. 1996. *Down to Earth Sociology.* Boston: Allyn and Bacon.

Hersh, Seymour M. 1994. "The Wild East." *The Atlantic Monthly* (June): 61–86.

Hibbert, Chrisotpher. 1963. *The Roots of Evil: A Social History of Crime and Punishment.* Minerva Press.

Hickey, Eric W. 1997. *Serial Murderers and Their Victims,* 2nd ed. Belmont, CA: Wadsworth.

Higgins, Dennis. 1988. "When Tactical Responses are Necessary." *The Police Chief* (February): 42–44.

Hillmann, Michael. 1988. "Tactical Intelligence Operations and Support during a Major Barricade/Hostage Event." *The Police Chief* (February): 18–30.

Hochschild, Arlie. 1993. "The Second Shift: Working Parents and the Revolution at Home," in Laurel Richardson and Verta Taylor, eds. *Feminist Frontiers III.* New York: McGraw-Hill.

Hodgson, Douglas. 1994. "Sex Tourism and Child Prostitution in Asia: Legal Responses and Strategies." *Melbourne University Law Review* 19(3): 512–544.

Howard, Johnette. 1995. "Sending the Wrong Message." *Sports Illustrated* (May 15): 84.

Howell, James C. 1994. "Recent Gang Research: Program and Policy Implications." *Crime and Delinquency* 40(4): 495–515.

Huff, C. Ronald. 1996. "Historical Explanations of Crime: From Demons to Politics," in Robert D. Crutchfield, George S. Bridges, and Joseph G. Weis, eds. *Crime.* Thousand Oaks, CA: Pine Forge Press, pp. 12–23.

Human Rights Watch. 1985. *The Human Rigfhts Watch Global Report on Women's Human Rights.* New York: Human Rights Watch.

Hutchison, Ira W., and J. David Hirschel. 1994. "Limitations in the Pro-Arrest Response to Spouse Abuse." *Journal of Contemporary Criminal Justice* 10(3): 147–163.

"Imported AIDS." 1993. *Connexions* 33: 16–18.

Inciardi, James A. 1986. *The War on Drugs: Heroin, Cocaine, Crime, and Public Policy.* Palo Alto, CA: Mayfield.

Inciardi, James A., and Juliet L. Dee. 1987. "From Keystone Cops to *Miami Vice* Images of Policing in American Popular Culture." *Journal of Popular Culture* 21(2): 84–102.

Inciardi, James A., and Duane C. McBride. 1990. "Legalizing Drugs: A Gormless, Naive Idea." *The Criminologist* 15(5): 1,3–4.

Inciardi, James A., and Ruth Horowitz, and Anne E. Pottieger. 1993. *Street Kids, Street Drugs, Street Crime: An Examination of Drug Use and Serious Delinquency in Miami.* Belmont: Wadsworth.

Inciardi, James A., Dorothy Lockwood, and Anne E. Pottieger. 1993. *Women and Crack-Cocaine.* New York: Macmillan.

Inciardi, James A., and Anne E. Pottieger. 1995. "Kids, Crack, and Crime," in James A., and Inciardi and Karen McElrath, eds. *The American Drug Scene: An Anthology.* Los Angeles: Roxbury, pp. 245–254.

Irwin, John. 1970. *The Felon.* Englewood Cliffs, NJ: Prentice Hall.

———. 1980. *Prisons in Turmoil.* Boston: Little, Brown.

Irwin, John, and James Austin. 1994. *It's about Time: America's Imprisonment Binge.* Belmont: Wadsworth.

Jacobs, James A., and Kimberly A. Potter. 1995. "Keeping Guns Out of the Wrong Hands: The Brady Law and the Limits of Regulation." *The Journal of Criminal Law and Criminology* 86(1): 93–120.

Jacobs, James B. 1977. *Stateville: The Penitentiary In Mass Society.* Chicago: The University of Chicago Press.

———. 1990. "Imagining Drug Legalization." *Public Interest* Fall(101): 28–42.

Jan, Lee Jan. 1983. "Deterrence and Social Control in the United States and China." *International Journal of Comparative and Applied Criminal Justice* 7(2): 195–200.

Joe, Karen A. 1994. "Myths and Realities of Asian Gangs on the West Coast." *Humanity and Society* 18(2): 3–18.

Johns, Christina Jacqueline. 1992. *Power, Ideology, and the War on Drugs: Nothing Succeeds Like Failure.* New York: Praeger, 1992.

Johnson, Robert. 1990. *Deathwork: A Study of the Modern Execution Process.* Monterey, CA: Brooks\Cole.

Jones, Landon Y. 1980. *Great Expectations: America and the Baby Boom Generation.* New York: Coward, McCann & Geoghegan.

Jones, Mark. 1992. "Islamic Law in Saudi Arabia: A Responsive View." *International Journal of Comparative and Applied Criminal Justice* 16(1): 43–56.

Kalstein, Michele H., Kirstie A. McCornock, and Seth A. Rosenthal. 1992. "Calculating Injustice: The Fixation on Punishment as Crime Control." *Harvard Civil Rights-Civil Liberties Law Review* 27(2): 575–655.

Kaminer, Wendy. 1994. "Crime and Community." *The Atlantic Monthly* (May): 111–120.

———. 1994. "Federal Offense." *The Atlantic Monthly* (June): 102–114.

Kania, Richard R. E. 1988. "Should We Tell the Police to Say 'Yes' to Gratuities?" *Criminal Justice Ethics* 7(2): 37–49.

Kant, Immanuel. 1995. "The Categorical Imperative." in Daryl Close and Nicholas Meier, eds. *Morality in Criminal Justice: An Introduction to Ethics* Belmont, CA: Wadsworth, pp. 45–50.

Kaplan, Edward H., Kaveh Khoshnood, and Robert Heimer. 1994. "A Decline in

HIV-Infected Needles Returned to New Haven's Needle Exchange Program: Client Shift or Needle Exchange?" *American Journal of Public Health 84*(12): 1991–1994.

Karnow, Stanley. 1983. *Vietnam: A History.* New York: Viking Press.

Kaufman, Irving R. 1990. "Reform for a System in Crisis: Alternative Dispute Resolution in the Federal Courts." *Fordham Law Review 49*(1): 1–38.

Kaufman, Michael. 1992. "The Construction of Masculinity and the Triad of Men's Violence," in Michael S. Kimmel and Michael A. Messner, eds. *Men's Lives,* 2nd ed. New York: MacMillan, pp. 28–49.

Keilitz, Susan, Geoff Gallas, and Roger Hanson. 1988. "State Adoption of Alternative Dispute Resolution." *State Court Journal 12*(2): 4–11.

Kelling, George L. and Mark H. Moore. 1988. "The Evolving Strategy of Policing." *Perspectives on Policing* November(4): 1–15.

Keve, Paul W. 1992. "The Costliest Punishment—A Corrections Administrator Contemplates the Death Penalty." *Federal Probation 56*(1): 11–15.

Kim, Chin, and Gary D. Garcia. 1989. "Capital Punishment in the United States and Japan: Constitutionality, Justification and Methods of Infliction." *Loyola of Los Angeles International and Comparative Law Journal 11*(2): 253–279.

King, Dr. Martin Luther, Jr. 1984(1958). "Pilgrimage to Nonviolence," in Judith Clavir Albert and Stewart Edward Albert, eds. *The Sixties Papers: Documents of a Rebellious Decade.* New York: Praeger, pp. 108–112.

———. 1958. *Stride Toward Freedom: The Montgomery Story.* New York: Harper Brothers.

———. 1969 (1963). "Letter From a Birmingham Jail," in Hugo Adam Bedau, ed. *Civil Disobedience: Theory and Practice.* New York: Pegasus, pp. 72–89.

Kleck, Gary, 1986. "Policy Lessons from Recent Gun Control Research." *Law and Contemporary Problems 49*(1): 35–62.

———. 1991. *Point Blank: Guns and Violence in America.* New York: Aldine de Gruyter.

Kleck, Gary, and E. Britt Patterson. 1993. "The Impact of Gun Control and Gun Ownership Levels on Violence Rates." *Journal of Quantitative Criminology 9*(3): 249–287.

Kleck, Gary and Marc Gertz. 1995. "Armed Resistance to Crime: The Prevalence and Nature of Self-Defense with a Gun." *The Journal of Criminal Law and Criminology 86*(1): 150–187.

Klein, Lloyd, Joan Luxenburg, and Marianna King. 1989. "Perceived Neighborhood Crime and the Impact of Private Security." *Crime and Delinquency 35*(3): 365–377.

Klein, Malcolm W. 1995. "Gang Control by Suppression: The Misuse of Deterrence Principles," in Malcolm W. Klein, Cheryl L. Maxson, and Jody Miller, eds. *The Modern Gang Reader.* Los Angeles: Roxbury, pp. 304–313.

Klockers, Carl B. 1991. "The Modern Sting," in Carl B. Klockers and Stephen D. Mastrofski, eds. *Thinking about Police: Contemporary Readings,* 2nd ed. New York: McGraw-Hill, pp. 258–267.

Klofas, John, and Charles Cutshall. 1985. "Unobtrusive Research Methods in Criminal Justice: Using Graffiti in the Reconstruction of Institutional Culture." *Journal of Research in Crime and Delinquency 22*(4): 355–373.

Klofas, John M. 1991. "Considering Prison in Context: The Case of the People's Republic of China." *International Journal of Comparative and Applied Criminal Justice 15*(2): 175–186.

Knopp, Fay Honey. 1991. "Community Solutions to Sexual Violence," in Harold Pepinsky and Richard Quinney, eds. *Criminology as Peacemaking.* Bloomington: Indiana University Press, pp. 181–193.

Kopeny, William J. 1985. "Capital Punishment—Who Should Choose?" *Western State University Law Review 12*(2): 383–416.

Kohl, Herbert. 1967. *36 Children.* New York: New American Library.

Kozol, Jonathan. 1967. *Death at an Early Age.* New York: Bantam.

Kozol, Jonathan. 1991. *Savage Inequalities.* New York: Crown.

Krasnow, Diane-Michele. 1992. "To Stop the Scourge: The Supreme Court's Approach to the War on Drugs." *American Journal of Criminal Law 19*(159): 219–266.

Lab, Steven P., and John T. Whitehead. 1990. "From 'Nothing Works' to 'The Appropriate Works': The Latest Stop on the Search for the Secular Grail." *Criminology 28*(3): 405–418.

_____. 1994. "Avoidance Behavior as a Response to In-School Victimization." *Journal of Security Administration 17*(2): 32–45.

Leavitt, Fred. 1982. *Drugs and Behavior,* 2nd ed. New York: Wiley-Interscience.

Lee, Felicia R. 1992. "Suing for Peace in a Neighborhood of Violence." *The New York Times,* December 27.

Leheny, David. 1995. "A Political Economy of Asian Sex Tourism." *Annals of Tourism Research 22*(2): 367–384.

Leland, John, and Vern E. Smith. 1995. "Back on the Chain Gang." *Newsweek* May 15: 58.

Lerman, Lisa G. 1984. "Mediation of Wife Abuse Cases: The Adverse Impact of Informal Dispute Resolution on Women." *Harvard Women's Law Journal 7*(1): 57–113.

Levy, Leonard W. 1996. *A License to Steal: The Forfeiture of Property.* Chapel Hill, NC: University of North Carolina Press.

Lewy, Guenter. 1978. *America in Vietnam.* New York: Oxford.

Li, Vickie F. 1995. "Child Sex Tourism to Thailand: The Role of the United States as a Consumer Country." *Pacific Rim Law and Policy Journal 4*(2): 505–542.

Light, Julie. 1995. "Needle Exchange on Trial." *Progressive 59*(3): 13.

Lilly, J. Robert, Richard A. Ball, G. David Curry, and John McMullen. 1993. "Electronic Monitoring of the Drunk Driver: A Seven-Year Study of the Home Confinement Alternative." *Crime and Delinquency 39*(4): 462–484.

Lively, G. Martin, and Judy A. Reardon. 1996. "Justice on the Net: The National Institute of Justice Promotes Internet Services." *National Institute of Justice* (March): 1–8.

Logan, Charles H., and Gerald G. Gaes. 1993. "Meta-Analysis and the Rehabilitation of Punishment." *Justice Quarterly 10*(2): 245–263.

Lombardo, Bennett J. 1986. "The Behavior of Youth Sport Coaches: Crisis on the Bench," in Richard E. Lapchick, ed. *Fractured Forms: Sport as Reflection of Society.* Lexington, MA: Lexington Books, pp. 199–206.

Lurigio, Arthur J., and Wesley G. Skogan. 1994. "Winning the Hearts and Minds of Police Officers: An Assessment of Staff Perceptions of Community Policing in Chicago." *Crime and Delinquency 40*(3): 315–330.

Luttwak, Edward N. 1985. *The Pentagon and the Art of War.* New York: Simon and Schuster.

MacKenzie, Doris Layton, 1990. "Boot Camp Prisons: Components, Evaluations, and Empirical Issues." *Federal Probation 54*(3): 44–52.

MacKenzie, Doris Layton, and James W. Shaw. 1990. "Inmate Adjustment and Change During Shock Incarceration: The Impact of Correctional Boot Camp Programs." *Justice Quarterly 7*(1): 125–150.

MacKenzie, Doris Layton, James W. Shaw, and Claire Souryal. "Characteristics Associated With Successful Adjustment to Supervision: A Comparison of Parolees, Probationers, Shock Participants, and Shock Dropouts." *Criminal Justice and Behavior 19*(4): 437–454.

Mainardi, Pat. 1993. "The Politics of Housework," in Alison M. Jaggar and Paula S. Rothenberg, eds. *Feminist Frameworks: Alternative Theoretical Accounts of the Relations Between Women and Men,* 3rd ed. New York: McGraw-Hill.

Malone, Julia. 1995. "Crackdown Fails to Cut Ranks of Hard-Core Users." *The Atlanta Journal/The Atlanta Constitution,* May 14, p. A6.

Manning, Peter K., and Lawrence J. Redlinger. 1986. "Invitational Edges of Corruption: Some Consequences of Narcotic Law Enforcement," in Thomas Barker and

David L. Carter, eds. *Police Deviance.* Cincinnati: Pilgrimage.

Marcuse, Herbert. 1976 (1965). "Repressive Tolerance," in Paul Connerton, ed. *Critical Sociology: Selected Readings.* New York: Penguin, pp. 301–329.

Marquart, James W., Madhava Bodapati, Steven J. Cuvelier, and Leo Carroll. 1993."Ceremonial Justice, Loose Coupling, and the War on Drugs in Texas, 1980–1989." *Crime and Delinquency 39*(4): 528–542.

Marwick, Charles. 1995. "Released Report Says Needle Exchange Work." *JAMA 273*(13): 980–981.

Marx, Gary T. 1992. "Under-the-Covers Undercover Investigations: Some Reflections on the State's Use of Sex and Deception in Law Enforcement." *Criminal Justice Ethics 11*(1): 13–24.

Mastrofski, Stephen D., R. Richard Ritti, and Debra Hoffmaster. 1987. "Organizational Determinants of Police Discretion: The Case of Drinking-Driving." *Journal of Criminal Justice 15*(5): 387–402.

Mastrofski, Stephen D. 1991. "Community Policing as Reform: A Cautionary Tale," in Carl B. Klockers and Stephen D. Mastrofski, eds. *Thinking about Police: Contemporary Readings,* 2nd ed. New York: McGraw-Hill, pp. 515–530.

Maxfield, Michael G. 1992. "Pretrial Home Detention With Electronic Monitoring." *Evaluation Review 16*(3): 315–332.

Maxfield, Michael G., and Terry L. Baumer. 1992. "Pretrial Home Detention with Electronic Monitoring: A Non experimental Salvage Evaluation." *Evaluation Review. 16*(3):315–332.

Maxson, Cheryl L. 1995. "Research in Brief: Street Gangs and Drug Sales in Two Suburban Cities," in Malcolm Klein, Cheryl L. Maxson, and Jody Miller, eds. *The Modern Gang Reader.* Los Angeles: Roxbury, pp. 228–235.

Maxson, Cheryl L. 1995. "Street Gangs and Drug Sales in Two Suburban Cities." *National Institute of Justice* (September): 1–14.

McCall, Patricia L., Kenneth C. Land, and Lawrence E. Cohen. 1992. "Violent Criminal Behavior: Is There a General and Continuing Influence of the South?" *Social Science Research 21*(3): 286–310.

McClintock, John M. 1992. "Sex Tourism in Cuba." *Hemisphere 5*(1): 27–28.

McDermott, M. Joan. 1994. "Criminology as Peacemaking, Feminist Ethics and the Victimization of Women." *Women and Criminal Justice 5*(2): 21–44.

McDonald, Kim A. 1995. "Peacemaking among Primates." *The Chronicle of Higher Education* July 7: A6–7,A11.

McKenzie, Ian. 1990. "Discretion in Danger." *Policing 6*(2): 422–439.

McNamara, Joseph D. 1996. "The War On Drugs is Lost." *National Review 48*(2): 42–44.

McPhail, Clark. 1994. "Presidential Address. The Dark Side of Purpose: Individual and Collective Violence in Riots." *The Sociological Quarterly 35*(1): 1–32.

Meehan, Patrick J., and Patrick W. O'Carroll. 1995. "Gangs, Drugs, and Homicide in Los Angeles," in Malcolm Klein, Cheryl L. Maxson, and Judy Miller, eds. *The Modern Gang Reader.* Los Angeles: Roxbury, pp. 236–241.

Mendez, Salvador. 1992. "Community Struggles to Prevent Youths from Joining Growing Numbers of Gangs." *Corrections Today* (July): 72–77.

Messner, Michael A., and Donald F. Sabo. 1990. "Toward a Critical Feminist Reappraisal of Sport, Men, and the Gender Order," in Michael A. Messner and Donald F. Sabo, eds. *Sport, Men, and the Gender Order: Critical Feminist Perspectives.* Champaign: Human Kinetics Press, pp. 1–15.

Messner, Michael. 1992. "Boyhood, Organized Sports, and the Construction of Masculinity," in Michael S. Kimmel and Michael A. Messner, eds. *Men's Lives,* 2nd ed. New York: MacMillan, 161–175.

Messner, Michael A., Margaret Carlisle Duncan, and Kerry Jensen. 1993(1992). "Separating the Men from the Girls: The

Gendered Language of Televised Sport," in D. Stanley Eitzen, ed. *Sport in Contemporary Society, 4th ed.* New York: St. Martin's Press, pp. 219–233.

Miller, Alden D., and Lloyd E. Ohlin. 1985. *Delinquency and Community: Creating Opportunities and Controls.* Beverly Hills: Sage.

Miller, Kent S., and Betty Davis Miller. 1989. *To Kill and Be Killed: Case Studies from Florida's Death Row.* Pasadena: Hope Publishing House.

Miller, Walter B. 1996. "Why the United States Has Failed to Solve Its Youth Gang Problem," in Joseph G. Weis, Robert D. Crutchfield, and George S. Bridges, eds. *Juvenile Delinquency.* Thousand Oaks, CA: Pine Forge Press, pp. 218–224.

Moore, David B. 1993. "Shame, Forgiveness, and Juvenile Justice." *Criminal Justice Ethics* 12(1): 3–25.

Morash, Merry, and Lila Rucker. 1990. "A Critical Look at the Idea of Boot Camp as a Correctional Reform." *Crime and Delinquency* 36(2): 204–222.

Morganthau, Tom, Susan Miller, Patrick Rogers, Ward Pincus, and Jeanne Gordon. 1994. "Why Good Cops Go Bad." *Newsweek* (December 19): 30–34.

Morris, Norval and Michael Tonry. 1990. *Between Prison and Probation: Intermediate Punishments in a Rational Sentencing System.* New York: Oxford.

Mulholland, David. 1994. "Judges Finding Creative Ways of Punishing." *The Wall Street Journal,* May 24.

Mushanga, Tibamanya mwene. 1992. "Introduction." *Criminology in Africa.* Rome: United Nations Interregional Crime and Justice Research Institute.

Musto, David F., M.D. 1987. *The American Disease: Origins of Narcotic Control.* New York: Oxford University Press.

Nack, William, and Lester Munson. 1995. "Sports' Dirty Secret." *Sports Illustrated* (July) 31: 64–74.

Nadelmann, Ethan A. 1988. "The Case for Legalization." *The Public Interest* 92(Summer): 3–31.

_____. 1996. "The War On Drugs is Lost." *National Review* 48(2): 38–40.

Naess, Anne. 1965. *Gandhi and the Nuclear Age.* Totowa, NJ: The Bedminster Press.

Nathanson, Stephen. 1987. *An Eye for an Eye?* Totowa, NJ: Rowman and Littlefield.

National Council of Juvenile and Family Court Judges. 1989. "Alternative Dispute Resolution: A Juvenile and Family Court Perspective." *Juvenile and Family Court Journal* 40(2): 51–98.

National Criminal Justice Commission. 1996. "Ten Recommendations to Shift the Fundamental Direction of U.S. Crime Policy." http://www.ncianet.org/ncia/FIND.HTML

Neimark, Jill. 1993. "Out of Bounds: The Truth about Athletes and Rape," in D. Stanley Eitzen, ed. *Sport in Contemporary Society: An Anthology,* 4th ed. New York: St. Martin's Press. pp. 130–137.

Neubauer, David W. 1979. *America's Courts and the Criminal Justice System.* North Scituate, MA: Duxbury Press.

Newman, Graham. 1983. *Just and Painful: A Case for the Corporal Punishment of Criminals.* New York: Macmillan.

New York Times. 1994. "War on Marijuana Draws Complaints in California," September 19, p. A12.

O'Malley, Pat. 1993. Review of "Criminology as Peacemaking," Hal Pepinsky and Richard Quinney, eds. *Canadian Journal of Law and Society* 8(1): 253–256.

Orwell, George. 1949. *1984.* New York: Signet.

Osler, Mark W. 1991. "Shock Incarceration: Hard Realities and Real Possibilities." *Federal Probation* 55(1): 34–42.

Palmer, Ted. 1992. "Growth-Centered Intervention: An Overview of Changes in Recent Decades." *Federal Probation* 56(1): 62–67.

Palmeri, Christopher. 1994. "The Texas Lockup." *Forbes* (September): 48,50.

Parrinder, Geoffery. 1971. *World Religions: From Ancient History to the Present.* New York: Facts on File Publications.

Paternoster, Raymond. 1987. "The Deterrent Effect of Perceived Certainty and Severity of Punishment: A Review of the Evidence and Issues." *Justice Quarterly* 4(2): 174–217.

Paternoster, Raymond, and A. Kazyada. 1988. "The Administration of the Death Penalty in South Carolina: Experiences Over the First Few Years." *South Carolina Law Review* 39: 245–414.

Payne, Robert. 1969. *The Life and Death of Mahatma Gandhi.* New York: Smithmark.

Peltason, J. W. 1976. *Corwin's and Peltason's Understanding the Constitution.* Hinsdale: Dryden Press.

Pepinsky, Hal. 1994. "Penal Abolition as a Human Birthright." *Humanity and Society* 18(4): 19–34.

Pepinsky, Harold E., and Richard Quinney. 1991. *Criminology as Peacemaking.* Bloomington: Indiana University Press.

Petersilia, Joan, and Susan Turner. 1994 (1993). "Evaluating Intensive Supervision Probation/Parole," in Peter C. Kratcoski, ed. *Correctional Counseling and Treatment,* 3rd ed. Prospect Heights: Waveland, pp. 31–53.

Platt, Anthony M. 1969. *The Child Savers: The Invention of Delinquency.* Chicago: The University of Chicago Press.

Polsby, Daniel D. 1994. "The False Promise of Gun Control." *The Atlantic Monthly* (March): 57–70.

Portner, Jessica. 1994. "Making the Best of a Bad Habit." *Education Week* 14(1): 37–38.

Potter, Gary, Larney Gaines, and Beth Holbrook. 1990. "Blowing Smoke: An Evaluation of Marijuana Eradication in Kentucky." *American Journal of Police.* 9(1): 96–116.

Powell, Dennis D. 1990. "A Study of Police Discretion in Six Southern Cities." *Journal of Police Science and Administration* 17(1): 1–7.

Powell, Lewis F., Jr. 1989. "Commentary: 'Capital Punishment'." *Harvard Law Review 102*: 1035–1046.

Pronger, Brian. 1990. "Gay Jocks: A Phenomenology of Gay Men in Athletics," in Michael A. Messner and Donald F. Sabo, eds. *Sport, Men, and the Gender Order: Critical Feminist Perspectives.* Champaign: Human Kinetics Press, pp. 141–152.

Pugsley, Robert A. 1981. "A Retributivist Argument Against Capital Punishment." *Hofstra Law Review* 9(5): 1501–1523.

Quinney, Richard. 1993. "A Life of Crime: Criminology and Public Policy as Peacemaking." *Journal of Crime and Justice* 16(2): 3–9.

Radelet, Michael L., and Glenn L. Pierce. 1985. "Race and Prosecutorial Discretion in Homicide Cases." *Law and Society Review* 19: 587–621.

Radelet, Michael L., Hugo Adam Bedau, and Constance E. Putnam. 1992. *In Spite of Innocence.* Boston: Northeastern University Press.

Raphael, Ray. 1988. *The Men from the Boys: Rites of Passage in Male America.* Lincoln, NE: University of Nebraska Press.

Ray, Oakley, and Charles Ksir. 1993. *Drugs, Society, and Human Behavior,* 6th ed. St. Louis: Mosby.

Reekie, Gail, and Paul Wilson. 1993. "Rape, Resistance and Women's Rights of Self-Defence." *The Australian and New Zealand Journal of Criminology* 26(2): 146–154.

Reiman, Jeffrey. 1995. *The Rich Get Richer and the Poor Get Prison: Ideology, Class and Criminal Justice,* 4th ed. Boston: Allyn and Bacon.

Reitan, Eric. 1993. "Why the Deterrence Argument for Capital Punishment Fails." *Criminal Justice Ethics* 12(1): 26–33.

Reskin, Barbara F. 1993. "Bringing the Men Back In: Sex Differentiation and the Devaluation of Women's Work," in Laurel Richardson and Verta Taylor, eds. *Feminist Frontiers III.* New York: McGraw-Hill.

Reuter, Peter. 1992. "Hawks Ascendant: The Punitive Trend of American Drug Policy." *Daedalus 121*(3): 15–52.

Reynolds, Diane E. 1988. "The Use of Pretrial Diversion Programs in Spouse Abuse Cases: A New Solution to an Old Problem." *Ohio State Journal on Dispute Resolution* 3(2): 415–436.

Riley, Sgt. William. 1992. "Taking and Two-pronged Approach To Managing Washington's Gangs." *Corrections Today* (July): 68–71.

Robinson, David, Alan Maynard, and Robert Chester, eds. 1989. *Controlling Legal Addictions.* New York: St. Martin's Press.

Rogers, Christopher. 1993. "Gang-Related Homicides in Los Angeles County." *Journal of Forensic Sciences 38*(4): 831–834.

Rojas, Aurelio. 1987. "Gang Life—The Way It Was and the Way It Is in Los Angeles." *Crime Control Digest 21*(2): 6–7.

Rorabaugh, W. J. 1979. *The Alcohol Republic: An American Tradition.* New York: Oxford University Press.

Rosenbaum, Dennis P. 1991. "The Pursuit of 'Justice' in the United States: A Policy Lesson in the War on Crime and Drugs?" *Canadian Police College Journal 15*(4): 239–255.

Rosenbaum, Dennis P., and Arthur J. Lurigio. 1994. "An Inside Look at Community Policing Reform: Definitions, Organizational Changes, and Evaluation Findings." *Crime and Delinquency 40*(3): 299–314.

Ross, Floyd H., and Tynette Hills. 1956. *The Great Religions by Which Men Live.* Greenwich: Fawcett.

Rothman, David J. 1995. "More of the Same: American Criminal Justice Policies in the 1990s," in Thomas G. Blomberg and Stanley Cohen, eds. *Punishment and Social Control.* New York: Aldine De Gruyter, pp. 22–44.

Rotundo, E. Anthony. 1993. *American Manhood: Transformations in Masculinity from the Revolution to the Modern Era.* New York: Basic Books.

Sadd, Susan, and Randolph M. Grinc. 1996. "Implementation Challenges in Community Policing." *National Institute of Justice* (February): 1–19.

Sanad, Nagaty. 1991. *The Theory of Crime and Criminal Responsibility In Islamic Law: Sharia'.* Chicago: The University of Illinois at Chicago.

Sanborn, Joseph B. 1993. "Philosophical, Legal, and Systemic Aspects of Juvenile Court Plea Bargaining." *Crime and Delinquency 39*(4): 509–527.

Sanders, William. 1995. "Drive-bys," in Malcolm Klein et al., eds. *The Modern Gang Reader.* Los Angeles: Roxbury, pp. 211–219.

Scheidegger, Kent. 1987. "Capital Punishement in 1987: The Puzzle Nears Completnoi." *Western State University Law Review 15*(95):95–126.

Schichor, David. 1992. "Following the Penological Pendulum: The Survival of Rehabilitation." *Federal Probation 56*(2): 19–25.

Schine, Eric. 1995. "The Explosion in Private Justice." *Business Week* (June 12): 88–89.

Schlaadt, Roger G., and Peter T. Shannon. 1986. *Drugs of Choice: Current Perspectives on Drug Use,* 2nd ed. Englewood Cliffs, NJ: Prentice Hall.

Schlesinger, Philip, and Howard Tumber. 1993. "Fighting the War Against Crime: Television, Police, and Audience." *The British Journal of Criminology 33*(1): 19–32.

Schlosser, Eric. 1994. "Reefer Madness." *The Atlantic Monthly* (August): 45–63.

Schmidt, Annealey K. 1994(1986). "Electronic Monitors," in Peter C. Kratcoski, ed. *Correctional Counseling and Treatment,* 3rd ed. Prospect Heights: Waveland, pp. 548–555.

Schmoke, Kurt. 1996. "The War On Drugs is Lost." *National Review 48*(2): 40–42.

Schur, Edwin. 1973. *Radical Non-Intervention: Rethinking the Delinquency Problem.* Englewood Cliffs, NJ: Prentice Hall.

Schwartz, Martin D. and Walter S. DeKeseredy. 1991. "Left Realist Criminology: Strengths, Weaknesses and the Feminist Critique." *Crime, Law and Social Change 15*(1): 51–72.

Schwartz, Martin D., and David O. Friedrichs. 1994. "Postmodern Thought and Criminological Discontent: New Metaphors for Understanding Violence." *Criminology 32*(2): 221–246.

Scott, Ellen Kaye. 1993. "How to Stop the Rapists? A Question of Strategy in Two Rape Crisis Centers." *Social Problems 40*(3): 343–361.

Sechrest, Dale K. 1989. "Prison 'Boot Camps' Do Not Measure Up." *Federal Probation* 53(3): 15–20.

Selke, William L. 1991. "A Comparison of Punishment Systems in Denmark and the United States." *International Journal of Comparative and Applied Criminal Justice* 15(2): 227–242.

Selva, Lance, H. 1980. "Treatment as Punishment." *New England Journal on Prison Law* 6(3):265–288.

Selva, Lance H., and Robert M. Bohm. 1987. "A Critical Examination of the Informalism Experiment in the Administration of Justice." *Crime and Social Justice (29)*: 43–57.

Serio, Joseph. 1992. "Organized Crime in the Soviet Union and Beyond." *Low Intensity Conflict and Law Enforcement* 1(2): 127–151.

Severson, Margaret M. 1992. "Redefining the Boundaries of Mental Health Services: A Holistic Approach to Inmate Mental Health." *Federal Probation* 56(3): 57–63.

Shaidi, Leonard P. 1992. "Traditional, Colonial and Present-Day Administration of Justice," in Tibamanza mwene Mushanga, ed. *Criminology in Africa.* Rome: United Nations.

Shapiro, Bruce. 1996. "How the War on Crime Imprisons America." *The Nation* (April): 14–21.

Shaw, William. 1973. "Vandalism Is Not Senseless." *Law and Order* (February): 14–19.

Sherman, Lawrence W., and Richard A. Berk, et al. 1990. "The Specific Deterrent Effects of Arrest for Domestic Assault," in Neil Alan Weiner, Margaret A. Zahn, and Rita J. Sagi, eds. *Violence: Patterns, Causes, Public Policy.* San Diego, CA: Harcourt Brace Jovanovich, pp. 422–431.

Sherman, Lawrence W., James W. Shaw, and Dennis P. Rogan. 1995. "The Kansas City Gun Experiment." *National Institute of Justice* (January): 1–11.

Shichor, David. 1992. "Following the Penological Pendulum: The Survival of Rehabilitation." *Federal Probation* 56(2): 19–25.

Shuster, Robert M., Daena R. Levine, Philip R. Harris, and Herbert Z. Wong. 1995. *Multicultural Law Enforcement: Strategies for Peacekeeping in a Diverse Society.* Englewood Cliffs, NJ: Prentice Hall.

Sielaff, Wolfgang. 1988. "Organized Criminal Activity in the Federal Republic of Germany." *The Police Chief* 55(11): 76–79.

Sipes, Richard Grey. 1993(1976). "Sports as a Control for Aggression," in D. Stanley Eitzen, ed. *Sport in Contemporary Society,* 4th ed. New York: St. Martin's Press, pp. 78–84.

Skolnick, Jerome H. 1992. "Rethinking the Drug Problem." *Daedalus* 121(3): 133–159.

Skolnick, Jerome H. 1995. "Gangs and Crime Old as Time; But Drugs Change Gang Culture," in Malcolm Klein, Cheryl L. Maxson, and Jody Miller, eds. *The Modern Gang Reader.* Los Angeles: Roxbury, pp. 222–227.

Skolnick, Jerome H., and David H. Bayley. 1991. "The New Blue Line," in Carl B. Klockers and Stephen D. Mastrofski, eds. *Thinking about Police: Contemporary Readings,* 2nd ed. New York: McGraw-Hill, pp. 494–504.

Skolnick, Jerome H., and Richard A. Leo. 1992. "The Ethics of Deceptive Interrogation." *Criminal Justice Ethics* 11(1): 3–12.

Skolnick, Jerome H., and James J. Fyfe. 1993. *Above the Law: Police and the Excessive Use of Force.* New York: The Free Press.

Smith, Brent L., and Edward H. Stevens. 1984. "Sentence Disparity and the Judge-Jury Sentencing Debate: An Analysis of Robbery Sentences in Six Southern States." *Criminal Justice Review* 9(1): 1–7.

Smith, Clayton L. 1988. [Review of *Capital Punishment and the American Agenda,* by Franklin E. Zimring and Gordon Hawkins. Cambridge, England: Cambridge University Press, 1986.]. *American Journal of Criminal Law* 14: 297–299.

Smith, Huston. 1958. *The Religions of Man.* New York: Harper and Row.

Spangenberg, Robert L., and Elizabeth R. Walsh. 1989. "Capital Punishment or Life Imprisonment? Some Cost Considerations." *Loyola of Los Angeles Law Review 23* (November): 45–58.

Spergel, Irving A. 1995. *The Youth Gang Problem: A Community Approach.* New York: Oxford University Press.

Spitzer, Robert J. 1995. *The Politics of Gun Control.* Chatham, NJ: Chatham House Publishers.

Sproule, Catherine F., and Deborah J. Kennett. 1989. "Killing With Guns in the USA and Canada 1977–1983: Further Evidence for the Effectiveness of Gun Control." *Canadian Journal of Criminology 31*(3): 245–251.

Stack, Steve. 1993. "Execution Publicity and Homicide in Georgia." *American Journal of Criminal Justice 18*(1): 25–39.

Stark, Rodney. 1972. *Police Riots: Collective Behavior and Law Enforcement.* Belmont, CA: Focus Books.

Stahl, Marc B. 1992. "Asset Forfeiture, Burdens of Proof and the War on Drugs." *The Journal of Criminal Law and Criminology 83*(2): 274–337.

Stevens, Dennis J. 1992. "Research Note: The Death Sentence and Inmate Attitudes." *Crime and Delinquency 38*(2): 272–279.

Stinchcombe, Andrew J. 1994. "The Acceptability of Executing the Innocent." *The Howard Journal of Criminal Justice 33*(4): 304–318.

Stitt, B. Grant. 1991. "Practical, Ethical and Political Aspects of Engaging 'Man's Best Friend' in the War on Crime." *Criminal Justice Policy Review 5*(1): 53–65.

Stitt, B. Grant, and Robert H. Chaires. 1993. "Plea Bargaining: Ethical Issues and Emerging Perspectives." *The Justice Professional 7*(2): 69–91.

Substance Abuse and Mental Health Services Administration News. 1995. 3(1).

Sutton, L. Paul. 1991. "Getting Around the Fourth Amendment," in Carl B. Klockers and Stephen D. Mastrofski, eds. *Thinking about Police: Contemporary Readings,* 2nd ed. New York: McGraw-Hill, pp. 433–444.

Sweet, Robert W. 1996. "The War On Drugs is Lost." *National Review 48*(2): 44–45.

Szasz, Thomas. 1996. "The War On Drugs is Lost." *National Review 48*(2): 45–47.

Taylor, Ian, Paul Walton and Jock Young. 1973. *The New Criminology: For a Social Theory of Deviance.* New York: Harper and Row.

Thomas, Jim, and Aogan O'Maolchatha. 1989. "Reassessing the Critical Metaphor: An Optimistic Revisionist View." *Justice Quarterly 6*(2): 143–172.

Tifft, Larry. 1982. "Capital Punishment Research, Policy, and Ethics: Defining Murder and Placing Murderers." *Crime and Social Justice* (Summer): 61–68.

Tittle, Charles R. 1980. "Evaluating the Deterrent Effects of Criminal Sanctions," in Malcolm W. Klein and Katherine S. Teillman, eds. *Handbook of Criminal Justice Evaluation.* Beverly Hills: Sage, pp. 381–402.

Tobolowsky, Peggy M. 1992. "Drugs and Death: Congress Authorizes the Death Penalty for Certain Drug-Related Murders." *Journal of Contemporary Law 18*(1): 47–73.

Tolstoy, Leo. 1967. *Tolstoy's Writings on Civil Disobedience and Non-Violence.* New York: Bergman.

Trebach, Arnold S. 1990. "A Bundle of Peaceful Compromises." *The Journal of Drug Issues 20*(4): 515–531.

Trout, Craig H. 1992. "Taking a New Look at an Old Problem." *Corrections Today* (July): 62–66.

Troyat, Henri. 1967. *Tolstoy.* Garden City: Doubleday.

Uelmen, Gerald F., and Victor G. Haddox. 1983. *Drug Abuse and the Law: Cases, Text, Materials.* New York: Clark Boardman.

"Use Prison Televisions to Give Serious Education." *The Atlanta Journal/The Atlanta Constitution,* September 12, p. A6.

Vago, Steven. 1988. *Law and Society.* Upper Saddle River, NJ: Prentice Hall.

Vaughn, Michael S. 1993. "Listening to the Experts: A National Study of Correctional Administrators' Responses to Prison Overcrowding." *Criminal Justice Review 18*(1): 12–25.

Viano, Emilio. 1983. "Victimology: The Development of a New Perspective." *Victimology 8*(1–2): 17–30.

Vlahov, David, Caitlin Ryan, Liza Solomon, Sylvia Cohn, Maude R. Holt, and Muhommad N. Akhter. 1994. "A Pilot Syringe Exchange Program in Washington, DC." *American Journal of Public Health 84*(2): 303–304.

Von Hirsch, Andrew. 1976. *Doing Justice: The Choice of Punishment.* New York: Hill and Wang.

Walker, Richard D. 1988. "SWAT Training/ Reorganization." *The Police Chief* (February): 46.

Walker, Samuel. 1994. *Sense and Nonsense about Crimes and Drugs.*Belmont, CA: Wadsworth Publishing Comapny.

Wallace, Harvey. 1996. *Family Violence: Legal, Medical, and Social Perspectives.* Boston: Allyn and Bacon.

Weisheit, Ralph. 1992. *Domestic Marijuana: A Neglected Industry.* Westport, CT: Greenwood.

Weisman, Jacob. 1993. "Big Buck Basketball: Acolytes in the Temple of Nike." in D. Stanley Eitzen, ed. *Sport in Contemporary Society: An Anthology,* 4th ed. New York: St. Martin's Press, pp. 164–168.

White, Welsh S. 1993. "Capital Punishment's Future." *Michigan Law Review 91* (May): 1429–1441.

Whitfield, Tom. 1995. "Chain Gang Chic may be Fashion Fad." *The Atlanta Journal/The Atlanta Constitution* December 21, p. D9.

Williams, John W., Jr. 1992. "Understanding How Youth Gangs Operate." *Corrections Today* (July): 86–88.

Wilson, Deborah G., and Susan F. Bennett. 1994. "Officers' Response to Community Policing: Variations on a Theme." *Crime and Delinquency 40*(3): 354–370.

Wilson, A. N. 1988. *Tolstoy.* New York: W. W. Morton.

Wilson, James Q. 1972. *Varieties of Police Behavior: The Management of Law and Order in Eight Communities.* New York: Atheneum.

_____. and George L. Kelling. 1993. "Broken Windows," in Roger G. Durham and Geoffrey P. Alpert, eds. *Critical Issues in*

Policing: Contemporary Issues, 2nd ed. Prospect Heights: Waveland.

_____. 1994. "What To Do About Crime." *Commentary 98*(3): 25–34.

Wiltfang, Gregory L., and John K. Cochran. 1994. "The Sanctuary Movement and the Smuggling of Undocumented Central Americans into the United States: Crime, Deviance, or Defiance?" *Sociological Spectrum 14*(2): 101–128.

Wolfgang, Marvin. 1995. "A Tribute to a View I Have Opposed." *The Journal of Criminal Law and Criminology 86*(1): 188–192.

Wooden, Wayne S. 1995. *Renegade Kids, Suburban Outlaws: From Youth Culture to Delinquency.* Belmont: Wadsworth.

Wooten, Jim. 1996. "For Safety, No Price Is Too High." *The Atlanta Journal/The Atlanta Constitution,* (January 7), p. D7.

"WTO to Combat Sex Tourism." 1995. *Travel Indonesia 17*(12): 18.

Yuille, John C. 1984. "Research and Teaching with Police: A Canadian Example." *International Review of Applied Psychology 33*: 5–23.

Zahn, Margaret A. 1990. "Intervention Strategies to Reduce Homicide." in Neil Allen Weiner, Margaret A. Zahn and Rita J. Sagi, eds. *Violence: Patterns, Causes, Public Policy.* San Diego, CA: Harcourt Brace Jovanovich, pp. 377–390.

Zampa, Fred. 1991. "Some Efforts of Extreme Overcrowding in Peruvian Prisons." *Criminal Justice Policy Review 5*(2): 133–141.

Zhang, Lening, and Dengke Zhiu, Steven F. Messner, Allen E. Liska, Marvin D. Krohan, Jianhong Liu, and Zhou Lu. 1996. "Crime Prevention in a Communitarian Society: Bang-Jiao and Tiao-Jie in the People's Republic of China." *Justice Quarterly 13*(2): 199–222.

Zimmer, Lynn. 1990. "Proactive Policing Against Street-Level Drug Trafficking." *American Journal of Police 9*(1): 43–74.

Zimring, Franklin E. 1995. "Reflections on Firearms and the Criminal Law." *The Journal of Criminal Law and Criminology 86*(1): 1–9

INDEX